BUSINESS CONSULTING IN A
MULTICULTURAL AMERICA

Business Consulting
IN A
Multicultural America

REVISED AND EXPANDED EDITION

Thaddeus Spratlen

Leslie Lum

Detra Y. Montoya

Michael Verchot

CONSULTING AND BUSINESS DEVELOPMENT CENTER

Foster School of Business   University of Washington

DISTRIBUTED BY THE UNIVERSITY OF WASHINGTON PRESS

Printed and bound in the United States of America

Design by Ashley Saleeba and Thomas Eykemans

Composition by Integrated Composition Systems, Spokane, Washington

Consulting and Business Development Center

Foster School of Business, University of Washington

www.Foster.UW.edu/consult

Distributed by

University of Washington Press

www.washington.edu/uwpress

Library of Congress Cataloging-in-Publication Data

Spratlen, Thaddeus.

    Business consulting in a multicultural America / Thaddeus Spratlen, Leslie Lum, Detra Y. Montoya, and Michael Verchot. — Revised and expanded edition.

        pages   cm

    Includes bibliographical references and index.

    ISBN 978-0-295-99497-0 (pbk. : alk. paper)

    1. Marketing—Cross-cultural studies.   2. Multiculturalism in advertising.   3. Marketing consultants.   4. Business consultants.   I. Lum, Leslie, 1952–   II. Multicultural marketing and business consulting.   III. Title.

    HF5415.S727   2015   001—dc23

The paper used in this publication is acid-free and meets the minimum requirements of American National Standard for Information Sciences—Permanence of Paper for Printed Library Materials, ANSI Z39.48–1984.∞

Contents

Preface

This textbook has grown out of twenty years of consulting that undergraduate and MBA students at the University of Washington Foster School of Business have done with small businesses in diverse communities. In 1995 the Foster School established the Consulting and Business Development Center under the leadership of then dean William Bradford. Two of this book's co-authors were among the founders of the Center. Thaddeus Spratlen was the founding faculty director. Michael Verchot was the founding director and continues in that role today.

Since its inception, the Center has had the same mission: linking students, faculty, and staff from the Foster School with racially and ethnically diverse business and nonprofit communities to expand students' knowledge and skills, help small businesses grow, create and retain jobs, open educational opportunities for underrepresented minority students, and stimulate innovative economic development research.

Today, a growing number of business schools are offering classes that engage students in solving real-world business challenges while also seeking new opportunities for small businesses. This textbook was written specifically to instruct students who are engaged in applying business theory and practice in their consulting work to assist and grow small businesses. As Jerome Williams, Prudential Chair in Business and research director of the Center for Urban Entrepreneurship and Economic Development at Rutgers School of Business says, "In today's economy it is widely recognized that the size and growth of multicultural populations are closely linked to successful marketplace performance of business on a national level, and especially in urban com-

munities. This book combines business case studies, theory, historical context, public policy implications, statistical data, and financial management concepts to provide students a full range of information and tools to address issues of how business can effectively reach multicultural marketing in urban areas and beyond."

For more information about the Consulting and Business Development Center, visit our website at www.Foster.UW.edu/consult.

ACKNOWLEDGMENTS

The Consulting and Business Development Center and co-authors of this book are grateful for financial support from the JPMorgan Chase Foundation, without which this book would not have been possible.

The University of Washington Foster School has consistently provided strong support to the Consulting and Business Development Center. We thank the numerous enterprises, nonprofit entities, and individuals whose funding and other forms of support have contributed to the Center's success. Last, but certainly not least, we extend gratitude to the many students who offered well-developed applications of their consulting experience as well as deeply reflective evaluations of our teaching, all of which are reflected in this textbook. Their insights were invaluable to our understanding of how students learn. As a result, we hope this book captures the essence of their experiences and is appropriately student centered as an instructional tool in multicultural business consulting.

ABOUT THE AUTHORS

Thaddeus Spratlen is professor emeritus of marketing at the University of Washington and founder of the Consulting and Business Development Center. He has authored numerous articles and is considered one of the nation's experts on multicultural marketing and business assistance for urban enterprises. The American Marketing Association Foundation established the WilliamsQualls-Spratlen Multicultural Mentoring Award of Excellence, named equally for Spratlen, Jerome D. Williams, and William Qualls for their pioneering work in mentoring multicultural students and junior faculty and doing advanced research on issues of racial, ethnic, and cultural diversity.

Leslie Lum has worked in corporate development for a Fortune 100 company as part of the team that restructured the company from manufacturing to financial services. She has worked in mergers and acquisitions with HSBC (the global bank) and has been general manager for a retail start-up. Her print and Web book *Personal Investing*, which teaches novices how to invest, was published by South-Western in 2002. She has led student teams at Bellevue College for the past twelve years, where the multicultural student consulting program won a 2004 award from the Community College National Center for Community Engagement.

Detra Y. Montoya is clinical associate professor of marketing in the W. P. Carey School of Business at Arizona State University. Her research focuses on multicultural consumer behavior. She has worked in Procter and Gamble's multicultural business development organization, with an emphasis on developing national multicultural merchandising programs. She has taught student consulting teams at the University of Washington as part of the Consulting and Business Development Center's Business Assistance Program, and she has taught marketing student consulting teams at Arizona State University. In addition, she has taught marketing courses to small business owners across the state of Washington.

Michael Verchot is the founding director of the Consulting and Business Development Center at the University of Washington Foster School of Business. Under his leadership, the Center has moved from a start-up to a major focal point for business development in underserved communities in the Pacific Northwest. Its varied educational programs and services now include student consulting projects that last from one week to one academic year; faculty-led small business classes that include an eighteen-hour certificate program course; a weeklong residential executive education class; and a ten-credit management certificate program. The Center has been recognized by the US Minority Business Development Agency, the US Small Business Administration, and the NW Mountain Minority Supplier Development Council for its impact on growing businesses and supporting student learning.

BUSINESS CONSULTING IN A
MULTICULTURAL AMERICA

1. Strategy

ABOUT THIS CHAPTER

Strategy and strategic planning are often viewed as the purview of large corporations. Knowledge and practice have centered on national and multinational companies with complex portfolios of business units. Yet strategy is important for businesses of all sizes, because it provides a road map to help firms reach their goals. Trying to grow a company without an overarching strategy is like trying to travel from one city to another without directions.

Most small firms do not have a written business plan but still make it through their first five years. Some founders of successful fast-growing firms acknowledge that they had no strategic plan in the early stages. Detailed written plans play a relatively small role when agility is needed to survive and thrive.

In the experience of student consulting teams, creation of a strategic vision is crucial for businesses moving from promising to long-lived. A good strategy is also important to the survival of businesses with strong competition or low barriers to entry. Without the direction that the accompanying plan provides, business owners are often distracted by the unevaluated opportunities presented to them. This creates a number of pitfalls, including the pursuit of unprofitable opportunities, the siphoning of resources away from key goals that will advance the business's long-term success, or the distraction of attention that prevents strategies from being pursued to completion. A plan keeps the business owner focused on the mission of the business. It keeps the firm's destination clear and provides direction and guidance for getting to it. A strategic plan also guides managers in making decisions to keep all employees working toward the business's goal. Further, research shows that having a plan should increase the effectiveness of efforts to achieve business success.[1]

This chapter gives an overview of strategic planning and defines the role of the student consulting team in the strategic planning process. A brief introduction is given to the most cited business strategies. Keep in mind that strategic planning is contextual. It depends on where the business is in its life cycle, the industry it competes in, the type and level of skill of its human capital, the financial capital it has or can access, the market segments and geographies it can reach, and its mission. In large companies, strategic planning is sometimes tasked to a highly innovative and knowledgeable team that has established strong trust within the organization. Large companies have the human capital to provide all the skills needed to create, execute, and measure a strategic plan. They also have deep experience with having iterated and learned through this process many times. Even so, it is estimated that only 10% of strategic plans are successfully implemented.[2]

Small businesses often do not have the resources, the experience, or the need for a highly detailed strategy, but they still need a strategic direction. Often the business is in the throes of defining what it is. Sometimes the business has defined its strategy incorrectly. Even in cases where the business owner has a clear vision of where the business should go, that vision has not been formalized nor communicated to the rest of the team. Therefore, the student team can play a crucial role in defining and moving the business toward its vision.

Good strategic planning happens when those who know the business best design and implement programs based on research, analysis, and the effective use of tools. There is no optimal way of learning this process, because it requires a combination of knowledge and iterative practice. Strategic planning frames this book. How-

Chapter 1 - A primer on strategy

Chapter 2 - Consulting, teaming, project management to achieve goals

Define Vision

Develop Mission Statement

Chapter 3 - Context of multicultural America

Complete Situation Analysis

Chapter 4 - What makes multicultural businesses succeed

Assess Firm's Environment

Define Strategic Direction

Set Goals and Objectives

Describe the Business Model

Chapter 5 - Marketing, segmentation, target, positioning, consumer decision making, branding, customer value proposition, marketing mix, CRM

Design Strategic Action Plans and Programs

Implement Strategies and Programs

Chapter 6 - Research and data gathering

Measure Performance Results

Chapter 7 - Business Processes, technology, service blueprints, and metrics

Evaluate and Revise Strategies

Chapter 8 - Accounting and financial analysis, managing cash flow

Epilogue - Communicating results effectively

FIGURE 1-1. Strategic Planning Process

ever, be aware that no set order exists for learning the concepts. Often the student will be introduced to a concept and will not know how it is applied until he or she encounters it in the consulting engagement. Students will come back to concepts repeatedly. At various stages of the consulting experience, team members will benefit from reading ahead as the need arises to use tools explained in later chapters. Figure 1-1 presents an overview of how the chapters in this book relate to the process of strategic planning.

After Studying This Chapter

After reading this chapter, students will be able to:

- Differentiate between strategic planning in a large enterprise and small business.
- Articulate why small businesses should plan, and describe the process and elements of planning for small businesses.
- Select the appropriate strategy for a business from among alternatives such as cost advantage, differentiation advantage, focus, vertical and horizontal integration, growth strategies such as the Ansoff Matrix, and harvesting or divestiture strategies based on portfolio analysis from the Boston Consulting Group.
- Understand when to apply exit strategies.
- Use strategic planning tools such as Porter's Five Forces, SWOT (strengths, weaknesses, opportu-

nities, and threats), PESTLE (political, economic, social, technological, legal, and environmental), and various business models to analyze a business and its environment.

STRATEGIC PLANNING IN SMALL BUSINESSES

Henry Mintzberg, a management professor at McGill University, argues that strategy is often defined differently from how it is practiced. Additional confusion ensues with the myriad definitions for *strategy*. For many, strategy is defined as a plan with goals and action steps to reach those goals. Others use *strategy* to describe a position, such as the position of the business's products in a market segment. Still others define the word broadly, as a perspective—a way of doing business. A more narrow definition has strategy as a "ploy" or tactic, similar to a military strategy on the battlefield to outmaneuver an opponent. Mintzberg asserts that strategy is more expansive and appears as a pattern, rather than blending intended responses of the business with responses that emerge out of the dynamic environment.[3]

The many definitions of *strategy* give rise to many purposes, similarly as broad or as narrow. Planning can be seen as future thinking. It can be a way of controlling the future. Some perceive planning as decision making or a formal process to produce an articulated goal. In this view, planning assumes rationality—that knowing the attributes of the future, determining the characteristics of the business that drive success or failure, and managing change are all possible.

There is much debate about the role that strategic planning plays in the success of small businesses. Small businesses often adopt a narrow definition of strategic planning, crafting a business plan that may cover a limited period of time and deal with specific markets. Some researchers have found a connection between planning and business success, while others have found no linkages or that the effectiveness of planning varies across industries. In 1994, Mintzberg completed a comprehensive review of planning and concluded that planning differs depending on contextual influences. He argues that planning is more appropriate for "machine" organizations, or businesses with a formal hierarchy, routinized work, clearly defined jobs, and centralized decision making. These organizations are mature and their processes are established, therefore there is a fair amount of certainty in planning. In contrast, for entrepreneurial or innovative organizations that are early in their life cycle, Mintzberg contends that planning should be minimal.[4] Formalized planning will actually inhibit the enterprise from finding and pursuing opportunities in an unknown and changing environment.

A survey of 220 Inc. 500 businesses (small but fast growing) found that 51% did not have formal business plans when they started, and of those who did, 70% had created business plans solely to secure external funding.[5] However, the main conclusion of this and other research is that, although there is little formal planning in small businesses, firms that engage in planning are less likely to fail than firms that do not.[6] For example, in one student project's experience with a restaurant, the owners wanted to expand into the ancillary business of catering. Yet they also faced challenges with respect to improving their facility and determining ways of building customer volume in a community with changing demographics. Sorting out the options and opportunities clearly represented a situation in which a business plan was needed to determine the best course of action for their business.

Here are six reasons why a firm should have a business plan:

1. A business plan helps the owners and managers determine where the company should go, given its strengths, resources, and other capabilities.
2. The process of developing the plan identifies possible obstacles and opportunities in the marketplace, along with ways of responding to them. By knowing what the obstacles are, a firm can better prepare to overcome them. Similarly, a business is be more likely to realize the available opportunities if it anticipates them as a result of having a plan.
3. Developing contingencies and alternatives for responding to the market environment is best accomplished through a business plan.
4. A plan is usually required to obtain a loan or other sources of financing.
5. Since the plan is a kind of guide for showing where a business is headed, it helps the owner, managers, and employees stay on track (or at least helps avoid being derailed). The destination is likely to be reached sooner when a firm has and follows a well-developed business plan.
6. Finally, an effective plan helps the firm reduce the risks of failure.

Role of Strategic Planner

As noted earlier, about half of small businesses do not have a strategic plan. In some cases, the plan resides in the mind of the business owner but is never communicated to others in the firm. Defining, formalizing, and communicating the plan can do much to pull the business together to achieve its long-term goals.

It is a misconception that the outcome of strategic planning is a document. The document may be the least important part of strategy formulation. Many other factors contribute to the successful execution of strategy, including gathering the correct data, involving the right people, and finding the right strategy. Often the process is emergent, meaning that strategic planners must have the flexibility to consider other options as the process progresses. By assisting in this process, the student team can provide the important service of enhancing business sustainability.

Figure 1-2 shows the roles of strategic planning as articulated by Mintzberg, and the following describes each role.[7]

Strategy analysis. The bulk of a strategic planner's time is spent gathering data and conducting analyses, which are especially required for small businesses. Most small business owners are occupied with day-to-day operations. Although they have a sense of the competitive environment, they lack the time to complete objective and com-

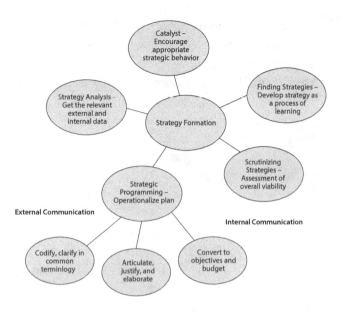

FIGURE 1-2. Strategic Planning Roles

prehensive research that can lead to implementing a solution to a problem. Internal research can be lacking as well. For example, one student team conducted an employee survey to determine how to reduce staff turnover in a Hawaiian restaurant. It was assumed that low wages might be a factor; however, the survey pointed to lack of training. That was easily remedied by providing weekly training to the staff.

Catalyst. It is natural to see the role of an outside consultant as one of change agent who encourages the organization to engage in strategic planning. Mintzberg cautions that a catalyst does not promote strategic planning—which is a process that may or may not benefit the organization—but strategic thinking. Strategic thinking is a learning process, and the catalyst will encourage forms of strategic behavior that consider the future in innovative ways. As a catalyst, the student consultant is in a unique position to bring new ideas into the firm. The student can raise difficult questions—diplomatically, of course—that will help the business consider how to define its future.

Finding strategies. Strategy can be deliberate (the business has a clear idea of where it will go and how it will get there) or emergent (a pattern emerges from different actions that the business takes). These are not mutually exclusive. Businesses can engage in various combinations of deliberate and emergent strategic planning. In fact, a

business cannot operate without elements of both styles. An innovative firm that cannot be deliberate in executing its strategy will not be successful, and a firm that engages only in well-thought-out strategies may miss an opportunity. Strategies can also come from all levels of the organization. A customer service representative may have good ideas for a customer relationship management strategy. A factory worker could be the source of supply chain management strategy. Strategies can even come from organizational failures. It is the role of the strategic planner to "find" the effective strategies.

Scrutinizing strategies. The net benefit or value brought to the organization from any given strategy is the ultimate proof of its worth. Planners should develop metrics in tandem with strategic plans. These may be quantitative measures of increased market share or profit. Quantitative evaluation is often done after the fact, but there is a need to scrutinize or conduct an assessment of its overall viability when the plan is being conceived. For example, a business owner entered into a contract with a Chinese supplier of stainless steel tanks and targeted the fast-growing craft beer industry. The strategy was based on low-cost sourcing from the supplier. After surveying several craft beer companies, the student team determined that long-term relationships with local suppliers were very important to the craft beer companies, which prided themselves on their culture of being local and US-made. A strategy of low-cost overseas sourcing was not viable in that industry.

Strategic programming. Once the strategy has been selected, strategic programming is the process of cleaning up and packaging the strategic plan so that it can be communicated to all stakeholders for execution. Codification involves clarification and conveyance in a form and terminology that can be understood. Any inconsistencies and lack of coherence are ferreted out. The translation must capture nuances and qualifications. Elaboration is the disaggregation of the codified strategies to substrategies, such as action plans to realize the strategy. Finally, conversion would translate the strategy to objectives and budgets that most businesses understand. Procedures may have to be reworked to accommodate the strategy.

First and foremost, the strategic plan serves as a communication device to get all stakeholders on the same page in achieving the business's vision. It communicates up, down, and across the business what each unit, subunit, and individual has to do to accomplish the business's mission. It also can be used to bring influential external partners into the fold. Concurrently, the strategic plan serves as a control function in that actual performance is fed back into the strategic plan to determine how successful the business has been. External players such as government regulators and accreditation bodies may require this control function. The acronym SMART (specific, measurable, attainable, relevant, and time-bound) is often used to describe the best-crafted goals. Performance feedback ensures that goals adhere to being SMART.

Small Business Strategic Planning

The strategic planner must be clear about the process of strategy formulation. At the same time, she or he must be equally clear about what the end product will include. While the process of developing a strategic plan is more important than the final document, the written document provides an excellent learning opportunity for students as well as a tool for the business owner to use after the student team has completed its work. Additionally, as noted earlier, many businesses use this document to secure capital.

Figure 1-3 maps out the components of the strategic plan, and the following describes each component.

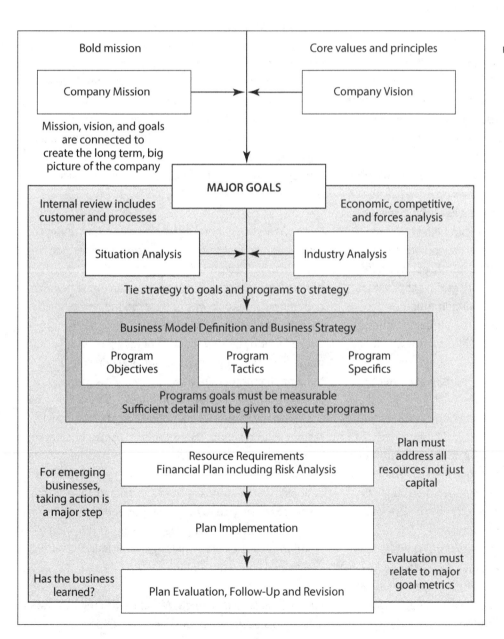

FIGURE 1-3. Strategic Plan

Mission. The firm's mission is the broadest, most forward-looking expression of where the business is headed and what its future is expected to be. It can be represented as a theme for the future. The mission of one home health care provider, for example, is to be the preferred provider for home-based health care. A mission can be expressed for a period of three to five years or for much longer periods, such as ten or more years. Despite its long-term orientation, a mission should be based on and informed by realistic assessments of what a firm might accomplish. Those responsible for leading the firm should share in the development and pursuit of the mission; they should be committed to doing what is necessary to realize the vision. Drafting a mission statement is not a trivial task, as even Fortune 500 companies often have difficulty expressing their mission.[8]

Vision. The vision of the firm encompasses the company's core values and guiding principles. Core values reflect a few of the firm's deeply held values and are independent of current environment or fads. Like many large enterprises, small businesses often have core values that involve giving back to their communities or otherwise supporting underserved populations. One African American home health care company's vision is that all its workers should earn a good living wage. This benefits the firm because, in an industry with high staff turnover, the company is able to retain its workers because of higher wages. Similarly, tribal enterprises have different core values than other enterprises. The core values of tribal enterprises are to lift their communities economically and provide employment to tribal members. Although tribal enterprises might hire outsiders who are initially more qualified than tribal members, such enterprises often choose to hire tribal members in order to develop internal capacity and skills. Such guiding principles can figure prominently in a company's major goals and are not necessarily counter to profitability.

The firm's vision articulates the company's long-term goals and may require a decade to achieve. J. Collins and J. Porras state that building a company vision consists of two parts: core ideology, which combines core values and core purpose, and a vision framework.[9] To operate successfully, a company must understand what its core values and purpose are. Core values define the enduring identity of the company. If the company operates such that it contradicts its core values, there will be dissonance. Core ideology also holds the company together

as it grows. Companies tend to have only a few (three to five) core values. It is essential to dig deep to determine core purpose. Often, superficial purposes like customer service or profitability are not the ones that will guide and inspire the employees to excel.

A vision framework is a bold mission that inspires the company to commit to a daunting challenge. Collins and Porras coined the term BHAG (big, hairy, audacious goals) to identify long-term and stretch goals that for a business are the equivalent of climbing Mount Everett. At its best, the firm's vision is clear and provides focus. It motivates employees to work together. Student consulting teams often do a great service to their businesses when they are able to articulate the business vision.

Situation and industry analysis. Generally, this part of business planning covers industry analysis, an internal analysis of the firm, and an evaluation of the market conditions and circumstances facing the company. During this part of the process, various stakeholder groups and influences are acknowledged. Of special importance are competitors, customers, suppliers, government regulators, technological developments, and any other influential groups or factors that will affect how the company performs over time.

Goals. Goals are general outcomes and expectations of results. In contrast to the firm's vision, goals are operational in a defined period of time (typically in one, three, or five years). For the African American home health care company, its mission was to become the home health care market leader in the state. The company accomplished that by setting the goal of taking on large urban markets in its first years of business. Then smaller cities became the target markets.

The purpose of establishing major goals is to enable the company to align all its actions and dedicate all its resources to reaching these goals. If a small business has a major goal, then once a consulting team collects data and information, the team's challenge is to determine actions that the company needs to take to align all its resources in service to reaching that goal. Thus, it is crucial for student consulting teams to either fully understand the firm's existing major goals or help the company define goals prior to planning a course of action.

Business model and strategy. Working with the business to articulate a business model can open up possibilities for the company. As described later, at its simplest level the business model describes how the business generates revenues and sustains profit in the competitive marketplace. The student consulting team can evaluate a firm's strategies according to each strategy's applicability to the business model. A very important aspect of market strategy, for example, is for the firm to differentiate itself from its competition. Entrepreneurs are often enticed by the many available business opportunities. Unless these opportunities align with the strategic focus and core competencies of the business, they can detrimentally distract from the business's success. For the African American home health care company, the move into a pharmacy business was a means of diversifying into another business within health care. This move leveraged its home health care business, which provided the pharmacy with a ready customer list. It was part of a long-term strategy to selectively enter other related businesses that would allow the firm to establish a dominant position as a diversified quality health care provider.

When creating a strategy, the focus is on intention and direction. Intention defines what goal will be accomplished, and direction includes the action steps necessary to achieve the goal. A strategic plan is one that details the pathways that will be followed in pursuit of the firm's stated objectives. When done properly, a strategic plan should be conceptual, visionary, and directional. Conceptually, it captures the essential characteristics of the firm as a successful enterprise. In being visionary, the plan reflects future directions and aims beyond the current business thinking. An effective plan gives direction to those responsible for pursuing the firm's objectives. See the "Strategies" section below for short descriptions of the most popular strategies.

The strategic plan serves as a framework within which management decisions are made. Its content makes clear to all the business's stakeholders what the plan is about. Besides informing these stakeholders, the plan may help build relationships that will improve the performance of the business.

Program strategies, objectives, specifics. While strategy is associated with thinking, acting, and making decisions that are focused, forward looking, company-wide, and directed toward specific performance objectives with outcomes beyond one year in duration, the terms program, tactics, or initiatives apply to within-year activities. A program is a defined set of steps that in aggregate forms an overall strategy to achieve business goals. Examples of programs include an advertising campaign, a direct mail campaign, public relations events, or a Web marketing plan.

Program objectives are the measurable performance results, or metrics, that are expected to be achieved within a given time period. They are most commonly stated with respect to such outcome measures as sales, market share, profit, return on investment, or other performance measures for a given time, such as month, quarter, or year. Objectives are also stated as changes and improvements. An example could be a 3% increase in same-store sales over the previous year.

Resource requirements. When a business plan is created, it is important to determine whether resources can be obtained to achieve the plan. Emerging businesses always grapple with limited resources. If the business does not have the resources to implement its programs, alternatives must be sought.

Risk analysis. Typically, when financials for a business plan are compiled, sensitivity analysis (covered in chapter 8) is undertaken to accommodate for uncertainty. However, there may be other risks that cannot be translated to financial statements. It is incumbent upon the business to list all potential risks and consider contingency plans to mitigate or deal with each risk.

Evaluating the plan. A good plan always includes a comprehensive method for measuring its success. Any feedback about the plan should be incorporated into future versions in a continuous improvement loop.

STRATEGIES

Because small firms compete in the same industry marketplace as large firms, understanding the strategies of large firms can better position small firms for success. What follows is a compendium of the most referenced tools that companies use to develop their strategic, or business, plans.

Porter's Competitive Strategies

The first line of strategic analysis consists of identifying the dynamics of an industry and the strategies necessary to compete in that industry. The firm's position within the industry is another important determinant of success.

TABLE 1-1. Porter's Competitive Advantage Strategies

Target	Advantage	
	Low Cost	Product Uniqueness
Broad (industry wide)	Cost leadership strategy	Differentiation strategy
Narrow (market segment)	Focus strategy (low cost)	Focus strategy (differentiation)

Harvard Business School professor Michael Porter specializes in industry analysis, and firms have used his competitive strategies for the past three decades. He asserts that, ultimately, only cost advantage and differentiation constitute a firm's strength and determine its position. By applying these two strengths in a broad market or a narrow segment, three strategies result: cost leadership, differentiation, and focus.[10] Table 1-1 summarizes how this is applied.

Cost leadership. A low-cost business achieves its cost advantage through process efficiencies, sourcing better materials at lower cost, effective outsourcing, or avoiding some costs altogether. These firms may have access to cheaper capital, be innovative in designing products or services, or have efficient operations or economical distribution systems. Proprietary learning may help their employees perform at higher levels. They may have intellectual property or technology that reduces costs.

The low-cost producer has several significant advantages in the marketplace. It can sell products at the same price as other firms but earn a greater profit. It can gain market share by lowering prices while maintaining profitability. As the product matures and prices decline, the low-cost leader can continue to accrue more profit than other firms. A good example of a low-cost leader in the fast food industry is a ramen or noodle shop. The menu is limited to a few items, making kitchen operations efficient. A proprietary recipe for the broth can be used for a number of different menu items. Large amounts of the same raw materials (e.g., noodles) are purchased, giving the business leverage for sourcing high-quality raw materials at lower prices from its suppliers. Profit margins are higher than at other restaurants because not as many food ingredients are used. Although the average customer tab is smaller, customers turn over in 30 to 45 minutes (as opposed to 2 hours in a typical restaurant), resulting in higher revenues per table. Other small businesses may have a real challenge in being the low-cost

producer, as they do not typically have the ability to control input costs or access low-cost capital. While many small businesses want to compete on price, student teams need to help the owners determine if they can sustain the low-cost strategy over many years.

Differentiation. Drivers of differentiation include unique product features, higher performance, more intensity, distinct content, proprietary or first-mover technology, better-quality raw materials, superior service, more skilled employees, or better information.

For example, a woman-owned photography studio distinguished itself with high-quality photography. Different from other studios that have gravitated to digital media, this business continued to use film. Film requires that the photographer understand exposure and shutter speed; it captures highlights and shadows. The use of film differentiated the business's photographs as high quality. Clients were willing to pay a significant premium for what they consider to be fine art as opposed to an ordinary photograph. In another example, a firm differentiated itself by having direct and ongoing relationships with a small number of Chinese factories that ensured quality while meeting international labor standards.

Focus. Focus is the application of cost leadership or differentiation to the broad market or narrow market segments. Student consulting teams may work with firms whose market segments can be pinpointed to emerging micromarkets. For example, small businesses have fewer constraints than large corporations in that they can explore very small markets and develop a strong competitive position.

Growth Strategies

Businesses can use a variety of growth strategies to expand. Not all strategies involve acquiring more customers. Here are some highlights of frequently used growth strategies.

Vertical integration. A business often exists as part of a supply chain. A supply chain is a system of processes, people, information, and other resources that move a product or service from its origins to the customer. It can stretch across businesses and other entities. Professor Leonard Greenhalgh of the Tuck School of Business at Dartmouth teaches that winning companies are those that have the most competitive supply chains. A company that purchases raw materials or products from its vendors and sells to customers may be able to take over functions it did not previously have and thus grow by reducing costs or increasing revenues.

Asian supermarkets are a good example of using vertical integration to reduce costs. (These stores often generate more than $10 million in revenue.) One Asian supermarket was purchasing its fresh produce from wholesalers. It also sourced Vietnamese foodstuffs from manufacturers in Vietnam. By purchasing produce from Californian farmers directly, the supermarket cut out the middleman. This significantly reduced prices and gave the business direct communication with the farmers, resulting in a more accurately predictable supply. The business vertically integrated its Vietnamese sourcing by sending extended family back to Vietnam to start manufacturing operations. This lowered prices, improved quality, and also allowed the business to specify exactly how the product was manufactured. The business was also a major vendor for local restaurants. It vertically integrated by opening a prepared food section that provided quick meals for shoppers and by catering for large parties.

Horizontal integration. Horizontal integration is the acquisition of businesses across markets. For example, the owner of a nail salon may acquire other nail salons in the area to expand its market. With several nail salons, the owner can effect economies of scale, for example, in terms of scheduling manicurists and purchasing supplies. Manicurists could be sent where demand was highest, ensuring that customers are not turned away.

New product (Ansoff). The Ansoff Matrix (see Table 1-2) is one method of determining risk in approaching markets

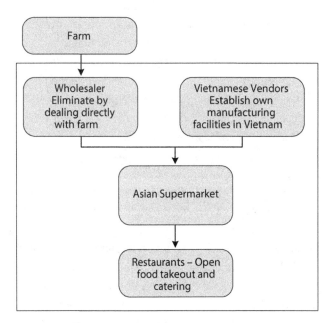

FIGURE 1-4. Vertical Integration of Asian Supermarket

with products. It details four product or market growth strategies: market penetration, market development, product development, and diversification. Market penetration presents the least risk, as it uses the business's existing resources and products to reach more of the same market. Market development involves selling current products or services to a new customer segment, for example, selling to women and then moving to teens, or expanding into a new market, for example, a new geography. Diversification presents the most risk, as in developing a new product or service for a new market. A Latino-owned promotional products company based in Los Angeles was successful in supplying bobble heads to the professional baseball team in its city. The company penetrated the market by selling other promotional products to the team. It leveraged this relationship and developed a division to focus on other baseball clubs, growing its sales across clubs. Without developing any new products, the company was able to use its industry expertise to acquire new customers.

Product development requires taking on the increased risk of developing new products. By targeting existing customers, the firm reduces the risk of having to penetrate

TABLE 1-2. Ansoff Matrix

	Existing Products	New Products
Existing Markets	Market Penetration	Product Development
New Markets	Market Development	Diversification

another market segment. An African American–owned payment processing company recognized that it had a competitive advantage in document imaging and records management with health care customers. It began to offer a document scanning and management service to these same customers, which deepened the client relationship in addition to increasing sales.

Strategic alliances. Businesses can foster more growth by developing strategic alliances with larger companies, peer companies, governmental bodies, or nonprofit institutions. For example, the National Minority Supplier Development Council provides certification and forums that help minority businesses compete for corporate purchasing dollars. The Women's Business Enterprise Alliance (WBEA) and the Gay and Lesbian Chamber of Commerce offer similar services to their constituent groups. Once such links are established, a business can often expand its market share through information exchange. Research has shown that entrepreneurial support systems can be created when minority peer companies cluster.[11] The same strategy can be used in the nonprofit sector. A nonprofit that focuses on environmental issues was able to increase funding by forming strategic alliances with schools.

Sustainability and Exit Strategies

Growth may not always be the objective of the firm. In some cases, the owner may want to harvest or collect the cash flow but not grow the business. For example, some small business owners may harvest cash from a retail operation to fund real estate investments. What follows are some guidelines for choosing whether or not to harvest a business or product line. Some businesses may be on a downward trend and need a turnaround. Others may require an exit strategy, as continued operation may only drain the business owner's resources.

Harvest. Businesses go through a life cycle. They start, go through a phase of growth, mature to slow growth, and then go into decline. Products and services within a business experience a similar product life cycle (discussed in detail in chapter 5). One strategy adopted by declining businesses is the harvest strategy. This means that the business will continue to operate but will input no new resources. Instead, the cash flow from operating the business is harvested.

The Boston Consulting Group developed a model for managing four categories of businesses or product lines (Figure 1-5). A star (top left) is a business or product line with a large market share in a fast-growing industry. Stars may require investment to grow, investment that is well spent because it will generate return. A cash cow (bottom left) is a business or product line with a large share in a slow-growing market. Cash cows require little investment but will generate cash that can be used to grow other businesses or products. A question mark (top right) is a business or product line with small market share but in a growing market. Investment is needed but success is not certain. A dog (bottom right) is a business or product line with small market share in a slow-growing market. Dogs are the businesses or product lines that should be divested from, because investment will not generate return.

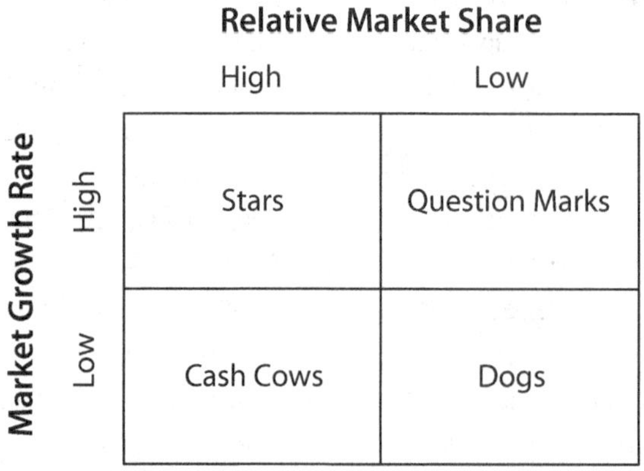

Relative Market Share

	High	Low
Market Growth Rate High	Stars	Question Marks
Market Growth Rate Low	Cash Cows	Dogs

FIGURE 1-5. Boston Consulting Group Matrix

Turnaround. A business or product line may be distressed and require action to turn the business or product line around. In private equity or leverage buyout, companies may be purchased by investors who install an interim team of turnaround specialists to right the business. The team assesses the situation, determines needs, and restructures and stabilizes the business. The actions taken by these specialists often seem brutal. Turnaround teams terminate employees, including top management, and cut costs. Success is measured by financial indicators, and often the goal is to sell the company on the public market or to other investors for a significant profit. The outcome is not always successful. Some businesses go into terminal decline or continued failure.

Turnaround strategies include retrenchment, which focuses on the firm's core competencies and shrinks the business; repositioning by tackling new products or markets; replacing the top management team; and longer-term strategies to restructure the company. As the business is already in dire circumstances, turnarounds are difficult to implement. Only about one-third of corporate turnarounds are successful.[12]

Be acquired. Student teams often approach their consulting projects with the preconceived idea that they must propose strategies for a business to continue. In some cases, a business may generate more value by being acquired by another company. For example, an Asian entrepreneur had developed a health website in 2005. The website won awards, but the student team was unable to come up with a business model that would generate profits. Users were unwilling to pay for use of the website, even though it provided valuable information. Health care facilities such as hospitals and clinics did not have the funds to buy the service as a subscription. The team's final recommendation was to make the business attractive for acquisition. The business owner was advised to continue to pour resources into developing the website. In fact, the website was acquired by a media company in 2007. It was of value to the media company because the cost of developing a similar website from scratch was significantly more than the acquisition cost.

Liquidation. The mortality rate of small businesses is high, especially in recessionary times. Statistics (given in chapter 4) indicate that only slightly more than half of businesses survive to five years. In some cases, it may be incumbent upon the student team to recommend that the business close. For example, a successful African American business owner opened a café as his second business solely based on securing inexpensive rent. The location proved to be difficult for customers to reach, and there were a large number of competitors in the vicinity. All food was purchased or prepared by other vendors, making food costs high. The business owner was drawing funds from his successful business to keep the café afloat. After careful deliberation with faculty and mentors, the student team recommended that the owner wind down the business to stop the outflow of cash. Then the business owner could refocus on his successful business.

Liquidation recommendations and how they are communicated should be carefully thought through. Owners can react emotionally to rational recommendations, as they have invested more than capital in their businesses. Often it is more effective to persuade the business owner

that a huge effort would be required to turn the business around. Hopefully, the business owner will come to the conclusion that such a path might not be worth the commitment of time and money.

TOOLS FOR STRATEGIC ANALYSIS

Different from strategy itself, tools for strategy formation allow the consultant to analyze the business or its environment. The best tools will prompt out-of-the-box thinking about how the business can compete successfully or will point to opportunities that the business had not considered.

Porter's Five Forces

Michael Porter's Five Forces approach enables analysis of forces present in a business's competitive environment.[13] Porter's model (Figure 1-6) involves five competitive forces that affect prices, costs, and firm investment in an industry and thus may determine a firm's profitability. For the small business, this includes its local competition, customers, and vendors. When all of these forces are working in the firm's favor, the firm can earn healthy profits.[14] The significance of each of these five forces depends on a given industry's structure, making it essential to consider the forces within the firm's industry. Firms can influence the impact of these five forces with their competitive strategies.

Threat of new entrants. New entrants in the marketplace can put pressure on existing firms to drive down prices and costs and can threaten to steal market share. When the threat of new entrants is high and new businesses are constantly emerging, this indicates low barriers to entry. This likely occurs when there is a common technology, little brand loyalty, easy access to multiple distribution channels, and low production costs. The rapid growth in online retailing, for example, has increased the ability of small firms to enter the marketplace. Existing firms in an industry can deter new entrants by maintaining prices or increasing investment.[15] A low threat of new entrants is characterized by high barriers to entry, which can make it more difficult for new businesses to emerge and compete with existing firms. Such barriers could include patented technology, little brand switching, restricted access distribution channels, and high production costs. Additional entry barriers include capital requirements, government policy, and

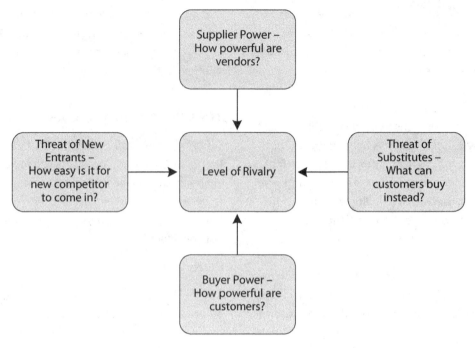

FIGURE 1-6. Porter's Five Forces

expected retaliation from a larger competitor, such as price cutting.[16]

Threat of substitutes. The presence of substitute products can limit profits within an industry. Although product substitutes or alternatives are difficult to avoid, firms should strive to differentiate their products by emphasizing unique product attributes and superior product performance, quality, or service levels. Taken together, such actions will likely result in higher switching costs to a firm's buyers as buyers expend more money, time, effort, or psychic costs in seeking substitute brands, products, or suppliers. Low switching costs promote a threat of substitutes (Table 1-3).

Bargaining power of suppliers. Powerful suppliers have the ability to charge higher prices or provide limited supplies, causing firms to either absorb the increased costs or pass them along to customers. Suppliers have more power when there are few of them, when resources are scarce, or when there are high switching costs between suppliers. Suppliers also gain power when their products or services are highly differentiated or when few or no substitutes are available (Table 1-4).

Bargaining power of buyers. Buyers have more power when they are price sensitive, when there are substitute products available, and when buyers have easy access to information. Powerful buyers have low switching costs between firms, and they are able to demand higher

TABLE 1-3. Threat of New Entrants or Substitutes

Threat of New Entrants Is Lower When	*Threat of Substitutes Is Lower When*
Firm has cost advantage through economy of scale or other means Government policy may limit entrants Firm has specialized technology Industry has large capital requirements Firm has strong brand identity Industry has high switching costs Firm has access to effective distribution Firm has proprietary products or intellectual property Retaliation is threatened	Industry has high switching costs Customers are not inclined to substitute Firm has better price performance Industry has low level of innovation

TABLE 1-4. Supplier Power

Supplier Powerful	Supplier Weak
Few suppliers High concentration—a few suppliers have most of market share High switching costs Suppliers can forward-integrate and absorb function of the firm	Many suppliers Product is commodity—standard, easily copied Customer can backward-integrate and absorb function of supplier Concentrated customers—a few customers are a large percentage of sales

levels of quality and service. Products in such cases tend to be standardized or undifferentiated. Powerful buyers have increased bargaining power with firms and can often achieve concessions such as lower price and service that is more costly for the firm to provide to the buyer (Table 1-5).

Level of rivalry. Rivalry or competition among firms increases when there are a large number of firms in the industry. The result can be an industry shakeout in which firms start to consolidate, as they did in banking following the 2007–2008 housing market collapse. High exit barriers that make it difficult for a firm to leave a market can increase competition. Even if the business is unprofitable, it might feel obligated to stay in the marketplace, creating more rivalry. If the market is growing slowly, firms will compete more strenuously for a slice of the pie. Following the housing market collapse, for example, large construction and architectural firms began competing for contracts previously considered unattractive because of their low profit margins. With the economic slowdown, low profit margins became better than no profit margins. The entrance of larger firms in small-profit-margin sectors forced out many smaller firms who used to compete successfully in this market.

Other circumstances also increase competition: High fixed costs increase competition because a firm must produce near capacity to absorb fixed costs at the lowest unit cost. High levels of production lead to an increase in supply and thus competition. When a firm must sell goods

as soon as possible, as with perishable goods such as food, competition to move the product intensifies. When customers can easily switch from one firm to another with lower costs, more competition ensues. And finally, if customers are unable to differentiate between one firm's product and that of its competitor, rivalry increases.

Core Competency

C. K. Prahalad, former professor at the University of Michigan, and Gary Hamel, a management consultant, coined the term *core competency* in a 1990 article.[17] Prior to this, many practitioners visualized a business as the products and services that it sold. This was limiting because as products and services go through life cycles and go into decline, so does the business. Markets are dynamic and businesses must make choices about what to pursue. Prahalad and Hamel argued that chasing markets based solely on growth was not sustainable. Rather, they proposed that a business should identify its core competencies—what it does best—and pursue markets based on this assessment.

Ascertaining core competencies has practical application in small and emerging businesses. Often business owners are opportunistic and want to chase every attractive business venture. Matching the opportunity with the business's capabilities is what produces success. Operating based on core competencies can provide access to a wide variety of markets. A firm's core competencies should be perceived by the customer as bringing value, and such attributes should be difficult to imitate.

TABLE 1-5. Buyer Power

Buyer Powerful	Buyer Weak
Few customers High concentration—a few customers have most of output Customer can backward-integrate and absorb function of the firm	Many customers Customers are fragmented High switching costs Firm can backward-integrate and absorb function of customer Firm is critical to customer's supply chain

Defining core competencies is not always simple. For example, an African American and women-owned engineering firm wanted to expand into new markets. The firm considered document control, a small part of its services, as a core competency. It wanted to penetrate new markets by offering this service. However, upon further investigation, the student consulting team found that many firms offered document control, often with much more sophisticated software. The student team found that clients valued the ability of the firm to get the job done in the often bureaucratic transportation sector. As it turned out, a number of lucrative transportation contracts were in the pipeline; the transportation market was growing at a much higher rate than the new markets the firm was considering for its document control strategy. The firm was able to redirect its efforts with a clear understanding of its core competencies.

Value Chain

The term *value chain* was coined by Michael Porter almost three decades ago, and the concept has since become standard in the business practitioner toolkit (Figure 1-7).[18] While Porter's value chain is relatively simple compared to more current models discussed in chapter 7, it does address the primary activities in a firm: getting raw materials from suppliers, manufacturing, distributing, marketing, and providing service for the product. In support of these primary activities, firms use procurement, technology, human resources, and other infrastructure. This model provides a framework to analyze a business's internal activities so that the firm can determine where value is being added. Porter's model defines value as profit margin. More sophisticated and complex mapping breaks down activities to a more granular level, but the question to answer is the same: where is value added? For example, typically most companies do not consider

providing information to a customer as an activity that produces value. However, in the case of one company, providing information about how to use and maintain the product reduced the risk of injury that customers might face when using the product. It also affected profitability by reducing customer returns 25%. Making this information accessible was less than 1% of the cost of the product, yet it reduced customer dissatisfaction and led to more repeat purchases.

A product's value to the customer is of critical importance. And for the customer, value is not always about the lowest price. Many HVAC (heating, ventilation, and air conditioning) companies serving commercial, industrial, and government markets have been able to win business by helping customers understand that while some systems may be more costly to install, they may save money in the long run, with lower energy costs. Some customers may also want the added status of being perceived as "green." Customers may value design, status, cost reduction in their own processes, risk reduction in decreasing risk of lawsuit or government fine, convenience, ease of use, accessibility, or simply the ability to get the job done effectively.

The concept of looking for where value is added in the activities of a business has been extended and elaborated in customer relationship management, business process analysis, project management, business model generation, and other concepts discussed later in this book. Some of these tools, which have origins in marketing or operations, have become overall business strategies.

SWOT Analysis

A commonly used tool to determine the mission-critical issues facing a company is an assessment the company's strengths, weaknesses, opportunities, and threats (SWOT). A SWOT analysis structures group discussion

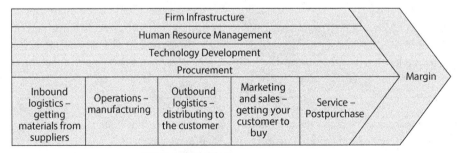

Primary Activities

FIGURE 1-7. Porter Value Chain

to identify the internal and external forces that drive a company's position in the market. Used effectively, a SWOT analysis can organize relevant information and determine what areas a company should focus on in order to move forward. Student consulting teams find it helpful to conduct a SWOT analysis early in the consulting process, and most include this analysis in their final report.

The first step in developing a SWOT analysis is to gather the entire consulting team together to discuss information collected to date. Then, using a flip chart or white board, the group identifies the following:

- Strengths. Existing resources and capabilities within the company that provide a competitive advantage within the market in which the company operates.
- Weaknesses. Existing internal forces that lower or limit current or future asset value that would build competitive advantage within the market in which the company operates.
- Opportunities. Existing or emerging forces external to the company that, if captured, could provide the company with a competitive advantage.
- Threats. Existing or emerging forces external to the company that could inhibit the company's ability to gain a competitive advantage or maintain its current advantage.

Once a comprehensive list is developed, ideas should be clarified to ensure that all team members understand all concepts listed. Then the challenge for the team is to determine which are the most important strengths, weaknesses, opportunities, and threats. Teams can use a five-point Likert scale to rank each item, with 5 being "most important" and 1 being "not at all important." The items receiving the highest overall ranking become those for which the team develops strategies to enhance, alter, ward against, or capitalize on.

Although a SWOT analysis allows the student consulting team to develop a comprehensive picture of the business, caution must be exercised in how results are communicated to the business owner. In presentations and reports, SWOT analyses often come across as negative. Since the primary role of the student team is to communicate and effect change, it is imperative that the SWOT analysis does not provoke resistance in the business owner. Some consulting firms advise that a SWOT analysis should not be presented to the client but rather

used by the consultants as a tool to understand the business. For example, a weakness (i.e., lack of accounting skills) may be an opportunity for the business (i.e., outsource to a bookkeeper). However, the business owner may not perceive an analysis of weakness as an opportunity to improve but as a criticism of his or her management style. It is important to keep in mind that the SWOT analysis is simply a tool one can use to understand a business; it is more important to communicate the outcomes of this analysis and its implications for the company's strategy than to focus on presenting the SWOT analysis itself.

PESTLE Analysis

A more extensive SWOT analysis can be created by combining it with another form of strategic analysis that considers political, economic, social, technological, legal, and environmental (PESTLE) factors. The PESTLE analysis examines trends in the greater economy or society that may have an impact on the business, thus expanding analysis to include environmental factors and generating a picture of the firm's macro environment. Although all these factors are external to the firm, business owners should take note of them and approach them proactively rather than reactively.

First, business owners should consider political factors that may affect their business operations. Political factors could include government regulations and policies, such as labor and tax laws, tax policies, trade policies, and environmental regulations. For example, a small business that wants to conduct business across borders could be significantly affected by international trade policies.

Second, firms should monitor economic factors. Such factors may include interest rates, unemployment levels, rate of inflation, and exchange rates. A higher unemployment rate, affects consumer spending behavior but may create opportunities in the marketplace. For example, new car sales may decline because consumers are postponing new car purchases, but an auto repair shop may benefit because consumers are spending money on maintaining their current cars longer.

Third, business owners should pay attention to changes in the social environment, which can affect small and large businesses alike. Social factors include demographic trends such as age, ethnicity, birth rate, religious beliefs, education and career paths, and cultural beliefs. For example, some cities are becoming more racially diverse, and small businesses may need to adapt their products or services to serve a more diverse marketplace. In addition, consumers' general view of society (i.e., conservative or liberal) can shift and may affect their overall shopping behavior. For instance, consumers may increasingly favor companies that are more socially responsible, that is, companies that are more environmentally friendly and support social causes.

Finally, firms must regularly monitor the changing technological environment. Technological factors include technical infrastructure and innovation that may increase productivity and the firm's ability to reach more consumers. For example, some small businesses lack a strong presence on the Internet, yet their customers may be very tech savvy and prefer to communicate with the business online or through social media.

Combining SWOT with the expanded PESTLE analysis encourages students to think divergently and to consider all factors in a firm's internal and external environment. In addition, Michael Porter's Five Forces analysis assesses elements in a business's micro environment that can help the firm compete. For the small business, this can include its local competition, customers, and vendors. Assessing special internal factors can assist the student team in identifying core competencies within the business. The business can best grow by capitalizing on core competencies. It must also develop and enhance its core competencies so that it can continue to compete effectively.

Tables 1-6, 1-7, and 1-8 incorporate strategic planning tools that student teams can use in order to think strategically. Each individual team member should make his or her own assessments, to encourage a variety of perspectives. Caution: Such analysis should not be done in a perfunctory manner. Student consultants should take the time to gather enough information from external sources as well as internal business sources to complete a careful analysis.

The Business Model

The business model is a tool that allows the firm to look at itself holistically while opening up the possibility of innovative future thinking. At its most rudimentary level, the business model is an articulation of how the company makes a profit and competes in the marketplace. More sophisticated business modeling includes formulation of how the firm brings value to the customer. Even more sophisticated models add resources, processes, partners, and channels.

At the outset, the student consulting team should have a clear description of the firm's business model, because it is a guide to what the consulting project should or should not focus on. Often the business model will illuminate how the firm will create barriers to entry or how it will compete effectively against larger competitors. The business model should provide a good indication of how the firm will make money, including the level and timing of profit generated over the projected life of the business.

The business model is defined by some as a summation of the core business decisions and trade-offs used by a company to make a profit.[19] The Business Model Canvas is one tool to generate the business model.[20] The nine building blocks in this model are shown in Table 1-9, for a Latino systems integrator.

Customer segments. Customers are core to the success of a business. However, businesses, particularly small businesses, cannot serve every market. Minority business enterprises (MBEs) are more likely to find a segment or niche that they can serve. But long-term success depends

TABLE 1-6. Macro Environment SWOT

Macro Environment	Opportunities	Threats
Political/legal	Tax incentives for hiring	Reduction in government spending; strict labor laws; higher corporate taxes
Economy	Low inflation; low interest rates	Low consumer confidence; high cost of acquiring loans
Social	Aging population; growth in multicultural market	Population shift to sunbelt; unfamiliarity of multicultural consumers' needs
Technology	Growth in consumers' mobile use; online customer reviews	Outsourcing to international firms; higher cost for smaller firms to implement new technology; competitors with proprietary technology

TABLE 1-7. Micro Environment SWOT

Micro Environment	Opportunities	Threats
Competitors	Distinctive products and services that are not easily replicated	Product technology may not be patentable; competitors have access to more capital
Buyers	High switching costs; loyal customer base	Customers are price sensitive; customers are concentrated in a declining market
Suppliers	Healthy competition among suppliers; efficient distribution channel	Suppliers are concentrated in a narrow market
New entrants	High barriers to entry created by product differentiation or high cost to enter	Low barriers to entry; low switching costs Potential for new entrants to capture market share
Substitutes	High product differentiation makes substitution difficult	Little product differentiation to encourage use of substitutes; potential for pricing wars

TABLE 1-8. Internal Environment SWOT

Internal Environment	Opportunities	Threats
Management	Good management team with ability to learn and grow	Small management team with limited expertise
Marketing	Excellent reputation in the community; good sales skills	Limited budget to promote brand message; outdated website
Operations	Efficient production process; high-quality products	Basic operations that cannot accommodate growth
Finance/accounting	Good accounting and financial systems; generation of good cash flow	Business owner is not well versed in accounting and financial systems; lack of cash flow to fund growth
Human resource	Well-trained and motivated employees; employee training is used effectively	Lack of human capital in certain functions

TABLE 1-9. Business Model Canvas for a Latino-Owned Systems Integrator

Key Partners	Key Activities	Value Proposition	Customer Relationships	Customer Segments
Technology companies in cloud, computing, storage, network and big data Bank	IT services IT consulting Cloud consulting Turnkey operations Data analytics	Full-service systems integrator that delivers innovative data center infrastructure and cloud solutions tailored to meet your business goals	High personal touch with clients High trust level to develop secure solutions	Gaming industry Banking
	Key Resources Experienced, committed, and diverse employees		Channels Direct sales International partners	

Cost Structure	Revenue Streams
Low fixed costs Lean operation Servers purchased as ordered Variable employee costs	Consulting fees Solution purchases Management fees Maintenance fees

on being able to compete for customers across racial and ethnic markets. At the same time, the business must specify which segments it cannot serve. The selection of the market segment is the first driver in a business model. Once the segment is selected, the business must obtain a strong understanding of what that customer needs. This is true in both business-to-consumer (B2C) and business-to-business (B2B) companies.

Value proposition. The customer value proposition is why a customer will choose one business over another. If the business can clearly define how it brings value to the customer, then it will operate effectively. Beware that the customer value proposition derives from the mix of products and services offered by a company, not from the products and services themselves. An example is the growth of smartphones. Apple has gained significant market share because its customers can fulfill many needs with one electronic device that provides multiple functions. Phones based on less popular operating systems are struggling to gain market share, because customers are unable to fulfill as many needs given the smaller number of apps available (e.g., software for messaging; playing music, games, or movies; reading or editing documents; exchanging photos; etc.). The value proposition for smartphone customers is an enhanced and easier lifestyle. As stated before, value is not just about price. It can be about status, performance, design, risk reduction, cost reduction, or convenience. The student consulting team often has to dig deep to determine exactly what the customer values.

Channels. Channels are the means for marketing, servicing, delivering, or otherwise engaging with customers. They include advertising, direct mail, websites, direct sales, mobile, stores, events, social media, television, telephone, and public relations. Channels raise awareness about the company's products and services, communicate and deliver the customer value proposition, allow for purchase, and provide postpurchase service. Channels can also involve partners such as wholesalers or brokers. The business must determine how best to reach its target segment both to initiate sales and to ensure customer loyalty.

Customer relationships. Customer relationship management (CRM) is a systematic way by which the company takes the customer from not knowing about the company to being a loyal customer. The business has to have a clear understanding of the quality and type of relationship the customer wants. Each touchpoint with the customer should be evaluated to insure its effectiveness. Chapter 5 addresses CRM in more detail.

Revenue streams. The nature of the relationship with the customer can give rise to different types of revenue streams. Businesses can sell a physical product and/or charge fees for usage, subscriptions, rent, brokerage services, or licensing. The firm can also generate revenues from advertising. Fixed or dynamic pricing can generate revenue streams of different characteristics.

Key resources. Some business models require heavy investment in physical assets. Others require innovative or highly skilled employees. Still others require intellectual property or financial resources for financing customer purchases. The business model articulates the resources needed to be successful.

Key activities. Each business has a process by which it delivers to the customer. For a manufacturing business, for example, this includes its supply chain and the process by which products are made. A service firm may have a service blueprint that defines interaction with the customer. The business model should define the key activities performed by the business in order to fulfill its customer value proposition. Chapter 7 discusses how to achieve this with business processes.

Key partners. Partnerships can be formed with other companies in the supply chain to effect cost savings or ensure reliable purchasing. They can be formed with competitors to deliver on a project that could not be completed by one firm. They can be joint ventures with foreign companies. Often partnerships can be struck with various levels of government or with nonprofits.

Cost structure. Creation of the business model should include an assessment of the firm's important cost drivers. Are costs fixed, semi-variable, variable, or nonrecurring? What is their relative size and importance? How do they change over time? Do economies of scale affect costs? Chapter 8 discusses cost structure in more detail.

In the example of the Latino systems integrator, partnership with large technology companies played an important role in ensuring that the firm was not highly

Redapt Systems Strategy for Exponential Growth

Back in 1996, Latino brothers Rick and Dave Cantu started a business (called Redapt) rebuilding Sun Microsystems servers and selling them to business clients. To differentiate their product, the brothers spent time and money making their refurbished computers appear like new, wrapping them in custom-made bags and delivering them in boxes printed with the company logo. By 2009, Sun Microsystems servers were no longer manufactured; the business was at $23.5 million in annual revenue and on a declining trend. The brothers were advised to adopt an end-of-life strategy, in which they would harvest the remaining cash flow from the refurbishing business until it dried up.

Instead, the company began a huge growth trajectory driven by its customers' interest in cloud services. They diversified their business from refurbished machines to building specialty servers and helping customers manage their public/private cloud services. Redapt responded to its customers' needs by figuring out whether clients needed public or private cloud storage, determining how much storage clients needed, and assessing how best to quickly expand storage capacity. Redapt assisted companies in keeping their more sensitive information in private storage.

Redapt does work for application and game-development companies such as the California game-maker Zynga. Redapt also builds servers for companies to use in-house. Twenty years ago, Redapt rebuilt only Sun Microsystems machines, but now the firm provides servers from a number of companies. Dell, the firm's largest vendor, represents only 40% of its business. Redapt also works with IBM, HP, F5, EMC2, and other manufacturers and service providers. The firm helps its clients select systems and manage them efficiently.

Redapt survived through the recession and a major shift in strategy because the Cantu brothers did not perceive themselves as a server refurbishing company. They determined that their core competency was being able to serve clients' storage needs. Then the Cantus built their business around that by learning what they had to know to provide cloud services. Despite the huge learning curve for technology, the brothers felt that learning how to run a business was even more challenging. They teamed up with local companies, such as the Puget Sound Bank, to help them manage cash flow and other day-to-day operations.

The Cantus do not define their firm as a cloud services or storage company. They say that the area of big data—or information being collected through apps, smartphones, search, and online traffic—is the next big business opportunity. Redapt is gearing up to be there for its clients.

In addition to its Redmond, Washington, office and warehouse, Redapt has expanded worldwide, with offices and facilities in California, Virginia, Hong Kong, and Amsterdam, and the firm was on track to generate $200 million in revenues in 2014.

dependent on one vendor. The firm also looked to financial services partners, such as its bank, to provide financial expertise in running the business. The key activities and the strength of its human capital were well known to the company. Surprisingly, it was relationships with customer that provided the key to its growth trajectory. The company had thought of itself as providing specific hardware and software services defined by the business itself. When it transitioned to a customer value proposition of providing services that the customer valued, exponential growth ensued. The business also selected market segments that were growing. This included mobile gaming and banking, where the business's core competency of secure solutions came into play.

DISCUSSION

1. Use the macro, micro, and internal environment SWOT tables to analyze a business. Do this individually and then meet as a team to compare your analyses.
2. Complete the business model canvas for your business or a business in your community.

3 Many large accounting firms have horizontally integrated past providing just accounting services. Research and discuss how they have done this.

NOTES

1   Stephen C. Perry, "The Relationship between Written Business Plans and the Failure of Small Businesses in the U.S.," *Journal of Small Business Management* 39, no. 3 (2001): 201-8.

2   Henry Mintzberg, *The Rise and Fall of Strategic Planning* (New York: Free Press, 1994).

3   Ibid.

4   Ibid.

5   Gary J. Castrogiovanni, "Pre-Startup Planning and the Survival of New Small Businesses: Theoretical Linkages," *Journal of Management* 22, no. 6 (1996): 801-22.

6   Perry, "Relationship between Written Business Plans and the Failure of Small Businesses."

7   Henry Mintzberg, "Rethinking Strategic Planning, Part II: New Roles for Planners," *Long Range Planning* 27, no. 3. (1994): 22-30.

8   A sampling of mission statements can be found at www .missionstatements.com/fortune_500_mission_state ments.html.

9   J. Collins and J. Porras, "Building Your Company's Vision," *Harvard Business Review* 74, no. 5 (1996): 65-77.

10 Michael E. Porter, *Competitive Strategy: Techniques for Analyzing Industries and Competitors* (New York: Free Press, 1985).

11 Cathy Yang Liu, Gary Painter, and Qingfang Wang, *Lessons for US Metro Areas: Characteristics and Clustering of High-Tech Immigrant Entrepreneurs* (Kansas City, MO: Kauffman Foundation, March 2014).

12 D. B. Bibeault, *Corporate Turnaround: How Managers Turn Losers Into Winners* (New York: McGraw-Hill, 1982).

13 Michael E. Porter, "How Competitive Forces Shape Strategy," *Harvard Business Review* 57, no. 2 (1979): 137-45.

14 Michael E. Porter, "The Five Competitive Forces That Shape Strategy," *Harvard Business Review* (January 2008): 1-17.

15 Porter, "How Competitive Forces Shape Strategy."

16 Michael E. Porter, *Competitive Advantage: Creating and Sustaining Superior Performance* (New York: Free Press, 1998).

17 C. K. Prahalad and Gary Hamel, "The Core Competence of the Corporation," *Harvard Business Review* 68, no. 3 (1990): 79-91.

18 Porter, *Competitive Strategy.*

19 J. M. Roberts, H. H. Stevenson, W. A. Sahlman, P. W. Marshall, and R. G. Hamermesh, *New Business Ventures and the Entrepreneur* (Boston: McGraw-Hill/Irwin, 2007).

20 Alexander Osterwalder and Yves Pigneur, *Business Model Generation: A Handbook for Visionaries, Game Changers, and Challengers* (Hoboken, NJ: John Wiley and Sons, 2010).

2. Consulting, Teaming, and Project Management

ABOUT THIS CHAPTER

The key role played by consultants in any enterprise is that of change agents. Consultants are employed when the business does not have the knowledge resources to capitalize on an opportunity or solve a business problem. The consultant provides that knowledge, but knowledge in itself is not enough. More often than not, the business needs to transform itself to take full advantage of the opportunity. The process of change involves education, commitment, and execution. It is the consultant who must spark this within the enterprise. With small business consulting, the relationship between the consultant and the business owner is pivotal to the consultant being an effective change agent. The first part of this chapter deals with fostering a productive client-consultant relationship. Once the relationship has been established, the consultant moves to executing the consulting project through data gathering and proposing an action plan. As a change agent, the student consulting team must communicate recommendations in such a way that the business owner will use them to transform his or her business.

Most consulting projects are of such magnitude that they cannot be completed by any one individual. They require not just a group of people but a team working collaboratively to complete the often complex tasks. Typically, consulting projects have tight deadlines, and the goal is to maximize client value and project a clear plan that identifies all tasks. For financially constrained small businesses, reducing costs associated with hiring outside consultants is often important but can lead to less effective results. Attention must be paid to both plan and tasks in order for the project to be successful. Focusing on one to the exclusion of the other can hinder the level of accomplishment. This chapter discusses both the teaming process and the project management plan.

Consulting projects undertaken in an academic setting present challenges to the student team beyond what students typically face in a class and beyond what professional consultants face. Unlike other academic assignments, where the parameters are defined and presented in a classroom setting, these projects are open ended in a fluid environment. For students unfamiliar with working on such projects, this can be unsettling, and they may spend an inordinate amount of time honing in on goals and performing the work. The nature of the academic term requires that the project be substantially completed in the designated time frame. The student team must thus make full use of project management tools to keep the project on track. Student teams also tend to be diverse, and the team is often working with a business owner of a different culture.

With student consulting projects, the worst outcome is to consume the extremely valuable time of the students, advisors, mentors, faculty, and business owners while accomplishing little of value for the business because of teaming issues. This is particularly harmful to a small business, which can scarcely afford the time and distraction. Student members suffer as well. An unpleasant team experience can foster dysfunctional team behavior that individuals may carry to the next team experience. Team conflict inhibits learning and development. A poorly executed project reflects badly on the school or other sponsoring organizations, as well as on all team members, including the faculty, advisors, or mentors who are guiding the students.

Good teams, however, have the chance to add value to a business and contribute to regional economic development. The majority of student consulting teams produce projects that are of great benefit to their businesses.

The goal of teaming and project management is to make the teaming experience rewarding and project management effective. In order to accomplish this, team members have to spend as much time working and reflecting on teaming skills as on completing the tasks of the project.

After Studying This Chapter

The objective of this chapter is to prepare students for the teaming experience by presenting theory and practice about the teaming process and project management. After reading this chapter, students will be able to:

- Understand key components of the consulting process.
- Describe the attributes of high-performance teams.
- Identify and use techniques of divergent thinking.
- Articulate how culture can affect communication in a team.
- Explain the stages of teaming and describe what actions must be taken at each stage.
- Identify and use the concepts and tools of project management, including project planning, work structure breakdown, Gantt charts, critical path analysis, and project control systems.

NATURE OF EMERGING BUSINESS CONSULTING

Major differences exist between approaches for consulting with small enterprises and approaches with large enterprises. Most small businesses do not have the financial resources to pay for highly specialized departments with highly skilled teams. For example, family-owned restaurants, construction companies, and manufacturing firms will often have a management team of one to three generalists who are responsible for setting the company's vision and direction. Even IT services companies with $25 million in annual revenue that serve Fortune 50 companies typically have up to three executives charged with oversight of the entire company. These senior leaders will oversee all aspects of marketing, accounting, financial management, operations, and human resources. In smaller businesses, it is the entrepreneur who performs these business management functions.

The vast majority of entrepreneurs bootstrap the start-up and growth of their companies and make effective decisions with limited information, capital,

and human resources. When working with small enterprises, the consultant has to address all business and operational processes rather than delving deeply into one area of the business. For example, in a large enterprise a consultant may complete research to identify new market niches for a company to enter. The consultant can assume that, once the new direction is identified, the large company has the skilled managers to examine and plan for the impact this expansion will have on company operations, financing needs, and staffing. The small business consultant, however, cannot assume that the business has managers with these skills and so must address them herself. It follows that the small business consultant must be more of a generalist than a specialist and must be able to address all areas of the business. This consultant also understands that his or her role is to help the business owner learn and transform.

Entry

The entry phase of the consulting project is when the goal and scope of the project are defined. Prior to defining this, consultants must learn as much as possible about the small business to determine its primary area of need. Be aware that often what the business owner initially articulates may not be the actual goal. Often business owners are acutely aware of symptoms but may not have worked through causes. As an example, a four-person architectural company sought help from a team of student consultants to conduct market research and develop a marketing plan to reach private commercial development clients. Through discussions with the CEO over a four-week period, it became clear that the lead architects knew whom to target and how to target them, but they lacked sales and networking skills. As a result of digging deep into the company's operations and history, the student consultants were able to focus on the underlying issue rather than limit themselves to the initial surface concern.

Throughout the initial interview, the consultant is creating ground rules for the consulting engagement. These may include establishing expectations of the consultant-client working relationship. Issues that may surface include the amount of information the business owner is willing to share with the consultant. Obviously, the more information made available to the consultant, the more effective she will be. However, business owners are often hesitant to be forthcoming with certain information, such as financial statements. Unlike with public companies, where financial disclosure is required, outsiders are not privy to the financial information of small businesses. Often small business finances are tied very closely to the personal finances of the business owner. Disclosure about earnings becomes a very sensitive matter. The consultant needs to be aware of this privacy concern. This is often dealt with in the consulting contract. A confidentiality clause will state that information will not be shared with any outside parties.

In order to be an effective change agent, the small enterprise consultant needs to develop a strong bond of trust with the business owner. The first step is to ensure that confidentiality will be maintained. The consulting team cannot betray this trust by discussing business matters with any outside parties.

At the entry phase, the consultant has the exciting task of finding out as much as he or she can about the business and crafting an agreement that will become the signpost for the entire engagement. Often the leader of the consulting team will be tasked with finding out about the business and developing the consulting contract. This involves an in-depth interview covering history, legal structure, and a broad range of business functions. A framework for an initial in-depth interview that uses concepts described in chapter 1 follows:

1. What is the mission of the business?
2. Who are the stakeholders?
3. What is the existing business model?
   - Industry? Size of industry? Number of competitors? Mature or growth industry? How many new entrants? Nature of competition (large or small)?
   - How does the business fit in? What products or services will it offer? What is its history? Is the legal structure appropriate?
   - What trademarks or patents does it hold? Who are the key managers, and what do they contribute?
   - What products and services does the business offer? What are its brands? What segment of the market does the business target? What are its prices, and how do they compare to those of competitors? How does the company manage the customer life cycle? What kind of customer service is given?
   - What is its revenue model? What drivers are key to profitability?

4. What is the market?
   - What market is being targeted? Who are the customers—demographics, geographic location, and psychographic profile? What is the customer value proposition? How is the value proposition presented to the customer? What is the relationship with the customer? What is the quality of the buy experience? How do customers feel about the firm? How does the business acquire customers? How does it measure customer satisfaction? What is customer profitability? What is customer retention? Describe the customer life cycle using relevant measures. What is the sales cycle?
   - What is the existing market share? How is the business positioned in the marketplace? What is the image and reputation of the business? Does it have brand equity? Describe how the business is positioned on functionality, quality, and price measures.

5. What are company processes?
   - How does the company develop new products and services? How long does it take? How much does it cost? When is breakeven reached?
   - Who are the key vendors? What resources (materials, etc.) have to be used?
   - What is the distribution system?

6. How does the company learn and grow?
   - Who are the employees? Do they understand the mission of the business? How productive are they? Are they empowered to make decisions and if so what can they decide on their own? Do they have the skill sets to succeed? What is employee turnover?
   - What kind of technology does the company use? What steps are taken to use technology to achieve goals?

When working with any small business client, it takes time to build trust in order to get to the place where real information about the struggles and opportunities that a company faces can emerge. Consultants need to learn about facets of the business that a business owner may not wish to reveal during initial conversations. This hesitancy comes from the fact that the business is often the "owner's baby." All of the business's strengths and weaknesses are the result of the actions of the owner and the management team. Many business owners are reluctant to reveal the true weaknesses to outside "experts" for fear of being viewed negatively or considered inadequate as an owner or manager. Student teams will often spend considerable time hearing about the business owner's personal history. In certain cultures, this is an important part of trust building.

Experience also shows that the racial and ethnic background of the client, as well as the consultants, plays a role in how easily and quickly information is shared. For example, due to generations of mistrust on financial issues, Native American–owned companies may be reluctant to show financial statements to white consultants working with government agencies. Similarly, new immigrants from Latin America, Asia, Africa, or Eastern Europe find that the systems of financial management and record keeping in their home country are very different from the systems in the United States. Thus consultants operating from a US-based system of accounting find it a challenge to get the necessary financial information from these prospective clients.

Another challenge is that early-stage enterprises often lack experience in working with consultants. Typical of their bootstrapping nature, owners of small enterprises will seek to get as much from a consultant as possible. This can lead to conflict for any project, but especially one where the time frame is fixed. During the entry phase, a careful discussion of the scope of the project and timelines will greatly aid work throughout the rest of the engagement. Project deliverables should be clearly articulated. Of course, it is important to be somewhat flexible in the process. Conditions, problems, and needs of the client may change, or unforeseen circumstances may occur. Adaptive responses must be made in order to be effective in the consulting process. First and foremost, consultants must be professional even when they are firmly drawing the line on what will be done.

Business Case

Just as the business model described in chapter 1 provides the beneficial rationale for the business, the business case provides the beneficial rationale for the consulting project. The business case must convincingly argue the value that the consulting project will bring to the business; and the value must be measurable. Typically, the consultant will conduct research, gather data, analyze the data, draw conclusions, and then come up with a solution at the end of the engagement. In fact, good consultants determine very early in the consulting

assignment what the business needs and the shape of the solution. They accomplish this by conducting a very quick market, financial, and operational analysis. Even though information may be incomplete, the team uses it to apply judgment in coming up with the business case. The business case must be compiled with objectivity. The key is to come up with the business case early and to reevaluate it several times throughout the course of the project to ensure that it remains valid.

One restaurant owner thought his key issue was attracting new customers to his existing customer base of low- to moderate-income families. Through discussion and analysis of the previous two years' performance, it became clear that food and labor costs had escalated. In response, the restaurant needed to raise its prices. But the price increases were more than what the customer base could afford, since many customers had jobs that paid less than $30,000 per year on average. Additionally, because of gentrification, many of the restaurant's clients had moved out of the surrounding neighborhood. The neighborhood had been transformed from a low- and moderate-income neighborhood into one with above-average rent and housing prices.

In order for the restaurant to continue to serve its traditional customers, it had to reduce prices below a profitable level. An alternate strategy of pursuing the newer upscale residents in the neighborhood seemed self-defeating as well. The restaurant would have to change its product mix and restaurant atmosphere, which would result in a loss of many of the company's traditional clients. The consulting team considered all these factors and identified the goal of developing a strategy for a catering division. By creating a new division, the business would not alienate its current customers, yet it could pursue the opportunity to sell to business clients for whom quality food and service, rather than price, were the drivers.

In summary, the business case will state the problem or opportunity in a very succinct manner, outline the benefits or how money will be made, and point toward solutions. Once the business case has been outlined, the team can move productively into gathering information and evidence and formulating the detailed action plan. If a business case is clear and logical, the consulting team can proceed very efficiently.

Contracting

Once the business challenge has been identified and the scope of a project has been discussed, the consultant drafts a contract that clearly defines work areas, timelines, and resources needed from the client. For some student teams, this contract has been discussed and partly developed through prior work with faculty or staff from a sponsoring institution. This may occur because of the short time frame involved in a quarter- or semester-long project. These work areas will focus on specific results that will benefit the client.

Student consulting projects most often focus on marketing opportunities (feasibility of a new market, moving into adjacent markets, providing consistent branding through websites and other marketing materials, etc.) or on analyzing the company's financial performance by comparing profitability in one area of the business against another. Reviewing business processes and recommending improvements is another prime area. This includes streamlining operations, standardizing procedures, and acquiring systems so that the business can expand. Although the menu of possibilities is quite large, the selection of student projects is based on a fit with the skill level and expertise of the student consultants and compatibility with the resources available to the client. Additional consideration is given to the constraint that actionable solutions must be delivered within the time frame required by the business and consultants.

Many small business owners have little or no experience working with a consultant and thus often hope that all of their organizational needs can be addressed by one consultant. In a real-world consulting engagement this is possible, as the client will be paying on an hourly basis for the work to be completed. When working with student consultants whose time is limited by the academic quarter or semester and who have numerous other competing priorities, it is important for the client and the student consultants to strike a balance between all the client's needs and the depth of investigation and analysis. With the fluid nature of fledgling enterprises, it is strategically more beneficial to address all areas of the business at a moderate level of depth than to address only one area very deeply.

Another primary challenge for student consulting teams is that they may lack the skills necessary to fully meet the desires of the business owner. Client satisfaction is maximized when the full scope of work can be accomplished. Thus, it would be better to deliver benefits to the client from a small project that is well done than to deliver partial results from a broad-based project. Having one success leads to others. Failure very likely would keep the business at a standstill. It could also set the business back. Often, student teams can access additional expertise from their advisors.

A statement of the work areas addressed in the student consulting engagement process defines the project goals. Typically, two to four work areas are specified, with subtasks listed. In selecting the work areas, attention should be placed on projects that can be completed by student consultants and that the business commits to executing. The business owner and student consultants must keep these goals clearly in mind throughout the life of the engagement.

Bearing all this in mind, the contract may include the following:

- Agreement of the business owner to provide information and to attend meetings (typically scheduled weekly).
- Commitment of the students and mentors to keep all business information confidential except for discussion in class.
- An understanding that the work is provided pro bono and that execution of any solutions is the sole responsibility of the business owner. No claims on gains can be made by students, faculty, or advisors, and no claims for liabilities can be made by the business owner.
- Obligation of the student consulting team to complete the work within the academic period.

When finalizing a contract, consultants should remember that written agreements are understood differently in low-context cultures and high-context cultures. In low-context cultures (such as white non-Hispanic or European cultures), where the emphasis is on the written word, e-mailing the contract for the client to read is often an effective review method. Groups such as Asians, Hispanics, Native Americans, and African Americans are high context. In high-context cultures, the interpretation of the message is heavily dependent on the nature of the relationship between the sender and the receiver, as well as on all previous communication. A face-to-face meeting to review and agree on the contract is recommended. Even revisions need to be discussed and agreed upon in face-to-face interactions. In one case, the consulting team was composed primarily of non-Hispanic white students, and their client was the owner of a multimillion-dollar African American insurance brokerage company. The team sought to clarify the contract language regarding research the students would undertake to help design a new line of services. The students were focused on the exact words of the contract, whereas the client was focused on the underlying meaning and the possibility that the scope might be extended. Not until a face-to-face meeting was held could the different interpretations be understood and clarified.

It is important to note that in a very few instances, business owners are unable to overcome trust issues or to commit fully or agree to the scope and objective of the project. Given the limited time of the project and the need to complete the requirements of the course, student consulting teams may have to proceed without the full input of the business owner. Although this is less than optimal, student teams can still engage in a good learning experience.

DATA COLLECTION AND ANALYSIS

Figure 2-1 outlines phases of research, analysis, decision making, and action steps. Each phase is essential to a good consulting product. Keep in mind that the process of gathering data is one of continuous improvement. The vigilant team will evaluate data well in advance of the deadline and gather new information as necessary.

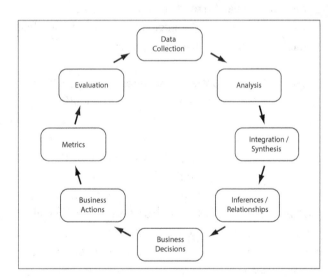

FIGURE 2-1. Overview of Data Gathering and Analysis Process

Data Collection

The majority of a consulting team's work is spent collecting data and assembling information about the client, the business environment, and the strengths, weaknesses, opportunities, and threats faced by the company. A good

motto for this phase is "leave no stone unturned." Student consultants are often eager to develop recommendations, but the emphasis early on should be on gathering data to support such recommendations. Prior to meeting with the client for the first time, the consulting team should have already conducted thorough secondary research to better understand the industry and marketplace in which the client is operating. Be aware that this research can take a significant number of hours when individuals are inexperienced in researching these areas. Unlike academic research, which is more accessible, research into businesses is often challenging due to proprietary information and requires ingenuity to accomplish.

Novice consulting teams commonly make two major mistakes when it comes to gathering data. The first is that once the project plan is created, individual team members perform their tasks without maintaining adequate communications with other team members, mentors, and advisors. As a result, teams may produce deliverables that are disjointed and do not contribute to a viable solution for the business.

The second major mistake is that, in the haste and pressure to complete the project, the team fails to budget enough time for information and data synthesis. The equally unfortunate result is that much of the data generated will lack coherence or relevance for business. Unless extensive work is done to sift, sort, and integrate data late in the process, the business receives a data dump as a finished product rather than an action plan that will capitalize on an opportunity or solve a problem.

Integration/Synthesis

Novice teams are often proficient at developing project plans and conducting secondary research via database and Internet searches, and they may even do well at creating and conducting primary research. Once all this hard work has been accomplished, these same teams may hit a roadblock when it comes to completing meaningful analysis of the information they worked so diligently to collect. Even more teams struggle to come up with viable and effective solutions or action steps for the business. Finally, with the rush to close, teams may fail to come up with suitable metrics to measure future results once their recommendations are implemented. All these phases are crucial to an effective solution. If analysis is flawed, the action steps will be wrong. If action steps are not viable, the business could waste time, effort, and money. If metrics are not defined, follow-up, which is critical to emerging businesses, cannot be performed. The business does not learn and will not be able to move to the next level. Fortunately, with knowledge and experience, these obstacles can be overcome.

Once students have collected all the data they need, the team should meet to review what has been learned. Often, novice consulting teams will find that they have to collect additional data because the information they have points to other areas of inquiry or opportunities for the company. Sometimes more data needs to be collected because the wrong type of information was inadvertently collected the first time. It is important for the team to collect as much information as early as possible in the project and to do continuous assessment as a team so that there will be sufficient time to gather additional data if needed.

It is possible to spend too much time collecting data, because data collection has to be balanced against other tasks that need to be accomplished in the short time frame of the project. Deciding when enough data have been collected is a judgment call. In terms of resources, consider the constraints of time and money and the importance of the decisions that are to be made. With respect to content, the information must be accurate and timely, and there must be adequate information to explore several possible options or solutions. A further consideration is to avoid collecting misinformation and to minimize missing and redundant information.

One student team was researching the feasibility of purchasing a $1 million printing machine for a package manufacturing company. The team had collected significant demand data and trend analysis from competitors and industry trade journals. When team members met to determine their recommendation to the client, they realized that they had failed to collect product pricing and equipment operating cost data. Although the project time was half over, they still had sufficient time to collect this information. If they had done their data analysis later in the project, they likely would have had insufficient time to conduct the additional research.

After initial data collection and analysis, the team must go through a process of analyzing the business. The consultant has a responsibility to take a cold, hard, objective look at the business and what it does. It is important to focus on asking and getting complete answers to the right questions. When delivering the results of the cold, hard, objective look to a business owner, remember that the role of the consultant is to help drive change. How a

message is delivered can lead to a greater or lesser willingness to change. Thus, careful preparation for client meetings and assessing how information will be received is critical to any consultant's success.

Inferences/Relationships

Working for a small business is such a rich experience for student consultants because most small business needs are mission-critical. Numerous student consulting projects have had a major impact on a business, with benefits ranging from increasing sales by 50% to the very survival of the company. Small enterprises do not have the financial resources to redo the work of consulting teams; for the most part, they will implement the recommendations that the teams develop. However, if consultants do not get it right, the business can suffer. The key is to deliver a product that benefits the client. In order to be of beneficial gain, the product must be actionable and accompanied by the necessary resources for implementation. Expected outcomes and benefits must be measurable.

As the team conducts its analysis, it should be briefing the business owner. These briefings serve to verify information, educate the business owner, and test the limits of what is achievable. Caution must be exercised with how analysis is communicated. Most business owners are not accustomed to the objective and often harsh way in which analysis is conducted in academic settings. Presenting the business owner with a written report that heavily criticizes management practices can be destructive. In one case, presenting this report to a Somalian business caused the business owner to abandon the project completely. The business owner was not accustomed to looking at his business in an objective and analytical manner. He took the feedback as an insult. In general, it is best to present feedback face-to-face, being sensitive to the business owner's response to each issue. Any results and meetings of this sort should be reviewed with faculty and advisors prior to meeting with the business owners.

Business Decisions and Actions

Most small enterprise projects will require that the consultants carry them through to implementation. The team will develop action steps and get business owners started on implementation. For small enterprises, these steps may have to be specified in more detail than for larger enterprises. The team must devise a means of measuring gains and work with the business owners to ensure that they know what the gains are and how they will be measured. With minority businesses, because of language or cultural differences, it may be necessary (but in any case helpful) to take time to communicate carefully and clearly. At times it may be useful to repeat a point or issue and ask a question of the client to make sure that effective communication has occurred. Remember what is at stake in consulting outcomes: implementing results that solve problems to provide new opportunities and other value-added benefits.

Because small enterprises often do not have the human resources needed to follow up on solutions and recommendations, consultants may be directly involved in the implementation of a project plan. This type of involvement can lead to potential problems. Team members may be unclear as to what implementation means. There may be a lack of communication between the team and the business owners as to how far the team will go in the implementation. Other problems arise when the consulting team is not specific and detailed in the implementation steps. Finally, if individual team members have not totally committed to the officially proposed solution, this will make implementation more complicated and challenging. In the worst case it could get in the way of or prevent effective implementation.

To reiterate, the presentation and final report are important to developing the skill sets of the student consultants; these consulting products provide a road map for implementation and an audit trail for measuring success. However, in themselves they will not communicate effectively to the business owner and, in fact, if given in isolation, they may thwart the effort.

More often than not, student teams that discover that a particular product line (or an entire company) can never become profitable find it difficult to recommend that the business divest itself of the product line or close entirely. The difficulty comes from the fact that the business owner likely spent many hours and much expense to launch and maintain the business or product line. The student team should consult extensively with advisors and faculty as to how such a situation should be handled. Additionally, the business owner must be part of the entire process in making such a decision, so that it is as much his or her decision as the student team's. Sensitivity must be considered in how to communicate such findings. Under no circumstances should the student team begin to propose such steps without in-depth analysis and review by faculty.

Metrics

For small business consulting the goal is helping companies adapt to changes and become more competitive. Peter Block, founder of Designed Learning and author of numerous books on consulting, talks about being an authentic consultant, one who is objective and will not make recommendations that are detrimental to the client.[1] The authentic consultant will not hide who he or she is nor will the consultant ever hide the truth. Care, honesty, depth, and saying no to commercialism is key to being authentic. In a sense, the consultant-client relationship is akin to the physician-patient relationship. The doctor takes an oath to do no harm. For most small businesses, participating in the consulting project can in itself be a drain and detract from day-to-day essential operations. Vague analysis, nonactionable recommendations, or incorrect conclusions can do substantial harm to the business. This is especially true for small enterprises that do not have the reserves or resources to absorb and survive mistakes the way large enterprises can.

Metrics should be selected that match the work areas of the project. Teams can select from the large library of metrics or key performance indicators (KPIs) that has grown with the increasing use of continuous improvement and analytics in large enterprises. For example, in the category of sales, such indicators include sell-through percentage, market share, repeat business turnover/revenue, conversion rate of marketing/sales campaigns, customer attrition or churn, average spent per customer, and average order size. In the area of production, key performance indicators include inventory turns, average production costs, manufacturing schedule adherence, defect or spoilage rate, on-time delivery rate, freight cost per unit, transit time, and customer order cycle time. Chapter 7 discusses these elements in detail.

Follow-Up Evaluation

Although the student team may complete its work with the delivery of the final report, advisors may continue to track the business after the project has been completed, and certainly the business owner will continue with the change process. Advisors encourage the business owner to overcome resistance to change and implement the recommended changes. They enhance the recommendations with additional information or by linking the business to networks that will increase its chances of successes. Often referrals are made to other sources of technical assistance or education. The bar is set significantly higher when the double bottom line—profitability and social value—is to be achieved.

TEAMING

Amy Edmondson, a professor of management at Harvard Business School, argues that in the knowledge economy, teaming is a dynamic activity in which participants learn as the team itself becomes the engine of organizational learning.[2] In this teaming scenario, the environment is fast changing and organizations must adapt quickly. The means by which they adapt is the team. The team and the organization exist in a constant state of learning. As the team learns, it teaches the organization how to innovate and transform so that it can thrive in a global, fast-moving, and competitive marketplace. This description is also true of multicultural student consulting teams. Students are often participating in their first team experience of grappling with a real problem or opportunity. They are learning how to work as a team where stakes are higher than a typical assignment. The situation is complex. There is a tremendous amount of knowledge to learn and apply—some of which students have learned in theory and much of which they have not encountered. There are no correct answers. Students must also learn to get the best work from diverse team members. The team's goal is not only to learn all this but to concurrently teach a business how to transform its business model so that it can survive and thrive.

Teams cannot be static entities or stable structures. Team members must understand their traditional tasks of recognizing and clarifying interdependence, establishing trust, and learning how to work together. But diverse teams do not have the luxury of spending time to bond or share personal history. Each team member must come into the team with openness to diverse viewpoints and a willingness to ask questions frequently to learn quickly.

In the case of student teams working with client businesses, the students are required to deliver a quality result (product) that meets established professional standards. The product should be presentable to a client as well as to other stakeholders in the business community. Meeting these expectations presents opportunities to display or demonstrate important skills. But the process may also be a source of stress and turmoil for the team.

High-Performance Teams

High-performance teams produce extraordinary results often under significant constraints. They are the appropriate model for student teams because the students are also being asked to perform against the odds to assist an underserved business in pursuing an opportunity. Projects must be completed under very tight timelines, with none of the resources available to employees of large corporations.

High-performance teams can produce results far above and beyond what prior teams have been able to accomplish. They solve the world's most difficult problems (e.g., low-cost and effective vaccination of children in underdeveloped countries) and often include experts. Care and time should be taken in putting together such teams; choosing the right team members is crucial to success. It is also important to create the right context for the team to succeed. The process of a high-performance team was documented in a 2001 case study and key attributes were identified.[3] Other characteristics and conditions associated with high-performance teams are summarized briefly.

Commitment to excellence. It stands to reason that high-performance teams typically consist of high-performance individuals. In order to complete projects of extraordinary quality, all team members must have the highest expectations for success. They will not tolerate a substandard product from themselves or the team. Members will go to extraordinary lengths to achieve the best outcome. For student teams this is likely to happen when every student commits to excellence.

Mutual respect. With high expectations and short timelines, team members work under stressful conditions. Difficult situations and conflicts may occur. Emotions may run high, and team members may communicate in ways that they later regret. It is imperative that the team work in a context of mutual respect. Individuals understand that no matter how difficult the situation, they will emerge from the team experience with respect for each other and their contribution to the team effort.

Shared risk and reward. The leader of the team is not the only individual responsible for the performance and failings of the team. All team members feel accountable for all actions of the team. If an individual team member cannot complete a task, other team members will put forth the extra effort needed to assist so the project can continue moving toward on-time task completion.

Flexibility. Contrary to conventional wisdom, high-performance teams do not have plans that are created at the beginning of the project and followed religiously until the end. New information is generated and shared continuously. The usual linear model for completing projects gives way to the rapid generation of ideas that are exposed and evaluated while still in a relatively immature state. If they are deemed appropriate, the plan is changed to adapt to the new input. Experienced team leaders suggest that agile development techniques be used, in which the team leader will check in every day with all team members, asking the following three questions: What did you do yesterday? What are you doing today? Do you need help?

Atmosphere of cooperation. As unfamiliar ideas and analyses are encountered in exploring solutions to problems, team members are likely to make mistakes. In the team environment, the mistakes are visible to everyone. Therefore, it is important to have an atmosphere of cooperation where team members understand that mistakes will be made and the team can learn from them and move on to successful results.

Acknowledged interdependence. Some students may assume that a few strong team members can complete the project, and this small group may break off from the team so that they can "more efficiently" get the job done. This is a mistake, as it will lead to producing a lower volume and typically a lower quality of work for the client. Acknowledging interdependence means that every team member is necessary to the success of the project. It is the combined efforts of all team members that will result in the best product.

Trust. Many teaming experts believe that the success of the team depends on how quickly trust is established among the members. Most challenging projects involve what seems like an inordinate amount of work, willpower, and creativity. The more one can count on team members to meet project goals, the higher the level of team trust reached. When first presented, innovative solutions may seem off the wall or even ludicrous. It is trust in the team member that will lead to exploration and the most

creative solutions. Trust is essential to team members performing at the highest level of excellence.

Heroism. Team members on a high-performance team will do what it takes to get the job done regardless of position or title outside of the team. A difficult situation or conflict may arise that calls for someone to show courage. Often one or more team members will perform acts of heroism that will get the team through a rough spot. Good team members reward acts of heroism.

Focus on shared performance outcomes. Each team member has a clear vision of the outcomes and a common commitment to achieve it. No time is spent on extraneous activities. Team time is used to accomplish team work. Meetings are not spent reviewing or summarizing the work of individual members. Any such review should be completed prior to the meeting. The team meeting is used to advance the project by completing other work. No distractions are tolerated.

Beyond these attributes, high-performance teams can be chaotic. They undergo large and small changes because team members are constantly experimenting and generating new ideas. A team may seemingly make no progress and then come through with a breakthrough in its eleventh hour. Often the process is the most disruptive just before such a breakthrough. As conflict is a vital part of the creative process in teaming, it should not be stifled. At the same time, the teaming environment should be a safe place to speak up, question, or experiment. Team members should be held accountable for their work. Learning happens when individuals feel psychological safety and are held accountable.

Task behaviors help the team stay focused and accomplish its goals, as shown in Table 2-1.[4]

Equally important are relationship behaviors. They help maintain a healthy environment for team members and keep communication open and flowing, as shown in Table 2-2.

There is a third set of behaviors—self-oriented behaviors—that generally disrupt team functioning. They include depending on others instead of doing one's own work, resisting the direction chosen by the team, withdrawing from the group, pairing off, putting others down, getting off topic, complaining, moping, being silent, triangulating, and dominating the discussion. For novice teams, it is important for the team to name such behav-

TABLE 2-1. Team Task Behaviors

Task Behaviors	Behavior	Purpose
Initiating	Define task, goal, or process	Helps team find direction when floundering
Seeking information and opinions	Collect more data or ask for individual opinions or ideas	Inadequate data gathering can lead to poor problem solving and decision making
Giving information and opinions	Provide data, relevant information, opinions, and ideas	Ensures the team has all the information it needs to accomplish the task
Clarifying and elaborating	Ask for clarification, build on other's ideas, or clarify an idea	Provides focus for team and builds on other's ideas
Summarizing	Restate key points, decisions, action plans, or themes	Focuses discussion and establishes closure
Evaluating	Assess whether group is performing tasks or using procedures effectively	Determines if team is functioning effectively
Testing for consensus	Poll the group and determine if there is consensus. Open discussion on objections	Determines if every team member supports decision

Source: R. Blake and J. Mouton, Spectacular Teamwork: How to Develop the Leadership Skills for Team Success (New York: Wiley, 1987)

TABLE 2-2. Team Relationship Behaviors

Relationship Behaviors	Behavior	Purpose
Gatekeeping	Ask individuals for their input and control individuals who wish to monopolize the discussion	Balances communication and includes all team members
Active listening	Paraphrase what was heard, indicate understanding, and ask clarifying questions	Values contribution and ensures correct understanding
Setting and maintaining standards	Set standards and define norms. Require that team members adhere to norms.	Defines how the team should work together and ensures that members maintain their standards
Harmonizing	Articulate common elements of conflicting viewpoints	Promotes compromise and collaboration
Encouraging	Give recognition and point out accomplishments	Creates positive team environment
Giving feedback	Give constructive feedback on behavior that is having a negative effect on the group	Supports effective behavior and discourages dysfunctional behavior
Receiving feedback	Actively listen without reacting or judging. Formulate a plan to change ineffective behavior.	Continuous feedback on team effectiveness

Source: R. Blake and J. Mouton, *Spectacular Teamwork: How to Develop the Leadership Skills for Team Success* (New York: Wiley, 1987)

iors so that team members understand that they are not acceptable. Table 2-3 summarizes communications that create and destroy value.

Team Development

In traditional team development, researchers and practitioners have identified four stages through which a team progresses. These phases are commonly referred to by the terms *forming, storming, norming,* and *performing.*[5] (See Figure 2-2.)

Forming. Individuals meet and become acquainted with other team members. The purpose and direction of the team is made clear. Team members find out what the team can and cannot do. They begin to establish trust with each other.

TABLE 2-3. Team Communication

Communication That Creates Value	Communication That Destroys Value
Asks questions frequently	Blaming, judgmental, accusative
Shows respect	Demanding
Acknowledges limits of knowledge	Denies choice
Uses direct and authentic language	Withholds information
Shares information	Contains labels
Invites participation	Silent
Seeks help	Crosses boundaries
Experiments	Penalizes for mistakes
Admits mistakes and sees as learning opportunities	Defers to hierarchy
Holds people accountable	

Storming. The difficulty and complexity of the task may start to overwhelm some team members. Conflict arises, and team members begin to argue about what should be done. No progress is made toward task completion. Teams may backpedal on work done previously.

Norming. The team moves to develop ground rules (norms) by which the team will operate and communicate. Each team member adopts a role. Expectations and standards are defined. Relationships between team members are strengthened, and commitment to the team is fostered. The team will begin to make significant progress toward project goals.

Performing. Team members incorporate individual strengths and weaknesses and work together. The focus is on completing the project. Roles become flexible. Relationships are strong. There is continuous improvement of the process.

Most depictions of these stages, assume that there is linear progression through each stage. In a real-world environment, teams actually move both forward and backward through these stages. A move backward may be the result of the team having insufficiently addressed issues relevant to the previous stage of development or, often,

disruptive events such as breakthroughs can trigger movement backward.

Forming Stage

The names of five students are called, and they are told they will be a student consulting team. With this unceremonious start, the forming stage begins. These five individuals must progress from knowing nothing about each other and the business with which they will work to being a team that will commit 400 to 500 hours (5 to 10 hours a week per person) to completing a challenging consulting project that will bring substantial value to a business. Although they will be successful in achieving this, at this early stage the students are full of insecurities.

Because they do not know each other, establishing their personal identity within the team is a major concern of each team member at the forming stage. Individuals may want recognition from others on the team. They may seek status. In doing this, they ask themselves questions such as: What role will I play in this group? How do I want others to perceive me? What can I contribute? Who is the leader? What is supposed to happen?

Part of the sense of insecurity arises from unfamiliarity with the consulting process. Like professional consultants when they begin a new project, the students start with very little knowledge about their project. They may have the name of the business and a list of work areas, but there are many unknowns. Students lack a sense of direction and are trying to get their bearings in this new situation. They feel self-conscious.

Being grouped with four strangers only adds to the uncertainty. There may not be any shared history. Team members may be from different cultures and some may

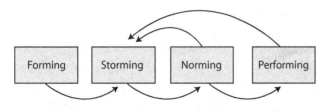

FIGURE 2-2. Team Phases

feel uncomfortable communicating in a group. Lack of trust prevents deep interaction between team members. Communication stays on a superficial level. Often the individuals look to faculty to provide leadership and direction. They will look to the mentor to guide them. At this initial phase, faculty will outline requirements and provide information. Experienced mentors will model leadership behavior, but both faculty and mentors will quickly turn the reins over to the team. In order to learn, the team must undergo the processing, planning, and executing of the project without too much intervention from faculty and mentors.

Each team member's goals in the forming stage are to get to know one another and to address questions about the process and the project. A team contract is usually drawn up once individuals have had a chance to interact with each other. The team contract includes a "code of cooperation" for the team and should establish team expectations, such as:

- Attend all meetings and be on time.
- Listen to and show respect for the views of other members.
- Critique ideas, not persons.
- There are no stupid questions.
- Avoid disruptive or distracting behavior.
- Carry out assignments on schedule.
- Resolve conflicts constructively, and always strive for win-win solutions.
- All team members are responsible for the team's progress.

Task issues may include:

- What is the best way to reach team members on a regular basis and in case of emergency?
- What are constraints on scheduling (including time away, other projects, or studying for exams)?
- How often, when, and where will the team meet?
- Is there a template for meeting agendas, minutes, and action items?
- How will data be collected, archived, and distributed?
- How will the workload be shared?
- How will each team member's effort and contributions be evaluated?
- How will work be circulated for review?
- How will action items be followed up?
- What is the standard for team work?

Relationship issues may include:

- What is the protocol for communication and response to communication?
- What is each team member's role (leader, facilitator, knowledge manager, etc.)?
- How will the team deal with members missing or being late to meetings?
- What are the rules for discussion and decision making during team meetings?
- How will team members' educational and professional developmental needs be addressed?
- What mechanism will the team have for flagging problems?
- How will a team member signal for help?
- When will outside help be sought?
- How will team members be rewarded?
- How will the team experience be evaluated?

Even with the short time frame, it is important to take the time to bond and establish trust. Once team members know each other, a leader should be chosen. Typically the role of the leader is to ensure the success of the rest of the team. There are no set ways to choose a leader. Some teams allow individuals to volunteer; others vote for a leader. The question of who will be team leader is often a point of contention for novice teams. Be aware that natural leaders may emerge later in the teaming process.

Most student teams define the role of the team leader as supervising the rest of the team. They see the team leader as someone who will tell the team what to do. In actual fact, the most important function of the leader is to open lines of communication with all team members and remove obstacles so the team can complete its job. Each team member must establish a relationship with the team leader. It is the responsibility of the team leader to ensure that time is taken to communicate with all the individuals. It is also important to remember that, even though the team may have a titular leader, different leadership may emerge as needed. Leadership issues and leadership roles must be discussed and agreed upon.

Be aware that consensus is not the goal of a team completing a small business consulting project, because consensus does not always lead to a good product. All team members must be heard. Team members should restate to the speaker what was heard and confirm that it is correct. Even if team members did not vote for a team decision, they will be asked if they can buy into it. It is essential that team members make the distinction and act accordingly.

Each team member must clarify her or his perception of the project mission. When the team members have a clear vision of their goals, the rules and procedures with which they will operate, the standards with which they will perform, and their expectations of each team member, they will have moved to a later phase of teaming: norming. Be aware that during the forming phase, little may be done to advance the project goals. However, time invested in establishing trust and eliminating uncertainty allows the team to be more productive in later phases.

Professional consultants often spend time in a planning retreat, where they discuss both the project and the team responsibilities and roles. While it is not necessary to spend an entire day in an off-site planning session, team members can discuss many of the same issues related to work styles and project goals. A candid discussion of each team member's strengths and weaknesses can go a long way toward establishing trust.

Novices often move through the forming stage in a superficial manner. This results from a lack of critical self-assessment and the desire to fit in with other team members. While it is commendable to try to fit in, honest communication is the best strategy. Without honest communication the team will never really form, and thus performance will be hindered later in the consulting process.

As the team moves toward developing its norms, cultural and personal differences will come into play. For example, team members for whom English is not their first language may be less vocal in expressing opinions. For some cultures, arriving on time means arriving no more than fifteen minutes late. For other cultures, arriving on time means arriving five minutes early. As team members commit to arriving on time to all meetings, it is important to clarify what "on time" means. It is equally important to iron out other matters of team protocol, keeping in mind that cultural perceptions may differ.

It is also important to recognize that, in a less diverse team, those who are in the minority might feel inhibited about offering opinions; likewise those in the majority might be tempted to bend over backward to accommodate what they perceive as differences. The keys to good team formation are honest self-assessment, open communication, appreciation of differences, and acknowledgment and full utilization of all of the skills and attributes of all team members.

The importance of speaking up in a team cannot be overstated. Research has shown that major issues and catastrophes have emerged because team members did not speak up when they foresaw a problem.[6] Reasons for not speaking up include deferring to a hierarchy or reluctance to look foolish. A key driver to team success is to ask questions and speak up often. In order for more reticent team members to speak up, the team may have to implement a practice of equal airtime. All team members should be asked for their feedback. Each team member should take on the responsibility of coming up with authentic questions that move the project forward and share any information he or she has. Team exercises have shown than even if separate team members have been given the information to solve a problem, the problem will not be solved because team members do not share the information. Lack of sharing can come about because team members assume that others know what they know or because team members want to exercise power by withholding information. Team members should provide the space to make mistakes and learn.

Team formation culminates with the drafting and signing of a team contract. The purpose of the team contract is to document the rules and regulations under which the team will operate. Expectations of each team member are disclosed, task and work standards are defined, communication protocols are outlined, and scheduling conflicts are identified and resolved. Other conflict resolution procedures are specified and accepted by the team. For novice team members, the significance of the contract is that it facilitates complete discussion of these issues and should help in gaining compliance from all team members.

Storming Stage

The storming stage is necessary for groups if they seek to reach a high level of performance. For some teams this stage will be short and uneventful, with only slight adjustments in expectations and roles. For others this stage can consume significant time and energy.

During the forming stage, team members have become familiar with each other and some of the work has been done. Secondary research will likely have begun and the first fruits of teamwork begin to trickle in. At the same time, traces of discontent may surface. As tasks are undertaken, differences in perceived quality and standards will arise. Individual team members may feel that others are not producing to the standards or quality agreed to by the team. They may feel that some team members are digressing on tangents not pertinent to project goals. Expressing this dissatisfaction brings up defensiveness or counterattacks. A faction of team members may question the legitimacy of the team leader.

There may be duplication of effort because some team members choose to assume the roles assigned to others. Team members jockey for position and status. Frustration builds from perceived violation of boundaries. The storming phase is characterized by lack of productive work; this results in additional consternation for the team.

As team members become more familiar with each other and develop their own views of where the project is going, disagreements often surface. The storming phase signals that team members are expressing their own viewpoints, and diversity in a team leads to superior results. The difficulty lies in teams not being able to move through this stage.

To move through the storming stage, the team must learn how to manage and resolve conflicts. The leader may play a key role in fostering a win-win resolution of disagreements. Faculty and advisors will redirect the team's focus to the project goals and successful completion and away from personal differences. At the same time, team members will be encouraged to express any ideas that advance project goals.

Using a diagnostic checklist for early detection of team conflicts can be extremely helpful. Teams are encouraged to use such a checklist frequently enough so that the team can develop solutions in consultation with faculty and other mentors before team problems become serious and much more difficult to manage or resolve. The evaluation tool in Table 2-4 can be used by all team members to rate team interaction.[7] For example, a score of more than 43 signals that the team requires more team building.

Frequently, persons in teams either misunderstand assignments or simply fail to follow through on what is requested. A feedback system (even a simple one such as the three questions, What did you do yesterday? What are you doing today? Do you need help?) can help to ensure that the project wheel keeps turning. If the team plans in advance how to handle members who do not meet their team obligations, there is less confusion about how to deal with poor performance. Additionally, if a team member fails to perform, wasting time on recrimination is unproductive. Rather, time should be taken to work out a way to help the team member to succeed. This is not to say that all work should be taken away from the team member, nor should the team member be shut out of the process in any way. In these consulting teams and projects, a major goal is to develop businesses, stu-

TABLE 2-4. Team Diagnostic Tool

	1 Low Evidence	2	3	4	5 High Evidence
Loss of production					
Grievances or complaints					
Conflicts or hostility					
Confusion about assignments or relationships					
Lack of clear goals or low commitment					
Apathy or lack of interest					
Lack of innovation, risk taking, imagination, or initiative					
Ineffective meetings					
Problems working with client					
Poor communication					
Lack of trust					
Decisions not understood or agreed with					
Good work is not recognized or rewarded					
People are not encouraged to work together					

Source: W. G. Dyer, *Team Building Issues and Alternatives*, 2nd ed. (Reading MA: Addison-Wesley, 1987)

dents, and advisors so they can make value-added contributions to project task completion.

Punishments do not develop teaming skills. Often they ensure that individuals who have not participated never will. If team members are unmotivated in the first place, punishment just excludes them completely. It is much more important to develop a system of reward. Business owners, mentors, advisors, and faculty can contribute to determining and offering effective rewards.

The nature of student teams—whose work is bounded by the start and end of a semester or quarter—can discourage efforts to work through the storming stage, because some students might prefer to simply count the days until the project ends. In the real world, where people work with each other on a repeated basis or seek to build a reputation that will advance their careers, working through the storming stage is critical. Using the opportunity provided by a student consulting project to learn how to navigate this stage can position a future business professional well for "the real world." The student should take some ownership of his or her role in any conflict and be proactive and cooperative in trying to move on to the norming stage.

Norming Stage

When the team has worked through the storming stage, several things happen: (a) the original team contract is revised to reflect what was learned in the storming stage, (b) newly defined roles and responsibilities are assumed by team members, and (c) the focus shifts away from group dynamics to reaching the team goal.

The norming phase is characterized by the strengthening of relationships between team members. Team members begin to put team goals above personal goals. All team members have agreed on how they will work together, who will provide leadership in what areas of the project, and how they will handle future conflicts. Teams enter the norming stage by resolving conflicts, developing unwritten rules for team interaction, and developing trust in each other. Individual team members will become more comfortable with their role in the team. Each member relies less on the leader and takes more responsibility for completing tasks, solving problems, and resolving conflicts.

It is important to remember that there is no right way for the team to function. Experienced team members know that each team will develop its own communication

protocol and operational process. Each team will have its own normative behaviors, a combination and synthesis of those of its members. Norming happens when team members can contribute their unique perspectives and skills and when those perspectives and skills are embraced for the good of the project. The more time the team spends together, the more team members should be able to collaborate and resolve issues. It is also important to note that some teams may revert to the storming stage, where issues need to be addressed again.

Throughout the consulting project, the team needs to be mindful of being focused on overall mission and goals. This does not mean the goals cannot change. Every project will undergo some amount of adjustment or "tweaking" as more knowledge is gathered. When key information is uncovered, the project plan needs to be changed to reflect this. Another continuing question is whether the client remains committed to the mission of the project. If commitment wavers, the team needs to deal with this by communicating, clarifying, and perhaps even helping with client motivation. After all, client buy-in is critical to the acceptance and implementation of project results and team recommendations.

Team Roles

During the forming stage, team members agreed to assume various team roles. Keep in mind that team roles can be interchanged or assumed by two members at the same time. When teams enter the norming stage, it is advisable to revisit these roles, which can include the following.

Team leader. The team leader is responsible for ensuring the success of each team member in delivering her or his work on behalf of the client. Because learning can be a stressful activity, the team leader must create a safe learning environment. Leadership in the team must create a psychologically safe environment because this encourages speaking up, clear thinking, and productive conflict. It also mitigates risk, promotes innovation, ties goals to performance, and increases accountability. There can be no recrimination when team members are unfamiliar with what is being done. The role of the team is to help each team member learn. It is especially important that the team learns from failure rather than simply ignoring it. The leader must be supportive and foster commitment from all team members. He or she must create win-win resolutions out of conflicts by identifying the nature of the conflict, modeling good communication, identifying shared goals, and encouraging difficult conversations.

In novice project teams, it is sometimes difficult to get individuals to step up to be team leader. Often students may not want to appear aggressive. In some cases, the individual who volunteers to be team leader may not be the best choice. He or she may envision the leader's role as autocratic. In fact, the leader must often fill in to complete day-to-day tasks in order to maintain the confidence and cooperation of team members. He or she may be responsible for keeping lines of communication open when there is conflict. Student teams tend to operate with little formal hierarchy so that trust and leadership needs to be earned.

Team facilitator. The team facilitator may assist the leader in planning team meetings, leading meetings, and handling meeting logistics and administrative tasks. The facilitator creates awareness of the process and manages discussion flow and strategic moments. Additionally, the facilitator may be the main contact person between the team, the business owner, mentors, and advisors. As the contact or point person, the facilitator is responsible for keeping everyone informed of all interactions. Withholding this information or becoming a gatekeeper can cause both conflict and lack of productivity. For example, one team facilitator had collected competitive price lists from the client business but failed to share this with other team members. The team member who was doing the pricing analysis wasted a significant number of hours trying to find the information.

Team knowledge manager. The team knowledge manager documents the team process, captures key points of the analysis, highlights decisions and action items, and distributes information often through a shared site. This role facilitates frequent communication between all team members by ensuring that all knowledge and communication is shared.

Devil's advocate. The devil's advocate asks questions that challenge the majority and present different points of view. Often this role is assumed on an ad hoc basis. Experimentation is one of the drivers of team success. It leads to more learning. Often in the rush of completing the project, team members will opt for the easy route or

succumb to groupthink. Having a team member who asks the hard questions is crucial to keeping the team learning and the project on the right path.

Mentors or advisors. Industry mentors or advisors may be used in student consulting projects. As working professionals, these individuals have a high level of technical expertise and can often provide linkages to larger enterprises in the area. In challenging times, students may look to mentors to lead the effort. However, mentors are not the "responsible party" for the deliverables in student projects. They provide guidance without taking leadership. Mentoring is further discussed later in this chapter.

Cultural Considerations in Teaming

Frequently, during the data gathering process consultants must move away from a familiar cultural perspective toward an understanding of different cultural perspectives. In this context, different cultures can mean racial/ethnic cultures, business/industry cultures, and corporate/organizational cultures. To be effective in creating change, the team needs to understand and respect the business owner's viewpoint. Much of the knowledge management in some businesses is not in databases or documents. It comes out of the client's experiences and skill set and the environment in which the firm operates. In order to elicit this knowledge, the team must be sensitive to verbal and nonverbal communication. Often teams working with different cultures will engage culture coaches to understand what distinctions must be made. Table 2-5 highlights the differences between individualism (often characteristic of mainstream cultures) and group collectivism (often characteristic of minority cultures).

Although not entirely without controversy, Geert Hofstede of the Institute for Research in Intercultural Communication at Tilburg University identified five dimensions of cultures that are relevant to multicultural consulting engagements.[8] They are presented here for reference.

Power distance. Many cultures give high respect to authority and believe that rank and status are very important. Many Asian immigrant business owners have been very desirous of having university students assist their companies because of the respect they have for education. Some African American business owners have placed a

TABLE 2-5. Individualism and Collectivism as Perspectives in American Business Culture

Individualism	Group Collectivism
Independence and individual achievement. In American business press, business success is equated with individual entrepreneurial achievement (e.g., Michael Dell, Bill Gates, Sam Walton) rather than the collective efforts of a team of many individuals.	Interdependence and group success. Minority businesses often involve many people who support the venture.
Ideas and business activity out of social context. Maximizing profit is the ultimate goal. It is acceptable to push the envelope on the rules and violate relationships to achieve maximum profit.	Ideas and business activity in social context. Business is to enhance human relationships, such as strengthen family or community.
Self-expression, individual thinking, and personal choice. American media and business myth often glorify the maverick or individual who goes against the grain to succeed.	Adherence to norms, respect for authority, and group consensus. Multiple members of the community may be consulted before a decision is made.
Private property. Ideas belong to the business and are protected by copyright and intellectual property laws. Time is private property and a resource to be allocated.	Shared property. Businesses may not understand that ideas cannot be copyrighted. They may not protect their own intellectual property.
Egalitarian relationships and flexible roles. It is acceptable for individuals to interrupt, assert their ideas, and assume the role of leader.	Stable, hierarchal roles. Rules of protocol apply to social and business interactions. Elders command respect.

Source: Geert Hofstede, *Culture's Consequences: Comparing Values, Behaviors, Institutions, and Organizations across Nations*, 2nd ed. (Thousand Oaks, CA: Sage Publications, 2001)

higher value on prior business experience or knowledge of the African American consumer market. Consultants entering cross-cultural consulting relationships should determine the power-distance dimension that is most relevant and seek to build confidence with the client by having the appropriate team composition.

Masculinity/femininity. Masculine cultures tend to be more materialistic and to value assertiveness, whereas feminine cultures value concern for others and relationships among people. In seeking to help a male-owned professional services firm, one consulting team successfully identified that the firm operated from a feminine-culture orientation when it came to approaching prospective clients. Through early recognition of this orientation, the team was able to reorient its consulting contract to focus on building a more assertive approach for the firm's sales strategy rather than on designing a broad marketing strategy.

Individualism and collectivism. Individualist-oriented cultures and businesses focus on taking care of the individual, whereas collectivist-oriented cultures and businesses focus on groups of people taking care of each other. A number of African American business owners state that the reason they started their business was as a means of contributing to their community. They operate from a collectivist perspective. Other African American firms, and many firms owned by non-Hispanic whites, are launched as a means of creating economic well-being for the founder and thus come from an individualist approach. A team's effectiveness is usually enhanced when there is some understanding of the client's value orientation.

Uncertainty avoidance. This dimension refers to the degree to which people feel threatened by and attempt to avoid ambiguous situations. Corporate cultures that desire to avoid uncertainty are resistant to change. Even for many bootstrapping entrepreneurs, change can be hard. They have built a business to a level of success and, though such business owners may communicate a desire to change, consultants might encounter hesitancy to implement change.

Long-term orientation. This dimension refers to the trade-offs that individuals and organizations make between focusing on long-term or short-term gain. Many fledgling companies are focused on making monthly payroll; they are fixated on increasing sales or decreasing costs immediately. More established firms can take a longer-term approach.

In addition to the issue of high- and low-context cul-

TABLE 2-6. Intergenerational Differences

	Silent Born 1928–45	Boomers Born 1946–65	Generation X Born 1965–80	Millennial Born after 1980
Perceived uniqueness	Shared WWII and depression	Work ethic	Technology	Technology
Median number of friends	50	98	200	250
Diversity (non-Hispanic white)	79% white	72% white	61% white	57% white
Education (percent with some college or more)	28% (21% for females)	38% (34% for females)	46% (52% for females)	49% (60% for females)
Married at age 18-32 (%)	65	48	36	26
Political independents (%)	32	37	39	50
Religious (%)	61	55	52	36
Patriotic (%)	81	75	64	49
Support gay rights (%)	32	33	37	51
Want bigger government (%)	22	32	43	53
Most people can be trusted (%)	40	37	31	19

Source: Paul Taylor and Scott Keeter, eds., *Millennials in Adulthood: Detached from Institutions Networked with Friends* (Washington, DC: Pew Research Center, March 2014)

tures (discussed earlier in this chapter), consideration should be given to generational differences between team members. These differences affect a range of work-style issues, including the use of technology, value systems, and collaborative styles. If the differences are understood, there is less likelihood of conflict. Table 2-6 gives generational differences as described by the Pew Research Center.[9] Thus, the Millennial student team may be more educated, more diverse, less likely to value loyalty, more open to government solutions, and more likely to incorporate technology than earlier generations. Such teams may be dealing with a business owner of an older generation. Misunderstandings can happen unless the team understands possible intergenerational differences.

Divergent Thinking

Novice and experienced teams alike can fall prey to other constraints of effective analysis. It is essential at every phase of the project, from initial planning to conclusion, to encourage divergent thinking. Teaming literature provides many examples in which the opposite of divergent thinking, or groupthink, led to disastrous results.[10]

The best solutions are likely to emerge outside the "box" in which teams routinely think. These solutions do not necessarily come from the people who are most likely to assert their thoughts. Therefore, it is important throughout the process to include all individuals who

have a stake in the outcome and to keep all team members in the loop. Consultants use several techniques to encourage both divergent thinking in the generation of ideas and refining of abundant ideas that might be generated for any one topic.

Brainstorming. Brainstorming is a technique familiar to most people who have worked in groups. The goal of brainstorming is to encourage a large number of ideas on the given issue or topic. The atmosphere should be freewheeling. Participants should be encouraged to come up with wild ideas. Nothing should be discounted. Participants are not allowed to evaluate or criticize ideas. This rule must be enforced in order for brainstorming to be effective. By brainstorming in a group, members are more likely to think of related ideas, which can in turn be built upon. Ideas are improved as they are transformed into various combinations.

The process involves first generating the ideas, then clarifying and categorizing them, and finally narrowing the list. To avoid getting bogged down, set strict time limits for each of these steps. When clarifying or categorizing the ideas, avoid evaluation and criticism. When categorizing and narrowing ideas, make sure that everyone is in agreement.

The facilitator should ensure that everyone participates in the process and that participation is equal. Domineering individuals allowed to monopolize the process will stifle creativity. Setting a goal for the number of ideas can keep team members going.

Brainwriting. In diverse teams, it is important to keep in mind that some team members may come from cultures where open oral discussion is not commonplace. Additionally, some team members may think or express themselves better in writing. A variation of brainstorming is to have all participants write a few ideas on one sheet of paper. One team member writes an idea on the paper. It is then placed in the middle of the group, where another team member may take it and write at least one more idea on the same sheet. This process is repeated until all ideas are collected. Then ideas can be clarified, categorized, and narrowed.

Another writing variation is to have enough sheets for every member of the group. Each team member is given five minutes to write three ideas on the paper. The sheet is then passed to the next team member, who also writes three ideas, and so on, until all team members have written three ideas on all the sheets.

Visualizing ideas is sometimes helpful in coming up with creative solutions. In this scenario, each team member is given a sheet of paper and asked to draw the solution to the issue in question. Again, a time limit is given. When all team members are finished, they show their drawings and explain them to the group.

Mind mapping. Mind mapping involves putting ideas in the form of a web or network that shows the relationships among ideas. Starting with a central idea or topic, branches representing different aspects of the main topic are added. This creates a "map" of the topic that can be used for further development. Often mind maps are used to develop project plans or organize notes, bringing divergent thinking into convergent organization.

In creating a mind map, individuals can use other

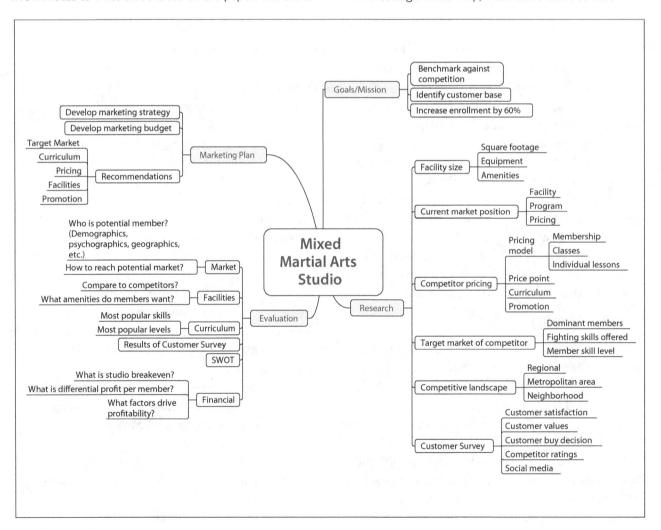

FIGURE 2-3. Mind Map of Mixed Martial Arts Studio

divergent thinking tools such as reframing the problem or opportunity from a different perspective, focusing on the ultimate purpose, listing attributes, or creating other checklists of factors. Figure 2-3 shows a mind map created by a student consulting team working with a mixed martial arts studio. The objective was to increase membership by 60%. In order to achieve this goal, the student team mapped all the tasks needed to acquire more members. Although not mapped at this early phase, promoting the brand image of the business owner (a mixed martial arts champion) turned out to be the driving factor.

Performing Stage

Toward the middle of the project, the team moves into high gear. Team leadership has been strong and focused on accomplishing team goals. Even team members who were not completely in agreement with some decisions are feeling comfortable that their ideas were considered. Every team member knows that the final deadline looms and they must produce.

About 75% of the project is completed in the final few weeks of a typical student consulting project. Teams synthesize and summarize their secondary research, administer surveys, and compile the results. Data are collected and feedback is obtained from the client. Team members support each other. When a team member is unable to complete a task, others pitch in. There is no assignment of blame, although team members are held accountable for their work. Meetings are scheduled to arrive at a consensus about findings and recommendations. Discussion is spirited, but opinions and ideas are treated with respect. Feedback is solicited from all team members. Rough findings and recommendations are compiled. The team "sleeps" on the results and has one more meeting to reconsider and then prioritize recommendations.

The number of hours spent on the project increases as the team moves into the rough draft of the final report and the presentation. Instead of relying on the team's strongest writers to carry the load, the team divides the writing among all members so that each can work on improving writing skills. The draft report often exceeds thirty pages, with up to an additional fifty pages of appendices. The draft report is proofed and submitted for faculty review.

The final presentation is drafted several days before the day of the presentation, and the team's advisors are asked to review evidence used. Revisions are made, and the day prior to the presentation is spent rehearsing in front of a mock audience. Final revisions are made, and individual team members spend the evening rehearsing their part of the presentation. Rehearsals often run several hours for a twenty-minute presentation.

The final presentation goes smoothly. Team members know their material and speak with confidence. The client is thrilled with their commitment and work. The team's mentors are proud. However, as much as the team would like to rest on its laurels, it cannot. The reviewed draft of the final report has been returned to the team, full of corrections and requests for clarification. It is tempting for the team to ignore the requests for clarification, but members collectively review and revise the report one last time. The final report is submitted on the due date.

Without exception, all team members are extremely proud of the work they completed. They understand that they have contributed to the success of a business and increased the vibrancy of the economy. A tremendous number of hours have been contributed to creating this original and unique work. Business owners express their appreciation and mentors give a nod to the professionalism with which the team conducted itself.

In this stage, teams perform efficiently. Team members understand and appreciate their roles and the roles of others. They operate at their highest level and support the work of others. In the final stages of the project, a tremendous amount of work must be completed. Pressure mounts as the deadline approaches, but a performing team will rise to the challenge, expressing unconditional commitment to getting the job done. Team members will motivate each other to keep the energy level high. They will coach and mentor each other. They will encourage new ideas and innovation because these will help maximize the achievement of goals.

Performing teams exhibit a variety of task and relationship behaviors. Modeling these behaviors can help the team move in the right direction. When a team is undergoing the storming phase, it is helpful to provide a list of these behaviors and ask all team members to monitor how often the behaviors are exhibited.

Teaming Postscript

Although all teams go through a storming phase, most teams succeed in fostering good team spirit for most of the process and deliver an excellent product to the client. Out of hundreds of projects, a handful undergo a particularly difficult time throughout the life of the project.

Power struggles may ensue because ego is not an uncommon issue among novice teams. Jostling for personal status may take precedence over accomplishing project goals. Individuals may be assigned roles without their buy-in. This can further alienate individual team members and communication breaks down. Team members may violate their role boundaries, and some individual team members may stop working altogether. Despite all this, the team must deliver a project to the client. In these cases, a few team members will assume the role of team hero and deliver the product. This outcome is absolutely essential. Failure to deliver a quality product is not an option.

PROJECT MANAGEMENT

The goal of a project is to fulfill the stated objectives for the client within the budgeted time and expenses. Once the objectives are achieved, the project ends. A project can be as simple as planning a party or as complex as building a defense system. Horror stories abound of government or private contracting entities spending millions or billions of dollars on projects in which the end product does not work as well as the previous model or, even

worse, does not work at all. An effective team works to balance the project scope (what the project will and will not do) and the time and budget available.

Experience with more than five hundred student projects has shown that student teams will commit eight to ten hours per week outside of the classroom in performing the consulting engagement. Although the workload is higher than typical, students find it rewarding and satisfying. Working with a real business requires that more complex tasks be performed within a short timeline.

This section reviews all the phases of project planning, management, and control with respect to the student consulting engagement.[11] The project timetable in Figure 2-4 highlights the typical starting times for project tasks using an eleven-week schedule. The project timetable may differ, depending on how different institutions arrange the consulting engagements.

Project Mission

Discounting the amount of planning needed for a successful project is a mistake that novice teams often make. It is important to explore and define the scope of work needed prior to coming up with the project plan. When consulting with a company, the team should find

Week	1	2	3	4	5	6	7	8	9	10	11
	Prepare for kickoff with client										
	Assign teams										
	Team forming										
		Review and execute consulting contract									
		Interview and research business									
		Draft, revise, and execute team contract									
			Draft and revise project management plan								
			Start secondary research								
				Draft and revise business case statement							
				Analyze and organize secondary research							
					Plan, draft, and test survey						
					Administer survey						
							Analyze and organize survey results				
							Draft and revise preliminary recommendations				
								Draft final report			
									Draft, revise, rehearse presentation		
										Revise final report	

FIGURE 2-4. Typical Project Tasks and Timetable

out as much as possible about the company, its culture, resources, industry, and competitors before defining the project. Typically, companies prefer to hire consultants who are experts in their field, so the consulting team has to attain "expert" status. Recognize that a business owner might be skeptical about how a group of student consultants can help solve real business problems. If a solution to the problem is to be found, the first order of business is not lining up solutions; it is ensuring that the right problem has been defined. The team cannot rely on the client business to be clear about the problems or opportunities. Businesses are not attempting to be deceptive, nor do they disrespect the consultant. More likely the business may be too preoccupied with day-to-day operations to take a different perspective when approaching opportunities or problems. The business might be dealing with symptoms and not the root causes of difficulties faced.

If trying to capitalize on an opportunity, the team should ensure that it is the right opportunity. Entrepreneurs are opportunistic and may be quick to capitalize on any attractive proposition. All businesses have limited resources, so they need to focus on the best opportunities. Conducting research and analysis will help determine the top alternatives.

Once the research is done and the team has a good understanding of the client company, the team will develop a project mission statement. The project mission defines the scope, objectives, and overall approach for the consulting engagement. It is the single point of reference between the team and the client as to what will be delivered. For example, the mission of the project might be to increase market share for the company by developing marketing strategies and programs. The mission statement is specific about what will be done, for whom, and how. All team members and the business should be included in coming up with this mission statement. It is essential to enlist the entire team's buy-in from the start.

Otherwise, individuals may be confused about, disagree with, or knowingly or unknowingly work against the effort.

Although composing a project mission statement may seem redundant, it is an important step to ensuring that all team members are clear about the direction of the project. The mission statement serves as a guidepost for the inevitable confusion that occurs early in any project. It keeps the team on track when the team is enticed by the many opportunities that arise when research begins. It allows advisors, faculty, or others who need to know to quickly understand what the project is about.

Project Goals and Objectives

A project mission provides broad direction for the work to be done. The mission is then broken down into project goals that define what will be accomplished. The goals need to be attainable with the resources and within the time frame allocated. Project goals must also be measurable.

The goals are then broken down one more level to work objectives. Work objectives must tie directly to achieving project goals. As an example, a project team working with a small business in a suburban city outside of a major metropolitan area may have determined that adults aged fifty to sixty-five years old make up an affluent and profitable local consumer market to pursue. The project goal would be to capture a percentage of this demographic in the city. Specific goals would be to propose a customer survey to determine how best to capture this market.

For most student consulting projects, the project objectives comprise a list of deliverables for the client (Table 2-7). Deliverables must be accompanied by end-item specifications (Table 2-8). For instance, creating a website for a business is a deliverable. However, there is a difference between delivering a website that does or

TABLE 2-7. Sample Goal and Objectives

Goal	Objectives
Capture the over 50–65 market in the city of Bellevue	1. Conduct research and identify where the over-50 population is concentrated 2. Conduct research and identify activities in which the over-50 population may engage 3. Develop and administer a survey to a sample of 30 or more potential over-50 consumers to determine how to reach the over-50 market in Bellevue 4. Conduct competitive analysis of other businesses that serve the over-50 market in Bellevue

TABLE 2-8. Sample Deliverable and End-Item Specification

Deliverable	End-Item Specification
Business website	Website pages: Home page with mission statement, featured products, featured expert article, owner blog, customer quotes, top navigation to landing pages, social media
	Landing pages, including product information and description
	Mock layout of all pages and navigation bars, including copy and graphics
	Suggested keywords, page title, meta tags, links
	Results of usability test with three customers

does not capture customers. A clearly defined deliverable might include the number of pages in the website, any graphic work, any copy that must be written, and how customers will be guided through the website. There might be a stipulation that the site has to be approved by key people in the business. Another requirement might be that the website be tested successfully on customers and that it be compliant with any regulations. When the site is up, the number of hits and conversions to sales can be measured to determine if objectives were reached.

Project Scope

As the student team goes through the process of determining what it will deliver, it must at the same time have a clear idea of what it *cannot* achieve. A project that tries to be all things to all people ends up achieving little. This is especially pertinent to resource-constrained small businesses. As the project evolves, the business owner often comes to realize how skilled the student consultants really are. The owner may also think of additional, equally critical projects. Moving beyond the initial scope of the project is not limited to the business owner. It is also natural that the more the team learns about an area, the more ideas it will have about what to do. This enthusiasm on the part of both business owners and student consultants to take on more work than specified by the project mission is known as scope creep. It needs to be contained. One approach for containment is to delineate the relevance of options and their worth to the overall project goal. Clearly stating and restating priorities is another way of responding to scope creep.

This does not mean that the scope of the project will never change. As the team and business gain more knowledge, there might be good reason to change the scope. For example, the team might discover that a market segment initially thought to be attractive is not via-ble. In this case, it would not be effective to continue to develop a marketing plan for this segment. Rather, the team should choose another segment. However, there also needs to be a way of controlling such changes in scope. It could be that the new ideas are more attractive than the old ones, but unless the team focuses on the project mission, it runs the risk of accomplishing nothing of value to the business.

Project Team

In student consulting projects, students are generally preselected and industry advisors or mentors are preassigned. If advisors and mentors are used, the student team should give thought as to how they fit into the team. Having mentors or advisors who are experienced in the industry is beneficial, but they tend to be busy people with many other priorities. The best use of their time is often to call on them as needed or on a just-in-time basis. They may be consulted briefly by e-mail or telephone when a particularly difficult problem is encountered. They may be solicited to facilitate communication or add weight to decision making. The student team should learn how to use advisors and mentors selectively to get the most out of their expertise.

Following the initial period of research by the consulting team, core and extended team members hold a "kick-off" meeting, or a required face-to-face meeting with the business owner. The goal of the meeting is to build trust with the business owner. Teams need to have the full trust of the client. They can achieve this by informing the business owner of their credentials, outlining their role in the project and their working styles, and establishing personal rapport. More often it takes a personal bond between the business owner and individual team members to make the project successful. At the same time, the student team will build relationships with advisors or mentors. Contact with these individuals may be intermittent after the kickoff meeting, and it is important to have a basis for future interaction.

During the kickoff meeting, implicit agreements are reached and expectations are set concerning how often the team will meet and what communication protocols will be. This is especially important in a multicultural consulting environment where the business owner may be multilingual. Considerations of culture must be incorporated, ensuring that messages are conveyed correctly. Team members should differentiate between the social constructs of white individuals in large corporations and collectivists who are more often represented in minority businesses. Keep in mind that these constructs represent two opposing poles of a continuum, and businesses may fall anywhere in between.

Typical student teams complete a good portion of their work on weekends while business owners are either working in their businesses or spending time with their families. Finding an appropriate meeting time and setting expected turnaround time when additional information or feedback is needed should be discussed during the kickoff meeting. A student team working with a commercial moving company was frustrated that the owner was unavailable to meet on weekends, but this was the time when the owner, a divorced father, could spend with his son.

Knowing what skills and knowledge people have is important. If long-term viability of the enterprise is a concern, the consulting project can be used to build capacity within the organization. It can also be used to develop team members so they can lead other projects. All team members have to be committed to project goals. If they do not come with this commitment, the project leader must facilitate its development: the leader must communicate the importance of achieving the goals and create a connection between each team member and the project goals.

Key stakeholders must be involved in the project team. Unless they are involved, it is unlikely that the fruits of the project will have any staying power. For example, if the project aims to improve sourcing for a company, and the purchasing person is not involved in the planning, it is unlikely that the recommendations will be implemented. A project champion may be necessary to explain the project's role to the stakeholders. Often mentors and advisors have the clout to get this message across. Good project champions can make more resources available

to the project. Effective teams are aware of this dynamic and use it to optimal advantage. Getting the right people on the team will also take excellent persuasion and negotiation skills.

Inexperienced consultants may find it difficult to stay focused on the project goals. Business owners can come up with many other tasks that seem just as important. Team members may have differing opinions or be unable to focus on specific goals. Individuals may gravitate toward what is comfortable as opposed to what needs to be done. It is important to keep the project mission in clear focus. Distractions will be plenty, while time and resources are in short supply. Being unfocused during the planning process can cause the project to veer far off course by its conclusion. It is important to resist being discouraged or sidetracked by such an occurrence. Each problem is an opportunity to adapt to the situation and put the project back on schedule.

Knowledge Management

Knowledge management is an important concept not limited to data contained in digital media. It includes any relevant knowledge that can be mined to achieve the mission. With many businesses, especially small businesses, the knowledge within the enterprise often resides in people. For example, production workers might have their own method of troubleshooting a line breakdown that is never documented. This would be a crucial piece of information needed to understand operations. If enterprises could access all the knowledge their people possess, they could unlock a huge goldmine of resources. True knowledge management means that the consulting team can get to the knowledge where it resides.

Within-team knowledge management can be enabled with digital file sharing. This is an effective way of managing the large amounts of data common in most projects. If labeled properly, these files provide a chronology of data gathered and analysis completed. This is important because sometimes data gathered or analysis done, if not initially pursued, may gain prominence later. The project team needs to have access to this information. Good archiving of data when the project is completed also allows the business owner to reuse the knowledge. Rather than reinvent the wheel when a similar project is done, the business owner can draw on work previously done.

The project knowledge-manager role can be assigned to a team member to provide a focal point for archiving the material. The team should have templates for agendas, meeting summaries, and decision making to simplify the recording of repetitive tasks and ensure accountability for action items. A Web service such as Google Docs is a good option as a repository for files. For best results, the team will select collaborative tools that allow editing concurrently, measure team performance, and communicate regularly with each other.

Project Plan

A project plan is a detailed breakdown of milestones, tasks, interrelations, resources, and schedules. For unseasoned project managers, project planning may be seen as an "overhead" item. These managers think it important to pare project planning down to the smallest value possible. Carefully setting out what has to be done, how completion is to be measured, how one task might relate to another, and when each task is to be completed gives a blueprint for management.

The project plan is important for several reasons. It does the following:

- Specifies how the team will meet its ultimate goal within the allotted time frame.
- Shows that the team has access to the information it needs at the time that it needs it to remain on schedule.
- Provides the team with a tool to manage the client's expectations.
- Assigns resources to address the right issues at the right time.
- Determines the communications mechanisms needed to maintain progress on the project.
- Establishes team roles and responsibilities.
- Identifies leaders for each area of the team's work.
- Schedules deadlines and milestones.
- Ensures that the scope of work satisfies the mission of the project.

As a general rule, all individuals who are part of the consulting project, its execution, or the subsequent implementation of its recommendations should be part of the planning. It follows that greater commitment to the change process will be fostered when all team members and other responsible parties are involved. Those who participate in planning a task have a stronger stake in its execution. Additionally, getting as much input in the initial stages contributes to a better solution.

Once the project mission and deliverables are set, the student team typically begins creating its work breakdown structure. In this stage of planning, the team starts with the deliverables and identifies the milestones, tasks, assignments, and schedule for each deliverable.

Be aware that business owners, mentors, and advisors may not be able to meet deadlines for feedback or decision making as determined by the team unless these are established at the kickoff meeting, and even so that may change over the duration of the consulting engagement. Advisors and mentors in particular are likely to have other pressing tasks that draw their attention elsewhere. It is important for the team to seek out and solicit these team members when their feedback is required, while keeping feedback windows flexible so that contributions can be included. At the same time, discretion should be used in drawing lines as to when project issues should be closed.

Work breakdown structure. With the project mission clearly in mind, the team then breaks the project into objectives or deliverables. For each objective, the team determines the subtasks that must be accomplished. For example, under the objective "competitive analysis," one subtask might be to obtain a list of competitors. Another might be to review competitor price lists. Still another might be to survey customers about their assessment of competitors. Each of these subtasks may be broken down further. For example, the customer survey would be broken down into obtaining a list of customers, creating a survey, administering the survey, and analyzing the results.

Some tasks can be performed only if a predecessor task is completed. In the previous example of the customer interviews, the survey can be administered only after the customer list is available. Tasks that do not have linked predecessor tasks can be performed independently. This is important to document because it has an effect on resource scheduling. Independent tasks can be completed simultaneously by different team members, while linked tasks must be completed sequentially. If the customer list is outdated, incomplete, or otherwise unusable, the team cannot interview customers. If the team member charged with completing a task does not complete it on time, the scheduling of all subsequent tasks will be affected. Often project managers will identify critical paths or tasks that can delay the entire project; when they focus management efforts on these, they can reduce the risk of a project falling behind.

Along with the task itself, it is important to specify exactly what constitutes a standard for completion of the task. If specifications are not clearly spelled out at the beginning, team members may not complete what is required. For example, a survey of customers can be as simple as informally stopping ten customers when they shop or as extensive as completing one thousand surveys using random telephone sampling. Unless the requirements are mapped out, team members may inadvertently miss the target, client expectations will not be met, and the final product will be of no value to the business.

Within a team there often exist varying perceptions of what is acceptable. In order to keep the process smooth, take the time to be as specific as possible. This can enhance team functioning.

Go and no-go review. When exploring new territory, the team may not have a clear concept of whether the finished product will be feasible. Instead of automatically completing all tasks, project planning should include key points when the team reevaluates whether it should continue. For example, a project mission might be to develop a new product for a new market. There are several decision points at which the team can determine whether to go forward. After secondary research of the market, the team might decide there is not enough potential to proceed. One project team explored the feasibility of a Native American tribe opening a data center. While there was (and is) a growing demand for such centers, the cost of developing the infrastructure was such that the go and no-go review decision was to forgo that opportunity in favor of other more profitable opportunities.

Scheduling and resource allocation. Once all the tasks have been laid out in the project plan, the time requirement or duration (number of hours and end date) must be determined for each task. It follows that the more experienced the project planners are, the more accurate they will be in determining the amount of time each task requires. It also follows that the more experienced the team is, the less time it will take to complete the tasks. Conversely, a novice team must plan for some slack time so that everyone can complete their tasks effectively.

Once the time for completion has been determined, specific team members are assigned to each task. A team leader who knows the team well can relatively easily match the individual with the task. Keep in mind that the most highly skilled individual for the task may not be selected.

It may be in the team's best interest to develop these competencies in other individuals to increase skill depth.

In a consulting firm, each consultant has a specific billing rate based on technical expertise and experience. Student team members may not have the expertise to command high billing fees. However, it is still important to assign market billing rates to each team member. Quantifying the cost of such endeavors will always be a part of the formula for determining beneficial gain. Likewise, all other expenses of the project should be quantified, whether they are out of pocket or not. Formulating a budget that proves accurate is an important skill for all project managers. Budgets are a critical part of a request for proposal, and a consulting firm stands to lose significant profit if budgeting is not done properly. Budgets also provide the basis for management and control as the project progresses.

Most project management software packages, such as Microsoft Project, easily handle the input of tasks, task dependencies, duration resource allocation, and budgeting. Baseline budgets are automatically tallied based on the information given. The software also provides graphics such as Gantt and critical path charts to show project status visually (Figure 2-5). Even if a software package is not available, student consulting projects are usually of a complexity that can be easily handled with a spreadsheet program.

Review project plan for risks. Each project has risks that jeopardize its successful completion. Good planning anticipates these risks and develops contingency plans to mitigate the risks. For student consultants, one common risk is spending significant time on a task that turns out to be of little or no value. For example, a team decided that it was important to conduct a survey of former customers to determine how a business could improve its marketing strategy. The business assured the team that it had a comprehensive list of former customers. The team obtained the list, uploaded it to a database, divided the list into sections, created a survey, and proceeded to contact the customers by e-mail and then by follow-up telephone calls. After a few days it was determined that e-mail addresses were out of date and telephone numbers were disconnected. The project hit the halfway mark in its timeline, and the team had to start again with no other options for contacting former customers.

This risk could have been mitigated had the team spent some time testing the list prior to proceeding with

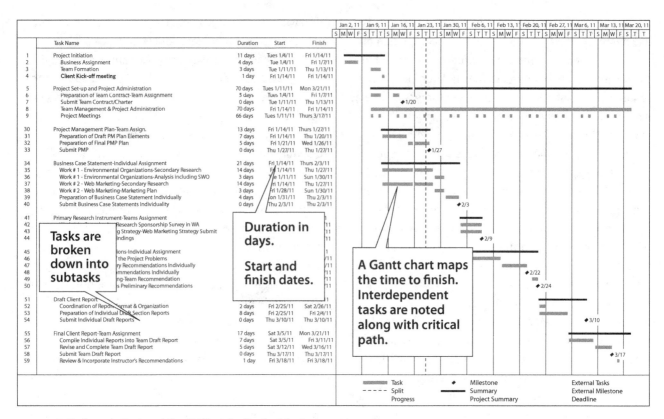

FIGURE 2-5. Sample Task and Gantt Chart for Student Project

the survey design. Additionally, once research suggests that a task may lead to a dead end, it is important that the team have a means of quickly changing the deliverable to make it relevant. Is it necessary to survey former customers? Would a list of potential customers be just as effective for getting information?

Project Management and Control

Projects, once started, move quickly, and they need to continue to progress in order to be completed successfully. The team should establish weekly meetings (or daily feedback via e-mail or telephone) to review project status. Project status reports need to be given to all interested parties, including mentors and advisors, on a regular basis.

Often teams find it more efficient to transfer tasks to a spreadsheet and track task completion and team member hours directly on the spreadsheet. This information can be kept in the shared document file so that all team members can access progress on the completion of tasks, milestones, and deliverables.

Dealing with Problems

Problems will arise in any project, no matter how well it is run. The team needs to establish a means of identify-ing problems. Catching the problem early can do much to counteract its impact. Often individual team members will not notice the start of a problem. They may be too involved in project details or too busy completing their own tasks to pick up on signals that something might be amiss. Team members need to be vigilant and aware of all aspects of the project to assist their colleagues in identifying the first signs of problems. Trust needs to be such that a team member will not be too polite, too embarrassed, or otherwise hesitant to call for help or point out issues.

Once problems have surfaced, there needs to be a process for dealing with them. If conflicts arise, rules for resolving them must already be in place. Determining rules of engagement in the heat of an argument rarely leads to resolution. Team members must be knowledgeable about the agreed-upon conflict-resolution procedures and must abide by them. Problems that are identified need to be monitored separately from normal project status to ensure satisfactory follow-through in resolving them.

From the outset, the team must set up a team culture conducive to having team heroes emerge. In the flurry of activities that characterize project work, it is not always the person with titular responsibility for a task who will be able to come through. Rather, another team member might step up to the plate to perform the heroic task to save the day. Team culture should allow this type of courage to be expressed. It should reward team heroes who contribute in this manner.

In some instances the team is better served by shared leadership, and this must be accommodated. These issues should be explored with faculty, mentors, and advisors to arrive at a solution that best serves the project and client.

Project Close

Project close is signified by delivery of the finished product to the client. Along with the final report, the team should have complete documentation of the project process, including the actual budget to complete the project. The documentation also provides a base of knowledge that will be invaluable in future consulting projects. It can provide direction for research that will not have to be redone or a critical analysis framework that will expedite problem solving.

Although the tendency is to physically and psychologically exit the project when the product is delivered to the client, it is best to resist this tendency. Taking time to reflect at project close on what went well and what could be improved is an important part of the developmental process of every team member. Reflecting can provide valuable knowledge for future consulting, teaming, and project management. Additionally, it is important to acknowledge the achievements and contributions of each and every team member. This type of reflection and recognition is vital to team member development and, according to many teaming experts, will lead to effective high-performance teaming.

MENTORING

One of the key messages of this book is that it is essential to create a support system around businesses to help them thrive. The same can be said for students. In some configurations of student consulting projects, mentors are used to guide the team. Typically the mentor is a professional who may have some expertise in the business's industry. Additionally the mentor values interacting to assist students in learning. A match of expertise and values is essential to a good mentor-mentee relationship.

Having mentors who are professionals or business owners as part of the consulting team can be an invaluable experience for students. In order for a student to thrive in a business career, it is important to create a support system or network of people who will assist in career development. Mentors are essential to learning the soft skills needed to navigate the business environment. Students may not have access to this type of mentor relationship nor understand how to nurture the relationship to their own benefit. Mentors also provide an invaluable source of expertise to the business owner and may model good leadership skills.

As mentioned before in this chapter, the mentor plays an important role in the team. Although the mentor will never take a directing role, his or her expertise can help guide the team on the right track and provide linkages to the larger entrepreneurial support system for the business. Unless there is conflict, the mentor will wait for the students to take the initiative in developing and sustaining the mentor-mentee relationship.

The mentoring process starts with the awareness that the team needs advice to move forward. It is important that the team take the initiative to contact the mentor and articulate the need. In some cases, a meeting may be necessary. Sometimes queries can be dealt with by e-mail or over the telephone. A face-to-face meeting with a mentor is the best way to learn, and teams can take advantage of this by scheduling regular meetings with their mentors. The frequency of these meetings will be determined by the availability of the mentor. As mentors are volunteers with very busy work schedules, the team needs to establish clear expectations with the mentor regarding meeting frequency and participation.

In addition to acting as a sounding board for issues encountered by the team, the mentor can model professional and problem solving behavior. Student consultants should:

- Ask questions of their mentors frequently.
- Identify issues that the team is struggling with and get feedback.
- Demonstrate to the mentor that the team is willing to learn and grow.
- Show how mentor guidance has been incorporated in team work.
- Be respectful of mentor time. Focus on small blocks of time and be prepared with enough information about what the team wants to achieve.
- Discuss and agree as a team what is needed from the mentor prior to a meeting.
- Coordinate all communication so the mentor is not

answering the same questions from different team members.

- Expect and require that the mentor be honest with the team.
- Keep in mind that mentors operate at a much higher business standard than the academic learning environment and their assessments may be more rigorous.
- Take all mentor feedback as an opportunity to correct mistakes and learn.
- Communicate status of the team project regularly even if the team does not meet with the mentor frequently.
- Be professional in dealing with conflict.

Although mentors understand that students are not as sophisticated in dealing with conflict as are people with decades of experience, mentors expect student consultants to be professional when conflict arises. Students should use good team communication skills in focusing on any problem and should not engage in blame. Responsibility for nurturing the mentor relationship rests with the student.

CREATING THE ACTION PLAN
Focus on Key Issues

Once all the data have been gathered and relevant analyses have been performed, it is the job of the team to begin focusing on key issues. In making recommendations, it is good to keep in mind the following:

1. Recognize pitfalls and biases in making recommendations. Too much ego involvement, excessive sense of ownership of a given idea or solution, and close-minded acceptance of a given tool or technique can misguide the process.
2. Be wary of using shortcuts and habit to guide recommendations. Such a route may be quick and easy but will likely lead to more bad decisions than good ones.
3. Use rules of thumb when they are likely to support correct decisions. Average ratios or margins, generally accepted industry performance standards, or other rules of thumb may be appropriate for routine, frequently made recommendations with low risk of much variability in outcomes. However, rules of thumb should be evaluated critically and used selectively.
4. Make sure that the recommendation is directly linked to the specific problem(s) for which the analy-

sis was completed. The right recommendation for the wrong problem is an obvious mismatch that should be avoided.
5. Process and integrate the best available data into the recommendation. Such data are the foundation of the analytical support for the decision.
6. Base recommendations on an informed, rational choice-making process and not on beliefs or assumptions. Use a "bounded rationality" approach as a guide, because it emphasizes analytical judgment based on facts, rational inferences, and consideration of other influences.
7. Recognize the value of intuition and creativity in the recommendation-making process. There are limits to analytical inferences and judgments. Insights and sound choice making can be formulated on hunches, imaginative insights, and other nonquantitative grounds.
8. Assess the value and impact of alternative recommendations. Cross-check the analysis and results to ensure accuracy and consistency.
9. Evaluate expected outcomes and develop contingencies for the consulting process. Recognize that assumptions can be inaccurate and that unpredicted and unexpected developments can block intended results.
10. Provide time, money, and other resources needed for implementation of and follow-up for a recommendation to make sure that it produced the expected results. This ensures that the right recommendation was made and that corrections will be made as needed.

Prioritize Findings and Analysis

The consulting team's research findings and analysis must be prioritized in order to make them understandable, acceptable, actionable, and usable for the client. The following guidelines should be of help to the consulting team: Group what has been done into general categories or topics, such as marketing, accounting, or finance. More specifically, the analysis could be problem-focused on new customers, cash flow, increased services, reducing operational costs, and so on. Using specific recommendations is another way of approaching a given task. Getting suggestions from faculty and mentors who have been there and done that should be helpful as well. Of course the team's own ideas are key. Based on the team's work and interactions with the client, what are the most persuasive or effective findings for what the team is proposing to the owner? Thinking along these lines should make a challenging task easier in gaining client buy-in and implementation of the team's recommendations.

Compile the Action Plan

Once the consulting team and the client have finalized a direction, the team needs to develop an action plan that will enable the company to reach its goals. Critical path analysis is an effective method of analyzing a complex project. It helps calculate the minimum length of time for completing the project and which activities should be prioritized to finish by that date.

Critical path analysis recognizes that some activities in the plan will take longer than others; some activities are dependent on other activities being completed first; and the dependent activities need to be completed in a sequence, with each activity needing completion before the next activity can begin. To develop the critical path, the team uses the same procedure as in any project plan.

The basic concept is illustrated in the timed layout of a human resource action plan shown in Figure 2-6. Whether using a formal critical path analysis or not, the team should be able to meet deadlines more consistently when tasks and activities are clearly delineated in terms of both people and time.

Describe Action Steps

The ultimate test of a project's value will be determined by how well decisions and action steps are implemented by the client. Hence, it is very important that a detailed plan for decision implementation be articulated. Be clear about what the proposed action will require of the client, how the action taken is to be directed and measured, and what markers will measure results. The business owner must know what is expected and how to determine what is, and is not, working over the course of decision implementation. In addition, the client or someone designated by her should be accountable for implementation. Therefore timelines, budgets, cash flow projections, or other measurement and control tools must be identified as part of the implementation process. If this is not done properly, accountability and follow-up are impossible.

If the client has been properly involved in the entire process, there should be approval and acceptance. But recognize that implementation of decisions will involve change. Some managers and employees in the business who will be affected by the change are likely to resist it. This should be anticipated as an aspect of the implementation plan. In this regard, some measure of cooperation and incentives for participation will be needed. Overall, the benefits and gains to individuals and to the firm as whole are likely to be important in gaining acceptance and support.

Realistically, very few things in business are certain. Contingencies should be built into the action plan for adjusting to the unexpected, including and some possible contingencies in the event that expectations are not met. The prospect of failure must be considered. Give thought to how contingencies can be built into decision implementation. With such consideration, the most relevant bases of decision implementation should have been covered.

In laying out the course of action, use these questions as guidelines:

1. What should the new arrangements/actions achieve? What level of performance? What quality of output?
2. How will the new situation differ from the old? Will

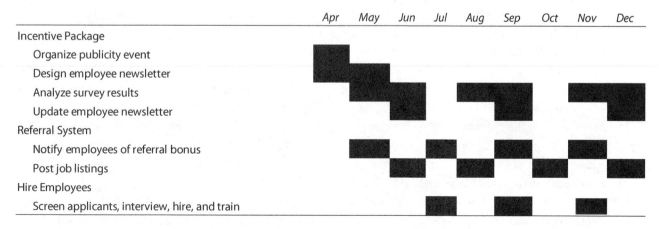

	Apr	May	Jun	Jul	Aug	Sep	Oct	Nov	Dec
Incentive Package									
Organize publicity event									
Design employee newsletter									
Analyze survey results									
Update employee newsletter									
Referral System									
Notify employees of referral bonus									
Post job listings									
Hire Employees									
Screen applicants, interview, hire, and train									

FIGURE 2-6. Sample Action Plan

there be different products, services, or activities, different processes, different equipment, and/or different locations?

3. Are the effects likely to last? Are the business and the target market changing so quickly that there may not be a need for the new product or service? Is there the possibility that people will revert to present practices?
4. What difficulties will arise in implementation? Will there be employee resistance or shortage of materials or other resources?
5. Who and what parts of the firm will be affected? Are employees receptive? What should be done to prepare employees? Do matching changes need to be made elsewhere?
6. When is the best time to change? Should it be at the end of a season, during down time, at the close of a financial period, or at the beginning of the calendar year?

Once the answers to these questions have been formulated, the timeline for the action plan can be developed. The action plan should provide enough detail that the business owner can implement it fully, and it should include visual representation of the timeline for implementation.

Follow Up

The special nature of these consulting projects makes follow-up essential. The purpose of the project is to effect fundamental and long-term change in emerging businesses such that they will operate in parity with all businesses. This cannot be achieved without diligent follow-up to ensure that recommendations are followed and change happens.

Decision follow-up should be guided by the performance expectations promised in the written client report. There must be sufficient detail and documentation so that anyone not part of the detailed work of the project can understand what is to be accomplished. Clear and concise financial, marketing, or other operational reports and documents should be integral to the follow-up process.

The directions that the client takes following completion of the consulting project depend heavily on the quality and persuasiveness of the team's recommendations and the level of buy-in the team has generated from the client during the consulting engagement. A final check to ensure that recommendations follow guidelines is important. Guidelines should:

- Address project goals.
- Be supported by the data and analysis.
- Add value for the client and the operations of the firm.
- Consider resource availability or provide means of obtaining resources.
- Provide enough detail to implement.
- Provide the metrics for measuring success.

Plan evaluations are best organized around or focused on specific functional programs. Generally the consultant would design an evaluation for each element of the marketing mix. Sometimes separate reports are prepared for specific campaigns or parts of a program. Follow-up should include the specific goal, the completion date, who was responsible for the goal, and some reflection on the results.

Carter McNamara, an author and organizational consultant, suggests using the following key questions for monitoring and evaluating plans. He also recommends that modifications be made to suit the circumstances and needs of the firm or organization.[12]

A major question is, Are goals and objectives being achieved? If they are, acknowledge, reward, and communicate the progress. If not, consider the remaining questions:

- Will the goals be achieved according to the timelines specified in the plan? If not, why not?
- Should the deadlines for completion be changed? (Be careful about making these changes; know why efforts are behind schedule before deadlines are changed.)
- Does the business have adequate resources (money, equipment, facilities, training, etc.) to achieve the goals?
- Are the goals and objectives still realistic?
- Should priorities be changed to put more focus on achieving the goals?
- Should the goals be changed? (Be careful about making these changes; know why efforts are not achieving the goals before changing the goals.)
- What can be learned from monitoring and evaluation in order to improve future planning activities and future monitoring and evaluation efforts?

The ultimate test of the worth or value of student consulting projects must be measured in terms of how well they accomplish their stated goals and objectives.

DISCUSSION

1. As a team, make a list of behaviors that the team should engage in and a list of behaviors the team should not engage in. Listing and naming these behaviors can lead to better team functioning.
2. Discuss differences within team member backgrounds, such as high- and low-context cultures or generational differences. What accommodations should be made to ensure that communication is open and clear?
3. Select two techniques for divergent thinking in coming up with project risks. Analyze and explain why one technique is more effective.
4. Have each team member compose the project mission and discuss similarities and differences. Did all team members buy into the same mission?
5. Develop a team meeting agenda template, including communication protocols.
6. Identify several skills and benefits that you expect to gain from your project learning experience.

NOTES

1   Peter Block, *Flawless Consulting*, 2nd ed. (San Francisco: Jossey-Bass/Pfeiffer, 2000).
2   Amy C. Edmondson, *Teaming: How Organizations Learn, Innovate and Compete in the Knowledge Economy* (San Francisco: Jossey-Bass, 2012).
3   Arvind Malhotra, A. Majchrzak, Robert Carman, and Vern Lott, "Radical Innovation without Collocation: A Case Study at Boeing-Rocketdyne," *MIS Quarterly* 25, no. 2 (2001): 229–49.
4   R. Blake and J. Mouton, *Spectacular Teamwork: How to Develop the Leadership Skills for Team Success* (New York: Wiley, 1987).
5   B. W. Tuckman and M. A. Jensen, "Stages of Small-Group Development Revisited," *Group and Organization Studies* 2, no. 4 (1977): 419–27.
6   Edmondson, *Teaming*.
7   W. G. Dyer, *Team Building: Issues and Alternatives*. 2d ed. (Reading, MA: Addison-Wesley, 1987).
8   Geert Hofstede, *Culture's Consequences: Comparing Values, Behaviors, Institutions, and Organizations across Nations*, 2nd ed. (Thousand Oaks, CA: Sage Publications, 2001).
9   Paul Taylor and Scott Keeter, eds., *Millennials in Adulthood: Detached from Institutions Networked with Friends*, (Washington, DC: Pew Research Center, March 2014).
10 James K. Esser, "Alive and Well after 25 Years: A Review of Groupthink Research," *Organizational Behavior and Human Decision Processes* 73, nos. 2/3 (February/March 1998): 116–41.
11 Project Management Institute, A *Guide to the Project Management Body of Knowledge*, 4th ed. (Newton Square, PA: Project Management Institute, 2008).
12 Carter McNamara, *Field Guide to Nonprofit Strategic Planning and Facilitation*, 3rd ed. (Minneapolis: Authenticity Consulting, 2007).

3. Multicultural Markets

ABOUT THIS CHAPTER

Several developments in the US economy and society help to explain the emergence of multicultural markets as an important aspect of the current business environment. The growth of multicultural populations is outpacing that of non-Hispanic whites and is projected to do so until midcentury, when minorities will outnumber non-Hispanic whites. There is a growing recognition in mainstream business of the significant spending power of multicultural communities. According to the Selig Center for Economic Growth at the University of Georgia, total annual buying power of African Americans, Asians, American Indians, and Hispanics in 2013 amounted to $3.2 trillion and is expected to reach $4.2 trillion in 2018.[1] This represents a 55% increase from 2013 to 2018. The 2013 lesbian, gay, bisexual, and transgender (LGBT) market was estimated at $830 billion;[2] while people with disabilities had $200 billion in discretionary income in 2010, with the government spending $357 billion on programs for people with disabilities in 2008.[3] The demographic trend toward greater cultural diversity in the population is creating new opportunities for businesses.

This chapter presents an overview of the size and characteristics of the larger multicultural markets, including African Americans (also referred to as blacks), Hispanics (also referred to as Latinos), Asians, and American Indians (also referred to as Native Americans). American Indians and Alaska Natives may be referred to by the US Census acronym AIAN. In most of this book, the term *American Indians* is used. Native Hawaiians and Pacific Islanders may be referred to by the US Census acronym NHPI. White populations that do not include individuals of Hispanic ethnicity are often compared with these groups; according to US Census terminology, they are referred to as non-Hispanic whites. Historically, they have been referred to as the dominant or majority population. Also included is a short description of the LGBT population. Although not a racial category, the LGBT population constitutes a growing and attractive market for business-to-consumer (B2C) companies.

As generally understood, culture includes language, the arts, customs, beliefs, institutions, and patterns of behavior in society. We recognize that specific categories of people (based on race, ethnicity, national origin, and other characteristics) differ culturally from the majority population. They may also embrace or share many of the elements of the dominant culture. However, the study of marketplaces has been multiplied by the number of different cultures within US society. Not only is it important to know the demographics of multicultural groups; it has become mandatory to understand the cultural context and the political, legal, and social factors of each of group. Racism is a process of racial/ethnic bias and related forms of discrimination that adversely affects our society with respect to the large cultural groups that we describe. All these factors must be included in a comprehensive understanding of the multicultural marketplace and the new paradigms that may emerge out of this cultural diversity. As a result of each population's experiences with discrimination, how each population interacts in the marketplace will be different from how the white population interacts. However, we encourage readers to view these challenges as opportunities for government, businesses, and foundations and other nonprofit organizations to meet multicultural needs for goods and services.

After Studying This Chapter

This chapter provides basic knowledge of multicultural markets. It provides a starting point for students to explore the complexity of multicultural groups. After studying this chapter, students will be able to:

- Explain the size and market potential of selected multicultural populations and project population trends in each group.
- Understand the environment in which multicultural populations have come to exist and thrive in the United States.
- Quantify and analyze the impact of multicultural populations on the marketplace.
- Describe the demography, geographic location, and purchasing power of the larger multicultural groups.
- Interpret other salient characteristics of multicultural populations that may affect the marketplace.

MULTICULTURAL MARKETS
Multicultural Marketing

Multicultural marketing has evolved since the early 1990s. Prior to that time, marketing to diverse racial and ethnic groups was generally referred to as minority marketing. While the phrase *marketing to minorities* is still used to refer to the targeting of racial/ethnic groups, diversity in multicultural terms extends far beyond race and ethnicity to people with disabilities and to lifestyles such as sexual orientation or distinctive value orientations associated with dietary practices (e.g., vegetarian and organic food preferences). Broadly, multicultural marketing can be defined as the *process of using market exchange concepts, methods, and techniques to recognize and respond to culturally distinct group characteristics and preferences of individuals, organizations, and communities.*

The essence of multicultural marketing requires that the target customer's culture and its complexities be placed at the core of management and strategy. Cultural distinctiveness of target groups is emphasized in contrast to the dominant and relatively standardized European American norms of traditional marketing. Cultural diversity is emphasized over cultural homogeneity. Whereas traditional marketing generally assumes assimilation into the dominant culture, multicultural marketing recognizes differences from the dominant culture in many forms—language, customs, music, food, folk art, and other forms of cultural expression. In addition, multicultural marketing recognizes the cultural affinity for certain norms, practices, and values that accompany a common pattern of geographic concentration. This is most noticeable in local

markets but is also reflected at the national level. Thus, Hispanics reside predominantly in five states—Texas, California, Florida, New York, and New Mexico.

The language characteristics and cultural traditions of many immigrant groups commonly lead to "high-context" relationships (discussed in chapter 2) that foster group centeredness, stronger social bonds, and more close-knit interactions than typically occur in the dominant culture. Immigrants have not assimilated into European American culture; indeed, attempts to persuade, seduce, or even force groups to assimilate have led to external and internal conflicts among minorities. As the United States becomes more diverse, the model of acculturation—in which cultures exist side by side and influence each other—may be more effective. According to the US Census American Community Survey in 2007, about 20% of the population spoke a language other than English at home.[4] The marketing implications are that communications media in languages other than English are needed to prevent market isolation because of language. Or, if English is the appropriate language, the focus might be on media that serve a community of color. There could be an emphasis on word-of-mouth messages or, alternatively, less emphasis on individualistic and self-centered messages and themes.

Multicultural marketing also embraces changing cultural traditions in the United States. Another reflection of the shift to multicultural marketing is illustrated in responses to changing demographics and increased market power of culturally distinct groups of consumers. For example, the growing presence and importance of Southeast Asians and Hispanics in Southern California have brought about noticeable marketing changes. Retailers in malls serving Southeast Asians have altered their merchandise assortments to reflect substantially higher proportions of petite sizes than in stores serving other population groups. Supermarkets catering to Hispanics (especially Mexican Americans) frequently alter store decor and musical programs and incorporate Spanish-language signage. Such responses illustrate how multicultural marketing benefits both consumers and enterprises. Consumers are better served with more appropriate choices in goods and services. Enterprises benefit by increased patronage and more competitive performance.

Adding even more complexity to this multicultural marketing concept, and essential for business leaders to understand, is that immigrant cultures evolve based on the number of generations a family has been in the United States. A third-generation Vietnamese American or Cuban American will differ from a newly arrived immigrant from the given country. Marketers targeting twenty- to thirty-year-old Cuban Americans in Miami cannot assume that they use Spanish-language media or hold the traditional values of their parents or grandparents who fled Cuba.

Along with culture, other factors that have shaped a group's history in the United States must be considered and understood. Racism is an integral part of the treatment and experiences of groups based on racial/ethnic and color differences as well as language and country of origin. It stems from beliefs, attitudes, and actions that consider norms, institutions, and other elements of the dominant culture to be superior, while people of color and many of their characteristics are considered and treated as inferior. Racism results in discrimination, disparity, and other negative outcomes. Historically, consider three of its most extreme forms: enslavement of African Americans, subjugation and genocide of American Indians, and internment of Japanese Americans during World War II. These are forms of institutional racism, because they go beyond individual bias and behavior and involve actions taken on an organizational and systemic or national level. In the present, institutional racism is evident in many forms of racial/ethnic profiling that lead to the highly disproportionate incarceration of African American and Hispanic males. Racism helps to explain the stark deprivation of large proportions of American Indians on most reservations and the glass ceiling commonly faced by even the most qualified Asian Americans. But recognize that these same invisible barriers affect other minority groups as well. Moreover, many statistical measures of the differences between these groups and the historically larger majority population reflect the continued influence of racism on multicultural groups in education, income, poverty, wealth, health, and crime.

Multicultural marketing broadens the marketing field in several ways. It assigns meaning and importance to groups and communities that have been neglected and traditionally underserved. Marketing becomes more culturally sensitive, inclusive, pluralistic, and progressive than was and is the case in traditional marketing. Multicultural marketing represents a forward-looking perspective in the theory and practice of marketing.

The main concepts and changes associated with multicultural marketing are illustrated in Figure 3-1.

CHANGES IN MARKETING PROCESS

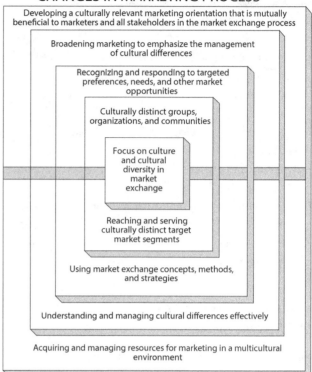

CHANGES IN MARKETING PRACTICE

FIGURE 3-1. Conceptual Framework for Multicultural Marketing. Source: Copyright Thaddeus Spratlen 2000

Context of Multicultural Markets

In terms of overall percentage of consumer groups, multicultural markets comprise as much as 60% of the US marketplace. One in five people in the United States speaks a language other than English at home. Racial and ethnic groups constitute more than 40% of the US population, segments by sexual orientation make up another 5% to 10%, and people with disabilities are yet another 18%.[5]

The hallmark of multicultural marketing has been an (insufficient) focus on four groups: Hispanics, African Americans, Asians, and American Indians. And historically, mainstream business has not paid much attention to any multicultural markets, because they were considered relatively small and seemingly difficult for business strategists of a predominantly white, non-Hispanic culture to understand.

Indeed, government and business have yet to come up with an effective means of categorizing these growing populations. The category "white" includes most Hispanics, while "black" commingles individuals born in

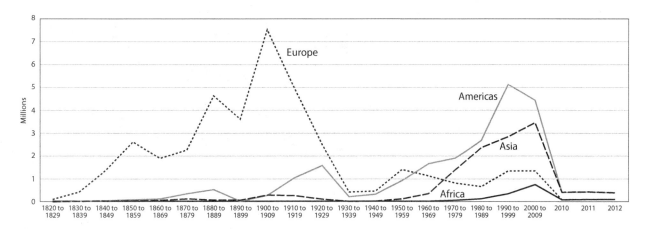

FIGURE 3-2. Number of Immigrants by World Region (Legal Status), 1820 to 2012. Source: US Department of Homeland Security, *Yearbook of Immigrant Statistics, 2012* (Washington, DC: Office of Immigration Statistics, July 2013)

or outside the United States of African, Caribbean, or South American descent. Asians originate from more than twenty countries with different languages, cultures, and histories. Populations that immigrated from South America, Central America, and Mexico are labeled Hispanic even though these individuals are not from Spain. Similarly, other indigenous people of the United States, such as American Indians and Alaska Natives, are categorized together although they represent more than five hundred tribes with different languages, cultures, and sovereign governments. The term *minority* is itself quickly becoming a misnomer because it suggests that there is a homogeneous majority population.

Until recently, mainstream business did not focus on these populations because they were small in number relative to the more established non-Hispanic white populations of mainly European origin or heritage. These more established populations had several generations to learn English and create the social and political infrastructure that supported business development. Over the years, the fusions of these originally multiethnic groups created a relatively homogeneous US culture that was approached by businesses using national demographics.

European populations were established in the United States through immigration. The wave of immigrants from the mid- to late 1800s included the Irish and Germans. Italians followed in the early 1900s. European immigrants came to the United States to escape harsh economic conditions, wars, or persecution. Race-based exclusion laws prevented the same scale of immigration from other parts of the world. In 1882 the US Congress passed the Chinese Exclusion Act, which was later

extended to all Asians until 1943, when it was repealed. Immigration quotas in the Immigration Act of 1924 effectively limited immigration until the 1965 Hart-Cellar Act lifted the discriminatory quotas. For many generations, racially oppressive policies prevented African Americans and American Indians from providing much more than low-wage labor. Moreover, slavery existed until 1865 and for generations afterward, Jim Crow laws and other forms of discrimination contributed to the further underdevelopment of African Americans as a group.

Twentieth-century immigration after World War II shifted dramatically, with increased immigration from Asian countries such as China, India, Korea, the Philippines, and Vietnam, some of which were engaged in conflicts such as the Korean and Vietnam wars. Immigration also increased from the Caribbean, Central America, South America, and particularly Mexico, which accounted for the bulk of the spike in 1991, as shown in Figure 3-2.

Multicultural Population Growth

Evidence to support and explain the shift to multicultural marketing is clear and convincing. In terms of overall size, in 2012 the five largest racial/ethnic groups that are referred to as minority groups comprised about 117 million people, or 38% of the US population as of the 2012 American Community Survey. In the same year, African Americans (alone or in combination with another race) numbered about 43 million; Hispanics about 53 million. Asians accounted for another 18.3 million, while American Indians (Native Americans and Alaska Natives) totaled more than 5.2 million. Native Hawaiians and other

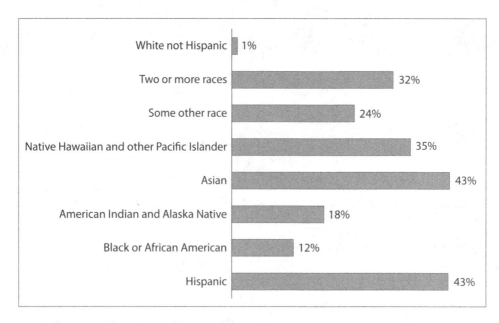

FIGURE 3-3. Multicultural Population Growth. Source: US Census 2010, Overview of Race and Hispanic Origin: 2010

Pacific Islanders accounted for 1.2 million. Multiple-race Americans, first allowed as a category in the 2000 census, numbered more 9 million in 2012. About 16.5 million identified themselves as some other race in 2012.[6]

Figure 3-3 shows that Hispanics, Asians, and mixed-race groups are growing the most, while the non-Hispanic white population has grown minimally during the ten years ending in 2010. In fact, the Hispanic population accounted for 56% of the growth in the total population between 2000 and 2010, while African Americans and Asians accounted for 16% each. More importantly, starting in 2014, public schools are projected to be majority minority, with Hispanics, Asians, African Americans, and multiracial students accounting for 50.3% of public school enrollment.[7]

According to the Selig Center for Economic Growth, African Americans, Hispanics, Asians, and American Indians accounted for $3.2 trillion, or close to 26%, of US purchasing power in 2013. In addition to the impressive dollar amount of spending power, marketers are attracted to the often disproportionate patterns of spending associated with specific groups. For example, African American consumption rates of apparel, shoes, cosmetics, and soft drinks can be up to three times their population proportion.

Going forward, the same patterns will persist. The US Census projects that Hispanic and Asian populations will account for 90% of the growth in population in the next fifty years. In fact, the US Census projects that after 2030, the non-Hispanic white population will actually be in decline. Figure 3-4 shows projected population growth to 2060.

Perhaps most significant is the demographic shift in the population of younger consumers, who are most coveted by marketers. In 2013, the US Census reported that the number of babies born into ethnic/racial minority families for the first time exceeded those born in Caucasian families. According to US Census projections for 2050, minorities will dominate the younger age categories, while non-Hispanic whites will constitute most of the older or retired population.[8] In fact, were not for minorities, the median age in the United States at midcentury would be 44 years. If that were the case, the United States would face the same problems as Japan and European countries, with their rapidly aging populations. The median age of developed countries is expected to reach 46.4 years by 2050. Japan, Italy, Switzerland, Germany, and Sweden already have median ages over 40. Some Western European countries and Japan expect a median age in the 50s by midcentury.[9] Without its diverse population, the United States would be in the same predicament (Table 3-1).

This is not to say that major change is not expected until the mid-twenty-first century. Already major urban areas, which are often the leading edge of demographic and cultural change, have shifted to become multicul-

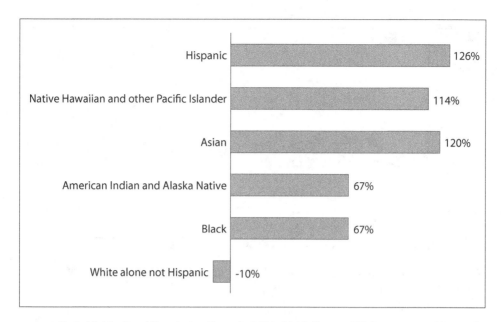

FIGURE 3-4. Multicultural Population Growth, 2014–2060. Source: US Census 2012, National Population Projections

tural areas in which no single cultural group dominates. In the three largest US cities—New York, Los Angeles, and Chicago—non-Hispanic whites constituted less than one-quarter of each city's population in 2012.[10]

It is a misconception that minority populations are static. Although they may suffer an economic disadvantage because of exclusion, discrimination, and lack of language skills or other resources, these populations are dynamic and quick to learn. Education levels have risen over the past twenty years and will continue to increase for populations that currently trail the non-Hispanic white population. Educational institutions that are run by black or American Indian educators for black or American Indian students have shown success rates exceeding those of mainstream educational institutions. Additionally, first-generation Hispanics are finding community colleges to be an effective gateway to education. In 2012,

for the first time, the proportion of eighteen- to twenty-four-year-old Hispanics who graduated from high school and enrolled in college exceeded that of non-Hispanic whites, as shown in Figure 3-5.[11] The second generation of Hispanics is following the pattern of other immigrants in increasing educational attainment.

Increases in education levels are often coupled with an increase in income. Median household income, as shown in Figure 3-6, grew more for Hispanics than it did for non-Hispanic whites prior to the 2007–9 recession. This growth was derailed in the recession, when median household income declined more for all minorities than it did for nonminority households. However, other factors may be in play. Within the Hispanic population, second-generation income levels exceed those of the first generation. Unlike the general US population, second-generation immigrants see their future as better than their parents'.[12] As rates of college education accelerate and as more role models emerge within their own communities, income levels will rise closer to those of non-Hispanic whites.

When the demographic trends are combined with the data on spending power, it is clear that multicultural markets represent a tremendous opportunity for both mainstream and minority businesses. It is also generally the case that minority markets are underserved. In some instances, brand loyalty has not been established for many of these segments. In addition, minority populations are

TABLE 3-1. Median Age, 2012 and 2060

	2012	2060
Two races	19	25
Hispanic	27	34
NHPI and AIAN	29	38
African American or black	32	39
Asian	35	42
Non-Hispanic white	42	47

Source: US Census 2013, 2012 National Population Projections

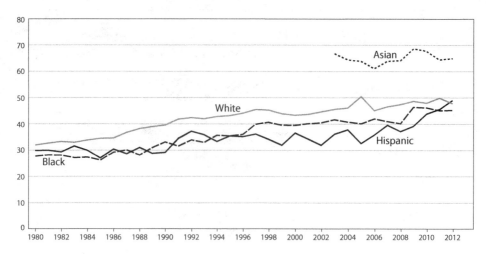

FIGURE 3-5. Proportion of 18 to 24 Year-Olds Who Graduated from High School and Enrolled in College, 1980–2012. Source: US Census, Historical School Data

already a major factor in the youth market and promise to increase their prominence in the years to come.

Multicultural Purchasing Power

Minority populations still trail the white population in income levels, but the purchasing power (as measured by personal disposable income) of Hispanic, African American, Asian, American Indian, and multiracial populations is significant, accounting for more than $3.2 trillion in 2013, or 26% of total buying power in the United States, according to the Selig Center for Economic Growth (Table 3-2). This is projected to grow 31% by 2018 to almost $4.2 trillion. At current levels of minority income, this purchasing power translates to 31%

of the growth in overall purchasing power between 2013 and 2018.

The geographic concentration and cultural traditions of Hispanics, African Americans, Asians, and American Indians give them substantial market potential in a variety of local and regional markets as well as in ethnically focused product categories. "Getting it" in the context of multicultural communities means understanding the potential and actual spending of customers who are members of diverse racial/ethnic groups so that targeted marketing efforts are more likely to be effective. "Getting it" also means acknowledging, responding to, and respecting the fact that these individuals (regardless of income, wealth, and class) are not "Caucasians in other than

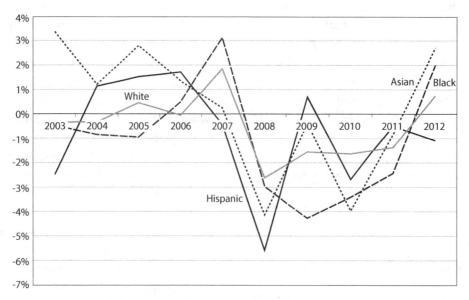

FIGURE 3-6. Annual Growth in Median Household Income, 2003–2004.
Source: US Census, Historical Income Tables H-9

TABLE 3-2. Multicultural Purchasing Power, 2013–2018

	2013 ($ billion)	2018 ($ billion)	Difference	% Change
Total	12,418	15,194	2,776	22
Hispanic	1,189	1,608	419	35
Black	1,071	1,333	262	24
American Indian	96	123	27	28
Asian	713	962	249	35
Multiracial	132	161	29	22

Source: L. M. Akioka, ed., *The Multicultural Economy 2013* (Athens, GA: Selig Center for Economic Growth, Terry College of Business, University of Georgia, 2013)

white skin." In order to be successful in the new America, there is no doubt that business enterprises must "get it" and respond to opportunities in expanding multicultural markets.

The goal of segmentation is to identify customer groups that have sufficient commonalities related to consuming a particular product or service and that are sufficiently large to generate profits for a company. Market niches can be attractive because they have characteristics that lend themselves to profitability or more frequent buying. Sometimes they are attractive simply because no other competitor has sufficiently served that market. All these arguments hold for multicultural markets. In the past, mainstream enterprises have not effectively targeted these populations because they were considered of insufficient size to be profitable or because they are difficult for mainstream marketers to understand. Large enterprises look for sales in the hundreds of millions as attractive potential markets. African American, Hispanic, and Asian/Pacific Islander markets are now of significant enough size to draw the attention of large national and multinational firms.

In addition, all these groups have faced discrimination as customers. A large body of research shows discrimination in major consumer purchasing such as housing and cars. A review of consumer racial profiling court cases outlined increasing discrimination, ranging from subtle degradation to overt denial of goods or services.[13]

What follows describes the larger segments of the multicultural market. It does so using the determinants of segmentation practiced in single-culture mass marketing, including demographics, geography, psychographic factors, and buying behavior. However, multicultural markets include myriad dimensions that define each culture and its relationship to the dominant culture. Such dimensions include sociological, psychological, and economic factors and racism. These all play a role in communicating to and determining the needs of the segment. Limited space does not allow full treatment of the complexity of these other dimensions, nor can we include all of the many cultures that make up the United States. Rather, this next section attempts to provide a brief overview for further exploration.

AFRICAN AMERICANS
Demographics

The 2012 American Community Survey counted more than 42 million African Americans, including the 2.3 million who identified as African American in combination with another race. Between 2000 and 2010, the group counting black or African American as their only race grew 12.3% versus 9.7% for the total US population. As with other races and ethnicities, the definition of the segment is itself complex. Of those who identify their race as African American alone, about 1.2 million are Hispanic blacks. Of those who identify themselves as black along with another race, the largest combination was black with white (1.8 million). Although it is estimated that up to one-third of African Americans are of multiple race, the struggle for lineage acknowledgment reaches as far back as the black descendants of Thomas Jefferson. In America's dominant culture, people with any portion of black heritage are typically identified as black.[14]

Immigration from Africa is increasing relative to historical rates. Almost 1.4 million Africans immigrated to the United States from 1990 to 2012, more than six times more than those who voluntarily came to the United States in the preceding two hundred years.[15] This tally of immigration, of course, excludes the estimated 8 million Africans who were forcibly brought to the Americas as part of the slave trade.

The gender split between male and female African Americans is 48% male and 52% female, compared with 49% male and 51% female for the general population. African American males actually outnumber females until age 20. After that point the number of females outpaces the number of males by a large margin. Although the same trend occurs in the white population, it does not start as early (females outnumber males starting at age 45), nor is the difference so pronounced until age 60. The smaller proportion of African American men plays itself out in family structure. Women head 48% of African American households (29% are households with children as compared to 10% of whites) and, similar to women in other groups, control more than two-thirds of the buying decisions.[16]

In 2012 the median age of all US males was 36.1 years; for black males, 31.1. Black females also had a lower median age than all US females: 34.6 years compared to 38.8.[17] A number of sociological factors, from lower access to health care to heightened victimization from crime, may account for these differences.

As a population, African Americans have more health risks, as manifested by an average life expectancy of 74.5 years for African American males versus 78.8 for all US males; and infant mortality rates of 11.5 per 1,000 births versus 5.2 for the white population.[18] These disparities are often caused by discrimination, cultural barriers, and lack of access to health care. Research documents the lack of access to healthy foods and the preponderance of environmentally unsafe conditions in both urban and rural areas where blacks live. Blacks are more likely to be obese (37.7% for black males and 51.8% for black females versus 34.7% for the general population).[19] Other studies have documented the preponderance of fast-food advertising in predominantly black areas.[20] There is a market opportunity for enterprises to provide products that address health needs specific to the African American population.

In 2012, African American households were slightly larger (2.68 persons per household) than those of whites (2.55) and were more likely to have children under age 18. Black women have a slightly higher fertility rate (65.1 of

1,000 gave birth versus 63 of 1,000 white women), and 71% of these women were unmarried compared with 29% of white women. Whites were more likely to be married (51%) compared to blacks (29%). Nearly 7% of blacks aged 30 and older were grandparents living with their grandchildren compared with only 2% of non-Hispanic whites. Approximately 52% of black grandparents were responsible for the care of their grandchildren compared with 45% of non-Hispanic whites.[21]

African Americans continue to lag behind the white population in educational attainment (see Figure 3-7), and this is of concern because education is one of the main determinants of wealth. It took a decade after the US Supreme Court's 1954 decision in *Brown v. Board of Education* for the government to start enforcing equal access to education. Many young African American students continue to learn under conditions that severely constrain their ability to perform. These include substandard schools or schools with far fewer resources than those in white neighborhoods. Being first in their families to attend higher education handicaps these students in navigating a complex, confusing, and expensive system.

The number of college-educated African Americans has increased by 135% since 1980 compared with 75% for the white population.[22] There are nearly 105 historically black colleges and universities (HBCUs),[23] such as Howard University and Morehouse (the alma mater of Martin Luther King Jr.). These universities graduate 20% of all African American degree holders while accounting for only 3% of higher education institutions. More than half of African American professionals are graduates of

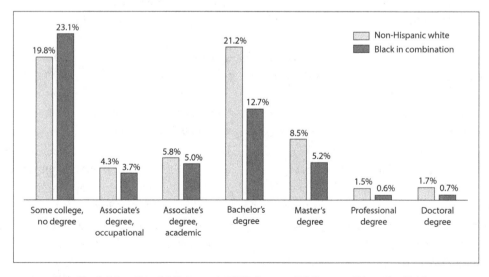

FIGURE 3-7. Black Educational Attainment, 2013. Source: US Census, Education Tables

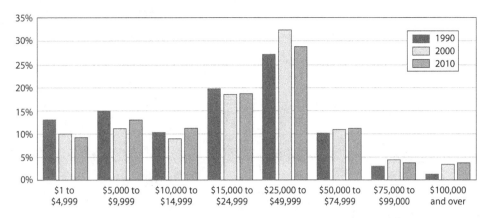

FIGURE 3-8. Black Income Growth, 1990–2010. Source: US Census, Historical Income Tables

HBCUs.[24] However, in the wake of the 2007–9 recession, many of these institutions encountered enrollment and funding problems. Blacks made up 6.4% of first-year medical students in 2011, less than in 1975, or half their proportion in the population.[25] Studies have shown that if personal factors are held constant, blacks are more likely than whites to both enter and graduate from college.[26] The disparities continue because of precollege personal factors, such as parents' educational levels and attending schools with lower per pupil spending, higher poverty rates, and lower average standardized test scores.

It is projected that educational attainment will continue to rise as African American youth find more role models among the increasing ranks of college-educated blacks, including a president who identifies as black. In 2010 about 28% of blacks were in management and professional occupations compared with 38% of whites.[27] Blacks continue to secure a broad spectrum of high-level, high-profile government and corporate positions, and this will also do much to raise the aspirations of the young. Similar to other multicultural segments, the demographics of African Americans are dynamic, fast changing, and often overlooked by mainstream marketers.

With rising educational levels over the long term, African American income levels are rising as well. This is particularly true for families with incomes of more than $75,000. Most of this growth accrued in the 1990s, as shown in Figure 3-8. The proportion of African American households with incomes of $75,000 to $99,999 grew 31% between 1990 and 2000 compared with a 5.3% increase for non-Hispanics whites; black households with incomes of $100,000 and over grew 59% versus 49% for non-Hispanic whites.

Although every downturn results in economic decline for all groups, minorities are affected to a greater extent. The 2007–9 recession had a disproportionate impact on African American wealth. In 2011 the median wealth of white households ($110,500) was twenty times that of black households ($6,314). From 2005 to 2009, median net worth fell 53% for black households versus a 16% drop for white households.[28] Black households were not affected as much as Hispanic and Asian households by the drop of real estate values; however, black households did experience drops in retirement accounts and in the values of the businesses they owned.

African Americans made significant inroads in reducing poverty rates in the 1990s, as shown in Figure 3-9. Black poverty rates remain significantly higher than those of the white population. In 2012, black poverty at 24.2% was slightly lower than for Hispanics at 25.3%, while whites had a 9.1% poverty level and Asians 9.8%.[29] The large proportion of single female heads in black households partially explains this. Within any group, families headed by single females tend to have a higher rate of

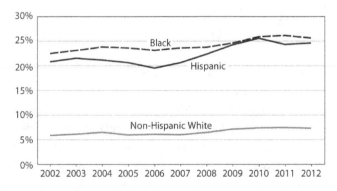

FIGURE 3-9. Poverty Rates, 2002–2012. Source: US Census, Table 2, Poverty Status of People by Family Relationship, Race, and Hispanic Origin: 1959 to 2012

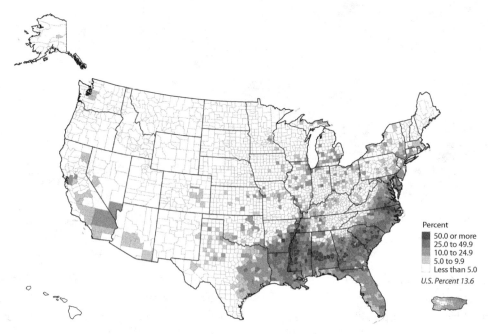

FIGURE 3-10. Black as a Percent of County Population, 2010. Source: US Census

poverty. As with Hispanic Americans, recessions tend to take a larger toll on African Americans, throwing more into poverty and stagnating income growth.

Geographics

African Americans are clustered in certain regions of the country. More than 55% of African Americans live in the south.[30] The US Census map (Figure 3-10) shows the high concentration of African Americans as a percentage of the population in the Mid-Atlantic and Southeast. African Americans are more than 50% of the population in 106 counties in the South (the only exception is St. Louis). The largest numbers of African Americans live in New York, Florida, Texas, Georgia, and California. Large growth occurred in the West and sections of the Midwest. The African Americans population in counties in Arizona, Nevada, California, Oregon, and Washington grew substantially between 2000 and 2010.

African Americans are more likely to live in metropolitan areas than the population as a whole. The cities with the largest African American populations are New York, Chicago, Philadelphia, Detroit, and Houston, totaling about 5 million. African Americans play a prominent political role in the cities where they have higher populations. Of the larger cities, six have African American mayors. According to the National Conference of Black Mayors, 650 US cities have black mayors, representing more than 48 million citizens.[31] As of 2014, the US Congress had 43 black representatives and 2 black senators compared with 33 Hispanic representatives and 3 Hispanic senators. There were 12 Asian American representatives and 1 Asian American senator.[32] Blacks were a formidable force in the 2012 elections, getting 66% of their eligible voters to the polls, a proportion that exceeded whites (64%).[33]

Other Factors

Along with the strong political involvement of African Americans, other psychological and sociological factors affect this segment's market potential. Poverty, criminal records, and single-female-headed households are more prevalent than in other groups. One in 13 black males between the ages of thirty and thirty-four has spent time in a correctional institution compared with 1 in 90 for white males and 1 in 36 for Hispanic males.[34] In 2011, 47% of prisoners were convicted of nonviolent drug, property, or public order crimes. Studies have documented wrongful convictions, lack of adequate legal representation, and racial profiling, particularly in the war on drugs. The 2001 report of the US Sentencing Commission found that African Americans constituted 13% of drug users but 35% of arrests and 53% of those convicted.[35] A criminal conviction has multiplier effects on families and household accumulation of wealth. It dismantles family structure and precludes higher-paying jobs.

Racism is a reality in the lives of most minority populations, and the competent enterprise will acknowledge and understand that racism is part of the complexity of marketing to minority cultures in the United States. It also represents an opportunity, because most minorities feel underserved in the marketplace. Most African Americans consider racial discrimination to be an important issue; 44% of African Americans report that they or a family member have experienced racial discrimination in the last few years.[36] African Americans overwhelmingly feel that they experience more discrimination than other groups. With regard to the enterprises that serve African Americans, the discrimination experienced has been widely documented in settlements with the Department of Justice over predatory lending and denial of credit.[37]

Homeownership is lower among blacks, with 43% owning homes in 2014 versus 73.4% for non-Hispanic whites. The gap is the largest since 1994.[38] Blacks had made major gains in homeownership, reaching 49.7% in mid-2004. However, they were targeted by subprime lenders. In 1993, subprime refinancing loans accounted for 8% of home loans in African American neighborhoods versus 1% in white neighborhoods. By 1998, 51% of the total loans in African American neighborhoods were subprime compared with 9% in white neighborhoods. This proportion remained constant until 2005, when 52% of loans in African American neighborhoods were subprime.[39] During the 2007–8 collapse of the housing market, the concentration of subprime loans among African American homeowners led to declines in homeownership and family net worth.

According to the Consumer Finance Survey, home equity continues to be the largest component of household wealth.[40] The barriers that restrict black homeownership, as well as the comparatively lower appreciation of homes in predominantly black neighborhoods compared with white neighborhoods, are the same barriers that stifle the accumulation of African American wealth. Predatory subprime lending and subsequent foreclosures inordinately set African American families back in their quest to build a secure financial future.

Recession takes its toll on the black population in other ways. From 2009 to 2013 more than half a million government jobs were lost. As African Americans are one-third more likely to be working in the public sector, these layoffs had more of an impact on blacks. Research shows that displacement rates for public sector blacks were similar to those in the private sector, where blacks are more likely to be terminated first.[41]

Religion, and particularly the church, continues to play a major role in the lives of African Americans. Eight historically black denominations represent sixty-five thousand churches and membership of more than twenty million people.[42] These denominations are African Methodist Episcopal (dates to 1787 and supports a dozen colleges); African Methodist Episcopal Zion (started in the late eighteenth century); Christian Methodist Episcopal (organized by forty-one former slaves in 1870 in the Wesleyan tradition); Church of God in Christ (founded in the early twentieth century); National Baptist Convention of America Inc.; National Baptist Convention, USA Inc.; National Missionary Baptist Convention of America; and Progressive National Baptist Convention Inc.[43] In addition to the customary role churches assume in other cultures, these ministries promote justice, affiliate relations, children and family development, economic development, antidrug and antiviolence campaigns, health issues, voter education, and leadership development. They continue to be a major means of communicating to the black population.

As with other minorities, the history, culture, and traditions of African Americans are not common knowledge to the American public because of the lack of inclusion in most school curriculums. Over the past four decades, Kwanzaa has emerged as a post-Christmas celebration among African Americans. Many individuals and families may celebrate both Christmas and Kwanzaa, while others choose to celebrate only or mainly Kwanzaa. In celebrating Kwanzaa (a Swahili word for "first fruits") between December 26 and January 1, much less emphasis is placed on giving presents. Greater emphasis is placed on family and community values. There are many examples of cultural differences in weddings, births, and other life events that spawn a host of new products and services—most of these provided by African American businesses that understand these customs and customer preferences.

Purchasing Power

The 2012 Consumer Expenditure Survey showed that, despite their lower income, African Americans spend more on telephone services, utilities, shoes, and children's apparel than whites. As a proportion of their total household income, blacks spend more on groceries, housing, utilities, apparel, and transportation. They spend less on alcohol, health care, entertainment, personal insurance, and pensions.[44]

TABLE 3-3. Comparative Black Consumer Spending, 2012

	All Consumer Units	Black or African American	All Consumer Units, % of Total	Black or African American, % of Total	% Difference
Number of consumer units (in thousands)	120,847	14,432			
Average annual expenditures	$49,067	$35,198			
Food at home	3,753	2,875	7.6	8.2	0.5
Food away from home	2,619	1,649	5.3	4.7	-0.7
Alcoholic beverages	435	201	0.9	0.6	-0.3
Housing	16,895	13,409	34.4	38.1	**3.7**
Shelter	10,075	7,847	20.5	22.3	**1.8**
Utilities, fuels, and public services	3,645	3,660	7.4	10.4	**3.0**
Household operations	1,011	618	2.1	1.8	-0.3
Housekeeping supplies	659	434	1.3	1.2	-0.1
Household furnishings and equipment	1,506	850	3.1	2.4	-0.7
Apparel and services	1,725	1,761	3.5	5.0	**1.5**
Transportation	7,658	5,269	15.6	15.0	-0.6
Health care	3,126	1,762	6.4	5.0	-1.4
Entertainment	2,693	1,406	5.5	4.0	-1.5
Personal care products and services	596	536	1.2	1.5	0.3
Reading	110	47	0.2	0.1	-0.1
Education	1,068	599	2.2	1.7	-0.5
Tobacco products and smoking supplies	380	232	0.8	0.7	-0.1
Miscellaneous	816	633	1.7	1.8	0.1
Cash contributions	1,723	1,277	3.5	3.6	0.1
Personal insurance and pensions	5,471	3,542	11.2	10.1	-1.1

Source: US Bureau of Labor Statistics, Annual Calendar Year Tables 2012, Consumer Expenditure Survey

Note: Bold figures indicate larger expenditures compared to the general consumer

Media

The ethnic press has long been a means for marginalized communities to give voice to their concerns and stories. As mainstream media become more concentrated, ethnic media perform an even more crucial role in providing different perspectives. Unfortunately, the contraction of print media is also having its impact on ethnic print media. About 30% of African Americans report getting their news from newspapers, similar to the general public. Nearly 69% of blacks receive their news from television compared with 56% of whites, according to the Pew Research Center's State of the New Media 2013. The Black Press of America identifies two hundred black-owned newspapers, including the Los Angeles Sentinel, the Chicago Defender, and the Washington Afro American. These newspapers cover recent news events from a black perspective. There are no remaining print dailies. In 2012, only one African American newspaper increased its circulation.[45]

Of the diverse magazines targeting black readers, five dominate. Ebony (1.3 million circulation) and Jet magazine (800,000 circulation) are owned by Johnson Publishing and target an upscale black audience. Essence (1.1 million circulation) is a Time Inc. magazine aimed at African American women. Black Enterprise (500,000 circulation) covers African American businesses and provides an annual ranking of the one hundred largest black-owned businesses. Uptown (100,000 circulation) is a national magazine with regional editions in New York, Philadelphia, Washington, DC, Charlotte, Atlanta, Detroit, and Chicago.[46]

In other media, the Black Entertainment Television (BET) network, a subsidiary of Viacom Inc., is broadcast to 92 million homes in the United States, Canada, and the Caribbean.[47] The BET brand includes CENTRIC, which reflects the newer trends in music, culture, and lifestyles, and BET Gospel and BET Hip Hop. TV One is another black cable station. The Oprah Winfrey Network got off to a rough start but is now profitable. ASPIRE was launched by Magic Johnson in 2012. Revolt, a music channel, was started by Sean Combs in 2013.

Several hundred black radio stations feature news and commentary by well-known personalities such as Tom Joyner and Tavis Smiley, as well as various genres of black music, including gospel, hip-hop, R&B, jazz and blues, and Caribbean.[48] Many of these stations are owned by large conglomerates that seek to target the black demographic and, given the ability of radio media to broadcast globally on the Internet, are reaching markets in Africa and the rest of the world. The number of stations with black owners peaked at 274 in 1995 and currently is about 68.[49]

In 2013, 80% of blacks were Internet users compared to 87% of whites. Older blacks and those who have not gone to college are less likely to use the Internet or have broadband service. Blacks, especially those between the ages of eighteen and twenty-nine, use social networking at rates equal to or higher than whites. In particular, tweeting seems especially popular among the young, with about 40% of blacks in this age group using Twitter compared to 28% of whites.[50]

HISPANIC AMERICANS
Demographics

Since 2000, Hispanic Americans have attracted the most attention among minority groups because of their high population growth rate and their surpassing African Americans as the largest US minority group. These trends are fueled by immigration since 1965 and higher birth rates than the overall US population, both of which have declined since 2010. The governments classifies *Hispanic* as an ethnic category (as opposed to race for whites, African Americans, Asians, American Indians and Alaska Natives, and Native Hawaiian and Pacific Islanders) to capture Spanish-speaking populations and persons from Brazil. Sometimes the term *Latino* is used, because it does not exclude non-Spanish-speaking South American countries such as Brazil. In 2014, the group numbered more than fifty-three million and constituted 17% of the US population. The Hispanic population grew fivefold since 1970 and accounted for half of US population growth from 2000 to 2012.

The term *Hispanic*, although used extensively by the government, media, and enterprises, is not a relevant term to the groups it categorizes. In fact, these populations identify most strongly with their country of origin. They include people from Mexico, South and Central America, and the Caribbean, as shown in Table 3-4. Most Hispanics do not see a common culture among US Hispanics nor do they feel that the categories used to identify them fit. Significant differences in identity exist between first- and second-generation Hispanics as they do for other immigrant groups.

With regard to race, in the 2010 US Census about 53% of Hispanics identified themselves as white alone and 2.5% as black alone. Approximately 37% identified themselves as some other race alone, while 6% identified themselves as two or more races. Millions of Hispanics changed their race category from "some other race" to "white" or vice versa between the 2000 and 2010 census reflecting the confusion in racial identity.[51] As a result, the US Census is drafting new questions to better capture this information. The assimilation of Hispanics appears to be following the same pattern as white immigrants groups, such as Italians and Irish, and may change the context of the race and minority discussion in the United States in the future.

With regard to gender, differences exist between Hispanic and white populations. Hispanic males account for 51% of the group versus 49% for whites. Young adult males outnumber females in the prime working-age groups (ages fifteen to forty).[52] This is similar to immigration patterns in Asian populations, where male workers predominated prior to 1980 due to restrictive immigration policies that prohibited the immigration of families. Immigration has been a dominant part of the political discussion since the 1990s, with various forms of immigration reform being debated in Congress. However, Hispanics also count education and healthcare as priorities.[53] By the mid-2010s, the curtailing of the flow of immigrants due to the 2007–9 recession, heightened border enforcement and deportations, and Mexican economic growth and decline in birth rates had reversed the largest immigrant flow to the United States. The Hispanic workforce has shifted to be made up of primarily US-born Hispanics.[54]

TABLE 3-4. Hispanic Groups by National Origin, 2000 and 2012

Country of Origin	Population, 2000	Population, 2012	Difference	% Growth, 2000–2012	% Foreign-Born
Mexican	20,640,711	34,038,599	13,397,888	65	35
Puerto Rican	3,406,178	4,970,604	1,564,426	46	100
Cuban	1,241,685	1,957,557	715,872	58	58
Dominican	764,945	1,656,960	892,015	117	56
Costa Rican	68,588	140,152	71,564	104	53
Guatemalan	372,487	1,241,560	869,073	233	64
Honduran	217,569	753,532	535,963	246	64
Nicaraguan	177,684	405,601	227,917	128	60
Panamanian	91,723	183,743	92,020	100	47
Salvadoran	655,165	1,992,754	1,337,589	204	60
Argentinean	100,864	248,823	147,959	147	62
Bolivian	42,068	103,296	61,228	146	68
Chilean	68,849	140,045	71,196	103	60
Colombian	470,684	1,039,923	569,239	121	64
Ecuadorian	260,559	662,633	402,074	154	62
Paraguayan	8,769	20,461	11,692	133	61
Peruvian	233,926	594,418	360,492	154	68
Uruguayan	18,804	60,178	41,374	220	65
Venezuelan	91,507	249,153	157,646	172	69

Sources: S. R. Ennis, M. Rios-Vargas, and N. G. Albert, "The Hispanic Population: 2010," Census Briefs C2010R-04, May 2011; US Census, "2012 American Community Survey: Hispanic or Latino Origin by Specific Origin," table B03001

The Hispanic population is younger than whites, blacks, and Asians, although differences exist within Hispanic groups. In 2011, the median age for Mexicans was 25, while for Cubans it was 40.6, a median age higher than the non-Hispanic white median age of 40.1. Other Central American groups had median ages from 28 to 32. South American groups had median ages from 32 to 35.[55] Hispanic youth (numbering seventeen million in 2012) constitute the largest ethnic segment (24%) of the under-18 population in the United States.[56]

Hispanic families are larger, with a median household size of 3.27 persons versus 2.38 for non-Hispanic white families. Mexicans have the highest average household size at 3.7. Cubans have the lowest at 2.7. The Hispanic marriage rate of 48% is lower than the 55% for non-Hispanic whites. Hispanic households have a larger number of single-parent households, with 23% having a female head of household versus 11% for non-Hispanic whites, and 10% have a male head of household versus 4.8% for non-Hispanic whites.[57] Hispanics have higher fertility rates: 74.4 per 1,000 women (2012) versus 63 per

1,000 for whites. However, fertility rates have fallen from 100 in 1994 and continue to decline. Hispanics out-marry in significant numbers, with nearly 20% marrying non-Hispanics.[58]

The majority (96.2%) of non-Hispanic whites are native US citizens, compared with only 60.8% of Hispanic Americans. Approximately one-third of all other Hispanic groups, except Puerto Ricans (births in Puerto Rico are classified as native US births), are native US citizens. Of the foreign-born heads of households, 48% entered the United States before 1990, 29% during the 1990s, and 22% in the year 2000 or later. Of those who entered before 1990, 58% own their homes, while only 20% of those who entered after 2000 report homeownership.[59]

The relatively recent immigration of most Hispanic Americans explains their lag in educational attainment. When coming to the United States, Hispanics have to grapple with a different language and social system. However, it is important not to discount the dynamism of minority populations. As noted earlier, in 2012 the percentage of Hispanics aged eighteen to twenty-four who

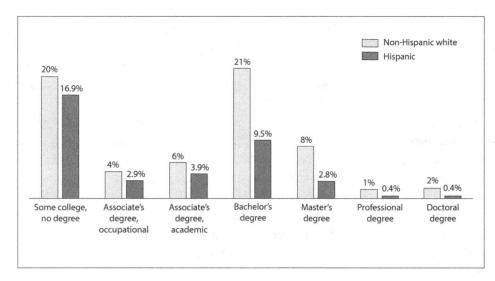

FIGURE 3-11. Hispanic Educational Attainment, 2013. Source: US Census, Education Tables

completed high school and enrolled in college was higher than for whites.[60] Hispanic high school dropout rates have declined from 27.8% in 2004 to 12.7% in 2012. High unemployment in this age group was a factor in rising enrollment among blacks and Asians.[61] However, Hispanics tend to favor community colleges, which accounted for 46% of their enrollment compared with less than 30% for whites and Asians and less than 40% for blacks.[62] The low college completion rate for Hispanics reflects the lower educational attainment of immigrants. The rate of college completion for US-born Hispanics aged twenty-five to twenty-nine is 20%, which is similar to the 19% for blacks.[63]

The strong correlation between education and income is reflected in the Hispanic population. In 2012, the Hispanic median income of $39,005 was lower than non-Hispanic whites' median income of $57,009.[64] From 1990 to 2000, approximately 6% of Hispanics increased their income from below $15,000 to higher levels. Almost 2% moved into income levels over $50,000 between 1990 and 2000. Half the increase in this group occurred between 2000 and 2010; however, 4% of households fell below $15,000. The 2007–9 recession had its greatest impact on middle-income Hispanic households.

While Hispanic income levels are 60% of those of non-Hispanic whites, it is important to note that Hispanic wealth (2011 median net worth $7,683) is one-eighteenth of non-Hispanic whites ($110,500). Hispanics experienced a 66% drop in median net worth between 2005 and 2009 compared to a 16% drop for whites. More than one-third of Hispanic households had zero or negative net worth in 2009. Homeownership is the major compo-

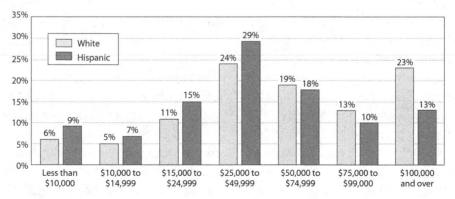

FIGURE 3-12. Hispanic Income Distribution, 2012. Source: US Census, American Community Survey, Data Set B19001I

nent in net worth, and the median level of home equity for Hispanics fell from $99,983 in 2005 to $49,145 in 2009. The geographical concentration of Hispanics in California, Florida, Nevada, and Arizona, the states that suffered the steepest decline in housing values when the housing bubble burst in 2007, accounts for this drop.[65]

It is important to keep in mind the demographic differences between Hispanics of different countries. Those from South America tend to have higher rates of college education (30% to 40%), higher median household income ($48,000 to $55,000), and lower poverty rates (11% to 18%) than those from Central America. Hispanics originating from Central America and Mexico have lower rates of attaining a bachelor's degree or higher (7% to 16%), lower household median incomes ($31,000 to $40,000), and higher poverty rates (18% to 29%).[66]

Immigration

As of 2010, approximately 65% of the US Hispanic population was from Mexico. Much of the Mexican-ancestry population preceded the English-speaking population in the Southwest, with Spanish-speaking settlers arriving in New Mexico as early as the 1600s, in Arizona and Texas in the late 1700s, and in California and Colorado in the early 1800s. These states continue to have high Hispanic populations, with 38% of Californians, 30% of Arizonians, 47% of New Mexicans, 23% of Floridians, and 38% of Texans being Hispanic.[67]

The Southwest experienced huge influxes of immigrants after the 1910 revolution in Mexico, providing the origins of the established Hispanic population. These settlers moved into the Midwest in the 1920s, where the Hispanic population of Chicago began to grow. Since 1965, and particularly in the 1990s, Mexican immigration has grown, with most of that new population settling in the Southwest and West.

Puerto Ricans accounted for 9.2% of the total US Hispanic population in 2010 (4.6 million). They began settling in the United States after Spain ceded the island as a result of the Spanish-American War of 1898. The first major settlements occurred in New York City in the 1920s. A large migration occurred after World War II. New York drew the most, but by the 1960s, Puerto Ricans began moving to Connecticut, New Jersey, Pennsylvania, Illinois, Massachusetts, south Florida, and California.

Large Cuban immigration happened after Fidel Castro took power in 1959, and there have since been continuing waves of Cuban immigrants, mostly into south Florida,

New York, California, and New Jersey. Cubans account for one-third of Miami's population, and many of the top Hispanic businesses in Miami are Cuban-owned. Major Cuban communities are also found in Chicago, New Orleans, and Atlanta.

Other than Mexico, the largest source of immigrants in the past two decades has been Central America. About one-tenth of the population of El Salvador is estimated to have entered the United States beginning in the 1970s, following internal strife and a major earthquake. Large numbers of Salvadorans live in Los Angeles, the San Francisco Bay Area, New York City, and Washington, DC. Guatemalans followed the same pattern. Nicaraguans settled in Miami. Dominicans account for the single largest group of recent immigrants to New York City. Of South American immigrants, Colombians have also established a major presence in New York City and Miami.

A major shift in the Hispanic population is marked by the increase in the number of native-born Hispanics. In 2013, 49.7% of employed Hispanics were immigrants, down from 56.1%. The recession that started in 2007 slowed the inflow of Hispanic immigrants. Growth in US-born Hispanics is fueling the increase in the Hispanic workforce.[68] The percentage of foreign-born Hispanics varies by group, reflecting the timing of the wave of immigration for each group. Mexicans reflecting inflow in the 1990s were at 35.6% foreign born in 2010. Central American immigrants who arrived later have a higher foreign-born percentage (52% to 66%), and South Americans who have arrived since the year 2000 have the highest foreign-born proportion (44% to 75%).

Mexico continues to be the largest source of unauthorized immigrants to the United States, numbering 6 million of the total estimated 11.7 million in 2012 (down from a peak of 12 million in 2007).[69] Other Latin American countries account for 23% (2.6 million) of unauthorized immigrants. Asia accounts for 11%, or 1.3 million. Europe, Canada, and Africa all account for fewer than 500,000 unauthorized immigrants. According to the Pew Hispanic Center, unauthorized immigrants made up 3.7% of the US population and 5.2% of its workforce in 2010. Most of these workers have arrived since 1990 and provide crucial worker requirements in several sectors, including half the agricultural workforce and one-quarter of meat and poultry workers. The number of unauthorized workers declined in 2008 due to the recession. However, the Pew Research Center estimates that the number of unauthorized immigrants from countries

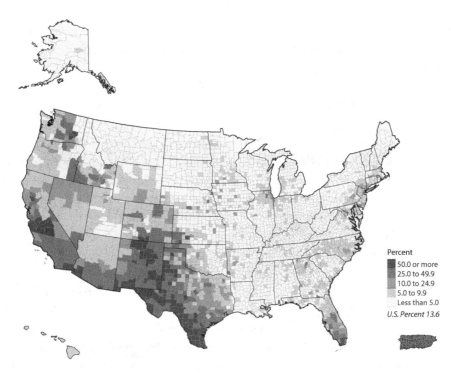

FIGURE 3-13. Hispanic as Percent of County Population, 2010.
Source: US Census, Hispanic Population: 2010

other than Mexico has been rising since then. Births to unauthorized immigrants (4% of the US population) accounted for 8% of all US newborns in 2009.[70]

Geographics

Like other minorities, the Hispanic population is concentrated in certain regions, as depicted in Figure 3-13. About half of all Hispanics live in two states: California (28%) and Texas (19%). With New York, Florida, Illinois, Arizona, and New Jersey, the seven states accounted for almost three-quarters of the US Hispanic population in 2010. With regard to subgroups, Mexicans are concentrated in California, Texas, Illinois, and Arizona; Puerto Ricans are in New York, Florida, New Jersey, and Pennsylvania; and the majority of Cubans are in Florida

Over 90% of Hispanics live in urban areas. The largest cities in the United States generally have the largest Hispanic populations. The influence of Hispanics is particularly felt in Los Angeles, San Antonio, and El Paso, where they represent a large portion of the population.

About 11 million Hispanics voted in the 2012 election, an increase of 15% over 2008. Hispanics accounted for 8.3% of US votes cast. However, this was only 48% of the 23.3 million eligible Hispanic voters, compared to 66% of eligible black voters and 46% of eligible Asian

voters. Younger and more educated Hispanics are more likely to vote, therefore it is anticipated that as Hispanics become more educated, they will wield more political force.[71]

Hispanics have increasingly become involved in politics. According to the National Association of Latino Elected and Appointed Officials, there are more than 6,000 Hispanic elected officials, a 53% increase over the fifteen years prior to 2011.[72] The bulk of these are local officials, with the largest number in Texas, California, and New Mexico. As of 2014, there were 33 Hispanic representatives in Congress and 3 Hispanic senators. However, despite all these gains, Hispanic voters make up the lowest proportion of eligible voters relative to population, due mainly to their youth and US citizenship status.[73]

Other Factors

Of all the racial and ethnic minority groups in the United States, Hispanics tend to have the largest families. Strong family values play an important role in the culture. For groups from Latin America, the Spanish conquest of some of their countries brought a colonial influence in religion (Roman Catholicism) and language. However, the indigenous Indian cultures (Maya, Inca, etc.) continue to permeate folk art, customs, and food. As noted earlier, Hispanic identity is shifting. In 2014, a survey found that one in four Hispanics have shifted from Catholicism (55% of Hispanics) to Protestantism (22%) or are unaffiliated (16%).[74]

According to the Pew Hispanic Center, the length of time Hispanics and their families have been in the United States is a key factor in their attitudes and behavior. About 40% of Hispanics are first generation or immigrants. Children of immigrants make up 29% of all Hispanics. The third generation is 31% of Hispanics. By 2020, demographers project that the second generation will be the largest segment at 36%. This second generation will fuel the workforce by adding 12.6 million workers by 2020, while the non-Hispanic labor force will increase by 11.6 million.[75]

Although recent immigrants and older people prefer to speak Spanish, most second- and third-generation Hispanics favor English. However, the proportion of second- and third-generation Hispanics who know Spanish is still high, and about 30% of Hispanics prefer Spanish in their media, as shown in Table 3-5. Marketers must also account for cultural differences in the Spanish language among subgroups. For example, Hispanic food manufacturers promoting beans refer to *habichuelas* for Puerto Ricans and *frijoles* for Mexicans.

TABLE 3-5. Language Preference by Media (%)

	Reading	TV	Radio	Online
Only English	37	29	26	43
Mostly English	24	33	29	20
Mostly Spanish	16	19	20	10
Only Spanish	19	12	19	12

Source: Simmons National Hispanic Consumer Study, Winter 2013

Second-generation Hispanics will drive population change in many ways. With increased English proficiency and acculturation, they will create more opportunities for themselves and the communities in which they live and work. Their educational attainment has increased compared to their first-generation counterparts as they attend college in greater numbers. Hispanic income levels have also risen, with the second generation earning more than the first generation. Like many other second-generation or later immigrants, 39% of US-born Hispanics and 57% of the third generation marry outside of their ethnicity compared to 12% of foreign-born Hispanics.[76] These are higher rates than for most Asian groups. Greater cul-

tural fusion is on the horizon for the US population, based on the sheer growth in numbers of second- and third-generation Hispanics.

Even with the acculturation of second- and third-generation Hispanics into the US population, Hispanics report that racial discrimination is a problem in their communities. Although the proportion of Hispanics who experience personal discrimination is lower than for blacks, they experience discrimination at a significantly higher rate than whites.[77] Hispanics who are less proficient in English also experience more discrimination.[78]

Purchasing Power

The purchasing power of Hispanics was estimated at over $1.3 trillion in 2013 by the Selig Center for Economic Growth. Barring the lingering effects of the 2007–9 recession, as the proportion of households in middle- and higher-income groups increases, Hispanic purchasing power is projected to increase at a higher rate than the population as a whole, reaching $1.6 trillion by 2018, a 35% increase compared to a 22% increase in total US buying power.

Even with lower incomes, Hispanics spend proportionately more on food, apparel, and transportation than the population as a whole (Table 3-6). They spend less on health care, entertainment, education, and personal insurance than the population as a whole. A smaller proportion of Hispanics own their own homes (45.5%) compared to non-Hispanic whites (73.4%).[79]

Of particular interest to marketers are Hispanic Millennials. These young US-born Hispanics tend to be English dominant but bilingual, as seen in Table 3-5, which shows that less than 20% of Hispanics prefer Spanish-only media. They live at home, have less debt, and have more disposable income. As noted earlier, they are more likely to be enrolled in college than whites; they prefer Spanish broadcasts and like older Hispanics are loyal to telenovelas (Spanish soap operas). They are more likely than their white counterparts to own a smartphone, they use social media at equal rates, and they are more likely to shop online.[80]

Media

In 2009, there were 1,323 Spanish-language radio stations in the United States, up from 1,224 in 2008. Radio has the strongest reach of all media, touching 95% of Spanish-dominant Hispanics and 93% of English-dominant Hispanics.[81] Hispanic men between ages 45

TABLE 3-6. Comparative Hispanic Consumer Spending, 2012

	All Consumer Units	Hispanic or Latino	All Consumer Units, % of Total	Hispanic or Latino, % of Total	% Difference
Number of consumer units (in thousands)	124,416	15,597			
Average annual expenditures	$51,442	$42,268			
Food at home	3,921	4,116	8	10	2
Food away from home	2,678	2,454	5	6	**1**
Alcoholic beverages	451	338	1	1	0
Housing	16,887	15,061	33	36	**3**
Shelter	9,891	9,215	19	22	**3**
Utilities, fuels, and public services	3,648	3,325	7	8	**1**
Household operations	1,159	728	2	2	-1
Housekeeping supplies	610	568	1	1	0
Household furnishings and equipment	1,580	1,225	3	3	0
Apparel and services	1,736	2,030	3	5	**1**
Transportation	8,998	8,306	17	20	2
Health care	3,556	1,893	7	4	-2
Entertainment	2,605	1,588	5	4	-1
Personal care products and services	628	556	1	1	0
Reading	109	40	0	0	0
Education	1,207	488	2	1	-1
Tobacco products and smoking supplies	332	157	1	0	0
Miscellaneous	829	553	2	1	0
Cash contributions	1,913	782	4	2	-2
Personal insurance and pensions	5,591	3,905	11	9	-2

Source: US Bureau of Labor Statistics, Annual Calendar Year Tables 2012, "Current Combined Expenditure, Share, and Standard Error Tables: Hispanic or Latino Origin of Reference Person," www.bls.gov/cex/csxcombined.htm

Note: Bold figures indicate larger expenditures compared to the general consumer

and 54 spend the most time listening to radio at 18.34 hours per week. Hispanic men between ages 55 and 64 (18.26 hours) and those between ages 35 and 44 (17.18 hours) are close behind. Hispanic women between ages 45 and 54 spend 15.49 hours per week listening to radio. Top-ranked radio stations in Los Angeles and New York have more than two million listeners.[82] Four in ten Hispanics who mostly speak English also listen to Spanish-language radio. A nationwide poll gave their reasons for listening as sports, entertainment, a cultural connection, and the belief that English-speaking media outlets portray Hispanics in a negative light.[83] Univision is a major media outlet, with the largest number of Spanish-language viewers in the United States, according to 2014 Nielsen ratings. Other significant outlets include Bustos Media (28 stations), Entravision (48 stations), Liberman Broadcasting, Spanish Broadcasting System, LA Public Media, and LA Forward.

Television advertising to Hispanic households accounted for $5.8 billion in 2012, and it grew 10% from the previous year. Univision remains the dominant force in Spanish-language television and garnered the number-one spot for summers from 2011 to 2014 for all viewers aged 18 to 49, beating out major mainstream broadcasters. The network's platforms include Univision, TeleFutura, Galavision Networks, Univision.com, Univision Movil, and Univision on Demand.

Telemundo, a division of NBC Universal Media, LLC (51% recently acquired by Comcast), reaches 94% of US Hispanic households. Telemundo is in 210 markets, with 17 stations, 46 station affiliates, and 1,000 cable affiliates.[84] It also offers content through mobile platforms.

In 2004, it began making its own telenovelas and has grown to the second-largest producer of Spanish-language content behind the large Mexican company Televisa.

Many mainstream media companies have been attracted to the size and growth of the Hispanic market. Fox has added Noticias Mundo Fox nationally and in the Miami and Los Angeles markets. Such ventures have mixed track records. Both NBC (Comcast) and CNN (Time Warner) ended their Latino broadcasts in January 2014. In 2013, Fusion was launched, a joint venture of Univision and ABC.

At the end of 2010, there were 26 Hispanic daily newspapers, down from 33 in 2007 and 38 in 2006 (2010 circulation 1.02 million). There were 428 weekly Hispanic newspapers (circulation 11.08 million), up from 417 in 2007. The number of biweekly or monthly news-papers in 2010 was 378 (circulation 4.92 million), down from 381 in 2008. Only 40% of Hispanics read a Spanish-language newspaper, while 60% read an English-language newspaper. About 33% read Spanish-language maga-zines, and 56% read English-language magazines, varying with acculturation. There is still a high level of engage-ment with Hispanic publications among Hispanics of all ages. The largest-circulation US Hispanic magazine is *People en Español*. Most Hispanic magazines are aimed toward women or entertainment.[85]

Hispanic media is moving to multiplatform, which encompasses online and mobile delivery. The proportion of Hispanics using social media and cell phones equals that of whites. Higher rates are experienced among native-born, English-proficient, and younger Hispanics than among Spanish-dominant, foreign-born, and older Hispanics.

ASIAN AMERICANS
Demographics

Asian Americans (alone or in combination with another race) numbered 17.7 million according to US Census esti-mates in 2012. This group experienced the fastest rate of growth of any demographic group between 2000 and 2010 (at 43%) and in 2010 accounted for 5.6% of the US population. Asian Americans are projected to grow to 44 million (or 10% of the population) by 2060, a 120% increase as compared to 30% increase for the pop-ulation as a whole.[86] With regard to market size, consider also the adjacent Asian Canadian population of close to

4.3 million in 2011.[87] The largest segments of the Asian American population are 1.3 million Chinese and 1.6 mil-lion South Asians.

This is the most diverse of all racial/ethnic categories. Significant numbers of Asians have immigrated to the United States from more than twenty countries, with the Chinese segment being the largest (Table 3-7). Each group has a different history and cultural heritage and, unlike Hispanics, members of this group do not generally share a common language. Often their countries of origin experienced strained relations with or outright hostility toward one another in the past.

Like Hispanics, Asians tend to identify most strongly with their country of origin rather than their US Census racial/ethnic category. About 60% of all Asians are for-eign-born. This ranges from 28% of Japanese (who were not part of the recent wave of immigration from Asia) to 77% of Sri Lankans. Of the foreign-born, the proportion who are naturalized US citizens also varies from 27% for Pakistanis to 63% for the Chinese, who tended to immi-grate earlier.

Asians value education and, as a group, educational

TABLE 3-7. Asian Population in the United States by Country of Origin, 2010

	Population	% of Asian Alone
Chinese/Taiwanese	3,347,229	23
Asian Indian	2,843,391	20
Filipino	2,555,923	18
Vietnamese	1,548,449	11
Korean	1,423,784	10
Japanese	763,325	5
Pakistani	363,699	3
Hmong	247,595	2
Cambodian	231,616	2
Other	218,922	2
Laotian	191,200	1
Thai	166,620	1
Bangladeshi	128,792	1
Burmese	91,085	1
Indonesian	63,383	0.4
Nepalese	51,907	0.4
Sri Lankan	38,596	0.3
Malaysian	16,138	0.1

Source: E. M. Hoeffel, S. Rastogi, M. O. Kim, and H. Shahid, "The Asian Population: 2010," US Census Briefs CB2010BR-11, March 2012

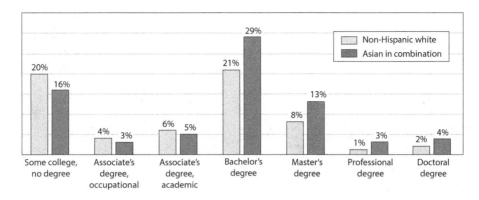

FIGURE 3-14. Asian Educational Attainment, 2013.
Source: US Census, Education Tables

levels outpace the rest of the population, as shown in Figure 3-14. Note that educational attainment varies across groups, with 68% of Indians and over 50% of Chinese and Koreans having bachelor's degrees or higher, a percentage that is 14% or less for Cambodians, Hmong, and Laotians.[88]

Asian immigrant and Asian American median household income levels are higher than those of any other racial/ethnic group, as seen in Figure 3-15. Concentration of Asians in professional occupations accounts for their high incomes. In 2010, 20% of medical school graduates were Asian compared to 6.7% black and 7.4% Hispanic.[89]

TABLE 3-8. Demographic and Socioeconomic Profiles of Asian Americans

	Foreign-Born (%)	US Citizen (%)	Other Than English at Home (%)	Bachelor's or Higher (%)	Median Family Income ($)	Median Household Income ($)	Per Capita Income ($)	Persons Under 18 in Poverty (%)
All Asians	60	32	71	49	78,565	68,549	28,342	11
Asian Indian	70	57	77	68	96,872	86,660	36,533	8
Bangladeshi	73	47	92	47	45,849	45,953	16,784	26
Cambodian	56	50	81	14	49,439	50,669	15,940	23
Chinese, except Taiwanese	61	63	75	50	80,369	68,420	30,061	10
Filipino	53	60	57	46	84,003	76,455	25,799	7
Hmong	44	64	91	14	47,339	47,038	10,949	32
Indonesian	66	57	67	47	69,577	60,906	25,729	11
Japanese	28	35	36	46	85,368	65,767	31,831	7
Korean	65	33	71	52	64,768	53,934	26,118	11
Laotian	55	54	81	12	56,296	55,119	16,585	14
Malaysian	73	62	65	57	82,777	63,269	33,264	9
Pakistani	65	27	86	55	67,379	62,744	24,663	19
Sri Lankan	77	57	72	56	83,638	73,927	32,480	8
Taiwanese	68	43	82	73	96,007	77,596	38,312	7
Thai	60	67	66	42	64,077	55,210	21,708	15
Vietnamese	64	49	84	27	59,456	54,799	21,542	15
Other Asian	76	73	81	37	55,609	51,514	20,114	28

SOURCE: ASIAN AND PACIFIC ISLAND AMERICAN HEALTH FORUM, "Demographic and Socioeconomic Profiles of Asian Americans, Native Hawaiians, and Pacific Islanders in the United States," July 2011

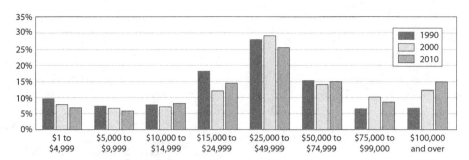

FIGURE 3-15. Asian Income Growth, 1990–2010.
Source: US Census, Historical Income Tables

Asians are 17% of scientists and engineers, or three times their proportion in the population.[90] For the most part, these individuals were first and second generation and part of the brain drain from places like Taiwan and India. Of the Asian-alone labor force in 2012, 48% of men and 46% of women were in managerial and professional occupations.[91]

Higher income levels are not consistent across all Asian groups (Table 3-8). On the other end of the spectrum, Southeast Asian refugees from Vietnam, Cambodia, and Laos—without the endowment that East Asians have (i.e., the physical, human, and cultural capital)—struggle with adapting to the United States. The 2010 per capita income of Hmong ($10,949), Cambodians ($15,940), and Laotians ($16,585) was lower than that of blacks ($17,459) and comparable to that of Hispanics ($15,506). Overall, Asian poverty rates (9.8% in 2012) are comparable to whites (9.1%). However, poverty rates among Bangladeshi, Cambodians, Hmong, and Pakistani are over 15%.

Immigration

The first Asian American settlers in the United States were recorded in the 1700s. The first significant groups of Chinese came to pan for gold in the 1850s leading to the United States being called Gold Mountain among the Chinese. Workers from China were brought over in the mid-1800s to build railroads. The Chinese became known for being industrious, but recessionary times in the late 1870s fired racist sentiment. White mobs attacked the Chinatowns of Los Angeles, San Francisco, Seattle, and, most horrifically, Rock Springs, Wyoming, killing Chinese people and destroying their businesses and homes. Starting in 1882, exclusion laws were enacted that prohibited the immigration of Chinese people and gradually

other Asians until after World War II. Even after exclusion laws were lifted, quotas continued to be levied on Asians, while there were no such quotas for immigrants from European countries. Immigration and the reunification of families continue to be issues for most first-generation immigrants, who constitute most of the Asian American population. Only 24% of Asian Americans were born in the United States.[92]

The Spanish-American War made the Philippines a protectorate of the United States in 1898. Filipinos joined the US military and became workers for US military bases. Japanese workers were brought over in the early 1900s, and immigration has been relatively small since then. Some Japanese women immigrated with their US military husbands after World War II. The Korean War brought a wave of immigrants from that country in the 1960s and 1970s, including children who were adopted by white families. The Chinese communist takeover sparked Chinese immigration from the 1960s onward, with another wave coming from Hong Kong in the 1970s, as refugees from the mainland sought to leave Hong Kong in anticipation of its handover to China. The Vietnam War brought Eurasian children of US military personnel and created refugees from the war, particularly supporters of the US military who found it difficult, if not impossible, to live under communist rule. Economic, social, and political hardship prompted other groups to seek a better life in the United States, including South Asians from India and Pakistan. Their reasons for emigrating varied depending on the circumstances they faced in their country of origin.

The earlier waves of Asian immigrants were low-wage workers who sought to escape war and economic hardship. In the 1970s, highly educated people who had the means to escape political turmoil immigrated to the

United States. Often they were college educated, owned businesses, or had wealth. The flight of these individuals from Asia was referred to as the "brain drain," because their emigration caused their home countries to lose highly educated human resources. Significant brain drain occurred, particularly with the immigration of Taiwanese and Indians. In 2010, approximately 68% of Indian Americans held four-year degrees compared to 51% for East Asians and 30% for non-Hispanic whites. Indian Americans were 3% of US engineers, 7% of IT workers, and 8% of doctors, while accounting for only 1% of the population.[93] Indian-trained engineers from educational institutions such as the Indian Institutes of Technology comprise a large proportion of the technology industry and were successful in founding 33% of Silicon Valley start-ups. Indian Americans were CEOs of nine Fortune 500 companies in 2014, with Satya Nadella heading Microsoft, a company with a workforce that is 33% Indian.

Despite the long history of immigration, 38.2% of foreign-born Asians entered the United States on or after 2000.[94] In 2010, of 60% of Asians who were foreign-born, 68% were not citizens.[95]

Geographics

Asian immigrants settled mainly on the West Coast, in Hawaii, and in pockets in the Northeast (New York and New Jersey) and Midwest (Figure 3-16). Hawaii has the highest concentration, with 58% of the population being of Asian descent, followed by California with 12%. California has attracted nearly one-third of Asian immigrants since 1980.[96]

Of all the larger racial/ethnic groups, Asians are the least politically involved. There are 108 local and state legislators, 6 statewide legislators, 3 governors, and 14 members of Congress.[97] California has the largest number of Asian American elected officials, with 204. Hawaii is next, with 84.

Other Factors

India is the birthplace of two world religions: Buddhism and Hinduism. Prior to the 1600s, China had preeminence over Europe and the rest of the world in science and government, and China consistently had the largest gross domestic product (GDP) for most years before 1800. It promises to regain that spot before 2020. Many Asian countries were subject to European military and economic conquest in the 1800s. The United States was engaged in several conflicts of major dimensions, including World War II against the Japanese, the Korean War, the Vietnam War (which included Cambodia and Laos), and hostilities toward communist China. These conflicts figure in mainstream attitudes toward Asian Americans and contribute to the stereotype of the perpetual foreigner. They also figure into the sensibilities and current circumstances of Asian Americans.

A number of laws and other government actions have also had an impact on Asian American economic opportunities. Internment of Japanese Americans during World

Percent
- 25.0 or more
- 10.0 to 24.9
- 5.0 to 9.9
- 1.0 to 4.9
- Less than 1.0

U.S. Percent 5.6

FIGURE 3-16. Asian as a Percent of County Population, 2010. Source: US Census

War II significantly interrupted the growth of their businesses. Internment meant being relocated to camps where they could take and keep only what they could carry with them. A pivotal incident for Chinese Americans was the murder of Vincent Chin in 1982, when two white men mistook him for Japanese and vented their rage at the Japanese auto industry by killing him. Recent expressions of Cold War attitudes led the US government to falsely accuse Wen Ho Lee of spying for China in 1999. In 2006 the charges were found to be false. The government, as well as several large media outlets, paid his legal fees and provided compensation for damages.[98] But the stereotyping and projecting of his alleged conduct affected other Asian American scientists in high-security posts. Aside from understanding what these various groups have experienced, the lesson here is that negative effects of pervasive racial bias and discrimination sometimes extend over many generations.

First-generation immigrants identify mainly with their country of origin and take great pains to preserve their culture within their families and communities. Immigrants from China number 2.3 million in 2011 and, next to Mexico, China is the leading country of origin for US foreign-born residents.[99] Chinese, Japanese, Korean, Vietnamese, and Indian American immigrant communities preserve religions, language, and traditions within their own homes. In the past twenty years, immigrant Asian communities have increasingly created their own religious institutions, language schools, and commercial centers in highly concentrated areas. First-generation Asian Americans continue to partake in their home country's culture by watching Asian-language television, enjoying films and television shows from their home country via an extensive media distribution system, reading Asian-language newspapers and Internet sites that report on home country events and listening to music from their home countries.

In all these cultures, the family continues to be the most important influence. Second-generation Asian Americans are discouraged from behaving like their white counterparts in terms of dating or experimenting with drugs. They are encouraged to value education, work hard, and respect their elders. The range of second-generation response has varied from outright rebellion to strict compliance.[100]

Indian Americans (98% of whom immigrated after 1970), notwithstanding their proficiency with English, are the least likely to out-marry. Japanese Americans, who immigrated prior to 1970, provide the best picture of cultural assimilation among immigrants. As Japanese move into their third and fourth generations with limited immigration, the effects of acculturation are apparent. Multiple-race Asians account for 15.3% of the population of any Asian descent.[101] The highest proportion occurs with Japanese and Filipino Americans. Despite this, there is a return to Japanese culture by third-generation and multiple-race Japanese Americans. Some want their children to learn the language. Others are interested in learning music and cultural activities such as taiko drumming, while others have an interest in Japan itself. Additionally, 2010 statistics show that the proportion of Asians who marry outside of the Asian race is dropping.[102]

With regard to religion, Asian Americans constitute 20% of Muslims in the United States, 32% of Buddhists, and 88% of Hindus. Chinese Americans are most likely to be unaffiliated (52%), Filipinos are most likely to be Catholic (65%), Indians are most likely to be Hindu (51%), Vietnamese are most likely to be Buddhist (43%), and Koreans (61%) and Japanese (33%) are most likely to be members of a Protestant denomination.[103]

Purchasing Power

The purchasing power of Asian Americans is estimated to grow to $962 billion in 2018 (a 35% gain from 2013), according to the Selig Center for Economic Growth. This growth rate mirrors the estimated growth in Latino purchasing power. High education attainment and larger households explain the higher level of disposable income per capita for the group. During the 2007–9 recession, Asian Americans were better able to retain their jobs and were therefore less affected financially than other minority groups.

Asian Americans tend to spend more on food, housing, clothing, education, and personal insurance compared to other ethnic or racial groups; they spend less on utilities, transportation, health care, and entertainment (Table 3-9). According to a Nielsen survey, their buying power per household is more substantial because their households are more likely to be multigenerational.[104] Ethnic supermarkets are an example of a good channel to satisfy Asian-specific culinary needs with fresh foods and good value. Asian Americans are also more likely to shop online and spend more. They have high smartphone penetration and are more likely to buy the latest technology regardless of price.

Northwest Asian Weekly
A Study of the Complexity of Cultural Markets

In 1982, Assunta Ng was volunteering for a Chinese radio station when she realized that the Asian community lacked access to information. At the time, there were no Chinese newspapers in the Pacific Northwest. Chinese immigrants were relying on San Francisco–based papers for news. Ng decided to create a Chinese-language newspaper for the Chinese community: the *Seattle Chinese Post*. Her first inclination was to set up the newspaper as a nonprofit. But she quickly learned that was a nonstarter as a basis for revenue generation or making a profit. So with just $20 for a business license, Ng launched a for-profit newspaper business. Within three months, the first issue was printed.

Other Asian groups (Japanese, Filipino, Vietnamese, Cambodian, Korean, and more) wanted a weekly paper that addressed the broader Asian community. In response, Ng established the *Northwest Asian Weekly*; it remains the only weekly English-edition newspaper serving Washington's Asian community. The two newspapers emphasize different content. After six years, Ng transitioned operations to a family-run business.

Similar to other small business owners, Ng faced many challenges as a woman entrepreneur. Although Ng was college educated and highly motivated, she did not have many strong community connections. However, through perseverance and dedication to serving the community, she began to establish herself as a leader in the Asian community. She also proved to be a savvy business owner. Within the first few years of operation, Ng had to make the decision to continue printing in black and white or convert to color. Because color printing was significantly more expensive, she opted for black and white. Instead she invested in her building, which

is nestled in the heart of Seattle's Chinatown/International District. Ng wanted to create a comfortable work environment and a place the community could be proud of. After about ten years in business, Ng added red print to the newspaper. In the Asian culture, red symbolizes good luck. She eventually converted to full color in 2002.

Ng continues to support the local community. In 1994, she founded the Northwest Asian Weekly Foundation, which provides a summer youth leadership program and diversity scholarships for high school students. In addition to her foundation, Ng hosts about eight events each year to honor women and others who have broken the glass ceiling. She is passionate about connecting people; she strives to meet three new people at each event. The newspaper has enabled her to build many bridges in the community.

After thirty years, Ng has built sufficient community support to sustain both newspapers. She still finds each day challenging but "takes every hurdle as an opportunity." Ng empowers her employees: "Everyone is a generalist, not a specialist." She brainstorms with her team to solve problems, and employees are not limited by their title or role. The *Northwest Asian Weekly* has earned a reputation for being fair, and it often runs stories not covered by mainstream news outlets, including political stories and issues related to the Asian community, with one simple goal: to empower the Asian community.

TABLE 3-9. Comparative Asian Consumer Spending, 2012

	All Consumer Units	Asian	All Consumer Units, % of Total	Asian, % of Total	% Difference
Number of consumer units (in thousands)	124,416	5,393			
Average annual expenditures	$51,442	$61,399			
Food at home	3,921	4,367	8	7	-1
Food away from home	2,678	3,613	5	6	**1**
Alcoholic beverages	451	360	1	1	0
Housing	16,887	20,821	33	34	**1**
Shelter	9,891	13,841	19	23	**3**
Utilities, fuels, and public services	3,648	3,456	7	6	-1
Household operations	1,159	1,469	2	2	0
Housekeeping supplies	610	497	1	1	0
Household furnishings and equipment	1,580	1,558	3	3	-1
Apparel and services	1,736	2,391	3	4	1
Transportation	8,998	10,117	17	16	-1
Health care	3,556	3,285	7	5	-2
Entertainment	2,605	2,303	5	4	-1
Personal care products and services	628	594	1	1	0
Reading	109	97	0	0	0
Education	1,207	3,295	2	5	**3**
Tobacco products and smoking supplies	332	161	1	0	0
Miscellaneous	829	849	2	1	0
Cash contributions	1,913	1,356	4	2	-2
Personal insurance and pensions	5,591	7,789	11	13	**2**

Source: US Bureau of Labor Statistics, Annual Calendar Year Tables 2012, "Current Combined Expenditure, Share, and Standard Error Tables: Race of Reference Person," www.bls.gov/cex/csxcombined.htm

Note: Bold figures indicate larger expenditures compared to the general consumer

Media

In 2007, Chinese was spoken in the home by 2.5 million Asian Americans (a 291% increase over 1980), Tagalog by 1.4 million (a 212% increase), Vietnamese by 1.2 million (a 511% increase), Korean by 1 million (a 299% increase), and Japanese by 459,000 (a 36% increase) (Table 3-10). Only Russian and Persian have similarly high rates of increase. Chinese is the third most spoken language in the United States after English and Spanish. (Chinese is the most spoken language in the world and is fast catching up to English as the number one language on the Internet. Spanish holds second place in terms of languages spoken in the world.)[105]

The number of Asian American media outlets increased 1,115% from 1999 to 2010, with 409 print, 136 television, 140 radio, and 554 digital.[106] Most Asian American households have access to Asian-language television through cable or satellite connections. There are more than 150 Asian satellite channels nationwide. These may broadcast content produced in Asia.

According to Nielsen, 73% of Asians are bilingual; therefore, Asian-language content is important to them.[107] A high proportion of Asians (67.8%) have access to the Internet, and they tend to go to overseas sites to look at Asian content. Asians bring brand consciousness in that global brands signify status in their home countries. Good price is part of their customer value proposition.

TABLE 3-10. Language Spoken at Home

Population 5 years and older	1980	1990	2000	2010	1980–2010 (% change)
Spoke only English at Home	210,247,455	230,445,777	262,375,152	289,215,746	37.6
Spoke other than English at Home	23,060,040	31,844,979	46,951,595	59,542,596	158.2
Vietnamese	197,588	507,069	1,009,627	1,381,488	599.2
Russian	173,226	241,798	706,242	854,955	393.5
Chinese	630,806	1,319,462	2,022,143	2,808,692	345.3
Korean	266,280	626,478	894,063	1,137,325	327.1
Persian	106,992	201,865	312,085	381,408	256.5
Spanish or Spanish Creole	11,116,194	17,345,064	28,101,052	36,995,602	232.8
Tagalog	474,150	843,251	1,224,241	1,573,720	231.9
Armenian	100,634	149,694	202,708	240,402	138.9
Portuguese or Portuguese Creole	351,875	430,610	564,630	688,326	95.6
Serbo-Croatian	150,255	70,964	233,865	284,077	89.1
French (incl. Patois, Cajun, Creole)	1,550,751	1,930,404	2,097,206	2,069,352	33.4
Japanese	336,318	427,657	477,997	443,497	31.9
Greek	401,443	388,260	365,436	307,178	-23.5
Polish	820,647	723,483	667,414	608,333	-25.9
German	1,586,593	1,547,987	1,383,442	1,067,651	-32.7
Yiddish	315,953	213,064	178,945	154,763	-51
Italian	1,618,344	1,308,648	1,008,370	725,223	-55.2

Source: Camille Ryan, "Language Use in the United States: 2011," US Census, American Community Survey Reports ACS-22, August 2013, www.census.gov/prod/2013pubs/acs-22.pdf

AMERICAN INDIANS AND ALASKA NATIVES

The unique history, status, and treatment of American Indians requires more background information on their circumstances and economic conditions than we have presented on the other groups. For many reasons their relationships with the US government have extended over a longer period of time and have been measurably more harmful than is generally the case for the other multicultural groups. Many of their barriers to economic and enterprise development are the direct result of the institutional controls, policies, and failures of education, land, and other resource management of the Bureau of Indian Affairs (BIA). Unfortunately, as we summarize in this section, the pattern of mistreatment and discrimination even precedes the BIA, which was established in 1824.

When Columbus "discovered" the Americas, it was estimated that there were several million (ranging from 2 to 7 million) indigenous people in North America. Since Europeans started settling in the Americas, American Indians have faced military violence, subjugation, epi-

demics (many brought by the European settlers, including smallpox, which decimated tribes), and government policies aimed at terminating their way of life. At the beginning of the twentieth century, American Indians numbered a few hundred thousand and were predicted to vanish by 1935.

American Indian tribes are sovereign entities. This is inherent within the tribes and was recognized by the European colonists and later by the US government in the Constitution. Indian tribes have their own lands (56.2 million acres held in trust by the United States for various tribes and individuals), cultures, languages, and governments. Tribes fought for decades to regain their right of self-governance as sovereignty. As a result of treaties signed with tribes, the US government held the lands of tribes in trust. Over the past two hundred years, much of the land has been lost because of federal government policies and practices. In particular, until its repeal in 1934, the 1887 Indian General Allotment Act distributed

90 million acres (of the best land of the 134 million acres held in trust) to non-Indian owners.[108]

Seizures of their lands and other assets brought about economic deprivation among American Indians. Mismanagement of the assets held in trust and outright fraud by the government and other parties has led to a ruling and court order for the government to properly account for the estimated $5 billion in payments due individual Indians for the use of their land held in trust.[109] Not just the economic value of the land is at stake. The crucial role that tribal lands play in the core of a tribe's identity is demonstrated by the dispute over the Black Hills of North Dakota. The Lakota tribes turned down money that now totals more than $400 million for the wrongful alienation of their lands, instead holding out for the return of their sacred Black Hills. This is especially telling, given that the Lakota tribes live on the Pine Ridge Reservation, located in one of the poorest counties in the United States.

Racism has taken its toll on American Indians in a variety of ways. Genocide in the form of forced relocation under inhumane conditions occurred in the 1800s. Prohibiting the use of tribal languages in American Indian schools, prohibiting religious practices, and expunging many other forms of their culture were common policies in the 1900s. For example, in the 1950s the US government adopted a policy of termination in which Indian children were forcibly removed from their families to "assimilate" them. These children were beaten if they spoke their own language and were put in Christian schools where they were not allowed to practice their own religions. Indians were encouraged to marry outside of their race, and incidents of sterilization were documented. The policy of termination resulted in the loss of one hundred tribes. Additionally, federal programs deprived tribes of sufficient funding for education and crime prevention while cultivating a culture of dependency.[110]

Since the mid-1960s, in response to the civil rights movement in which American Indians fought with other minorities for their rights, the US government has adopted a policy of self-determination and self-governance. After more than a century of broken treaties and ineffective government policies that plunged the tribes into poverty, destroyed their culture and identity, put their communities into disarray, disrupted their families, and dismantled their governments, many American Indian tribes are rebuilding their nations. More than five hundred distinct Indian nations continue to survive and grow in Indian Country.

In the twenty-first century, efforts have increased to gain formal recognition of the racism and injustices imposed on American Indians. But a formal apology by the head of the Bureau of Indian Affairs in 2000 is about as far as the government has gone to make amends for centuries of racism. Recent court decisions provide some compensation for fraudulent mismanagement and offer the prospect of supporting investments in American Indian communities that will bring a new era of enterprise and economic development.

As of 2012, there were 5.2 million American Indians and Alaska Natives (alone or in combination with other races) and 2.9 million declaring American Indian and Alaska Native alone. Many tribes cross the US–Canadian border, and adjacent Canada's aboriginal population of 1.17 million enlarges the market.[111]

Demographics

The American Indian population consists of more than 566 federally recognized tribes and a number of other tribes yet to achieve official recognition.[112] Tribal membership ranges from 330,000 to a few members. American Indians identify strongly with their tribes, and there are major differences in culture, language, and governing structures across tribes. The ten largest tribal groupings as of 2010 are shown in Table 3-11.

The population has shown rapid growth, due in part to persons acknowledging their American Indian heritage. The ability to select one or more race on the 2000 US Census also allowed individuals to fully disclose their

TABLE 3-11. American Indian Population by Tribe, 2010

Tribe	Population
Cherokee	819,105
Navajo	332,129
Choctaw	195,764
Mexican American Indian	175,494
Chippewa	170,742
Sioux	170,110
Apache	111,810
Blackfeet	105,304
Creek	88,332
Iroquois	81,002

Source: T. Norris, P. L. Vines, and E. M. Hoeffel, "The American Indian and Alaska Native Population: 2010," US Census Briefs C2010BR-10, January 2012

heritage. American Indian and Alaska Natives report the highest proportion (43%) in the multiple race category.

In 2012, the median age of American Indian and Alaska Natives was thirty-one years, about nine years younger than non-Hispanic whites. About 30% of American Indians and Alaska Natives were under eighteen in 2012 compared to 22% of non-Hispanic whites. They were less likely to be married (36%) compared to non-Hispanic whites (51.4%) and more likely to be divorced or separated than whites. Native women have lower birth rates compared to whites; 55% of Native women who gave birth were unmarried compared to 30% of non-Hispanic whites. Among American Indians there is a greater proportion of single-parent households and twice the proportion of women heads of household as among whites. Three times the proportion of American Indian households have grandparents living with grandchildren compared to whites; and 51% of grandparents living with grandchildren are responsible for their care, compared to 40% of whites.[113]

Among American Indians and Alaska Natives (AIANs), 17.4% have a bachelor's degree or higher compared to 30% of whites. Educational attainment lags behind that of the general population mainly because federal educational spending for AIANs has lagged behind that for the general population. Low educational attainment is a legacy of the Bureau of Indian Education boarding schools, created by the federal government to eradicate Native cultures and languages through Western education.[114] Native children were taken from their families and put into residential boarding schools or day schools run by the government or religious institutions.[115] Native ex-students have sued for the abuse suffered, which included brutal corporal punishment and rampant sexual abuse as late as the 1970s, and they won multimillion dollar settlements. Canada, which subjected Native children to similar treatment, has set aside $1.9 billion for payments to survivors of its residential schools. BIA schools with 2012 enrollment of 42,000 have produced generations of American Indians who are poorly educated, are unable to compete for jobs, have been separated for years from their tribal communities, and have been subject to various forms of abuse. All of this has contributed to the extreme poverty on many reservations throughout the country. Four of the poorest counties in the United States are on reservations, including Pine Ridge, where there is 80% unemployment.

Tribes have no tax base and are dependent on federal government funding, but they have been allocated half the funding typically necessary for educational needs. Additionally, regular public educational institutions, which teach the bulk of the 607,000 Native students in schools, do not understand the needs of American Indian students, causing low retention rates. About one-third of American Indians drop out before attaining a high school education, a rate one and a half times higher than other minorities.[116] Indian children are more likely to be in single-parent families, and Indian youth are seventeen times more likely to suffer alcohol-related deaths. Teen pregnancies are 180% of the national rate.[117]

With more self-government, the tribes have taken control of half of the BIA schools. Initial results show better performance and retention with the culturally sensitive curriculum and high-quality education. Enrollment in higher education doubled between 1976 and 2006.[118] In 2012, 28.1% of college-aged AIANs were enrolled in college versus 31.6% of whites (Figure 3-17). About 37% of AIAN males received a degree within six years, a rate comparable to blacks, while 41% of AIAN females received a degree within six years compared to 59% of white males and 64% of white females.[119]

In response to the high college dropout rates for American Indians, tribally operated colleges were created. In 2013 there were thirty-seven tribal colleges with about 20,000 students, or 75% of total enrollment, up from 2,100 students in 1982.[120] The bulk of tribal colleges are two-year institutions, with seven four-year institutions. They offer two-year degrees in more than two hundred disciplines and two hundred vocational certificate programs. Evidence shows that tribal colleges are increasing the employment rates and success in four-year institutions for American Indian students. Such institutions certainly have the potential to help sustain the expansion of human capital development in American Indian communities.

Native household income is lower than that of the US population. American Indian median household income in 2012 was $37,353 compared to $57,429 for whites (Figure 3-18). American Indians suffer poverty rates of 24.3%, which is equivalent to the rate for African Americans and more than twice that for white Americans (9.1%). Poverty rates are particularly high for the population under age eighteen. Median income and poverty levels can vary tremendously among tribes. The small number of tribes with gaming compacts near major metropolitan areas have met with economic success, while

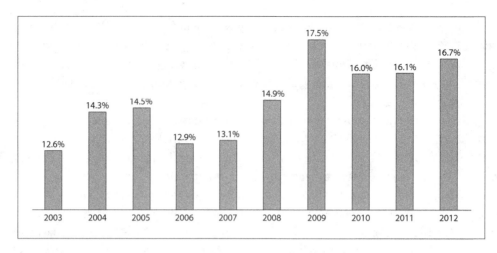

FIGURE 3-17. Percent of American Indians and Alaskan Natives with Bachelor's or Higher, 2003–2012. Source: 2012 Digest of Education Statistics

tribes far from population centers continue to seek other means to escape poverty and, generally, lack jobs and other sources of economic opportunity.

It is estimated that in the one hundred most populous tribes, about one-third of the people have knowledge of their native language. There are roughly 150 languages currently spoken or that could still be revived. Of the American Indian and Alaska Native tribes, the Navajo, Pueblo, Apache, and Eskimo are least likely to speak English at home.[121]

Geographics

About 36% of individuals who identify themselves as American Indians or Alaska Natives live on reservations or trust lands. Historically, reservations have higher rates of unemployment, poverty, health problems, and crime than other communities. This disparity can be attributed to a lack of resources. American Indian reservations are typically allocated half or substantially less than half of the health dollars, law enforcement, and other federal government support than the general population, despite treaties signed with the US government ensuring that tribes' health and education needs would be fully funded in exchange for tribal land.[122]

The highest concentrations of nonreservation American Indians are in the central and western United States. California ranks first as the state with the most American Indians. Half of all American Indians live in California,

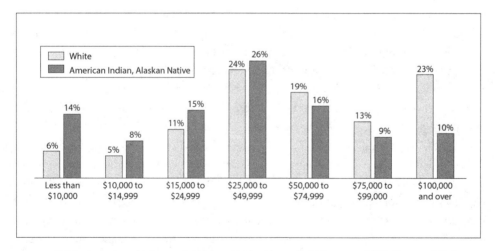

FIGURE 3-18. American Indian and Alaskan Native Household Income, 2012. Source: US Census, American Community Survey, Data Set B19001C

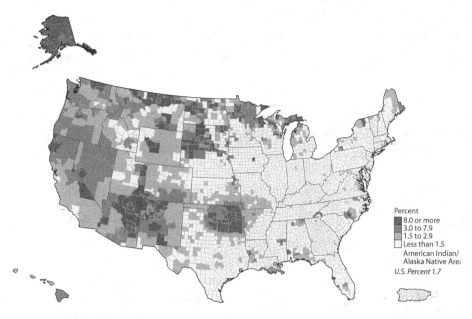

FIGURE 3-19. American Indians and Alaska Natives as Percent of County Population, 2010. Source: US Census

Oklahoma, Arizona, New Mexico, and Washington, as shown in Figure 3-19.

The sovereignty of tribes necessitates American Indian involvement in many levels of politics. Many tribes are governed by tribal councils, which are evolving with the integration of traditional tribal governing structures. Some traditional tribal structures are close to the US political structure (with a central constitution), while others are not. The Harvard Project on American Indian Economic Development found that when the governing structure emulates a more traditional structure, governance tends to be more successful.[123] As of 2014, three American Indians also serve as representatives in the 113th Congress.

Other Factors

Tribes continue to fight the effects of the policies and actions against them. According to the Indian Health Service, American Indians and Alaska Natives die at higher rates than other Americans from chronic liver disease and cirrhosis (368% higher), diabetes mellitus (177% higher), unintentional injuries (138% higher), assault/homicide (82% higher), intentional self-harm/suicide (65% higher), and chronic lower respiratory diseases (59% higher).[124] American Indians and Alaska Natives have suffered an epidemic of youth suicides, with rates in some communities of three to ten times the national average. In 2013, the US Justice Department created a

task force to study violence and its impact on Native American youth. Some officials on the task force view the epidemic as an outcome of pervasive despair brought about by the program of termination that took Native children away from their families. As more resources are invested in security and safety, this will improve the infrastructure needed to ensure better conditions for American Indians.[125]

Despite the legacy of BIA mismanagement as well as other policies at the federal, state and local government levels designed to limit the economic progress of American Indians, some positive developments should be noted. Since the 1980s the casino boom has brought substantial gains. On an annual basis, casino revenue has been as much as ten times the annual budget of the BIA. Total revenue was about $28 billion in 2013, and gaming provided an estimated 650,000 jobs in the same year.[126] To be sure, there are accompanying problems of saturation, overbuilding in remote locations, and competition with nonreservation gaming. But the overall results have been beneficial for tribal governments and communities..

Purchasing Power

American Indian purchasing power is estimated to grow to $123 billion in 2018, an increase of 28% over 2013. Spending power is concentrated in ten states: California ($23.3 billion), Oklahoma ($11.1 billion), Texas ($11.2 billion), Arizona ($6.8 billion), New Mexico ($4.8 billion),

Washington ($4.1 billion), Florida ($23.6 billion), North Carolina ($3.8 billion), Alaska ($3.3 billion), and New York ($7.2 billion).[127]

Media

Fifty-three tribal radio stations comprise the media within the American Indian population, according to Native Public Media.[128] Two national newspapers provide an important function in giving voice to American Indian values, concerns, and lives. Native radio stations often broadcast in English and in the native language of the tribe. Given the portrayal of American Indians in mainstream media, such media outlets are essential to providing a balanced picture of Native life and concerns.

NATIVE HAWAIIANS AND PACIFIC ISLANDERS

Similar to American Indians, Native Hawaiian people faced decimation with the influx of white settlers. In 1778, when Captain Cook arrived in Hawaii, it was estimated that between 400,000 and 800,000 people inhabited the islands. The Hawaiian monarchy was overthrown by US naval forces in 1893 and the islands were annexed in 1898, mainly due to the land's attractiveness in producing sugar. By 1900, the pure Native Hawaiian population had declined to 29,800, with 7,800 of mixed heritage, due to the introduction of cholera, measles, whooping cough, influenza, leprosy, and tuberculosis—diseases for which Native Hawaiians had no immunity. Although historical wrongs have been done to Native Hawaiians, unlike American Indians they do not have recognition as a sovereign people.[129] In fact, a 2000 court ruling questioned the status, rights, and protection of Native Hawaiians. The use of one-half blood quantum to define Native Hawaiians, per the Hawaiian Homes Commission Act of 1921, has undermined Hawaiian sovereignty claims.[130]

As of 2012, Pacific Islanders (alone or in combination with other races), numbered 1.1 million. As a group, the population grew 40% between 2000 and 2010. Polynesians—who are composed of Native Hawaiians (527,077), Samoans (184,440), and Tongans (57,183)—form the largest group, with Micronesians, mainly Guamanians (147,798), following. According to 2012 US Census projections, the Native Hawaiian and Pacific Islander (NHPI) population will grow to 3.2 million by 2060.[131] The top five states for the NHPI population are Hawaii, California, Washington, Texas, and Florida.

In 2012, Pacific Islanders had a median age of 29 (in combination with other races, the median age was 27.7), about 13 years younger than non-Hispanic whites. Pacific Islanders are less likely than non-Hispanic whites to marry, and they are more likely to be divorced or separated. About 56% of the NHPI population are multiracial compared to 3% of whites, 6% of Latinos, 7% of African Americans, and 15% of Asians Americans.[132] Pacific Islander women have a higher fertility rate and are also less likely to be married than non-Hispanic whites. Pacific Islanders are more likely to be in family and single-parent households than non-Hispanic whites. Pacific Islanders are four times more likely to have grandchildren in the household.[133]

Pacific Islanders are more likely to be native US-born than other groups discussed here simply because those born in Guam, American Samoa, and the Commonwealth of the Northern Mariana Islands are considered native-born Americans. About 43% speak a language other than English at home compared to 6% for non-Hispanic whites. For Pacific Islanders alone, 14% have bachelor's degrees, about half the rate of 30.5% for whites. Pacific Islanders are less likely to be in management and professional occupations than whites. In 2012, the Pacific Islander median household income was $51,322 compared to $54,729 for the US population.[134] The Pacific Islander poverty rate (18.3%) was twice that of whites (9.1%) in 2012. Only 40% owned their own homes compared to 69.2% of whites.[135]

In 2008, about 39% of inmates in Hawaiian jails were Native Hawaiians, which is disproportionate to their 24% proportion of the state population at the time. Controlling for other factors, Native Hawaiians are much more likely to get a prison sentence than almost all other groups except for Native Americans.[136]

In comparison to other groups, Native Hawaiians and Pacific Islanders have higher rates of smoking, alcohol consumption, and obesity. They have little access to cancer prevention and control programs. Some leading causes of death include cancer, heart disease, unintentional injuries (accidents), stroke, and diabetes. Other health conditions prevalent among Native Hawaiians and Pacific Islanders are hepatitis B, HIV/AIDS, and tuberculosis, which occur at a rate twenty-one times higher than for non-Hispanic whites.[137] Between 2005 and 2010, the number of NHPI suicide deaths increased 170%.[138]

In 2011, Hawaii governor Neil Abercrombie signed into law Act 195, which formally recognizes the Native Hawaiian people as the only indigenous people of Hawaii and establishes a Native Hawaiian Roll Commission

FIGURE 3-20. Native Hawaiians and Other Pacific Islanders by County, 2010. Source: US Census

(NHRC) to compile a roster of qualified Native Hawaiians, for use in determining who is eligible to participate in the process of reorganizing a Native Hawaiian government for self-governance. There has been a net migration of Native Hawaiians outside of Hawaii. Most have settled on the West Coast, with high concentrations in California, Washington, and Texas (Figure 3-20).

MULTIPLE RACE

Multiple-race group identity has only recently received official recognition. Yet this group provides substantial diversity, richness, and numbers of multiple-heritage people in the US population. Interracial marriage (illegal in some states until 1967) has resulted in the explosive growth of the multiple-race population. The 2010 US Census was the first to allow people to identify themselves as being of multiple races. In 2012, nine million people self-identified as more than one race (Table 3-12). Multiracial individuals account for more than 3% of the population but 5.9% of people under the age of eighteen. As previously stated, it is estimated that more than one-third of blacks are of multiple-race heritage, and US history shows documentation of accepted interracial marriages going back as far as the 1600s.[139]

Native Americans, Alaska Natives, and Native Hawaiians show a particularly high proportion of mixed race, which may be due to policies such as termination, which encouraged American Indians to marry outside of their race. Among American Indians, 51% of the population is multiracial, with white in combination with American Indian being the largest group. Hawaiians show an even higher proportion, with 56% of the population reporting multiple-race heritage. The states of Hawaii and California, both minority-majority states (only 27% of Hawaii's population is white, while 25% of California's population is non-Hispanic white), provide a glimpse of the multiracial future.[140] Native Hawaiians have intermarried with Asians and whites. The term *hapa*, used to describe

TABLE 3-12. Growth in Multiple-Race Population, 2000–2010

	2010 Population (million)	Growth, 2000–2010 (%)
One race	300	9
Two races	9	30
Three races	8.3	65
Four races	0.7	51

Source: N. A. Jones and J. Bullock, "Two or More Races Population: 2010," US Census Briefs C2010BR-13, September 2012

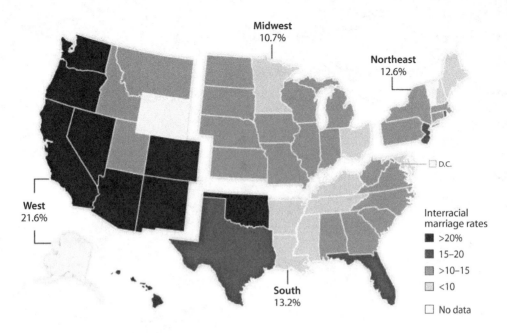

Midwest
10.7%

Northeast
12.6%

West
21.6%

South
13.2%

□ D.C.

Interracial
marriage rates
■ >20%
■ 15–20
■ >10–15
□ <10

□ No data

FIGURE 3-21. Interracial Marriage, 2010. Source: J. Passel, W. Wang, and P. Taylor, "Marrying Out: One-in-Seven New U.S. Marriages Is Interracial or Interethnic," Pew Research Center, June 15, 2010

individuals of multiple race or ethnicity, was first coined in Hawaii.

Interethnic marriages and pairings are increasing and create more complexity in the cultural landscape. The Pew Research Center estimates that 14.5% of marriages in 2008 were between spouses of different races or ethnicity.[141] There are also gender differences, with more black males and Asian females marrying outside of their race. First-generation immigrants are less likely to marry outside of their race compared to second and third generations. The trend is expected to continue with more-accepting attitudes toward race, the upward mobility of many minorities, and increased opportunity for social contact. The Pew study shows that acceptance of interracial marriages is 81% for whites, 75% for Asians, 73% for Hispanics, and 66% for blacks. Figure 3-21 shows interracial marriage rates by region as of 2010.

This breadth, magnitude, and speed of cultural fusion is likely unprecedented in any other country or society. Previously, interracial marriage with the dominant white culture was seen as a measure of assimilation. By marrying into the majority culture, the minority adopted the latter's norms. More interracial marriages signaled greater assimilation. Increasing evidence points to a different phenomenon in the United States with the fading of the dominant culture. Increasingly, the existence of acculturation or mutual influence of cultures upon each other is

recognized. Minority cultures are not subsumed by the majority. This has borne itself out in multiple-race individuals seeking to be connected to all of their heritages, not just their white heritage. It is also evidenced by transracially adopted children seeking their (often Asian) roots. It is manifest in third-generation immigrants wanting to retain their native languages or cultures. It is demonstrated in the slowing rate of Asians marrying outside of the Asian race. Psychological studies have also shown that mixed-race children are better adjusted and suffer less stress when they accept all of their heritages.[142]

According to the Selig Center for Economic Growth, the 2013 purchasing power of the multiracial population was $132 billion, and it more than doubled in the previous decade. Multiracial buying power is expected to grow to $161 billion in 2018. New York, California, and Florida have the largest multiracial populations.

LESBIAN, GAY, BISEXUAL, AND TRANSGENDER (LGBT)

The acronym LGBT describes a population that self-identifies based on sexuality and gender identity. Definition is complicated by how researchers categorize respondents and also by stigmatization. Some researchers categorize based on attraction, while others categorize by behavior. About 8.2% of the US population have engaged in same-

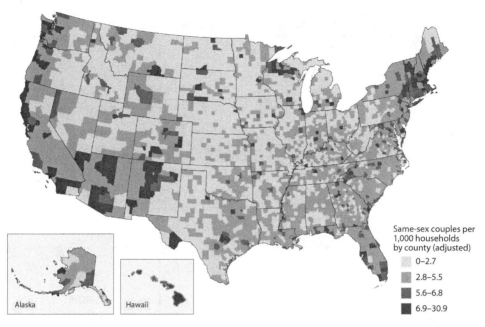

FIGURE 3-22. Same-Sex Population by State, 2010. Source: Williams Institute, UCLA

sex behavior and 11% acknowledge some same-sex attraction. Self-identified LGBT persons are estimated to be 3.5% of the US population. Gay men and lesbians comprise 1.7%, while the bisexual population is slightly larger at 1.8%. Approximately 0.3% of the US population is transgender. The population proportion of same-sex individuals varies by state, with North Dakota at 1.7% and Washington, DC, at 10%. Figure 3-22 shows same-sex population by state as of 2010.

The Pew Research Center's 2013 Survey of LGBT Americans found substantial change over the previous ten years in the social acceptance of LGBT individuals, as seen by the general population and the LGBT community. Pew attributes this to more interaction between LGBT people and the general population and increased advocacy by high-profile public figures and LGBT families.[143] The Pew survey also notes that younger individuals tend to be more accepting of LGBT individuals. Despite growing social acceptance, about 53% of LGBT individuals say they face significant discrimination, according to the survey. The Pew study reports that 79% of gay men were subject to slurs or jokes and 49% of gay men were threatened or physically attacked. Nearly 60% of lesbians were subject to slurs or jokes, while 22% were threatened or physically attacked. Even gaining acceptance from those close to them is difficult, as just 56% say they have told their mother about their sexual orientation or gender identity, and 39% have told their father.

The Williams Institute at UCLA conducted an analysis of the US Census American Community Survey and found 650,000 same-sex couples in 2011 (Table 3-13). Approximately 51% of these couples are female, representing a shift from 52% male in 2005. They tend to be younger than their different-sex counterparts. With regards to race and ethnicity, the proportion of black and Hispanic individuals is the same in both same-sex and different-sex couples. The proportion of same-sex couples who identify as Asian and Native Hawaiian and Pacific Islander is 2.6% versus 5.1% of the different-sex population. LGBT couples tend to be more educated, with 46% of same-sex couples reporting that they have a college degree compared to 32% of different-sex couples. Levels of employment are similar between same-sex and different-sex couples; and the difference between median personal income earned by same-sex and different-sex men has narrowed, while same-sex women continue to earn more ($8,000 more) than their different-sex counterparts. Lesbian couples are five times as likely to be military veterans as different-sex couples.[144]

In June 2013, the US Supreme Court struck down the federal Defense of Marriage Act, ruling that the government cannot deny benefits to same-sex couples legally married by the states. Two years later, in June 2015, the Supreme Court ruled that marriage is a fundamental right, affirming equal protections for gays and lesbians under the Fourteenth Amendment of the Constitution.

TABLE 3-13. Comparative Demographics of Same-Sex and Different-Sex Couples

2011		Same-Sex	Different-Sex
Percent female		51.50%	50%
Average age		**44.4**	**49.5**
Age (%)	< 30	**15.00**	**9.70**
	30–49	**50.40**	**41.60**
	50–64	28.30	31.30
	65+	6.30	17.40
Neither spouse/partner aged 65+		90.30	79.30
One spouse/partner aged 65+, one < age 65		6.70	6.40
Both spouses/partners aged 65+		3.00	14.20
Race/ethnicity (%)	White	76.10	73.20
	African American	7.40	7.30
	Latino/a	11.30	12.70
	Asian, Native Hawaiian, Pacific Islander	**2.60**	**5.10**
	AK Native/American Indian	0.50	0.50
	Other	2.00	1.30
Children under age 18 in the home (%)		**19.40**	**43.50**
College degree (%)		**46.10**	**32.20**
In the labor force (%)		81.70	69.40
Employed among those in the labor force (%)		92.70	93.50
Median annual personal income	Men in labor force	47,000	48,000
	Men not in labor force	13,000	22,600
	Women in labor force	38,000	30,000
	Women not in labor force	11,400	5,100
Median annual household income	Both in labor force	94,000	86,000
	One in labor force	59,600	60,000
	Neither in labor force	42,110	41,850
Industry sector (%)	Private	73.90	71.00
	Public	15.00	16.60
	Self-employed	10.50	11.70
Health insurance (%)	Neither insured	7.00	8.50
	One insured	16.50	7.90
	Both insured	76.50	83.50
Disabled (%)		10.90	11.50
At least one spouse/partner is disabled (%)		18.10	18.80
Veteran (%)	Men	9.30	21.40
	Women	**5.00**	**1.20**
At least one spouse/partner a veteran (%)		13.10	1.10
At least one spouse/partner on active duty in the last year (%)		0.70	5.50
Binational: One partner/spouse a US citizen and one a noncitizen (%)		5.00	5.40
Both partners noncitizens (%)		1.80	1.10

Source: G. J. Gates, *Same-Sex and Different-Sex Couples in the American Community Survey: 2005–2011* (Los Angeles: Williams Institute at UCLA School of Law, February 2013)

Note: Bold figures indicate notable differences

The decision swept aside fourteen state bans on gay marriage, entitling same-sex couples to marriage in all fifty states. Although 72% of Americans saw the legal recognition of same-sex marriage as inevitable, the issue continues to be divisive, with 42% opposing it. Despite same-sex marriage's prominence in the press, equal employment rights remains the top priority of LGBT.

According to the 2010 US Census, the top five states for LGBT individuals are California, Texas, New York, Florida, and Illinois. Many marketers covet LGBT consumers because marketing research has described the market as highly educated and high income. Because these marketers assume that LGBT individuals are less likely to have children, they conclude that the market has high disposable income. LGBT purchasing power is estimated at over $800 billion; however, given the problems with categorization and measurement, this cannot be confirmed. According to a Prudential survey, dining out, entertainment, and travel are the top three items for LGBT discretionary income spending.[145]

There are a small number of LGBT news outlets that marketers can use to target messages to this community. Examples include *Out* and the *Advocate*.[146]

CULTURE AND MARKETS

The influence of culture on interactions between businesses and customers is an important consideration as marketplaces continue to diversify.[147] Because ethnicity is a broad dimension of culture (including national origin, language, cultural heritage, and religion), it poses many challenges for business owners who are not attuned to diverse customer needs. Ethnic customers may respond differently to marketing campaigns compared to non-ethnic customers; businesses should have the cultural competence and resources to address ethnic customers' needs. A key component of this competence is to understand how ethnic customers commonly identify with and respond to individuals who are from their ethnic group and with whom they have a shared ethnicity.

Detra Montoya, of Arizona State University, and Elten Briggs, of the University of Texas, conducted research using a sample of Asians, Hispanics, and Caucasians to understand how shared ethnicity affects marketplace exchanges between businesses and ethnic customers.[148] When studying culture, researchers often classify groups based on the individualism-collectivism dimension (discussed in chapter 2). For example, people of Western cultures, such as US Caucasians, are considered to be more *individualist*, with an emphasis on individual differentiation. On the other hand, Hispanics and Asians are typically considered *collectivists*. Collectivists define themselves based on the groups to which they belong and emphasize their connectedness to others. The studies conducted showed that this important cultural distinction can influence ethnic customer expectations and actual service encounter experiences under conditions of shared ethnicity.

Montoya and Briggs's results provide preliminary evidence of important patterns of ethnic customer responses. Montoya and Briggs reported that:

1. Respondents representing collectivist groups (e.g., Asians and Hispanics) often expected more favorable service experiences when they shared ethnicity with a contact employee, compared to customers from individualist groups (e.g., Caucasian).
2. Asian and Hispanic respondents reported feelings of comfort and fondness during service exchanges when they shared ethnicity with a customer contact employee, more often than Caucasian respondents.
3. Asian and Hispanic respondents reported receiving tangible benefits such as discounts and free products when they shared ethnicity with a customer contact employee, more often than Caucasian respondents.
4. Regardless of ethnic group membership, respondents expressed loyalty to a business after having a service encounter involving an employee of the same ethnicity.

These results provide evidence that shared ethnicity is an important factor in a diverse marketplace. Business owners should be aware of cultural norms of behavior, especially related to the individualism-collectivism dimension. Businesses should consider hiring employees from the ethnic groups they are targeting and offering cultural training for their employees. Effectively addressing the needs of ethnic customers can be beneficial to both the business (increased loyalty) and customer (enhanced experience).

DISCUSSION

1. Analyze demographic information from the census tract or zip code of the client business. How does it differ from the demographics of the city, county, or state? Identify some of the main social, cultural, or other characteristics of the community where the client business is located. Visit the community where your client business is located. Based on your data analysis and your visit, describe how your results could be used by your client's business.

2. Select two groups and compare them based on a variety of demographic and other factors. Summarize their main multicultural characteristics. What are the main differences in reaching each of the groups? Which sociocultural factors would need to be considered? How will this change in ten years?

3. To make sure that you fully understand some of the terms introduced in this chapter, find some examples that illustrate the idea that people of color have been subject to racism, racial discrimination, or some kind of challenge or barrier associated with their race, cultural attributes, ethnicity, or national origin.

4. Pertaining to the cultural aspects of this course, how would you describe or define your own awareness of, exposure to, and tolerance of differences? Consider this with respect to race and ethnicity, disability, sexual orientation, or any other cultural distinction that you have had limited exposure to or experience with. How do you react to stereotyping or expressions of bias against these characteristics?

5. Based on your own ethnicity and experiences in service businesses, how do your judgments compare with those reported in the research concerning markets and culture?

6. What potential advantages or challenges might business owners from your ethnic group have in attracting and serving customers with whom they share ethnicity? What cautions would you suggest to your team regarding attempts to define expected relationships based on shared ethnicity?

NOTES

1   L. M. Akioka, ed., *The Multicultural Economy, 2013* (Athens, GA: Selig Center for Economic Growth, Terry College of Business, University of Georgia, 2013). Unless otherwise noted, all statistics from the Selig Center for Economic Growth are from this source.

2   Witeck Communications, "America's LGBT 2013 Buying Power Estimated at $830 Billion," press release, November 18, 2013, www.witeck.com/pressreleases/lgbt-2013-buying-power/18.

3   Matthew W. Brault, "Americans with Disabilities 2010," US Census, Current Population Reports P70-131, July 2012, www.census.gov/prod/2012pubs/p70-131.pdf.

4   Hyon B. Shin and Robert A. Kominski, "Language Use in the United States: 2007," US Census, American Community Survey Reports ACS-12, April 2010, www.census.gov/prod/2010pubs/acs-12.pdf.

5   Ibid.

6   US Census, "ACS Demographic and Housing Estimates: 2012 American Community Survey 1-Year Estimates," American FactFinder, http://factfinder.census.gov. Unless otherwise noted, US Census sources are available via searches at this American FactFinder website.

7   William J. Hussar and Tabitha M. Bailey, *Projections of Education Statistics to 2022* (Washington, DC: National Center for Education Statistics, February 2014).

8   Sabrina Tavernise, "Whites Account for Under Half of Births in US," *New York Times*, May 17, 2012.

9   "Field Listing: Median Age," 2014 estimate, in *The World Factbook*, https://www.cia.gov/library/publications/the-world-factbook/fields/2177.html (retrieved March 2, 2015).

10 US Census, "2012 American Community Survey."

11 Richard Fry and Paul Taylor, "Hispanic High School Graduates Pass Whites in Rate of College Enrollment," Pew Research Center, Hispanic Trends Project, May 9, 2013, www.pewhispanic.org/2013/05/09/hispanic-high-school-graduates-pass-whites-in-rate-of-college-enrollment.

12 Paul Taylor et al., "Second-Generation Americans: A Portrait of the Adult Children of Immigrants," Pew Research Center, February 7, 2013, www.pewsocialtrends.org/2013/02/07/second-generation-americans.

13 A. G. Harris, G. R. Henderson, and J. D. Williams, "Courting Customers: Assessing Consumer Racial Profiling and Other Marketplace Discrimination," *Journal of Public Policy and Marketing* 24, no. 1 (2005): 163-71.

14 S. Rastogi, T. D. Johnson, E. M. Hoeffel, and M. P. Drewery Jr., "The Black Population: 2010," US Census Briefs C1020BR-06, September 2011, www.census.gov/prod/cen2010/briefs/c2010br-06.pdf.

15 US Department of Homeland Security, *Yearbook of Immi-*

grant Statistics, 2012 (Washington, DC: Office of Immigration Statistics, July 2013).

16 Rastogi et al., "Black Population: 2010"; M. Miley and A. Mack, "The New Female Consumer: The Rise of the New Mom," *Advertising Age* white paper, November 16, 2009, http://adage.com/images/random/1109/aa-newfemale -whitepaper.pdf.

17 US Census, "2012 American Community Survey: Median Age by Sex and African American Alone," tables B01002 and B01002H.

18 *National Vital Statistics Reports* 62, no. 7 (Washington, DC: Centers for Disease Control and Prevention, January 6, 2014).

19 National Center for Health Statistics, *Health, United States, 2013: With Special Feature on Prescription Drugs* (Hyattsville, MD: National Center for Health Statistics, 2014).

20 J. D. Williams and S. K. Kumanyika, "Is Social Marketing an Effective Tool to Reduce Health Disparities?" *Social Marketing Quarterly* 7, no. 4 (Winter 2002): 14–31.

21 Rastogi et al., "Black Population: 2010."

22 US Census, "Table A-2: Percent of People 25 Years and Over Who Have Completed High School or College, by Race, Hispanic Origin and Sex: Selected Years 1940 to 2014," www.census.gov/hhes/socdemo/education/data/ cps/historical.

23 Alisa Cunningham, Eun Kyoung Park, and Jennifer Engle, *Minority Serving Institutions: Doing More with Less* (Washington, DC: Institute for Higher Education Policy, February 2014), www.ihep.org/sites/default/files/uploads/docs/pubs/ msis_doing_more_w-less_final_february_2014-v2.pdf.

24 Ibid.

25 Kaiser Family Foundation, "Distribution of Medical School Graduates by Race/Ethnicity," www.kff.org/other/state -indicator/distribution-by-race-ethnicity (retrieved March 3, 2015).

26 I. Hinton, J. Howell, E. Merwin, S. Stern, S. Turner, I. Williams, and M. Wilson, "The Educational Pipeline for Health Care Professionals: Understanding the Source of Racial Differences," *Journal of Human Resources* 451, no. 5 (2010): 116.

27 Rastogi et al., "Black Population: 2010."

28 US Census, "Detailed Tables on Wealth and Asset Ownership," 2005, 2009, 2011, www.census.gov/people/wealth/ data/dtables.html.

29 US Census, "Table 2: Poverty Status by Family Relationship, Race, and Hispanic Origin," www.census.gov/hhes/www/ poverty/data/historical/people.html (retrieved August 4, 2014); S. Travernise, "Soaring Poverty Casts Spotlight on 'Lost Decade,'" *New York Times*, September 13, 2011.

30 Rastogi et al., "Black Population: 2010."

31 National Conference of Black Mayors, http://ncbm.org/ 2009/04/our-mission (retrieved December 20, 2011).

32 J. E. Manning, "Membership of the 113th Congress: A Profile," Congressional Research Service, March 14, 2014, https://fas.org/sgp/crs/misc/R42964.pdf.

33 Mark Hugo Lopez and Ana Gonzalez-Barrera, "Inside the 2012 Latino Electorate," Pew Research Center, His-

panic Trends Project, June 3, 2013, www.pewhispanic .org/2013/06/03/inside-the-2012-latino-electorate.

34 Sentencing Project, "Facts about Prisons and People in Prison," www.sentencingproject.org (retrieved August 5, 2014).

35 US Sentencing Commission, *Sourcebook of Federal Sentencing Statistics*, 2001, www.ussc.gov/Data_and_Statistics/ Annual_Reports_and_Sourcebooks/2001/SBTOC01.htm.

36 Pew Hispanic Center and Kaiser Family Foundation, "2002 National Survey of Latinos," http://pewhispanic.org/files/ reports/15.pdf; Carroll Doherty, "For African Americans, Discrimination Is Not Dead," Pew Research Center, June 28, 2013, www.pewresearch.org/fact-tank/2013/06/28/ for-african-americans-discrimination-is-not-dead.

37 Remarks by Acting Assistant Attorney General Vanita Gupta at the CRA and Fair Lending Colloquium, November 3, 2014, www.justice.gov/opa/speech/remarks-acting-assistant-attor ney-general-vanita-gupta-cra-fair-lending-colloquium.

38 US Census, "Housing," www.census.gov/hhes/www/hous ing/hvs/historic/index.html (retrieved December 20, 2011).

39 C. L. Nier, "The Shadow of Credit: The Historical Origins of Racial Predatory Lending and Its Impact upon African American Wealth Accumulation," *Journal of Law and Social Change* 11 (2007): 131–94.

40 Brian K. Bucks, Arthur B. Kennickell, Traci L. Mach, and Kevin B. Moore, "Changes in U.S. Family Finances from 2004 to 2007: Evidence from the Survey of Consumer Finances," *Federal Reserve Bulletin* 95 (February 2009): A1–A55.

41 Kenneth A. Couch and Robert Fairlie, "Last Hired, First Fired? Black-White Unemployment and the Business Cycle," *Demography* 47, no. 1 (February 2010): 227–47.

42 Hartford Institute for Religion Research, "Historically African American Denominations," http://faithcommunities today.org/historically-african-american-denominations (retrieved July 15, 2014).

43 C. Eric Lincoln and Lawrence H. Mamiya, *The Black Church in the African American Experience* (Durham, NC: Duke University Press, 1990).

44 US Bureau of Labor Statistics, Annual Calendar Year Tables 2012, "Current Combined Expenditure, Share, and Standard Error Tables: Race of Reference Person," www .bls.gov/cex.

45 E. Goskin, A. Mitchell, and M. Jurkowitz, "African American: A Year of Turmoil and Opportunity," *State of the News Media 2013*, www.stateofthemedia.org/2013/ african-american-2.

46 Alliance of Audited Media, http://abcas3.auditedmedia .com/ecirc/magtitlesearch.asp.

47 Viacom, Form 10K for the fiscal year ended September 30, 2013.

48 See the lists of radio stations at www.radioblack.com (retrieved December 20, 2011).

49 Gail Mitchell, "Fewer and Fewer African-American-Owned Radio Stations Reports Show," *Billboard*, February 13, 2013, www.billboard.com/biz/articles/news/1539311/fewer-

and-fewer-african-american-owned-radio-stations
-reports-show.

50 Aaron Smith, "African Americans and Technology Use: A Demographic Portrait," Pew Research Center, Internet Project, January 6, 2014, www.pewinternet.org/2014/01/06/african-americans-and-technology-use.

51 Paul Taylor, Mark Lopez, Jessica Martínez, and Gabriel Velasco, "When Labels Don't Fit: Hispanics and Their Views of Identity," Pew Research Center, Hispanic Trends Project, April 4, 2012, www.pewhispanic.org/2012/04/04/when-labels-dont-fit-hispanics-and-their-views-of-identity.

52 US Census, "2011 American Community Survey: Hispanic or Latino Origin by Specific Origin," table B03001.

53 Jens Manuel Krogstad, "Top Issue for Hispanics? Hint: It's Not Immigration," Pew Research Center, Hispanic Trends Project, June 2, 2014, www.pewresearch.org/fact-tank/2014/06/02/top-issue-for-hispanics-hint-its-not-immigration.

54 Anna Brown and Eileen Patten, "Statistical Portrait of Hispanics in the United States, 2012," Pew Research Center, Hispanic Trends Project, April 29, 2014, www.pewhispanic.org/2014/04/29/statistical-portrait-of-hispanics-in-the-united-states-2012.

55 US Census, "2011 American Community Survey: Hispanic or Latino Origin by Specific Origin," table B03001.

56 US Census, "2012 American Community Survey 1–Year Estimates," table B01001.

57 Anna Brown and Eileen Patten, "Statistical Portrait of Hispanics in the United States, 2012," Pew Research Center, Hispanic Trends Project, April 29, 2014, www.pewhispanic.org/2014/04/29/statistical-portrait-of-hispanics-in-the-united-states-2012.

58 J. A. Martin, B. E. Hamilton, M. J. K. Osterman, S. C. Curtin, and T. J. Mathews, "Births: Final Data for 2012," *National Vital Statistics Reports* 62, no. 9 (December 30, 2013): 15.

59 Anna Brown and Eileen Patten, "Statistical Portrait of Hispanics in the United States, 2012," Pew Research Center, Hispanic Trends Project, April 29, 2014, www.pewhispanic.org/2014/04/29/statistical-portrait-of-hispanics-in-the-united-states-2012.

60 Richard Fry, "Hispanic College Enrollment Spikes, Narrowing Gaps with Other Groups: 24% Growth from 2009 to 2010," Pew Research Center, Hispanic Trends Project, August 25, 2011, www.pewhispanic.org/2011/08/25/hispanic-college-enrollment-spikes-narrowing-gaps-with-other-groups.

61 National Center for Educational Statistics, "Table 219: Percentage of High School Dropouts among Persons 16 through 24 Years Old (Status Dropout Rate), by Sex and Race/Ethnicity: Selected Years, 1960 through 2012," http://nces.ed.gov/programs/digest/d13/tables/dt13_219.70.asp.

62 Ibid.

63 US Census, "Table A-2: Percent of People 25 Years and Over Who Have Completed High School or College, by Race, Hispanic Origin and Sex: Selected Years 1940 to 2014."

64 US Census, "Income," www.census.gov/hhes/www/income/data/historical/families/index.html (retrieved December 20, 2011).

65 P. Taylor, R. Fry, and R. Kochhar, "Wealth Gaps Rise to Record Highs between Whites, Blacks, Hispanics," Pew Research Center, July 26, 2011, http://pewsocialtrends.org/2011/07/26/wealth-gaps-rise-to-record-highs-between-whites-blacks-hispanics.

66 Anna Brown and Eileen Patten, "Statistical Portrait of Hispanics in the United States, 2012," Pew Research Center, Hispanic Trends Project, April 29, 2014, www.pewhispanic.org/2014/04/29/statistical-portrait-of-hispanics-in-the-united-states-2012.

67 US Department of Homeland Security, *Yearbook of Immigrant Statistics, 2012.*

68 Rakesh Kochhar, "Latino Jobs Growth Driven by US Born," Pew Research Center, Hispanic Trends Project, June 19, 2014, www.pewhispanic.org/2014/06/19/latino-jobs-growth-driven-by-u-s-born.

69 Jeffrey S. Passel, D'Vera Cohn, and Ana Gonzalez-Barrera, "Population Decline of Unauthorized Immigrants Stalls, May Have Reversed," Pew Research Center, Hispanic Trends Project, September 23, 2013, www.pewhispanic.org/2013/09/23/population-decline-of-unauthorized-immigrants-stalls-may-have-reversed.

70 Jeffrey S. Passel and D'Vera Cohn, "Unauthorized Immigrant Population: National and State Trends, 2010," Pew Research Center, Hispanic Trends Project, February 1, 2011, www.pewhispanic.org/2011/02/01/unauthorized-immigrant-population-brnational-and-state-trends-2010.

71 National Association of Latino Elected and Appointed Officials, "The 2012 Latino Vote: Turning Numbers into Clout," www.naleo.org/latinovote.html (retrieved December 20, 2011).

72 National Association of Latino Elected and Appointed Officials, www.naleo.org/aboutnaleo.html (retrieved December 20, 2011).

73 Mark Hugo Lopez, "The Latino Electorate in 2010: More Voters, More Non-Voters," Pew Hispanic Center, April 26, 2011, http://pewhispanic.org/files/reports/141.pdf.

74 Alan Cooperman, Mark Hugo Lopez, Cary Funk, Jessica Hamar Martínez, and Katherine Ritchey, "The Shifting Religious Identity of Latinos in the United States," Pew Research Center, May 7, 2014, www.pewforum.org/2014/05/07/the-shifting-religious-identity-of-latinos-in-the-united-states.

75 Robert Suro and Jeffrey S. Passel, "The Rise of the Second Generation: Changing Patterns in Hispanic Population Growth," Pew Hispanic Center, October 14, 2003, http://pewhispanic.org/files/reports/22.pdf.

76 Jeffrey S. Passel, Wendy Wang, and Paul Taylor, "Marrying Out: One-in-Seven New U.S. Marriages Is Interracial or Interethnic," Pew Research Center, June 15, 2010, www.pewsocialtrends.org/files/2010/10/755-marrying-out.pdf.

77 *Washington Post*, Henry J. Kaiser Family Foundation, and Harvard University, "National Survey on Latinos in America," conducted July–August 1999, www.kff.org/kaiser polls/3023-index.cfm.

78 Ibid.

79 Robert R. Callis and Melissa Kresin, "Residential Vacancies and Homeownership in the Fourth Quarter 2013," US Census News Release CB14-09, January 31, 2014.

80 Monica Gil and Juan Carlos Davila, "Understanding Latino Diversity: New Insights into Three Important Hispanic Segments," presented at Hispanic Retail 360, Las Vegas, August 2013.

81 Center for Spanish Language Media, *The State of Spanish Language Media, 2010* (Denton: University of North Texas, 2011).

82 "Hispanic Fact Pack 2013," *Advertising Age*, July 22, 2013.

83 *The Associated Press–Univision Poll*, 2010, http://surveys.ap.org/data%5CNORC%5CAP-Univision%20Topline_posting.pdf.

84 Comcast Corp., Form 10K for the period ending December 31, 2013, filed February 12, 2014.

85 Emily Guskin and Amy Mitchell, "Hispanic Media: Faring Better Than the Mainstream Media," *State of the News Media 2011*, www.stateofthemedia.org/2011/hispanic-media-fairing-better-than-the-mainstream-media.

86 US Census, "2012 Population Projections: Summary Tables," www.census.gov/population/projections/data/national/2012/summarytables.html.

87 Statistics Canada, "Immigration and Ethnocultural Diversity in Canada: National Household Survey 2011," catalog no. 99, 2013, www12.statcan.gc.ca/nhs-enm/2011/as-sa/99-010-x/99-010-x2011001-eng.cfm.

88 Pew Research Center, "The Rise of Asian Americans," April 2013, www.pewsocialtrends.org/files/2013/04/Asian-Americans-new-full-report-04-2013.pdf.

89 Kaiser Family Foundation, "Distribution of Medical School Graduates by Race/Ethnicity, 2010," www.statehealth facts.org/comparetable.jsp?ind=454&cat=9.

90 National Science Foundation, "Women, Minorities, and Persons with Disabilities in Science and Engineering: 2011," www.nsf.gov/statistics/wmpd.

91 Pew Research Center, "The Rise of Asian Americans," April 2013, www.pewsocialtrends.org/files/2013/04/Asian-Americans-new-full-report-04-2013.pdf.

92 General immigration information in this section is from Iris Chang, *The Chinese in America: A Narrative History* (New York: Viking, 2003).

93 Paul Taylor, ed, "The Rise of Asian Americans," Pew Research Center, April 4, 2013, www.pewsocialtrends.org/files/2013/04/Asian-Americans-new-full-report-04-2013.pdf.

94 US Census, "Race Data 2010."

95 Won Kim Cook, Corina Chung, and Winston Tseng, "Demographic and Socioeconomic Profiles of Asian Americans, Native Hawaiians, and Pacific Islanders in the United States," Asian & Pacific Islander American Health Forum, July 2011, www.apiahf.org/resources/resources-database/profilesofaanhpi.

96 E. M. Hoeffel, S. Rastogi, M. O. Kim, and H. Shahid, "The Asian Population: 2010," US Census Briefs C2010BR-11, March 2012, www.census.gov/prod/cen2010/briefs/c2010br-11.pdf.

97 Asian Pacific American Institute for Congressional Studies, www.apaics.org (retrieved March 2, 2015).

98 P. Farhi, "US, Media Settle with Wen Ho Lee," *Washington Post*, June 3, 2006.

99 Thomas Gryn and Christine Gambino, "The Foreign Born from Asia: 2011," US Census, American Community Survey Briefs ACSBR/11-06, October 2012, www.census.gov/prod/2012pubs/acsbr11-06.pdf.

100 Wesley Yang, "Paper Tigers: What Happens to All the Asian-American Overachievers When the Test-Taking Ends," *New York Magazine*, May 8, 2011.

101 Hoeffel et al., "Asian Population: 2010."

102 C. N. Le, "Interracial Dating and Marriage: U.S.-Raised Asian Americans," Asian-Nation: The Landscape of Asian America, www.asian-nation.org/interracial2.shtml (retrieved June 29, 2014).

103 Cary Funk, "Asian Americans: A Mosaic of Faiths," Pew Research Center, Religion & Public Life Project, July 19, 2012, www.pewforum.org/2012/07/19/asian-americans-a-mosaic-of-faiths-overview.

104 Nielsen, *Significant, Sophisticated and Savvy: The Asian American Consumer*, Diverse Intelligence Insights Series (New York: Nielsen, 2013).

105 Ethnologue, "Summary by Language Size," www.ethnologue.com/statistics/size#2 (retrieved December 20, 2011).

106 Nielsen, *State of the Asian American Consumer: Quarter 3, 2012*, www.nielsen.com/content/dam/corporate/us/en/microsites/publicaffairs/StateoftheAsianAmericanConsumerReport.pdf.

107 Nielsen, *Significant, Sophisticated and Savvy*.

108 Harvard Project on American Indian Economic Development, *The State of the Native Nations: Conditions under U.S. Policies of Self-Determination* (New York: Oxford University Press, 2008).

109 *Cobell v. Salazar* settlement, Indian Trust Settlement, indiantrust.com (retrieved December 20, 2011).

110 Harvard Project on American Indian Economic Development, *State of the Native Nations*.

111 US Census, "2012 American Community Survey 1-Year Estimates," for American Indians and Alaska Natives, table S0201; Statistics Canada, "Aboriginal Identity Population," www40.statcan.ca/l01/cst01/DEMO60A-eng.htm (retrieved December 20, 2011).

112 Bureau of Indian Affairs, www.bia.gov (retrieved December 20, 2011).

113 US Census, "2012 American Community Survey 1-Year Estimates," for American Indians and Alaska Natives, table S0201.

114 *Findings and Recommendations Prepared by the Bureau of Indian Education Study Group Submitted to the Secretaries of the Departments of the Interior and Education*, June 27, 2014, www.doi.gov/news/upload/Study-Group-Blueprint-DOI-FINAL.pdf.

115 Stephanie Woodard, "South Dakota Boarding School Survivors Detail Sexual Abuse," *Indian Country*, July 28, 2011.

116 Education Trust, *The State of Education for Native Students*, 2012, www.edtrust.org/sites/edtrust.org/files/NativeStudentBrief_0.pdf.

117 Harvard Project on American Indian Economic Development, *State of the Native Nations*.

118 National Center for Education Statistics, *Status and Trends in Education of American Indian and Alaska Natives*, 2008, http://nces.ed.gov/pubs2005/2005108.pdf.

119 National Center for Education Statistics, *Higher Education: Gaps in Access and Persistence*, 2012, http://nces.ed.gov/pubs2012/2012046.pdf.

120 Higher Learning Commission, *Distinctive and Connected: Tribal Colleges and Universities and Higher Learning Commission Accreditation*, June 2013, www.aihec.org/our-stories/docs/reports/HLC%20TCU.pdf.

121 Julie Siebens and Tiffany Julian, "Native North American Languages Spoken at Home in the United States and Puerto Rico: 2006–2010," US Census, American Community Survey Briefs ACSBR/10-10, December 2011, www.census.gov/prod/2011pubs/acsbr10-10.pdf.

122 Harvard Project on American Indian Economic Development, *State of the Native Nations*.

123 Ibid.

124 Indian Health Service, "Disparities Fact Sheet," www.ihs.gov/newsroom/factsheets/disparities (retrieved June 28, 2014).

125 US Department of Justice, "Indian Country Accomplishments of the Justice Department, 2009–Present," www.justice.gov/tribal/accomplishments (retrieved March 2, 2015).

126 Tribal Gaming Commission, "Gaming Revenues 2009–2013," www.nigc.gov/Gaming_Revenue_Reports.aspx.

127 Akioka, *Multicultural Economy, 2013*.

128 Native Public Media, "Radio," www.nativepublicmedia.org/radio (retrieved March 2, 2015).

129 Office of Hawaiian Affairs, "Hawaiian History Timeline," www.oha.org/pdf/HwnHistoryTimeline.pdf (retrieved December 20, 2011).

130 J. Kehaulani Kauanui, *Hawaiian Blood: Colonialism and the Politics of Sovereignty and Indigeneity* (Durham, NC: Duke University Press, 2008).

131 US Census, "2012 National Population Projections: Summary Tables," table 4, www.census.gov/population/projections/data/national/2012/summarytables.html (retrieved April 13, 2015).

132 Asian Americans for Advancing Justice, *Native Hawaiians and Pacific Islanders: A Community of Contrasts 2014*, http://advancingjustice-la.org/sites/default/files/A_Community_of_Contrasts_NHPI_US_2014.pdf.

133 US Census, "The American Community—Pacific Islanders: 2004," American Community Survey Reports ACS-06, www.census.gov/prod/2007pubs/acs-06.pdf.

134 US Census, "Native Hawaiian and Other Pacific Island Population in the US."

135 US Census, "2012 American Community Survey 1-Year Estimates," for Native Hawaiians and Pacific Islanders, table S0201.

136 Office of Hawaiian Affairs, *The Disparate Treatment of Native Hawaiians in the Criminal Justice System*, September 28, 2010, available at the Justice Policy Institute, www.justicepolicy.org/uploads/justicepolicy/documents/10-09_rep_disparatetreatmentofnativehawaiians_rd-ac.pdf (retrieved March 3, 2015).

137 Office of Minority Health, "Profile: Native Hawaiians and Pacific Islanders," http://minorityhealth.hhs.gov/omh/browse.aspx?lvl=3&lvlid=65 (retrieved March 3, 2015).

138 Asian Americans for Advancing Justice, *Native Hawaiians and Pacific Islanders*.

139 Audrey Smedley, "The History of the Idea of Race . . . and Why It Matters," paper presented at the conference "Race, Human Variation, and Disease: Consensus and Frontiers," American Anthropological Association, Warrenton, VA, March 14–17, 2007.

140 US Census, "2012 American Community Survey 1-Year Estimates," for Native Hawaiians and Pacific Islanders, table S0201.

141 Passel, Wang, and Taylor, "Marrying Out."

142 D. Bowles, "Bi-racial Identity: Children Born to African-American and White Couples," *Clinical Social Work Journal* 21, no. 4 (1993): 417–28.

143 Pew Research Center, "A Survey of LGBT Americans: Attitudes, Experiences and Values in Changing Times," June 13, 2013, www.pewsocialtrends.org/files/2013/06/SDT_LGBT-Americans_06-2013.pdf.

144 G. J. Gates, *Same-Sex and Different-Sex Couples in the American Community Survey: 2005–2011* (Los Angeles: Williams Institute at UCLA School of Law, February 2013).

145 Prudential, *The LGBT Financial Experience: 2012-2013 Prudential Research Study*, 2012, www.prudential.com/LGBT.

146 "Top 10 Gay and Lesbian Magazines," www.cision.com/us/2012/06/top-10-gay-and-lesbian-magazines (retrieved March 3, 2015).

147 Detra Y. Montoya and Elten Briggs, "Shared Ethnicity Effects on Service Encounters: A Study across Three U.S. Subcultures," *Journal of Business Research* 66 (2013): 314–20.

148 Ibid.

4. Multicultural Entrepreneurship

ABOUT THIS CHAPTER

Most business knowledge and theory taught in business schools focuses on the administration of large enterprises with thousands of employees and billions in revenues. These long-lived enterprises are not representative of the majority of US businesses, which are significantly smaller. Recently, considerably more attention has been paid to small and medium enterprises (SMEs), which constitute the largest number of US businesses. Research has validated the role that these businesses play in job creation and innovation.[1] Access to larger and more in-depth databases has contributed to exponentially more evidence about characteristics of these businesses and factors that lead to success. In this chapter the focus is on the SME sector and how multicultural forces and conditions shape the environment in which entrepreneurs from diverse groups and backgrounds compete. Recognize that these entrepreneurs face all of the challenges and conditions of conventional or mainstream entrepreneurs. They also face risks, uncertainties, and other obstacles associated with their racial, ethnic, and socioeconomic characteristics.

In 1979 David Birch, who pioneered looking at small businesses as an engine for job creation, claimed that businesses with fewer than one hundred employees generated more than 82% of jobs.[2] Since that time, there has been considerable debate as to just how many jobs are generated by small businesses compared to large businesses. New research continues to show that small businesses generate the bulk of new jobs; however, they also contribute to job destruction. Businesses with fewer than one hundred employees created more than half of new jobs and about 40% of net jobs in the period from 1992 to the first quarter of 2010.[3] Recent research has shown that it is startup firms (which average fewer than five employees) that create the most net jobs.[4] According to the Kauffman Foundation, the dynamic cycle of the creation of new businesses generates net jobs in the United States.[5]

Since 1997, the majority of business growth has come from groups that previously exhibited lower proportions of entrepreneurship relative to their populations. Minority business enterprises (MBEs), immigrant-owned businesses, and women-owned business enterprises (WBEs) have shown growth rates that exceed those of white male businesses.

Monetary gain is not the only goal of all the businesses described in this chapter. With many American Indian tribes, for example, casino profits contribute directly to the social welfare of tribe members. Other MBEs provide employment within their underserved communities. A new business model, social entrepreneurship, has emerged in the last several years. This model combines the mission focus of nonprofits with the bottom-line profit goal of for-profit companies.

Despite the economic impact of entrepreneurship, for a variety of reasons the survival rate of small businesses remains dismally low. The positive news is that data collection has improved substantially, and a number of excellent centers are driving research that identifies the attributes of high-impact businesses. This chapter attempts to summarize this dynamic area in which more data continue to emerge.

After Studying This Chapter

Reviewing the material in this chapter will provide theory and knowledge about how different categories of businesses evolve. Not all student consulting teams will consult with MBEs. Some will work with WBEs, businesses in economically distressed areas, or nonprofits and social enterprises. Much of the knowledge provided here can be applied to all emerging or small enterprises. Understanding how businesses evolve will allow the consulting team to place the client business in a framework and devise a strategy that will propel the business to critical mass and survival.

This chapter also provides information specific to MBEs. Data are presented on the number and characteristics of these businesses. Comparisons are made to non-Hispanic white businesses so that key factors obstacles to success of the client firm can be discerned. In addition to having to beat the odds of survival for emerging businesses, MBEs face additional obstacles that often require substantial effort to overcome. The support and understanding of the consulting team can do much to assist the business in overcoming these obstacles.

After studying this chapter, students will be able to:

- Distinguish between the different kinds of firms and the drivers for business survival and growth.
- Articulate the key characteristics of self-employed individuals, employer firms, and high-impact firms and the role each plays in economic development.
- Describe entrepreneur support systems and how they foster business success.
- Determine sources of capital and their characteristics in relation to business startups.
- Describe the factors that inhibit or nurture business survival for MBEs.

MINORITY BUSINESSES, OTHER SMALL ENTERPRISES, AND NONPROFITS

It is generally agreed that multicultural markets will play an increasingly important role in the US economy. The first tremors of the cultural and ethnic shifts in the American population were felt throughout the 1990s, confirmed by the 2000 US Census and evidenced in the explosive growth of multicultural groups in the 2010 US Census. As these populations grow, the corollary growth in related business activity is affecting local economies. The effect of these businesses is much more complex than a simple increase in revenues. Minority business enterprises (MBEs) were a major factor in the revitalization of inner-city Los Angeles after the 1992 riots that following the Rodney King verdict. MBEs played a major role in the recovery of Houston after the decline in its oil

industry. MBEs, for a time, were the only bright spot in New York City's economy, after more than thirty thousand financial service workers left the city in the three years following the September 11, 2001, attacks on the World Trade Center. Utica, New York, has been revived by the influx of refugees from Bosnia, Vietnam, Belarus, and recently, Somalia (the Somali Bantu).[6] Some of the factors that enhance the success of MBEs are the same ones that enhance other small businesses.

In periods of downturn and austerity, local governments realize the importance of MBEs in providing a stable foundation for the economy. These businesses have ties to the community and are unlikely to move out of state to reduce costs or to merge with larger firms and eliminate jobs. Research by William Bradford at the University of Washington Foster School of Business and others shows that minority-owned businesses are more likely to hire minority workers, who consistently have higher unemployment rates, than are businesses owned by non-Hispanic whites.

Multicultural markets are inextricably tied to multicultural entrepreneurship, and thus both are the focus of this book. Many unique relationships exist between multicultural aspects of the marketplace and businesses owned by persons of color. It is commonplace for such businesses to predominantly serve customers of particular racial and ethnic backgrounds. Obviously, this is not true of all such businesses. Some have locations that serve mainstream customers. Some are positioned by strategies and operations to cross over into the larger or mainstream marketplace.

Crossover market opportunities are increasingly prevalent in cities with large ethnic populations where gentrification and revitalization are occurring. Such developments mean that communities are changing in ways that usually bring higher-income residents, increased property values, and other improvements that expand business opportunities.

Mirroring growth trends in multicultural populations in the past two decades, the number of minority businesses increased at a much faster rate than did firms as a whole in the United States. As shown in Table 4-1, in 2007 the number of black-owned businesses grew by 61% and their combined revenues grew by 53%; non-Hispanic-white-owned firms grew by 14%, with a combined revenue growth rate of 24%. All MBE categories grew faster than white firms. Women-owned businesses continue to grow at rates higher than male-owned businesses. These

TABLE 4-1. Firm Growth in Number and Revenues

Group	All Firms, 2007 (number)	All Firms, 2002 (number)	Percent Change (%)	Receipts, 2007 ($1,000)	Receipts, 2002 ($1,000)	Percent Change (%)
All firms	27,092,908	22,974,655	17.9	30,031,519,910	22,603,658,904	32.9
White	22,595,146	19,899,839	13.5	10,240,990,714	8,277,812,084	23.7
Black or African American	1,921,864	1,197,567	**60.5**	135,739,834	88,641,608	**53.1**
American Indian and Alaska Native	236,691	201,387	17.5	34,353,842	26,872,947	27.8
Asian	1,549,559	1,103,587	**40.4**	506,047,751	326,663,445	**54.9**
Native Hawaiian and Other Pacific Islander	37,687	28,948	**30.2**	6,319,357	4,279,591	47.7
Hispanic	2,260,309	1,573,464	**43.7**	345,183,070	221,927,425	**55.5**
Female-owned	7,793,364	6,489,259	**20.1**	1,190,057,451	939,538,208	26.7
Male-owned	13,909,064	13,184,033	5.5	8,507,846,994	7,061,026,736	20.5
Veteran-owned	2,447,608			1,219,551,078		

Source: US Census 2007 Survey of Business Owners

Note: Bold figures indicate larger than average changes

growth rates seem to have continued after the 2007–9 recession. The US Small Business Administration (SBA) estimates that minority businesses were 14.6% of businesses in 2012 compared to 11.5% in 2007.[7]

Although minority businesses are showing large growth rates, as a group they face some notable limitations based on their general characteristics compared to nonminority firms. MBEs tend to be smaller than nonminority firms. With the exception of Asian firms, minority firms are a larger proportion of microbusinesses (businesses with $10,000 or less in sales) than non-Hispanic white firms and they have fewer firms with more than $1 million in sales (Figure 4-1).

According to the Kauffman Index of Entrepreneurial Activity, in 2013, 280 businesses per 100,000 people were started in the United States. Entrepreneurial rates ranged from 210 per 100,000 for blacks, 310 per 100,000 for whites, 370 per 100,000 for Asians, and 560 per 100,000 for Hispanics. The intensity of activity by state is shown in Figure 4-2, with the heaviest activity in the West and South. Entrepreneurial activity did not decrease after the 2007–9 recession. In fact, it increased through

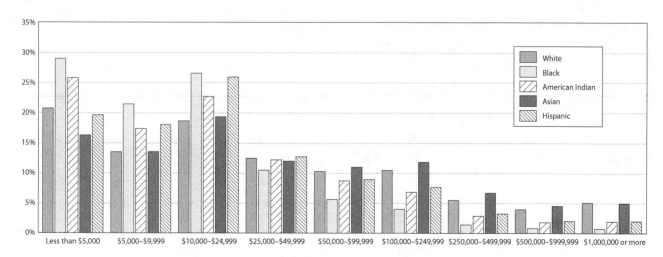

FIGURE 4-1. Proportion of Firms by Race and Revenues. Source: US Census 2007 Survey of Business Owners

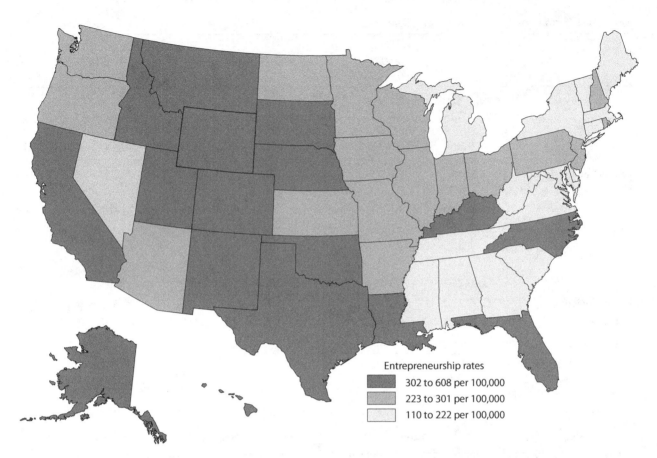

Entrepreneurship rates

■ 302 to 608 per 100,000

■ 223 to 301 per 100,000

□ 110 to 222 per 100,000

FIGURE 4-2. Location of New Entrepreneurs. Source: Robert W. Fairlie, *Kauffman Index of Entrepreneurial Activity, 1996–2013* (Kansas City, MO: Kauffman Foundation, April 2014)

2010, a phenomenon some attribute to divergent trends: a general increase in entrepreneurial rates and unemployed individuals looking for ways to earn money by starting a business. Table 4-2 shows that new entrepreneurs are increasingly diverse, immigrant, and older, mirroring changes in the US population. This is counter to the stereotype often portrayed in the media of entrepreneurs being young, white, and male. In fact, Figure 4-3 shows a drop in the number of younger entrepreneurs.

Some analysts postulate that the churning (birth and death) of firms is a ubiquitous and necessary feature of the US economy. New firms create the most jobs. At the same time, they drive productivity gains for all firms by competing with other small and large firms.[8] Firm termination is a natural part of the entrepreneurial ecosystem. This creative destruction opens opportunities for other entrepreneurs but it also eliminates jobs.

Even in periods of healthy birth rates for businesses, survival rates are daunting. According to the US Bureau of Labor Statistics, 80% of businesses make it to their second year of operation, 50% make it to their sixth year,

TABLE 4-2. Attributes of New Entrepreneurs (%)

	2003	2013
Race		
White	67.8	61.2
Black	9	8.8
Latino	16	20.4
Asian	4.4	6.1
Other	2.9	3.5
Age		
Ages 20–34	26.4	22.7
Ages 35–44	29.8	24
Ages 45–54	25.2	30
Ages 55–64	18.7	23.4
Nativity		
Native-born	80.9	74
Immigrant	19.1	25.9
Veteran	10.2	4.8

Source: Robert W. Fairlie, *Kauffman Index of Entrepreneurial Activity, 1996–2013* (Kansas City, MO: Kauffman Foundation, 2014)

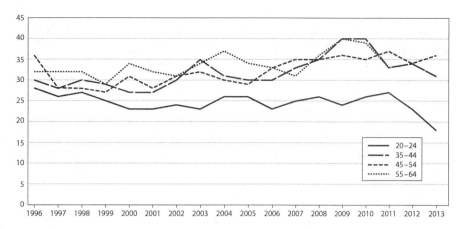

FIGURE 4-3. New Business Start-Ups by Age Group. Source: Robert W. Fairlie, *Kauffman Index of Entrepreneurial Activity, 1996–2013* (Kansas City, MO: Kauffman Foundation, April 2014)

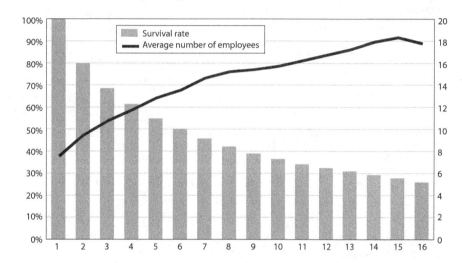

FIGURE 4-4. Business Survival Rates in Years. Source: US Bureau of Labor Statistics

and less than 30% make it to their fifteenth year (Figure 4-4). To begin the analysis of success factors, businesses have been divided into groupings of key characteristics: Figure 4-5 divides the universe of the thirty million US businesses into groups with characteristics described in Table 4-3.

Of all businesses, the great majority involve self-employment, with no employees beyond the business owner. The balance, about a quarter of the total, are employer firms that have people on their payrolls. Of the employer firms, there are about 350,000 *gazelles*, according to David Birch, who coined the term. Gazelles, or high-impact firms, represent the holy grail of business in that they are innovative, grow very quickly (over 20% per year), and generate employment as a result of their

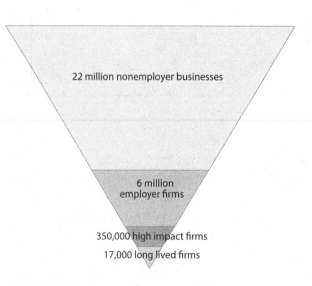

FIGURE 4-5. Universe of Businesses, 2012

TABLE 4-3. Characteristics of Businesses

	Self-Employed	Employer Firms	Gazelles or High-Impact Firms
Definition	Firms with one owner/ employee	Firms that have employees	High-impact businesses that grow quickly and are highly productive
Number	22 million	6 million	About 350,000, or 6% of businesses
Characteristics	Most self-employed start businesses to accommodate lifestyle choice	Most are small marginal businesses and continue to be small	Growth rates of over 20% per year. Growth rates may or may not be sustained over long periods of time
Capital	Low capital requirements: 75% start with less than $5,000. More than 90% start with less than $25,000.	Low capital requirements: About 75% start with less than $25,000. More than 50% required less than $5,000.	Most owners use own funds to start company
Industries	Professional and other services, retail, and construction	Most are low capital and low barrier industries	Range of industries, including declining ones
Owner or manager characteristics	Wants to be own boss, control over number of hours worked, and family reasons	Risk-averse	Educated, with many years of experience
Business characteristics	Marginal businesses with low-risk incremental opportunities	Most popular are restaurants, beauty salons, and construction firms	High revenues and innovation per employee. Most firms have 1–19 employees. Average age of these firms is 16 years.
Revenue generation	Most generate less than $50,000, and one-third operate at loss.	Most do not grow. Majority have less than $100,000 in sales	High revenue growth of over 20% a year
Job generation	None	Only 24% of employer firms tracked over ten years show any growth in employment	High job generation
Cycle	Self-employment increases during economic downturns	Growing at 1–2% a year. Follows business cycle, with more starts during expansions and more deaths during downturns.	Job creation is immune to business cycle
Survival	One study showed about half survive five or more years	About 500,000 started every year and about 500,000 terminated. Fewer are started and more terminate during recessions.	High-impact firms are in clusters where there is an entrepreneurial support system for their industry

Source: SBA Office of Advocacy, "Frequently Asked Questions," September 2012, www.sba.gov/sites/default/files/FAQ_Sept_2012.pdf

growth.[9] Unlike the "mice" (or microbusinesses) that do not survive, or the "elephants" (or large firms) that can shed jobs, gazelles typify the best in entrepreneurship in America. Gazelles may evolve or merge into long-lived businesses. Long-lived businesses command the most attention. They constitute the largest 17,000 firms, of which about 7,000 are listed on the public stock exchanges.

Most Small Businesses Want to Stay Small

While not all small businesses have the goal of becoming large enterprises, it is important that all small businesses be given the full set of strategies and tools to survive, as this is critical to wealth creation in multicultural and underserved communities. Small businesses are typically defined by number of employees. Businesses with fewer

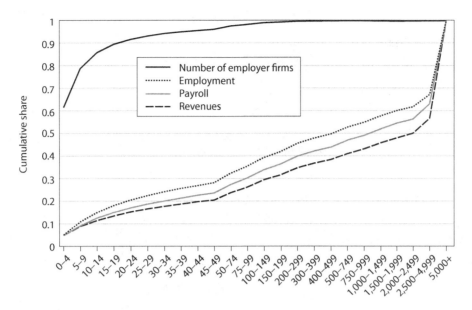

FIGURE 4-6. Cumulative Share of Number of Firms, Employment, Payroll, and Revenues by Size of Firm. Source: US Small Business Administration, Office of Advocacy, based on data from US Census 2007 Survey of Business Owners

than 100 employees account for 99% of businesses but only 40% of employment and 30% of revenues. Smaller firms (with fewer than 10 employees) account for 90% of businesses but less than 15% of revenues. The Small Business Administration defines small businesses as those with fewer than 500 employees, which account for more than half of US employment and more than 40% of revenues (Figure 4-6). Another distinction is between the self-employed and other small businesses. Gazelles, or high-impact firms, which grow at compounded rates of more than 20%, constitute a third category that is the focus of research. The following section outlines characteristics of the main categories of small businesses.

Businesses with No Employees

The great majority of small firms are the self-employed. Although they comprise 79% of businesses, they account for only 3% to 4% of all business revenues. Between 2002 and 2007, the number of self-employed firms grew 65% for blacks, 47% for Asians, 33% for Native Hawaiians, and 20% for American Indians, compared to 18% for white firms. This growth is consistent with previous studies that showed growth across all groups, with more growth in minority groups.[10]

In sheer numbers, the self-employed tend to be mostly male and mostly white, according to the US Department of Labor 2010 study of the self-employed (based on the joint Department of Labor and US Census Current Population Survey, with definitions and different totals for self-employed firms with no employees). About 58% of the self-employed are home-based businesses, while 22% are employer firms. Studies of the self-employed show that these individuals often start businesses for nonmonetary reasons, such as being their own boss or a desire for flexible work arrangements.[11] The self-employed tend to be concentrated in industries that have low capital requirements; services (29%), construction labor (16%), and retail trade (11%) dominate. The ranks of the self-employed include a broad spectrum of occupations, from construction workers to doctors and lawyers. Average revenues for all self-employed business were $45,300 in 2012 (Figure 4-7 shows revenues by sector). Most of these individuals have no desire to grow their businesses past self-employment.[12]

About 3% of nonemployer firms become employer firms within three years of operation, and nearly 2% of employers migrate to nonemployer status in the same period.[13] Of all nonemployer firms, 26% claim they do not need start-up capital compared to 10% of employer businesses. About 36% of nonemployer firms start their businesses with $5,000 or less, as shown in Figure 4-8. More than 80% start with $10,000 or less in capital. Although a small percentage of these businesses can

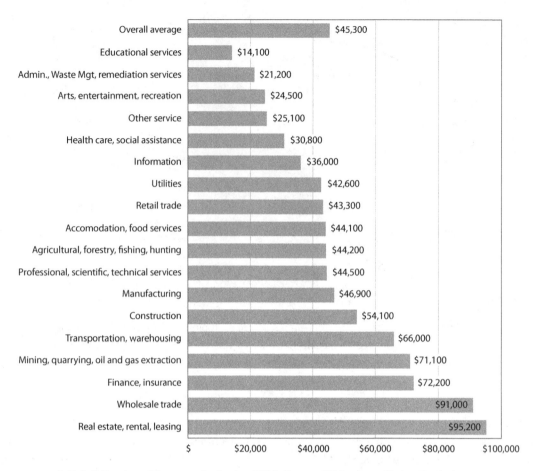

FIGURE 4-7. Self-Employed Revenues by Sector, 2010. Source: US Bureau of Labor Statistics

generate significant revenues and profit, 80% generate less than $50,000 in revenues, as shown in Figure 4-9. Some evidence suggests that the low revenue generation may be a result of the number of hours put into the busi-

ness. The birth rate (34.3% in 2003–4) and death rate (29.6%) for the self-employed are almost three times higher than for businesses with employees (12.6% and 10.8%, respectively).

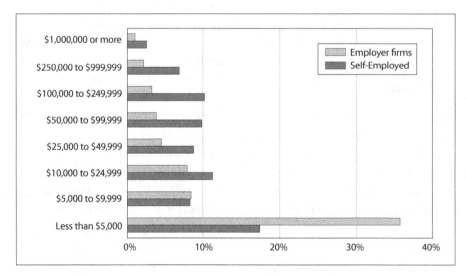

FIGURE 4-8. Start-Up Capital Is More for Employer Firms. Source: Statistics for all US firms by total capital used to start or acquire the business, US Census 2007 Survey of Business Owners

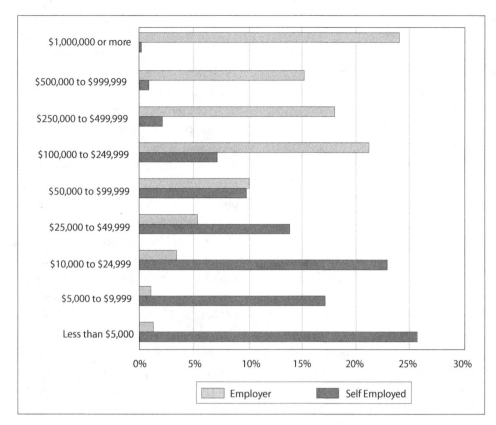

FIGURE 4-9. Employer Firms Have More Revenue. Source: US Census 2007 Survey of Business Owners

About 43% of nonemployer firms rely on business income for the owners' primary income, compared to 69% of employer firms. Research shows that the self-employed are divided into two very different groups. One group tends to be less educated and work in low-barrier industries such as agriculture, construction, and personal services.[14] The second group tends to consist of older, white, and married males who have the financial capital, social capital, and skills to enter high-barrier industries such as medicine, dentistry, and other professional services.[15] Populations with higher unemployment rates—such as American Indians, Native Alaskans, Native Hawaiians, Pacific Islanders, and Hispanics—have a higher proportion of nonemployer businesses (Table 4-4).

TABLE 4-4. Employer and Nonemployer Firms by Race/Ethnicity/Gender

	Businesses		Nonemployer Firms		Nonemployer Firms as Percent of All Businesses	
	Number (1,000)	Revenue ($ million)	Number (1,000)	Revenue ($ million)	Number (%)	Revenue (%)
All firms	27,093	30,031,520	21,357	972,691	79	3
White	22,595	10,240,991	17,955	834,441	79	8
Black or African American	1,922	135,740	1,815	38,595	94	28
American Indian and Alaska Native	237	34,354	213	6,860	90	20
Asian	1,550	506,048	1,152	52,474	74	10
Native Hawaiian and Pacific Islander	38	6,319	34	1,069	89	17
Hispanic	2,260	350,661	2,011	70,741	89	20
Women	27,110	30,176,155	21,357	972,694	79	3

Source: US Census 2007 Survey of Business Owners

Employer Firms

Employer firms numbered about 5.9 million in 2007 and have been growing at a rate of 1% to 2% a year. About 800,000 establishments were started in 2012. The highest number started (872,000) occurred in 2006. Establishment terminations were 732,000 in 2012, with the highest terminations (900,000) occurring in 2008, the midst of the recession.[16] Business termination does not always mean the business failed. About 25,000 to 65,000 business bankruptcies are filed every year. Bankruptcies trend upward during downturns and downward during expansions.[17]

Like nonemployer firms, the bulk of employer enterprises do not grow. In one study, only 32% of employer firms tracked over five years reported expansion.[18] Economists hypothesize that these businesses remain small because they choose to enter markets with standard offerings for an existing customer base. Most small businesses are restaurants, medical offices, construction firms, auto repair shops, accounting firms, and other service businesses with low barriers to entry. Low fixed costs relative to variable expenses and dependence on the skill of the business owner make it optimal to keep these businesses small. Most of these business owners do not innovate, and their main reason for starting the business is neither monetary nor growth.[19]

Table 4-5 shows that WBEs and MBEs tend to be younger compared to all employer firms (that is, a smaller proportion were started prior to 1990 and a larger proportion have started in recent years).

In 2007, more than two-thirds of business owners reported completing at least some college education by the time they started or acquired their business, as shown in Table 4-6. More than one-quarter (27.8%) had bachelor's degrees, and 20.4% had earned a master's, doctorate, or professional degree before starting or acquiring their business. These proportions were generally 2% to 3% higher than for nonemployer firms. The proportion of female business owners with a bachelor's degree was 1.3% lower than that of male business owners, while the proportion of women with a master's, doctorate, or professional degree was 3.7% lower than that of men. The US Census 2007 Survey of Business Owners (SBO) shows that both black and Asian business owners are more likely to have a college degree, while Hispanic, American Indian and Alaskan Native (AIAN), and Native Hawaiian and Pacific Islander (NHPI) business owners lag behind by 10% to 13% compared to white firms.[20] The increase in the number of educated blacks should have a positive impact on black entrepreneurship as more educated black entrepreneurs start larger businesses, which are more likely to be successful. In the past, education was noted as a factor in the success of Asian businesses. For all businesses, education was found to be correlated with increased rates of firm survival, more employees, increased sales, and profits.[21] Owners with bachelor's degrees have 25% higher sales than high school dropouts, and owners with master's degrees have 40% higher sales than holders of bachelor's degrees.[22] Other factors that portend success include having family-business background or having actually worked in a family business.[23]

TABLE 4-5. Proportion of Group by Year Business Started (%)

	All Firms	Female	Hispanic	Black	AIAN	Asian	NHPI
Before 1980	21	15	9	10	15	8	15
1980 to 1989	18	16	13	14	17	12	15
1990 to 1999	25	27	26	26	26	25	23
2000 to 2002	11	13	16	15	13	15	12
2003	4	5	6	6	4	6	0
2004	5	6	7	8	6	7	5
2005	5	6	8	8		9	11
2006	5	6	8	7		8	5
2007	3	4	5	5		6	4

Source: US Census 2007 Survey of Business Owners

TABLE 4-6. Highest Educational Attainment of Employer Firm Owners (%)

	White	Female	Hispanic	Black	AIAN	Asian	NHPI
Less than high school graduate	3	9	12	5	7	6	4
High school graduate: diploma or GED	21	26	25	16	22	17	21
Technical, trade, or vocational school	6	6	6	6	7	3	9
Some college, no degree	17	19	17	17	22	12	21
Associate's degree	6	8	6	6	7	5	8
Bachelor's degree	28	19	18	24	21	31	24
Master's, doctorate, or professional degree	20	14	16	27	16	27	14

Source: US Census 2007 Survey of Business Owners

Gazelles, or High-Impact Firms

Research on high-impact firms shows that they consistently number approximately 350,000 and represent about 6% of US firms. They are younger and more productive than all other firms and can be found across a variety of industries, even declining ones. Some researchers claim that they generate all net jobs, and their job creation seems immune to expansions and contractions of the business cycle.[24] Burgeoning research, including the study of gazelles in foreign and emerging economies, makes knowledge of this area fluid; caution should be exercised. Many of the theories related to gazelles are being tested by increasingly rigorous research and evidence.

Not all gazelles, or high-impact firms, show high growth through an extended period of time. A study of gazelles that issued an initial public offering found that their evolution could result in continued operation (33%), acquisition (55%), or bankruptcy (12%).[25] Following on Michael Porter's cluster theory,[26] which asserts that geographic clustering of businesses and industries accrue benefits, researchers have identified the importance of entrepreneurial support networks for high-impact firms. California and Silicon Valley stands out as the geographic location of high-impact firms that issued stock on the public markets. In particular, it is home to high-impact firms in the Internet, semiconductor, medical instruments, biotechnology, and retail industries. Massachusetts comes in second in terms of the number of high-impact firms that have gone public. Reasons include the availability of human (successful entrepreneur mentors, lawyers, skilled workers) and financial capital to fuel company growth. In looking at high-impact clusters throughout the rest of the United States, it seems that being close to a top-flight research university and government (in the case of the Washington, DC, area) are other success drivers.[27]

The greatest share (94%) of high-impact firms have from 1 to 19 employees. The remaining 5.5% have between 20 and 499 employees. Very few high-impact firms have more than 500 employees. High-impact firms are characterized by high productivity per employee in revenue generation and innovation as measured by patents per employee.[28] In 2008, the average age of a high-impact firm with 1 to 19 employees was 16.3 years. For firms with 10 to 499 employees, the average age was 25.9 years, while the average age for those with more than 500 employees was 37.5 years.[29]

A study of German gazelles found that they began growing immediately upon start-up. Typically they have 15 employees when they enter the growth period. Super gazelles (which grow at rates higher than 20%) start out with more employees (50) and grow faster. German gazelles are more likely to emerge in knowledge-intensive industries and to sell in international markets. Founders of gazelles are educated and have many years of experience, confirming assertions that human capital is important to business success. The average age of the business owners was between thirty and thirty-nine years. Slightly more than half of such firms had developed an innovation and operated in young, emerging, and growing markets.[30]

Most gazelle founders use their own money for start-up capital. Different from employer firms, gazelles intend to grow. Research has yet to identify consistent patterns for gazelles. A study of UK gazelles found that they tend to concentrate on a single product, are not dependent on international markets, and have marketing departments.[31] Gazelles hire more educated workers, and 11% believe that their human resource policy is the most important factor in their competitive advantage.[32]

Minority businesses face additional hurdles beyond those faced by any business. These hurdles fall into three categories: money (access to debt and equity financing), management (formal business education or prior industry management experience), and markets (limited access to potential customers). Even when holding constant for educational levels, the owner's net worth at the start of the business, and prior business experience, minority-owned firms still receive lower amounts of debt or equity financing or pay higher rates for this financing than do nonminority-owned firms. On average, minority-owned firms have lower levels of educational attainment, which is a result of higher dropout rates and lower college-attendance rates among African Americans, Hispanics, and Native Americans than among the US population as a whole. Similarly, minority-owned firms have less access to markets.

Sources of Capital

Accessing and securing sufficient capital is a key step in starting a business. The 2007 Survey of Business Owners revealed the overwhelming common source of capital for businesses to be the owner's personal savings, personal borrowing, or home equity. Women- and minority-owned businesses relied more on personal sources and less on bank loans than white male–owned businesses

(Table 4-7). Studies have documented large disparities in access to financial capital. MBEs are less likely to receive loans, or they receive loans of lower amounts, and they are more likely to be denied loans and to pay higher interest rates,[33] despite the fact that MBEs outpace the growth of white firms and garner similar returns. There is evidence that MBEs produce healthy returns equal to, if not slightly higher than, traditional investments in venture capital.[34]

SBA loans. The Small Business Administration (SBA) is charged by the federal government to enhance small business success. In 2013, the SBA made $25.5 billion in total loans, with 70% of loans in the 7(a) program, which provides general-purpose loans up to $5 million to help businesses that have difficulty obtaining loans from other sources. SBA 504 loans of more than $10 million accounted for 21% of loans used to acquire physical assets such as real estate or equipment.[35] There is some controversy about how successful these SBA programs have been. For example, following the 2007–9 recession, when credit froze for all businesses, SBA programs contracted instead of expanding and created more duress for small businesses.[36]

Additionally, it appears that the proportion of loans made to black and Hispanic businesses versus all SBA loans has decreased. The black share of SBA loans

TABLE 4-7. Source of Capital (%)

	All Firms	Female	Hispanic	Black	AIAN	Asian	NHPI
Owner personal savings	**62**	**65**	**67**	**68**	**64**	**69**	**67**
Family savings	**10**	**10**	**9**	**10**	**13**	**10**	**9**
Personal home equity loan	**8**	**10**	**10**	**10**	**9**	**11**	**13**
Personal credit card	**11**	**14**	**14**	**16**	**15**	**11**	**19**
Government loan	1	1	1	2	1	1	2
Government-guaranteed loan	2	2	1	2	3	2	2
Bank loan	19	17	14	16	18	18	17
Family/friends loan	5	5	4	4	5	6	5
Venture capital	1	0	0	1		0	
Grants	1	0	0		0	0	1
Other	4	3	3	4	4	3	5
Don't know	6	4	4	4	4	6	5
None needed	11	11	8	9	10	6	8

Source: US Census 2007 Survey of Business Owners

Note: Bold figures show that the majority of capital comes from personal sources

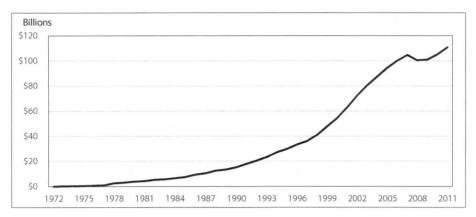

FIGURE 4-10. Corporate Diversity Purchases Slow. Source: National Minority Supplier Development Council

dropped from 4% to 2% of loans between the fiscal years 2006 and 2014, while the share of Hispanic businesses fell from 8% to 4%. Only Asian businesses, which have more access to capital, increased from 13% in 2006 to 21% in 2014 (equal to the level in 2006).

The general proportion of loans to minorities has fallen from 34% in fiscal year 2006 to 29% in 2014, despite the much larger growth rate in the number and revenues of MBEs.[37]

Federal contracting. Federal contracting dollars were $460 billion in fiscal year 2013, and small businesses accounted for 23.39% of the total. Disadvantaged businesses, which include MBEs, accounted for 8% of federal contracting dollars in 2013. Prior to 2000, an SBA program certified small and disadvantaged businesses, and these businesses could compete for federal contracts that were set aside for this group. These programs were discontinued in the mid-2000s, because the SBA found that they were not cost-effective; that is, costs outweighed benefits. Also, small businesses were not making inroads in obtaining more federal contracts. However, women-owned businesses continued to be part of the SBA's goals. In 2013, small WBEs accounted for 4% of federal contracting. Disabled veterans accounted for 3%. Historically underserved business zones accounted for 2%.[38]

Diversity programs. Despite the federal government's commitment to helping minority businesses, major increases in MBE revenues have come from the private sector, where there has been an almost sixfold increase (565%) since 1990 to $111 billion in 2011 (Figure 4-9). The Billion Dollar Roundtable is an association of twenty

large corporations that have documented first-tier (i.e., direct) purchasing of at least $1 billion from MBEs and WBEs. Collectively, these twenty corporations spend more than $64 billion with MBEs and WBEs. The National Minority Supplier Development Council, with its regional branches, advocates for large corporations to create opportunities for MBEs to compete for corporate purchasing dollars. It provides certification and forums for MBEs to improve their chances of becoming suppliers to major corporations. One of the main motivators for the corporations is fast-growing multicultural purchasing power. In recent years, the growth rate in diversity supplier dollars has also flattened.

Venture capital. Venture capital has been romanticized in the start-up stories of many Silicon Valley companies, including eBay, Google, and Facebook. Contrary to popular misconception, venture capital is a factor in only a small number of start-ups. Figure 4-11 shows that the peak of venture capital investing occurred during the late 1990s dot-com period. In 2013, approximately four thousand deals for $29.6 billion were completed, marking a $10 billion uptick since the recession.

According to the 2007 Survey of Business Owners, 1% of businesses use venture capital for financing. Among MBEs, 1% of black businesses use venture capital. Only particular kinds of businesses lend themselves to venture capital funding. Venture capital firms typically look for proprietary products and managers who are highly qualified or experienced in the industry. Ventures need to be first or second to market, and there is an urgency to scale up quickly and become the market leader. Businesses must have the potential for hundreds of mil-

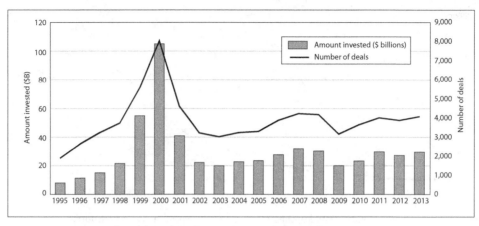

FIGURE 4-11. Venture Capital Funding. Source: PricewaterhouseCoopers/National Venture Capital Association MoneyTree Report, using data from Thomson Reuters

lions in revenues. The National Venture Capital Association estimates that 40% of venture-backed companies fail, 40% have moderate returns, and 20% or less have high returns.[39] The Cambridge Venture Capital Fund Index shows that for the ten years ending September 2013, returns were 8.58% for all venture capital, 7.63% for early stage, and 11.72% for late stage and expansion versus 7.57% for the Standard and Poors 500, a benchmark for the US market.[40] Researchers with the Kaufmann Foundation determined that venture capital investments did not outperform the stock market in the foundation's twenty-year history investing in venture capital funds.[41]

Venture capital firms also become intimately involved in the management of the enterprise, using their contacts and resources to assist the firm in getting to scale. The investment is premised on an exit strategy into an initial public offering (IPO) in about five years; therefore venture funding is highly dependent on a "hot" IPO market. The large majority of companies make public offerings without going through venture capitalists; examples include Oracle, Walmart, and Dell.

Venture capitalists expect a major "win" in only about one-quarter of their portfolio. Experienced venture capitalists typically will give a "haircut," or reduction of up to two-thirds, on financial projections. According to William Sahlman and colleagues, the most important factor for success is the people involved.[42] Venture capitalists look for individuals who have succeeded in bringing an innovative product to market. These individuals have the right experience, skills, and willpower to bring the venture to fruition. The role of the venture capitalist is to accelerate the process and profit handsomely along the way.

Regarding the distribution of venture capital financing,

CBInsights, a firm that analyzes venture capital, found that 87% of founders funded were white, 12% were Asian, and 1% were black. The small proportion of venture capital allocated to black firms is not related to the return on these firms. Research has shown that the return on minority-focused funds earned slightly higher returns than mainstream funds of the same period.[43]

Angel financing. The term angel in this usage was coined to describe wealthy investors in Broadway productions. It now refers to private individuals, typically successful entrepreneurs, who contribute their skills and money to start-up companies. Angel investors are typically hands-on people who bring industry expertise and contacts. Entrepreneurs frequently state that the value of an angel's expertise often exceeds the money put into the company.

The University of New Hampshire's Center for Venture Research estimates that about 298,800 angel investors put $24.8 billion into 70,730 ventures in 2013 (Figure 4-12). Like venture capital, active angel investors peaked in 2000 at 400,000. Since 2002, software has topped the list of sectors. Recently interest in social media has put media in second place. Health care, biotech, retail, and financial services round out the list of the top seven sectors. Individual investments by angels average just over $80,000. In 2013, angels increased their investments in the seed and start-up stage to 45%. In the same year the typical yield rate, or the percent of proposals accepted, was 21.6%, which is down from a peak of 23% in 2005. The Center for Venture Research estimates that the yield rate will revert to the historical average of 15%.

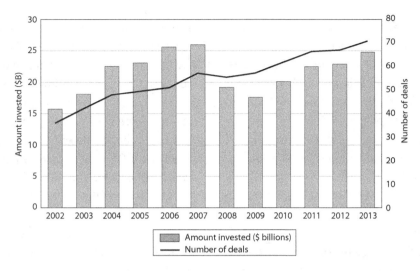

FIGURE 4-12. Angel Financing. Source: University of New Hampshire, Center for Venture Research

In 2013, 19.4% of angels were women. Women-owned ventures accounted for 23% of the entrepreneurs looking for angel capital, and 19% received angel investment in 2013, down from 25% in 2012. Minority angels were 4% of the angel population, and minority-owned firms represented 7% of the entrepreneurs seeking funding. The yield rate for these minority-owned firms was 13%.[44] Venture forums and personal networks are the most common types of organization for angels, providing evidence of the importance of personal connections, which are not typically available to MBEs. The small proportion of MBEs seeking angel capital continues to be a concern in the marketplace, given the market yields on angel investments in these businesses.

Crowdfunding. Started only in 2008, crowdfunding is a means for organizations and individuals to raise money for for-profit, cultural, or social projects by using platforms that allow them to market or promote their project to people who might contribute. A report prepared for the World Bank claims that crowdfunding is an innovation that can fuel "the rise of the rest" globally. Crowdfunding has been used successfully for donating to causes and projects as well as for investing. The World Bank report advocates its use for microfinance and microloans, for seeding start-ups, and for bridging the gap between start-up and the use of angel investors and venture capital in developed and emerging economies. The report estimates the total worldwide potential of crowdfunding to be $93 billion.[45]

One of the most successful examples of crowdfunding is Kickstarter. Since its founding, the Kickstarter platform (kickstarter.com) has raised close to $1.2 billion for about 65,000 projects from 6.5 million contributors. More than $100 million was raised in 2013 in each of the following categories: $225 million for games, $187 million for film or video projects, $150 million for design, $140 million for technology, and $105 million for music projects. In 2013, Kickstarter raised more money for art projects than the $140 million funded by the National Endowment of the Arts.[46] Indiegogo and Rockethub are two other crowdfunding platforms that have raised hundreds of millions of dollars. This success has sparked a movement for crowdfunding businesses, particularly businesses in the start-up phase where risk is highest.

In 2010, the Jumpstart Our Business Startups (JOB) Act was signed into law. Prior to this act, only accredited investors—those who have a net worth of more than $1 million or income exceeding $200,000 in each of the last two years—were allowed to invest in private equity. Per Title III of the act, individuals will be allowed to invest $2,000 or 5 percent of their annual income or net worth, whichever is greater.

Crowdfunding holds some promise for underserved businesses in the United States because of its roots in raising money for social causes. But because people who live in lower-income communities may not have the social capital to secure sufficient funding from crowdsourcing, new networks are emerging that create a marketplace to match lower-income entrepreneurs with investors who may also be their customers. There is concern that individuals who fund these projects may be subject to fraud or that ventures who seek funding in this fashion may fail to deliver. Preliminary research is promising, showing that less than 5% of projects funded are clearly fraudulent. Regarding completion, a review of design and technology projects on Kickstarter in 2012 showed that 24% of projects were delivered on time, 51% were delayed (with a mean delay of 2.4 months), and 33% were yet to deliver. Similar results were found in the film, food, and theater category.[47]

The Australian Small Scale Offerings Board is the largest equity crowdfunding platform, having raised $138 million since inception, with an average equity raised of about $500,000. Fees for using the platform are approximately $5,000, with a 1.5% success fee and other advisory fees that average $5,000. No evaluation has been done on the platform's impact on small and medium enterprise capital access nor return to investors. The UK-based Funding Circle has completed financing totaling over £156 million (about US$250 million), receiving an annualized return of 5.8 percent, with a 1.6 percent default rate.

Successful crowdfunding has similarities to raising capital in traditional environments. It is important to signal preparedness and quality. A smaller goal size increases the chances of achieving the goal. A large network enhances funding and endorsements that could lead to funding. Crowdfunding differs from traditional funding in that the entrepreneur will take advantage of video to communicate and social media to contact networks, which are predominantly personal networks. It is estimated that friends and family contribute $139 billion to business ventures.[48]

Similar to venture capital, crowdfunding success seems to be geographically determined, with the nature of the projects and their appeal related to the cultural geography of where projects are located.[49]

Microfinancing. Microfinance is a movement that is growing at 30% annually. It began with informal saving and credit systems in which group savings were used to finance small loan requests. In the 1970s it spread to Bolivia, Brazil, and Bangladesh and evolved in some models to being a principle economic development tool among very poor people in developing countries. Women were given small loans to start businesses that would sustain their families. The most replicated model is Grameen Bank in Bangladesh, where there are twenty-four million borrowers with $1.75 billion in loans. The average loan is $80.[50] Some microfinancing is provided by nonprofits, but as the movement has grown, more for-profit players have entered the market.

Microfinance in the United States began with the Economic Opportunity Act of 1964, which stipulated that Small Business Administration loans would be extended to people in poverty. While default rates were high (62.9% between 1967 and 1970), the program continued into 1984. Other nongovernmental programs started in the 1970s and 1980s. During the early years of microfinance in the United States, and continuing to today, expenses often exceeded return. Investments have been mainly in retail and services, such as restaurants, groceries, laundries, and taxis. Analysis has shown that performing loans have consistently been those disbursed to business owners who are not disadvantaged. For the truly disadvantaged, there have been low loan volume, high administrative costs (sometimes $4 in administrative cost for each $1 loaned), and high default rates.[51]

The Aspen Institute conducted a study of microenterprise development organizations and found that in 2011 microlenders sought to build their clients' credit scores by reporting their performance to credit bureaus; microlenders also offered services such as training and technical assistance to help business owners stabilize and grow their businesses. Microloans of up to $35,000 were the primary product offered: 97% of loans offered technical assistance, 60% offered training, 44% mentoring, 44% financial literacy, and 33% credit counseling.[52]

AFRICAN AMERICAN BUSINESSES

According to the 2007 Survey of Business Owners, African American firms totaled 1.9 million (double the 1997 total), or 7.1% of US firms. This was an increase of 61% in the number of firms and 53% in firm revenues over 2002, accelerating growth rates of 45% for the previous five years. Black firms employed 921,032 people and generated $137.5 billion in business revenues. Of these, 96% were nonemployer firms compared to 79% for white firms. Black firms show evidence of increasing critical mass for enterprise success as a greater proportion of African American college degree holders are starting businesses.

Geographics. In 2007, New York topped the states with the most black-owned firms (10.6% of all firms), followed by Georgia (9.6% of all firms), and Florida (9.4% of all firms). Higher concentrations of African American businesses as a percentage of all businesses are found along

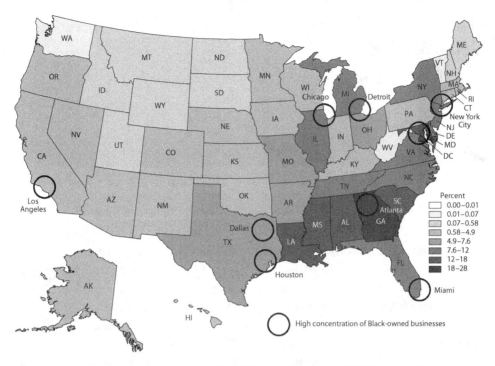

FIGURE 4-13. Black-Owned Firms by State, 2007. Source: US Census 2007 Survey of Business Owners

the East Coast, consistent with where the African American population is concentrated. The top metropolitan areas for black firms were New York City, Atlanta, Chicago, Miami, Washington, DC, Los Angeles, Houston, Dallas, and Detroit (Figure 4-13). Black businesses are more likely to locate in urban areas and have not moved to suburban environments like mainstream businesses have. *Inc. Magazine* maintains its own annual list of five thousand fast-growing companies (the Inc. 5000).[53] Of these, in 2013 eighty-two (2%) were African American firms. The bulk of these fast-growing black firms were located in the New York City to Washington, DC, corridor and Georgia. In some metropolitan areas the support system for black entrepreneurs may be stronger than in others.

Sectors. Note that in discussing sectors, the 2007 Survey of Business Owners (SBO) uses codes from the North American Industry Classification System (NAICS). Interested readers can look up these codes to get detailed descriptions of industries. According to the SBO, the number one industry for African American business owners was health and social assistance (36% of all black firms compared to 15% for all US businesses). Repair, maintenance, personal, and laundry

services were the next most common industries. Of all US firms in transportation and warehousing, 13.4% were black firms.

Black Enterprise, the business publication for black-owned businesses, ranks the largest black-owned firms every year in its BE 100 list. In 2014, auto dealerships remained the largest on the BE 100, as measured by total revenues, with technology second (Figure 4-14).

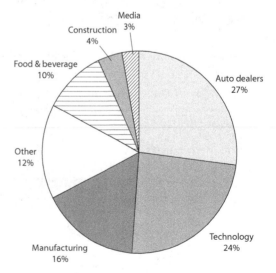

FIGURE 4-14. Black Enterprise 100 by Industry, 2014. Source: *Black Enterprise*

Retail Lockbox

An African American High-Impact Firm Reveals Factors in Its Success

Each day thousands of people submit payments for county taxes, medical bills, or credit card bills. Craig Dawson, co-founder and CEO of Retail Lockbox, makes it a priority to ensure that these payments are processed quickly and accurately.

Dawson began his career selling mainframe computer systems. During this time he saw a market opportunity for payment and remittance processing. In 1994, Dawson and co-founder Walt Townes launched Retail Lockbox Inc. Within the first thirty days, and with equipment still sitting on the floor, Dawson was awarded a city contract to process utility payments. The business grew to processing 100,000 payments in just six months.

Today, Retail Lockbox is the premier independent remittance processing, document imaging, and online payment processing company in the Pacific Northwest. It is entrusted with several billion client payment receivables each year as well as sixty million document images. Retail Lockbox has created unique and sophisticated processing services that save its clients valuable time, resources, and expenses associated with in-house processing.

Dawson believes in the importance of a strong brand identity. What do his customers associate with the brand Retail Lockbox? Outstanding quality, efficiency, and speed. The term *lockbox* originated in the 1940s. Retail stores provided "locked boxes," located on the wall, for customers to leave payments for bills. Today *lockbox* is a standard term for a secure payment portal.

Dawson describes two keys to the firm's success: delegation and quality control. Many small business owners may excel at one particular skill but may not be experts in every skill needed to successfully manage operations. He believes it is important to leverage the individual strengths in the organization. Dawson recruits, hires, and develops the brightest people. Quality is also an important ingredient in success. Dawson is fanatical about quality control while running a lean organization. His error rate is about 1 in 250,000 items processed.

After five years of courting a major health care provider, his persistence paid off. And it paid off for the client as well. The client's data were consolidated into a more efficient digital format, providing easy payment inquiry and research capabilities and reducing the need for multiple file cabinets and storage space. Dawson and his team succeeded in reducing the client's transaction costs, with a monthly savings of $50,000.

Retail Lockbox has reached more than $6.5 million in annual sales and continues to grow. Dawson predicts that the biggest growth will come from online merchant services, potentially doubling his business in the years to come.

Dynamics. Traditionally, black businesses developed in response to segregation. African Americans were segregated into specific neighborhoods and thus their goods and services needs were met by the African American-owned businesses in these neighborhoods. Sometimes described as ethnic or enclave economies, black businesses also provided employment for members of their own community who were unable to secure employment in white firms. As reduction in segregation occurred and gentrification of black areas proceeded in the 1980s, traditional black businesses suffered.[54] While national numbers are important, unique concentrations of business ownership in some geographic areas have emerged. A thirty-year longitudinal study of the largest black firms showed that those that competed in the business-to-business and business-to-government markets were more successful than those that competed in the business-to-consumer (B2C) market. Some industries, such as the auto industry, have recognized that by engaging with minority vendors they can also grow market share in a growing population demographic. Many of the most successful black firms have chosen to be acquired by mainstream companies.[55]

Regarding the clustering of black firms, the metropolitan Atlanta area provides the best example. Atlanta leads the nation for black business formation and has the highest density of black firms per capita. A study of small black-owned firms found that Atlanta also has a higher proportion of black gazelles than the nonminority gazelle concentration in California and Massachusetts. Government contracting opportunities, strong corporate diversity programs, population growth, a large black middle class, and in-migration of black business owners account for Atlanta's high black business formation rate. Of thirty-nine variables studied, four factors were associated with high growth: (1) the proportion of government contracting increased; (2) the company competed nationally or internationally; (3) the owner entered the business voluntarily, not because of job loss; and (4) the company did not engage in price competition.[56]

Other studies corroborate the benefit of commitments by government to foster competition that allows for diverse competition. Specifically, the African American community programs that promote a level playing field for competition have resulted in increased black male self-employment immediately after program implementation and a narrowing of the black-white employment-to-population gap by 3% during the first five years of the program. A reduction in the black-white gap persists even after the programs are well established.[57]

HISPANIC BUSINESSES

According to the 2007 Survey of Business Owners, Hispanic Americans owned 2.3 million businesses, or 8.3% of all US businesses, double the 1997 total and 43% more than in 2002. They employed 1.6 million people in 2007, with $226 billion in revenues. Employer firms numbered 77,222 and employed 496,870 people.

As with Asian American business owners, the country of origin of Hispanic business owners are disparate (Table 4-8). Mexicans and Cubans constitute the largest number of business owners. The number of Cuban businesses grew at the highest rate (65.5%) between 2002 and 2007, while Mexican business receipts grew the fastest (60%). On average, business owner education

TABLE 4-8. Hispanic Firms by Ethnicity

Ethnicity	Number of Firms, 2007	Percent of Hispanic Firms (%)	Number of Firms, 2002	Percent Change, 2002-7 (%)	Receipts, 2007 ($1,000)	Percent of Hispanic Firms (%)	Receipts 2002 ($1,000)	Percent Change, 2002-7 (%)
All Hispanic	2,260,309		1,573,464	44	345,183,070		221,927,425	56
Mexican (58.5% of Hispanics)	1,035,748	46%	701,078	48	155,534,140	45	96,735,081	61
Puerto Rican (9.6%)	156,546	7%	109,475	43	16,677,962	5	12,340,353	35
Cuban (3.5%)	251,070	11%	151,688	66	51,252,555	15	35,443,349	45
Other Hispanic (28.4%)	778,757	34%	596,125	31	113,892,563	33	74,219,213	54

Source: US Census 2007 Survey of Business Owners

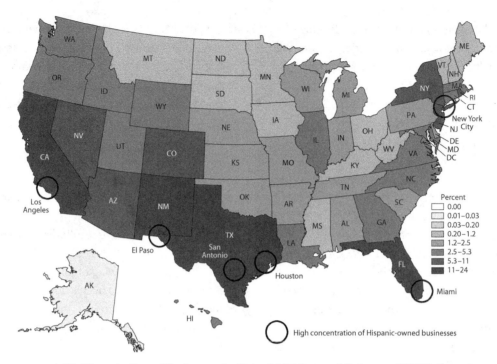

FIGURE 4-15. Hispanic-Owned Businesses by State, 2007. Source: US Census 2007 Survey of Business Owners

levels are lower than for non-Hispanic whites, with one-third fewer bachelor's degrees and one-fifth fewer master's or doctoral degrees. Cuban immigrants, who came to America with more endowment in terms of education and wealth, have the highest revenues per firm.

Geographics. California (36% of Mexican firms), Florida (74.5% of Cuban businesses), Texas (34% of Mexican businesses), and New York (22% of Puerto Rican businesses) all reported more than 100,000 Hispanic businesses in 2007 (Figure 4-15). The highest concentrations were in New Mexico, Texas, and Florida. New York City had the largest number of Hispanic businesses. The Miami metro area ranked second, with Los Angeles following. Houston was home to a cluster of Hispanic businesses, while San Antonio and El Paso had a large proportion. Inc. Magazine counted 158 Hispanic businesses, or 3%, among its fastest-growing businesses in its 2013 Inc. 5000 list. The bulk of these businesses were in Florida and California.

Sectors. Note that in discussing sectors, the 2007 Survey of Business Owners (SBO) uses codes from the North American Industry Classification System (NAICS). Interested readers can look up these codes to get detailed descriptions of industries. According to the SBO, the most prevalent industries for Hispanic-owned businesses are construction and repair, maintenance, and personal and laundry services, which together account for 10.4% of all firms in these sectors. Like in all immigrant groups, there is variability in the types of businesses that are started. For example, Puerto Rican firms are more highly concentrated in health care and social assistance than in the general Hispanic business sector. By industry, the 2014 Hispanic Business 100 showed a concentration in automotive, services, wholesale, and construction services, all of which also showed the highest growth rates from 2012 to 2013. However, technology and manufacturing constitute the third and fifth largest sectors, respectively. Of the 2014 Hispanic Business 100, 53 companies had revenues of more than $100 million. Figure 4-16 shows wholesale and construction as the largest sectors and Figure 4-17 shows the highest growth rates in automotive and construction.

Dynamics. With Hispanic firms, language, education, and access to capital are characteristics that frequently limit operations and growth. At the same time, Spanish-speaking Hispanic firms have an advantage in serving a fast-growing market. According to the 2007 Survey of Business Owners, more than one million businesses, with $6.3 billion in revenues, spoke Spanish to their custom-

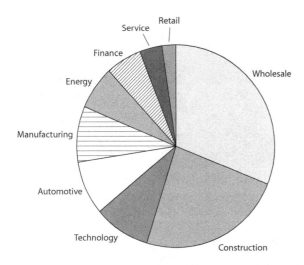

FIGURE 4-16. Hispanic Business 100 by Sector, 2014. Source: *Hispanic Business*

ers. Of these, 447,065 were employer firms, with $6.2 billion in revenue.

Very little study has been done on Hispanic businesses and, as more research is conducted, it can be anticipated that differences will exist depending on country of origin. Unlike immigrants from Asia or other parts of the world who start businesses at a higher rate than US natives, many Hispanic immigrants come with lower levels of educational attainment than Asian immigrant groups. Thus, although Hispanic immigrants start more businesses than Asian immigrant groups, the firms tend to be smaller in revenue and employee size. Education, wealth, and legal status have been found to explain the low formation rates for businesses and lower income levels for Mexican Americans.[58]

A study commissioned by the Hispanic Chamber of Commerce shows that Hispanic businesses grew at an annual rate of 6.6% from 2007 to 2013, which is twice the rate of all businesses. The study estimates that 29% of Hispanic business owners earn more than $100,000, twice the proportion of the overall US Hispanic population.[59]

ASIAN BUSINESSES

According to the 2007 Survey of Business Owners, Asians owned approximately 1.5 million businesses, or 5.7% of all firms, a growth of 40% over 2002. Asian firms employed 2.8 million people and generated $507.6 billion in revenues. Asian Indian, Chinese, Japanese, and Korean firms showed a greater percentage of employer firms than other Asian businesses. Chinese, Vietnamese, and other Asian groups showed the highest rate of growth in numbers, while Vietnamese, other Asian, and Asian Indian groups showed the highest growth in revenues (Table 4-9).

Geographics. In 2007, California had the most Asian businesses (33% of all Asian firms), with over half a million firms accounting for 15% of all firms in the state (Figure 4-18). New York and Texas are second and third in the number of Asian businesses. High concentrations of Asian firms are found in the metropolitan areas around

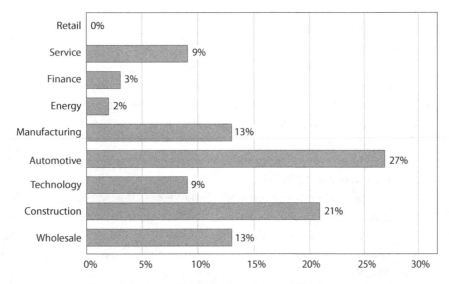

FIGURE 4-17. Hispanic Business 100 Growth by Sector, 2014. Source: *Hispanic Business*

TABLE 4-9. Asian Firms by Ethnicity

Ethnicity	2007 (number)	% Asian	2002 (number)	% Change 2002-7	2007 Receipts ($000,000)	% Asian	2002 Receipts ($000,000)	% Change 2002-7	2007 Employer firms (number)	2002 Employer firms (number)	% Change 2002-7
Asian	1,549,664		1,103,587	40	507,641		326,663	55	397,484	319,468	24
Asian Indian	308,514	20	223,212	38	152,468	30	88,128	73	109,196	82,422	33
Chinese	423,609	27	286,041	48	142,752	28	105,051	36	109,614	89,049	2
Filipino	163,217	11	125,146	30	20,217	4	14,155	43	21,071	19,888	6
Japanese	108,361	7	86,910	25	39,572	8	30,623	29	22,823	22,166	3
Korean	192,465	12	157,688	22	78,633	15	46,960	67	71,423	57,078	25
Vietnamese	229,149	15	147,036	56	28,800	6	15,512	86	29,782	25,591	16
Other Asian	153,565	10	89,118	72	45,142	9	24,275	86	37,367	24,835	51

Source: US Census 2007 Survey of Business

Los Angeles, San Francisco, and New York. Hawaii is the state with the largest concentration of Asian firms (47% of all firms in Hawaii).

Inc. Magazine counted 320 South Asian companies, or 6.4% of the Inc. 5000, its 2014 list of the fastest-growing companies; 125 firms (2.5% of the Inc. 5000) were East Asian business owners.[60]

Sectors. Note that in discussing sectors, the 2007 Survey of Business Owners (SBO) uses codes from the North American Industry Classification System (NAICS). Interested readers can look up these codes to get detailed descriptions of industries. According to the SBO, the top industries for Asian firms were repair, maintenance, personal and laundry services (45%), professional, scientific and technical services, and retail trade. Asian firms differ based on the owner's country of origin and endowment in terms of education and wealth. Of the highly educated Asian Indians, 49% of their firms were in professional, scientific, and technical services; retail; and health and social assistance. For Chinese firms, 40% were in professional, scientific, and technical services; accommodation and food services; and repair, maintenance, and personal and laundry services. Korean firms were concentrated in professional, scientific, and technical services and retail trade (40%). Vietnamese firms were concentrated in repair, maintenance, and personal and laundry services and retail trade (67%). Restaurants have a strong showing: According to Chinese Restaurant News, as of 2009 there were 43,000 Chinese restaurants in the United States—more than the number of McDonald's, Wendy's, and Burger Kings combined. As of 2014, there were about 7,000 Japanese, 5,000 Thai, 1,500 Vietnamese,

and 1,000 Korean restaurants listed in Manta's online directory (www.manta.com). While national numbers are important, unique concentrations of business ownership exist in some geographic areas. Of independent donut shops in Los Angeles, Cambodians operated as many as 80% of them.[61] Indians own half the motels in the United States; most of these owners come from the same part of India and 70% have the last name Patel.[62]

Dynamics. As of 2012, authorized Asian immigrants numbered about thirteen million, 88% of whom arrived after 1970, reflecting the easing of immigration laws and the H1B visa program used by large US corporations to attract high-skilled workers. The category Asian includes more than thirty-six countries, with the largest numbers of immigrants coming from China, India, Korea, the Philippines, and Vietnam. Among these immigrants are entrepreneurs who owned and managed successful businesses in their home countries. These individuals are able to start up businesses with their own capital and are successful in bringing the businesses to scale. However, many of these entrepreneurs meet barriers in breaking out of their ethnic communities. Barriers include language and understanding US marketing. Many of these owners have only recently emigrated from countries where cultural norms and business practices vary significantly from those in the United States.

There are marked differences in the size and number of Asian firms. Chinese American firms have the largest number and highest combined sales, while Vietnamese firms are the smallest. On average, Vietnamese business owners have the lowest education attainment, Japanese American business owners tend to draw the fewest num-

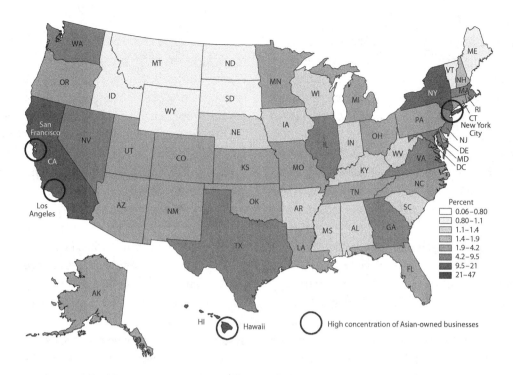

Percent	
	0.06–0.80
	0.80–1.1
	1.1–1.4
	1.4–1.9
	1.9–4.2
	4.2–9.5
	9.5–21
	21–47

High concentration of Asian-owned businesses

FIGURE 4-18. Asian-Owned Businesses by State, 2007. Source: US Census 2007 Survey of Business Owners

ber of customers from their own ethnic market, and Korean American and Vietnamese American business owners draw a large proportion from their co-ethnic markets.

In general, Asian businesses have performed better than white businesses. They have higher sales and profits and are more likely to hire employees and survive. Much of their success can be explained by the owners' education levels (a larger proportion of Asians have bachelor's and graduate degrees) and start-up capital (Asians are twice as likely to have over $100,000 in start-up capital).[63]

Immigrant entrepreneurs have attracted recent interest because immigrants are more likely to start businesses (25% of new businesses in the period 2007–11),[64] and immigrants have been at the helm of some high-profile start-ups, including Yahoo and Google. For earlier immigrants, business location was dependent on available recent immigrants as a source of customers and employees. Many of these businesses were restaurants or Asian supermarkets that served their own markets and hired recent immigrants, who might be unable to find work elsewhere because of limited education or language skills.

The impact of immigrant entrepreneurs is more prominent in technology companies. A 1999 study by AnnaLee Saxenian found that Asian immigrants were at the helm of 24% of technology companies started from 1980 to 1998 in Silicon Valley. The Asian share rose to 43.9% between 2006 and 2012. The proportion of Chinese or

Indian founders increased to 28% from 1999. Indians founded 15.5% of Silicon Valley start-ups, and Chinese immigrants (from both China and Taiwan) were key founders in 12.8% of start-ups. In 2013, the study estimated that 20% of the high-tech workforce and 17.3 percent of high-tech entrepreneurs were immigrants.[65]

This study also found that 25.3% of engineering and technology companies in the United States had at least one key founder who was foreign-born; Asian Indians were the largest proportion (26%). Almost 80% of immigrant-founded companies were in software and innovation/manufacturing services. The study estimated that foreign nationals were named as inventors or co-inventors of 24.2% of international patent applications filed in the United States in 2006, and the largest group was Chinese. In 2006, 16.8% of international patent applications from the United States had a Chinese-heritage name. Indian-heritage names constituted 14% of patent applications in the same year.[66]

One might assume that newer and more educated immigrants would not be constrained to ethnic enclaves as earlier immigrants were. However, research has shown that immigrant high-tech businesses are more likely to be located in metropolitan areas where there are a larger ethnic population and more ethnic diversity. These are the areas considered to be open, tolerant, and innovative.[67]

These immigrants are highly educated, with 47%

having a master's degree and 27% having a doctoral degree, with an emphasis on science and engineering. Most of the high-tech immigrants came to the United States to study and stayed to work; or they came through the H1B visa program that US technology companies use to attract high-skilled tech workers from around the world. However, in recent years there has been a reverse brain drain, with many of these highly skilled workers returning to India and China to start companies. Estimates of these returning entrepreneurs are in the tens of thousands. They cite better economic opportunities, access to local markets, and family ties as important considerations for their return. Many (72% of Indians and 81% of Chinese) believed there were better opportunities in their home countries, and they took pride in contributing to their countries' economic development.[68] These entrepreneurs continue to maintain ties with the United States, and there is speculation that "brain circulation from Asia to the United States" is a better description of this phenomenon.

AMERICAN INDIAN AND ALASKA NATIVE BUSINESSES

According to the 2007 Survey of Business Owners, American Indians and Alaska Natives (AIAN) owned 236,967 businesses, an 18% increase from 2002. They generated $34.4 billion in revenues and employed 184,416 people. These figures do not include tribally owned enterprises in energy, mining, wood products, gaming, hospitality, and entertainment.

Geographics. Non–tribally owned Native businesses are concentrated in California, Texas, Oklahoma, and Florida (Figure 4-19). The highest concentration is in Alaska, where they constitute 11% of all businesses. With regard to metropolitan areas, Los Angeles ranks the highest, followed by Tulsa, Oklahoma. Native businesses tend to be in construction, services (amusement, business, and engineering/management), and retail (auto dealers/service stations).

Sectors. According to the 2007 Survey of Business Owners, about 30% of AIAN firms were in construction and repair, maintenance, and personal and laundry services. AIAN business owners had lower educational attainment and less start-up capital (typically less than $5,000) than their non-Hispanic white counterparts. AIAN businesses also tended to be younger than non-Hispanic white firms.

Dynamics. US policies and actions have led to severe economic deprivation for many tribes. It was not until the past twenty-five years that tribes began to make much progress in restoring self-governance in the face of US government resistance. This progress has enabled tribes to relaunch economies that had been destroyed by federal government mismanagement of tribal assets.[69]

Even as Indian Country has made amazing advances in economic development, each tribe must also deal with a host of challenges inherent in nation building. Although some tribes can adopt the constitutional model of the US government, many other tribes find this structure inconsistent with their traditional ways of governing. Additionally, economic development and thriving enterprises are dependent on a fair system of dispute resolution. Along with the reestablishment of viable governance and court systems, tribes are taking over the health, education, and social service programs that had previously been controlled by the US government and that are now being funded by a combination of federal dollars and profits from tribal enterprises.

The Harvard Project on American Indian Economic Development states that it is easier to understand the economic development of American Indian tribes by comparing them to the communist economies of Eastern Europe and the former Soviet Union. Indian tribes are recovering from a century of a command-control economy imposed by the US government. On top of this, the US government used economic development, job creation, and poverty relief as incentives for assimilation, with the rationale that American Indians needed to learn white ways in order to be economically successful. Besides having a false premise, these policies have nurtured a culture of dependency that has distorted economic incentives.

American Indian reservations cover 55 million acres of land. Native villages and corporations account for an additional 44 million acres in Alaska. Excluding Alaska, this land contains 5,770 lakes; 765,706 acres of developed oil, gas, and mineral resources; 30% of the US coal reserve; 40% of US uranium deposits; and 4% of US oil and natural gas deposits.[70] Economic utilization of these natural resources varies among tribes and is sometimes dependent on culture and values. Even when tribes want to capitalize on their natural resources, it can take years to secure sufficient capital so that tribes can fully control how resources are extracted and utilized to maximize value for tribal members. Additionally, for any company seeking to profit in commodity markets, there are chal-

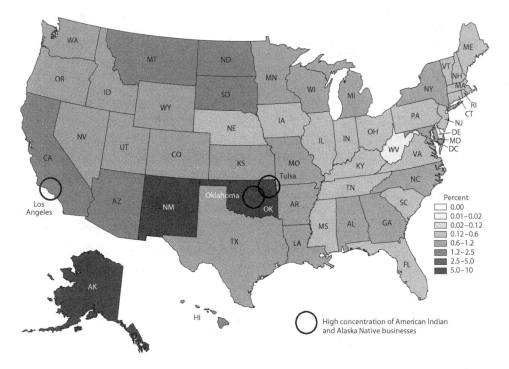

FIGURE 4-19. American Indian– and Alaska Native–Owned Firms by State, 2007. Source: US Census 2007 Survey of Business Owners

lenges in ensuring long-term profitability, making the timing of investments a challenge.

Tribal gaming has been a major factor in uplifting economic conditions in a few of the more than five hundred tribes. Gaming is a relatively new phenomenon that started in the 1970s with tribes using bingo games to raise funds to support local government services. This coincided with efforts by several states to develop gaming to generate state revenues. Conflicts continue to occur between tribal and state governments over whether tribes can conduct gaming independent of state regulations. The 1987 Supreme Court ruling in *California v.*

Cabazon Band of Mission Indians confirmed the authority of tribal governments to do so. Subsequently, Congress grappled with the issue and passed the Indian Gaming Regulation Act of 1988, which was a compromise between state and tribal gaming interests. Tribal gaming has grown tremendously since the early 1990s, and growth stabilized in 2009 (Figure 4-20).

When looking at data about American Indian and Alaska Native businesses, it is important to recognize that data for tribally owned enterprises are excluded. This is due to the sovereign status that tribal enterprises have. Many factors, ranging from access to markets and start-

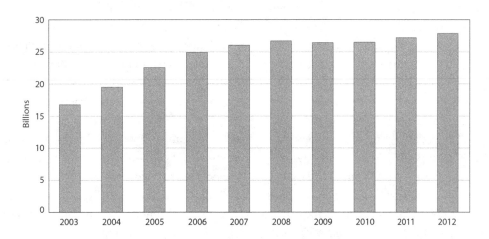

FIGURE 4-20. Tribal Gaming Revenues. Source: National Tribal Gaming Commission

up capital to legal structures, influence the ease with which individual American Indians can start businesses on reservations. Tribes that have developed environments that are conducive to business start-ups (reduced bureaucracy, technical support, etc.) have been successful.

In 2013, 240 American Indian tribes (just 42% of federally recognized tribes) operated 449 gaming operations, which accounted for $28 billion in gaming revenues. Revenues of tribal gaming must be used to fund the tribal government, provide for the welfare of the tribe, promote economic development, donate to charitable organizations, or fund operations of local government agencies. A study of the impact of casinos found a 7.4% increase in per capita income and reductions in child poverty rates.[71]

Although perceptions might be otherwise, only a few gaming operations generate high revenues. Seventy-eight of the 449 gaming operations generate over $100 million in revenues, because these enterprises have the advantage of being located near heavily populated areas.

Evidence is clear that gaming has had a beneficial effect, not just on the income of reservations but also on other social factors. According to a ten-year review of data conducted at the Harvard Project on American Indian Economic Development, in all but two categories, gaming reservations showed a remarkable improvement over nongaming reservations.[72]

WOMEN-OWNED BUSINESS ENTERPRISES

According to the 2007 Survey of Business Owners, women accounted for 28.7% of businesses in the United States. They owned 7.8 million businesses, employed 7.6 million individuals, and generated $1.2 trillion in revenues. There is evidence that women-owned firms fared better in retaining employees during the 2007–9 recession. Despite their presence, women-owned business enterprises (WBEs) do not match the proportion of women in the general population.

Geographics. In 2007, California had the largest number of WBEs (13% of all WBEs in the country), followed by Texas (7.8%), and New York (7.6%). Of US counties, Los Angeles, Cook (Chicago area), and Miami-Dade have the largest number of firms. New York City, Los Angeles, and Chicago were the cities that ranked the highest in the number of WBEs (Figure 4-21). *Inc. Magazine*'s 2013 list of the 5,000 fastest-growing companies included 12% that

were women-owned. California and the New York City to Washington, DC, corridor had the largest number of fastest-growing women-owned businesses.

Sectors. Similar to MBEs, WBEs are concentrated in low-capital, low-barrier-to-entry sectors. In 2007, women-owned businesses made up more than half (52%) of all businesses in health care and social assistance. Other top industries for women include educational services (45.9% of all such businesses are women-owned); administration and support; waste management; remediation services (37%); retail trade (34.4%); and arts, entertainment, and recreation (34%). WBEs are more likely to be home-based and less likely to have partners than are businesses as a whole in the United States.

Dynamics. With regard to entrepreneurial human capital, an SBA study shows that there are minimal differences between male and female business owners in education, experience, and preparedness. As more women enroll in college and obtain bachelor's degrees than men, it is expected that gaps in education will narrow and thus will contribute even less to the differences between male and female business owners. Managerial experience contributes to entrepreneurial success, and a lower percentage of women hold managerial positions. Previous entrepreneurial experience, especially with a family business and particularly with a mother who was an entrepreneur, can affect the probability of success. Women typically have less previous experience with entrepreneurship.[73] Studies of gazelles show that about 12% are women-owned, which is consistent with the proportion of all businesses owned by women.[74] However, the larger the business, the less likely it is woman-owned. About 4% of businesses with more than five hundred employees are women-owned. Women-owned gazelles succeeded at the same rates as male-owned gazelles.

Women-owned firms start with less capital, and a higher percentage of women owners have low credit scores.[75] On average, it takes women four attempts to obtain debt capital and twenty-two attempts to obtain equity capital.[76] Only 8% of active angel investors are women, and women angel investors are more likely to support women than are men.[77] Women owners in high-tech firms are much less likely to use external equity, and this may affect their firms' ability to grow as quickly as high-tech firms owned by men.[78]

The 2014 State of Women-Owned Business Report, a

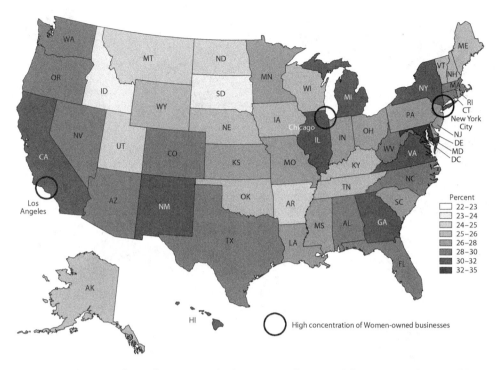

FIGURE 4-21. Women-Owned Businesses by State, 2007. Source: US Census 2007 Survey of Business Owners

study commissioned by American Express, estimates there to be 9.1 million women-owned businesses, or 30% of all US businesses, with $1.4 trillion in revenues and 7.9 million employed.[79] This study pays particular attention to businesses owned by women of color, which grew from 1 million in 1997 to 2.9 million in 2014, a 216% increase compared to 68% for all women-owned firms. Businesses owned by women of color are smaller than businesses owned by all women, and they employ on average 0.5 employee in addition to the owner. The study estimates that women of color own one in three women-owned businesses; the study further estimates that their firms grew employment 85% (versus 10% for all women-owned firms) and grew revenues 168% (versus 63%). The study also finds that black women owners account for 49% of all black firms and 28% of revenues; Asian, 35% of Asian firms and 28% of revenues; Hispanic, 36% of Hispanic firms and 16% of revenues; Native American, 45% of Native American firms and 28% of revenues; and Native Hawaiian and Pacific Islander, 41% of Native Hawaiian and Pacific Islander firms and 25% of revenues.

VETERAN-OWNED BUSINESSES

In 2010, 20.2 million men and 1.8 million women were veterans or individuals who served in the US military.

Veterans who served in Korea or Vietnam number 11 million, and those who served in the Gulf Wars from 1990 onward number 5.9 million. A million veterans were unemployed as of the end of 2011, and another million are expected to leave military service by 2016. For veterans in their early twenties, 27% were unemployed in 2011. The US Bureau of Labor Statistics claims that unemployment rates are consistent with those of the general population, with the exception of disabled veterans. About one-third of younger veterans are employed in the public sector.[80]

According to the 2007 Survey of Business Owners, veterans of the US military owned 2.4 million businesses, which accounted for 9% of all businesses. Employer firms (20%) were a larger proportion than employer firms among all US firms; they employed 5.8 million people and generated $1.2 trillion in revenues. A larger proportion of veteran firms were started prior to 1980, suggesting that more recent and younger veterans are less likely to start new firms. With regard to education, veteran business owners are more likely to have some college or advanced degrees than nonveteran white business owners. The distribution of revenues is similar to that among all US firms.

Geographics. In 2007, California had the highest proportion of veteran firms (9% of all veteran-owned firms), followed by Texas and Florida. Los Angeles County had

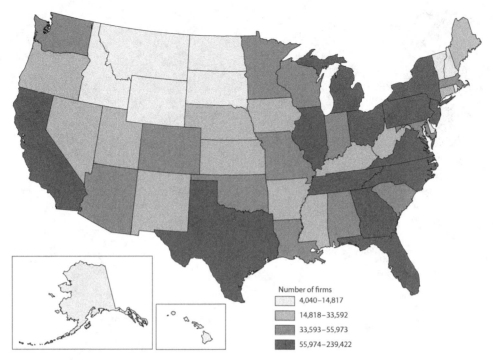

Number of firms
	4,040–14,817
	14,818–33,592
	33,593–55,973
	55,974–239,422

FIGURE 4-22. Veteran-Owned Businesses by State, 2007. Source: US Census 2007
Survey of Business Owners

the largest number among all US counties. Among cities, New York, Los Angeles, and Houston had the largest number of veteran-owned firms (Figure 4-22).

Sectors. In 2007, veterans owned 9% of all US businesses, with the following industries having the highest concentration: finance and insurance (13.2%); transportation and warehousing (12.7%); mining, quarrying, oil, and gas (12.4%); construction (11.1%); professional, scientific, and technical services (10.9%); and manufacturing (10.5%). Veteran-owned firms accounted for 4% of all sales but 9.2% of construction sales.

Dynamics. Veterans have a higher propensity for self-employment than other groups. However, veterans follow the patterns of other groups in that officers, who have bachelor's degrees or higher, are more likely to start businesses. It does not appear that anything inherent in military training, education, or culture predisposes a veteran to start a business. Length of service, age, and membership in the Marine Corps are positively correlated with self-employment.[81] Veteran-owned firms are overwhelmingly male (95%) and white (90%). Veteran businesses are more likely to have one owner (79%) than all US firms (61%). Veteran-owned businesses tend to have older owners (75% of owners older than fifty-five) than busi-

nesses as a whole (36.6%). Among veteran-owned business, 8.3% are classified as service-disabled.[82] There appears to be a difference between older veterans and those under age thirty-five. Older veterans are more likely to start a business, earn more money, and be successful.[83]

NATIVE HAWAIIAN AND PACIFIC ISLANDER–OWNED BUSINESSES

According to the 2007 Survey of Business Owners, Native Hawaiian and other Pacific Islanders (Guamanian and Samoans) owned 37,957 businesses, a very small percentage of total US businesses (Figure 4-23). They employed 38,750 people and generated $6.5 billion in revenues. Although spread more widely across sectors, construction, health care, and social assistance topped the list. Many of these businesses (30%) are located in Hawaii, while California is home to nearly 24% of NHPI businesses.

NONPROFIT ORGANIZATIONS

Nonprofit organizations are separate from the government (even though some receive government support), do not distribute profits to owners (even if they accumulate profit), are self-governing, and are voluntary. Some nonprofits provide services such as health care, educa-

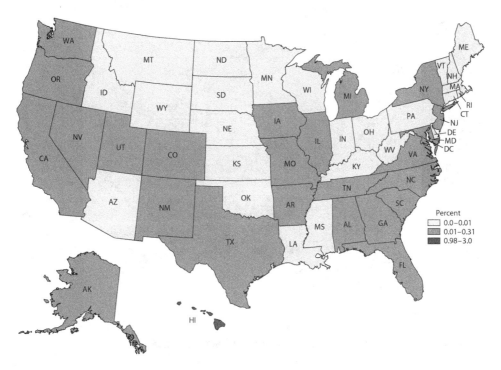

FIGURE 4-23. Native Hawaiian and Pacific Islander–Owned Businesses, 2007. Source: US Census 2007 Survey of Business Owners

tion, and family and social services. Others advocate or bring attention to issues, problems, or needs. A third category enriches by giving. Still others give expression to art, religion, culture, or recreation.

In 2010, there were about 2.3 million nonprofit organizations in the United States, of which 1.6 million were registered with the Internal Revenue Service (IRS), a 24% increase over the previous decade. The Urban Institute National Center for Charitable Statistics estimates that the nonprofit sector contributed over 5.5% to the US GDP in 2010. Nonprofits employed about 13.7 million people, had $2.1 trillion in revenues, and had $1.9 trillion in expenses, including about $600 billion in wages and salaries. Close to 27% of the US population, or 64.3 million people, volunteered at least once in 2011, with a median of 51 hours volunteered annually. From 2005 to 2011, the number of people volunteering has ranged from 61 million to 65 million, and median hours volunteered have been consistent. Although foundations command attention, individuals (including their bequests) make up over 80% of private giving to charitable organizations. Foundations account for 13% and corporations 3%. Congregations account for 35% of private giving.[84]

Geographics. The location of nonprofits may have little bearing on the money they raise or the services they pro-

vide. For example, Washington, DC, has the highest density of nonprofits of any city. Many of these are national organizations. The top three states for nonprofits are California, Texas, and New York. The metropolitan areas with the most nonprofits are Los Angeles, Chicago, New York, and Washington, DC (Figure 4-24).

Sectors. Nonprofits can include member-serving organizations (such as labor unions, business leagues, social/recreational clubs), lobbying organizations, and foundations such as the Bill and Melinda Gates Foundation. For the most part, the nonprofits that provide service or are in the arts and culture areas are more likely to be involved in social entrepreneurship. These are divided into health care, education, arts/recreation, social services, and civic/other (Figures 4-25 and 4-26). Health care generates the most revenue but includes a smaller number of entities because the category includes large hospital complexes. Education includes private and nonprofit schools at all levels. Social services account for the largest share of the number of organizations involved in social enterprises but generates less revenue compared to health care and education. In terms of funding, education generates the largest part of its funding from fees or tuition. Health care relies on government funding through programs such as Medicare and Medicaid.

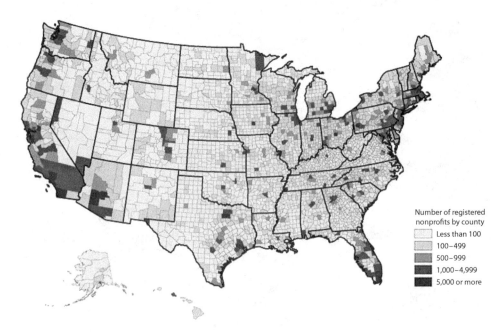

FIGURE 4-24. Number of Nonprofits by County, 2013. Source: Urban League

Social services rely almost equally on both fees and government funding.

Dynamics. Despite the well-publicized effort of major business figures such as Bill Gates and Warren Buffett to increase private giving among the wealthy, the Urban Institute estimates that the amount of contributions from private giving is essentially static. Although volunteer hours exhibit some volatility, they remain basically static as well.

Prior to 1970, education was the largest social welfare expenditure for all levels of government in the United States. The aging of the US population has driven government spending to social insurance and health care. The education sector has increased tuition substantially to mitigate cuts in government funding. For-profits have been entering every segment and are bringing business goals of cost efficiency and revenue maximization. This has created some conflict in that nonprofits may serve a larger proportion of the neediest and the least profitable populations. Additionally there have been issues with the use of federal funding, completion rates, and high student debt without commensurate salaries.

Judith Sharken Simon and J. Terence Donovan developed a model for the life cycle of nonprofit organizations that has been widely used.[85] Table 4-10 lists the five stages: imagine and inspire, found and frame, ground and grow, produce and sustain, and review and renew. Some nonprofits fall into decline and dissolution. This can happen at any stage. Within each of these stages, the model considers governance, staff leadership, financing, administrative systems, products and services, staffing, and marketing.

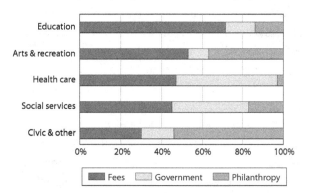

FIGURE 4-25. Nonprofits' Source of Revenue, 2007. Source: Lester M. Salamon, *America's Nonprofit Sector: A Primer*, 3rd ed. (New York: The Foundation Center, 2012)

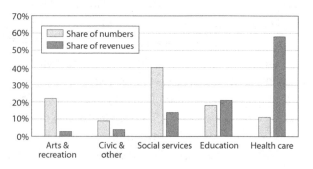

FIGURE 4-26. Number and Revenue Share by Nonprofit Category, 2009. Source: Lester M. Salamon, *America's Nonprofit Sector: A Primer*, 3rd ed. (New York: The Foundation Center, 2012)

TABLE 4-10. Five Stages of Nonprofit Organizations

Qualities	Getting Started Imagine and Inspire	Stage One: Found and Frame	Stage Two: Ground and Grow	Stage Three: Produce and Sustain	Stage Four: Review and Renew
Primary Question	*Can this dream be realized?*	*How are we going to pull this off?*	*How can we build this to be viable?*	*How can we sustain the momentum?*	*What do we need to redesign?*
Governance	Not yet a concern	Formal governance structure created, homogenous, small, passionate board of directors, working board	Expansion of the board size, first "outsider" on board, reactive rather than strategic	The governing role is in its prime, few founding board members remain, board discussions broadly focused, well developed committees, board role is to ensure well-being and longevity of the organization, board-staff roles are clearly defined, diverse composition	Turnover of board membership and leadership, development of formal linkages with other organizations, clarification of board roles and responsibilities
Staff Leadership	Entrepreneurial, visionary, no positional leader, often volunteer	Single-minded, driven, sole decision maker, visionary, entrepreneurial, charismatic	First paid executive director, who is directive, unavailable, high-energy, needed both internally and externally	Well-rounded executive director, needs good delegation skills, assistant director in place, complemented by good program managers, "founder's syndrome"	Founder likely to leave; change agent needed; a decisive, highly motivated individual whose strength is integrating diverse perspectives; has experience and knowledge of finances
Financing	Not yet a concern	Start-up funding granted, limited funds, no accounting systems, in-kind donations of expertise	Greater need for financial resources, a few funder relationships established, proficient use of in-kind donations, discussion of revenue-generating schemes	Stable funding, development of an operating reserve, need for exploration of new and expanded funding sources, fundraiser position added	Critical examination of funding sources, strategies, and systems; new funding sources located; growth of a development office
Administrative Systems	Not yet a concern	Few formal systems, a home office, small and agile	High need for administrative systems, first office space rented, first administrative staff hired, systems of accountability developed, technology and equipment purchased	In their prime, policies and procedures are well developed, multiple support staff, revamping of hardware and software	Administrative systems revamped, centralization of many aspects of the systems
Staffing	Not yet a concern	Dedicated group of volunteers, no paid staff	Paid staff hired, volunteers still critical part of staffing strategy, lack of job descriptions	Organization size is at its peak, program managers hired increased diversity of staff, volunteer structure self-perpetuating, volunteer coordinator hired, first staff firing may occur	Many changes in program staff, push for internal and external collaboration, new staff hired, existing staff reassigned, volunteer system reevaluated
Products and Services	Extremely informal or not yet a concern	One primary activity or a mix of varied, loosely related activities	One primary activity, refinement in program delivery, need to say "no" to program ideas due to lack of resources	Programs well-designed and functioning at high level, long-range program planning, core programs with new programs for expansion	Reexamination and redefinition of activities, longstanding programs may close, collaborative programs, new products and services

DISCUSSION

1. List factors that contribute to firm survival and escape velocity for promising businesses. Consider your business and business owner's attributes. Analyze background information regarding work experience, reasons for starting the business, competitive environment, start-up capital, previous experiences with lending institutions, or other aspects of your client's experiences. Can this business reach escape velocity? What are the barriers, if any, for achieving this level of growth? How can you communicate needed changes?

2. The US Census Survey of Business Owners has several categories for businesses. Are these categories sufficient for capturing, analyzing, and implementing business and economic development strategies? What other categories should be created to improve our analysis and understanding of small business and entrepreneurship?

3. Certification of minority businesses for federal contacts has been stopped at the SBA yet continues in the supplier diversity marketplace. Is your client business disadvantaged? Should initiatives in this area continue? Give your analysis of why or why not.

4. Tribal gaming often comes under attack for a variety of reasons. Analyze the need for and future of tribal gaming. Give your conclusions on what its future should be.

5. Should the United States attempt to stem the reverse brain drain? What should be the policy on immigrant entrepreneurs? How does immigration policy affect the reverse brain drain?

6. Identify a nonprofit organization and determine what stage of the life cycle of nonprofits it is in. Give reasons for your placement.

NOTES

1 D. Stangler and R. Litan, *Where Will the Jobs Come From?* Kauffman Foundation Research Series: Firm Formation and Economic Growth (Kansas City, MO: Kauffman Foundation, 2009).

2 David L. Birch, *The Job Generation Process* (Cambridge, MA: MIT Program on Neighborhood and Regional Change, 1979).

3 Kevin L. Kliesne and Julia S. Mavis, "Are Small Businesses the Biggest Producers of Jobs?" *Regional Economist*, April 2011, 8–9.

4 John Haltiwanger, Ron S. Jarmin, and Javier Miranda, *Who Creates Jobs? Small vs Large vs Young*, CES 10-17 (Washington, DC: US Census, Center for Economic Studies, August 2010).

5 Stangler and Litan, *Where Will the Jobs Come From?*

6 Susan Hampson, "A New Life for Refugees and the City They Adopted," *New York Times*, August 20, 2014.

7 Jules Lichtenstein, "Demographic Characteristics of Business Owners," *SBA Office of Advocacy Issue Brief* 2 (January 16, 2014).

8 S. Davis, J. Haltiwanger, and R. Jarmin, *Turmoil and Growth: Young Businesses, Economic Churning, and Productivity Gains* (Kansas City, MO: Kauffman Foundation, 2008).

9 Zoltan J. Acs, William Parsons, and Spencer L. Tracy, *High-Impact Firms: Gazelles Revisited*, SBA Office of Advocacy, June 2008, http://archive.sba.gov/advo/research/rs328tot.pdf.

10 Robert W. Fairlie, *Self-Employed Business Ownership Rates in the United States: 1979–2003*, SBA Office of Advocacy, December 2004, http://archive.sba.gov/advo/research/rs243tot.pdf.

11 Erik Hurst and Benjamin Wild Pugsley, *What Do Small Businesses Do??* NBER Working Paper, August 2011, www.nber.org/papers/w17041.pdf.

12 Ibid.

13 Zoltan J. Acs, Brian Headd, and Hezekiah Agwara, *Nonemployer Start-Up Puzzle*, SBA Office of Advocacy, December 2009, http://archive.sba.gov/advo/research/rs354tot.pdf.

14 Magnus Lofstrom, Timothy Bates, and Simon C. Parker, *Transitions to Entrepreneurship and Industry-Specific Barriers*, Institute for the Study of Labor, IZA DP No. 6103, November 2011, http://ftp.iza.org/dp6103.pdf.

15 Robert W. Fairlie, *Crossing the Employer Threshold: Determinants of Firms Hiring Their First Employee*, SBA Office of Advocacy, December 2013, www.sba.gov/sites/default/files/rs418tot.pdf.

16 US Bureau of Labor Statistics, "Table 8: Private Sector Establishment Births and Deaths, Seasonally Adjusted," Economic News Release, April 2014, www.bls.gov/news.release/cewbd.t08.htm.

17 US Courts, "Bankruptcy Statistics," www.uscourts.gov/Statistics/BankruptcyStatistics.aspx (retrieved July 2, 2014).

18 Ying Lowrey, *Dynamics of Employer Establishments, 2002–2003*, SBA Office of Advocacy, December 2009, www.sba.gov/sites/default/files/rs356tot.pdf.

19 Hurst and Pugsley, *What Do Small Businesses Do??*

20 US Census, "2007 Survey of Business Owners," www.census.gov/econ/sbo/07menu.html (retrieved September 25, 2011). See this source for all mentions of statistics from the 2007 SBO.

21 Robert W. Fairlie and Alicia M. Robb, *Race and Entrepreneurial Success, 2008* (Cambridge, MA: MIT Press, 2008).

22 Ibid., 91.

23 Ibid., 92.

24 Acs, Parsons, and Tracy, *High-Impact Firms: Gazelles Revisited*.

25 Martin Kenney and Donald Patton, *The Geography of Employment Growth: The Support Networks for Gazelle IPOs*, SBA Office of Advocacy, May 2013, www.sba.gov/sites/default/files/files/rs412tot.pdf.

26 Michael R. Porter, "Clusters and the New Economics of Competition," *Harvard Business Review*, November–December 1998.

27 Kenney and Patton, *Geography of Employment Growth*.

28 Spencer L. Tracy Jr., *Accelerating Job Creation in America: The Promise of High-Impact Companies*, SBA Office of Advocacy, July 2011, www.sba.gov/sites/default/files/rs381tot.pdf.

29 Ibid.

30 Kristi Dautzenberg, Marius Ehrlinspiel, Hardy Gude, Judith Käser, Philipp Till Schultz, Julian Tenorth, Michael Tscherntke, and Frank Wallau, *Study on Fasting Growing Young Companies (Gazelles): Summary*, on behalf of the Federal Ministry of Economics and Development of Germany (Ramboll Group and Creditreform, June 2012).

31 Simon C. Parker, David J. Storey, and Arjen van Witteloostuiju, "What Happens to Gazelles? The Importance of Dynamic Management Strategy," *Small Business Economics* 35 (2010): 203–26

32 Oriol Amat and Jordi Perramon, *Gazelle Companies: Growth Drivers and an Evolution Analysis*, working paper, Department of Economic and Business, Universitat Pompeii Fabra, 2011.

33 Robert W. Fairlie and Alicia M. Robb, *Disparities in Capital Access between Minority and Non-Minority-Owned Businesses: The Troubling Reality of Capital Limitations Faced by MBEs*, Minority Business Development Agency, January 2010, http://people.ucsc.edu/~rfairlie/presentations/Disparities%20in%20Capital%20Access%20Report%202010.pdf.

34 Timothy Bates and William Bradford, *Minorities and Venture Capital: A New Wave in American Business* (Kansas City, MO: Kauffman Foundation, 2007).

35 US Small Business Administration, "Business Loan Approval (Gross $) YTD Activity FY 2011 vs 2012 vs 2013, Period Ending: 07/31/13," www.sba.gov/sites/default/files/aboutsbaarticle/SBA%207a%20and%20504%20Gross%20Loan%20Approval%20Amount%20as%20of%207-31-2013.pdf (retrieved March 2, 2015).

36 Emily Matby, "Sharp Drop in Small Business Loans: The Small Business Administration Processed 57% Fewer Loans Last Quarter Than It Did a Year Ago," *CNN Money*, January 6, 2009, http://money.cnn.com/2009/01/05/smallbusiness/sba_loans_plunge.smb.

37 US Small Business Administration, "Business Loan Approval (Gross $) YTD Activity FY 2011 vs 2012 vs 2013, Period Ending: 07/31/13."

38 US Small Business Administration, "Government-Wide Performance: FY2013 Small Business Procurement Scorecard," www.sba.gov/sites/default/files/files/FY13_Government-Wide_SB_Procurement_Scorecard_Public_View_2014-04-28.pdf (retrieved March 6, 2015).

39 National Venture Capital Association, "Venture Capital Industry Overview," www.nvca.org/index.php?option=com_content&view=article&id=141<emid=589 (retrieved July 3, 2014).

40 Cambridge Associates, *U.S. Venture Capital Index and Selected Benchmark Statistics*, September 30, 2013, www.cambridgeassociates.com/our-insights/research/u-s-venture-capital.

41 Diane Mulcahy, Bill Weeks, and Harold S. Bradley, *We Have Met the Enemy and He Is Us: Lessons from Twenty Years of the Kauffman Foundation's Investments in Venture Capital Funds and the Triumph of Hope Over Experience* (Kansas City, MO: Kauffman Foundation, 2012).

42 William Sahlman, Howard H. Stevenson, Michael J. Roberts, and Amar Bhidé, *The Entrepreneurial Venture* (Boston: Harvard Business School Press, 1999).

43 Timothy Bates and William Bradford, "Venture Capital Investment in Minority Business," *Journal of Money, Credit and Banking* 40 (2008): 489–504.

44 Jeffrey Sohl, *The Angel Investor Market in 2013: A Return to Seed Investing* (Durham, NH: UNH Center for Venture Research, April 30, 2014).

45 infoDev/World Bank, *Crowdfunding's Potential for the Developing World* (Washington, DC: World Bank, 2013).

46 National Endowment of the Arts Appropriations History, http://arts.gov/open-government/national-endowment-arts-appropriations-history (retrieved July 15, 2014).

47 Ethan Mollick, "The Dynamics of Crowdfunding: An Exploratory Study," *Journal of Business Venturing* 29 (2014): 1–16.

48 Scott Shane, *Fool's Gold?* (New York: Oxford University Press, 2009).

49 Ibid.

50 Arvind Ashta and Djamchid Assadi, "Should Online Micro-Lending Be for Profit or for Philanthropy?" *Journal of Innovation Economics* 2 (2010): 123–46.

51 Timothy Bates, Magnus Lofstrom, and Lisa Sevron, *Why Have Lending Programs Targeting Disadvantaged Small-*

Business Borrowers Achieved So Little Success in the United States? Institute for the Study of Labor, IZA DP No. 5212, September 2010, http://ftp.iza.org/dp5212.pdf.

52 William Girardo and Elaine L. Edgcomb, *Key Data on the Scale of Microlending in the US* (Washington, DC: Field at the Aspen Institute, February 2011).

53 See *Inc. Magazine*, "Facts and Figures of the 2014 Inc. 5000," www.inc.com/inc5000/2014/facts-and-figures .html (retrieved March 5, 2015).

54 Timothy Bates, "The Urban Development Potential of Black-Owned Businesses," *Journal of the American Planning Association* 72 (2008): 227–37.

55 Thomas D. Boston and Linje R. Boston, "Secrets of Gazelles: The Differences between High-Growth and Low-Growth Business Owned by African American Entrepreneurs," *Annals of the American Academy of Political and Social Science* 613, no. 1 (September 2007): 108–30.

56 Ibid.

57 A. K. Chatterji, K. Y. Chay, and R. W. Fairlie, *The Impact of City Contracting Set-Asides on Black Self-Employment and Employment*, NBER Working Paper no. 18884, March 2013, www.nber.org/papers/w18884.

58 Robert W. Fairlie and Christopher Woodruff, *Mexican-American Entrepreneurship*, Institute for the Study of Labor, IZA DP No. 3488, May 2008, http://ftp.iza.org/ dp3488.pdf.

59 Geoscape, *Hispanics Businesses and Entrepreneurs Drive Growth in the New Economy*, 2nd annual report, 2014, www.geoscape.com/HBR/pdf/Geoscape_Hispanic BusinessOwners_FINAL.pdf.

60 *Inc. Magazine*, "Facts and Figures of the 2014 Inc. 5000."

61 Ethel Navales, "The History of Cambodian-Owned Donut Shops," *Audrey Magazine*, June 6, 2014, http://audrey magazine.com/the-history-of-cambodian-owned-donut -shops.

62 Pawan Dhingra, *Life behind the Lobby: Indian American Motel Owners and the American Dream* (Palo Alto, CA: Stanford University Press, 2012).

63 Robert W. Fairlie and Alicia M. Robb, "Determinants of Business Success: An Examination of Asian-Owned Businesses in the United States," *Journal of Population Economics* 22, no. 4 (2009): 827–58.

64 Robert W. Fairlie and Magnus Lofstrom, *Immigration and Entrepreneurship*, Institute for the Study of Labor, IZA DP No. 7669, October 2013, http://ftp.iza.org/dp7669.pdf.

65 AnnaLee Saxenian, *Silicon Valley's New Immigrant Entrepreneurs* (San Francisco: Public Policy Institute of California, 1999), www.ppic.org/content/pubs/report/R_699ASR .pdf.

66 Vivek Wadhwa, AnnaLee Saxenian, and F. Daniel Siciliano, *America's New Immigrant Entrepreneurs* (Kansas City, MO: Kauffman Foundation, 2007).

67 Cathy Yang Liu, Gary Painter, and Qingfang Wang, *Lessons for US Metro Areas: Characteristics and Clustering of High-Tech Immigrant Entrepreneurs* (Kansas City, MO: Kauffman Foundation, 2014).

68 Vivek Wadhwa, Sonali Jain, AnnaLee Saxenian, Gary Gereffi, and Huiyao Wang, *The Grass Is Indeed Greener in India and China for Returnee Entrepreneurs* (Kansas City, MO: Kauffman Foundation, 2011).

69 US Department of Justice, Office of Public Affairs, "Attorney General Holder, Secretary Salazar Announce Settlement of Cobell Lawsuit on Indian Trust Management," December 8, 2009, www.justice.gov/opa/pr/ attorney-general-holder-secretary-salazar-announce- settlement-cobell-lawsuit-indian-trust (retrieved March 6, 2015).

70 Harvard Project on American Indian Economic Development, *The State of the Native Nations: Conditions under U.S. Policies of Self-Determination* (New York: Oxford University Press, 2008).

71 Robin J. Anderson, "Tribal Casino Impacts on American Indians Well-Being: Evidence from Reservation-Level Census Data," *Contemporary Economic Policy* 31, no. 2 (April 2013): 291–300.

72 Harvard Project on American Indian Economic Development, *State of the Native Nations*.

73 Darrene Hackler, Ellen Harpel, and Heike Mayer, *Human Capital and Women's Business Ownership*, SBA Office of Advocacy, April 2008.

74 Tracy, *Accelerating Job Creation in America*.

75 Alicia M. Robb and Susan Coleman, *Characteristics of New Firms: A Comparison by Gender* (Kansas City, MO: Kauffman Foundation, 2009).

76 National Women's Business Council, *Launching Women-Owned Businesses onto a High Growth Trajectory*, 2010, www.nwbc.gov/research/launching-women-owned -businesses-high-growth-trajectory.

77 Kauffman Foundation, *Women and Angel Investing: An Untapped Pool of Equity for Entrepreneurs* (Kansas City, MO: Kauffman Foundation, 2006).

78 Alicia M. Robb and Susan Coleman, *Sources of Financing for New Technology Firms: A Comparison by Gender* (Kansas City, MO: Kauffman Foundation, 2009).

79 Womenable, *The 2014 State of Women-Owned Business Report* (American Express OPEN, March 26, 2014).

80 US Bureau of Labor Statistics, "Employment Situation of Veterans, 2010," www.bls.gov/news.release/vet.nr0 .htm (retrieved December 20, 2011).

81 John B. Hope, Brian Oh, and Patrick C. Mackin, *Factors Affecting Entrepreneurship among Veterans*, SBA Office of Advocacy, March 2011, www.sba.gov/sites/default/files/ files/rs384tot.pdf.

82 US Small Business Administration, *Veteran-Owned Businesses and Their Owners: Data from the Census Bureau's Survey of Business Owners*, SBA Office of Advo-

cacy, March 2012, www.sba.gov/sites/default/files/393tot.pdf.

83 Compendium Federal Technology, *An Exploration of Veteran Business Creation and Management Using the Census Bureau's Survey of Income and Program Participation*, SBA Office of Advocacy, February 2014, www.sba.gov/sites/default/files/rs420tot.pdf.

84 Katie L. Roeger, Amy S. Blackwood, and Sarah L. Pettijohn, *The Nonprofit Almanac 2012* (New York: Urban Institute Press, 2012).

85 Judith Sharken Simon and J. Terence Donovan, *The Five Life Stages of Nonprofit Organizations: Where You Are, Where You're Going, and What to Expect When You Get There* (St. Paul, MN: Amherst H. Wilder Foundation, 2001).

5. Marketing Analysis and Strategy

ABOUT THIS CHAPTER

Developing and implementing marketing strategies and programs are critically important activities in any business enterprise but are especially pertinent to all small businesses. The authors of this textbook have guided more than five hundred student teams working with small and emerging businesses. The firms' most frequently cited need is assistance with marketing. The success of the enterprise is ultimately measured in terms of how well it satisfies the needs and wants of its customers. That goal cannot be achieved effectively without defining a strategic direction and devising specific tactics to execute that strategy. For emerging businesses, moving from a bootstrapping mode of operation to one where planning is important is a pivotal transition in the company's lifecycle. This can be particularly challenging for growing minority business enterprises (MBEs) in the business-to-consumer (B2C) space because growth may dictate movement into market segments outside familiar cultures, into other minority cultures, or into the white culture. For any business-to-business (B2B) firm, movement into a new market may mean learning a new industry or expanding to a new geography.

Consultants use the standard tools of the marketing trade to help enterprises grow. Identifying the firm's target market segment is an important first step in developing a marketing strategy. Small businesses can do this through segmentation, targeting, and positioning (STP). Although commonplace in large enterprises, these concepts may be unfamiliar to small businesses. Often the business owner has come from a background or country where marketing may be approached differently or the business owner has grown her or his company without significant analysis of existing market segments. It may be the consultant's role to develop a plan for the

company's marketing efforts. Small businesses should take into account differences in the consumer buying decision process and factors that influence this process, particularly for multicultural consumers. Then, the small business can develop a marketing mix for its market segment or segments, including a strong brand identity and appropriate promotion and selling strategies for its target customers.

Promotion strategies are part of the marketing mix and should include a Web marketing component. Web marketing and social media are important for small businesses because these media are doing much to level the playing field in competition between small and larger businesses. Use of the Web is essential for small businesses that operate in the B2B sphere, as most large enterprises require the convenience and efficiency of the Web. Small businesses where the owners or decision makers do not have a corporate background are not likely to be as familiar with how to effectively communicate with corporate clients using these channels.

Often, emerging businesses build market share one customer at a time. The principles of customer relationship management are critical to success in acquiring new customers at a faster rate. Along with growing market share, small businesses must devise strategies to retain current, profitable customers and grow "share of wallet" by selling more to existing customers. Businesses need to articulate a customer value proposition, to both grow share of wallet and market share.

The purpose of this chapter is to provide a compendium of marketing tools that could be used. Given the breadth of topics covered in this textbook, there is insufficient space to provide comprehensive details about each tool. Thus the authors assume that student teams will find more detailed information about each tool in other sources.

After Studying This Chapter

With the tools in this chapter, teams will be able to use marketing concepts, define strategies, gather the appropriate data, and apply the correct analysis. The interrelatedness of marketing, operations, and accounting requires that the tools presented in this chapter must be used in tandem with business process (described in chapter 7) and financial analysis (described in chapter 8).

After reading this chapter, students will be able to:

- Describe effective segmentation, targeting, and positioning (STP) strategies for a business to reach its target market(s).
- Understand the consumer buying decision process and factors influencing this process.
- Understand and use all elements of the marketing mix to develop programs for a specific business.
- Describe the elements of customer relationship management and its relevance to business strategy.
- Identify and apply the techniques of designing and operating a business website, achieving search engine optimization, and using social media.
- Articulate the customer value proposition, analyze the stages of the customer life cycle, calculate customer

lifetime value, and develop appropriate marketing and customer service programs.

SEGMENTATION, TARGETING, AND POSITIONING

For small businesses, it simply may not be feasible to offer a product or service to the entire marketplace. Thus, a small business should break down the marketplace into smaller market segments, identify key characteristics of each segment, choose which segment(s) to target, and position itself appropriately within each segment. This is the STP process (Table 5-1). Once the target segment(s) has been identified, the small business can adjust its marketing mix (product/brand, price, place/distribution, promotion) to support its positioning strategy. The marketing mix components will be discussed later in this chapter.

Market Segmentation

When a B2C small business assesses the marketplace, it is important to consider the characteristics of each market segment. The usual dimensions of demographics (age, gender, education, and income), geographics, psychographics, and behavior are inadequate when it comes to understanding all potential market segments. This is especially true when looking at multicultural markets as a segment. For these market segments it is important to

TABLE 5-1. Segmentation, Targeting, and Positioning (STP)

Marketing Tool	Description	Opportunities
Segmentation	A process for identifying market niches that can be profitable to the enterprise. Typical segmentation identifies demographic, geographic, behavioral, and psychographic groups that interact with a product or service in a similar manner.	Multicultural or targeted geographic markets can be small compared to segments pursued by large enterprises and can provide opportunities for emerging businesses
Targeting	Strategies and programs for choosing market segment(s)	The full breadth of current social, psychological, economic, and other factors must be assessed in targeting multicultural market segments Cultural analysis (which includes history, art, music, etc., of the population and its home country) must be taken into consideration in targeting multicultural segments
Positioning	Strategy for setting the enterprise apart from competitors in the minds of consumers based on key attributes important to the customer value proposition. Could also include strategies for creating entry barriers for future competitors.	Small businesses seeking to expand beyond their initial market niche focus on building new value propositions that include benefits to a distinct market segment

understand history, culture, sociological context, discrimination, and languages as well as many other factors.

With regard to emerging businesses, especially those in the retail, hospitality, and personal service industries, their markets are often hyperlocal and require targeting smaller areas such as a city or even a neighborhood. It is important for the consulting team to take the time to conduct detailed research of these hyperlocal economies and focus on a segment that is understandable to the business owner. Defining the segment in terms of key characteristics and size can do much to help the business owner reach the market. Analyzing the potential revenues from the target market is also important. Newer business owners may have limited experience with the idea of business cycles, migration patterns, or other factors that might affect their business. In preparing this analysis, the team needs to incorporate the dynamic nature of segments and what factors may affect the success of reaching each segment.

B2B market segmentation uses the same principles as consumer market segmentation. But rather than focusing on issues such as demographics, B2B segmentation more typically focuses on industry clusters, unique processes, service needs, sales cycles, and the tier of contracting at which a small business will operate.

For all businesses, the highest growth potential exists within market segments that are growing. New markets do not have clearly defined requirements, and information is evolving. The emerging business may have advantages over larger enterprises in that it may be more flexible in responding to quickly changing market conditions. Additionally, it is important to recognize that an emerging business usually lacks the resources to compete head-on with large, well-endowed enterprises. For the emerging business, B2B marketing relies heavily on expensive one-on-one sales efforts. Often, segments are defined as the business owner encounters success with sales calls. In this fluid environment, constant assessment must be made of the profitability and cash flow generation of each opportunity.

Targeting and Positioning

Once the small business has identified viable market segments within the marketplace, the small business must decide whether to target one or several segments. For small businesses, it is more common to pursue one or just a few segments, which is referred to as a niche or concentrated targeting strategy. This approach may be more feasible for small businesses in light of their limited resources. For example, the small business may be able to focus on a smaller segment that includes fewer competitors. As small businesses grow, they are able to expand their offerings to more segments such as new geographies or demographics. When choosing specific target segments it is also important to determine if the segment allows for firm growth and if the segment can generate profitable returns, rather than simply focusing on the ease with which a segment can be reached.

Once the target market segment(s) has been identified, the small business can focus on how to position itself within the segment. Positioning refers to how customers perceive the business relative to other businesses. For example, if the small business specializes in a new technology with an emphasis on customer service, it must be able to brand itself accordingly and effectively communicate its value proposition to its target market. Volvo's positioning strategy of safety is well known, due to the firm's ability to produce cars with high safety ratings (product/brand), communicate good value (pricing) through effective advertising and selling (promotion), and make the cars available to customers (place/distribution). A small business can be just as effective in communicating its positioning through the use of the marketing mix. Moreover, small businesses should take the time to consider how consumers make purchase decisions, especially multicultural consumers who may add unique influences to the process.

CONSUMER DECISION-MAKING PROCESS

Small businesses should recognize that all consumers engage in a decision-making process. Multicultural consumers may have unique influencers in this process. Figure 5-1 shows the five-step process that the customer uses to make a decision. The consumer decision-making process can be simple or complex depending on the type of product, cost, and type of purchase. A more complex and expensive product such as a new car will require more information and processing. The consumer will likely spend less time gathering information and processing the decision for a routine product such as a soft drink from a vending machine.

Problem recognition occurs when a consumer becomes aware of an unmet need, either from internal or external factors. The consumer may see an online advertisement (external) or simply feel hungry (internal). Once the con-

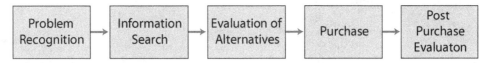

FIGURE 5-1. Consumer Decision-Making Process

sumer recognizes his or her unmet need, he or she enters the information search stage. The consumer may spend more time gathering information for new, expensive, or complex products or spend little time if he or she is familiar with the product. The most credible sources of information are trusted individuals such as family, friends, and neighbors. Other credible sources are nonmarketing authorities such as *Consumer Reports* or websites such as Trip Advisor and Yelp. Less credible sources include brand advertisements and product displays. Multicultural consumers who strongly value the opinions of their families and friends will place more weight on their opinions in the decision-making process.

Once consumers gather sufficient information, they begin to evaluate their alternatives. It is important to understand how a target market evaluates options. Are customers more likely to seek advice from family, friends, or salespeople? Do they buy impulsively or do they engage in a careful and logical analysis? There can be instances where the consumer fails to make the purchase. This could be due to unexpected circumstances (loss of income) or a consumer could be swayed by the opinions of others. Purchase intentions are not always acted upon.

Businesses must recognize that the process does not end when the purchase is made. Consumers often engage in postpurchase evaluation, which can lead to cognitive dissonance or buyer's remorse. This happens when a consumer experiences a discrepancy between his or her attitude and behavior. The discomfort can be reduced by either changing his or her attitude or altering her behavior. For example, a consumer may purchase a new television and, upon taking it home, discover that the image does not look as clear as it did in the store. She can accept that the image does not meet her expectations (attitude) or return the product to the store (behavior). Businesses can help minimize or reduce buyer's remorse by using strategies to reassure customers that they made the right purchase decision. For example, businesses can follow up with a phone call, provide adequate information to avoid product misuse, or be responsive to customer questions and complaints. These actions will convert a single purchase into one of many future pur-

chases, contributing to a higher customer lifetime value. Minimizing buyer's remorse can significantly affect long-term profitability.

Consumers may encounter several influences that affect the decision-making process, including situational influences such as physical and social situations; psychological influences such as motivation, attitudes, lifestyle, perception, or personality; or social influences such as reference groups, opinion leaders, family, and culture. For Hispanic consumers, the extended family may play an important role in purchase decisions. An urban consumer may choose to buy fewer or smaller products to accommodate a smaller home. Culture and subculture also play an important role in consumer decision making. Consumers may connect more with brands that they perceive share values similar to those of their social, ethnic, economic, or other reference group.[1]

Motivation theories can shed light on the attitudes, beliefs, and motives that drive purchase decisions.[2] Maslow's hierarchy of needs in Figure 5-2 suggests that people try to solve their needs in a predetermined order, satisfying each level of needs before moving up the hierarchy.[3] The most basic level of needs is physiological, such as thirst and hunger. Once a person's physiological needs are met, he/she moves up to the next level, which is safety. Safety needs may include security (physical and financial) and protection; a place to live (a house or apartment) would satisfy a person's safety needs. Next, people strive to satisfy their social needs, including a sense of belonging, love, and friendship. A cell phone, social group, or a Facebook account may satisfy a person's social needs. The next level is esteem, which refers to a person's desire for respect or the sense of making a contribution to society. Finally, people seek to satisfy a need for self-actualization, or their drive to reach their full potential. Very few people attain self-actualization, but for those who do, they are motivated by wisdom and look to find meaning around them. While some of the basic needs such as physiological and safety concerns would likely be pursued similarly across cultures, it is important to consider what unique factors may motivate multicultural consumer behavior.

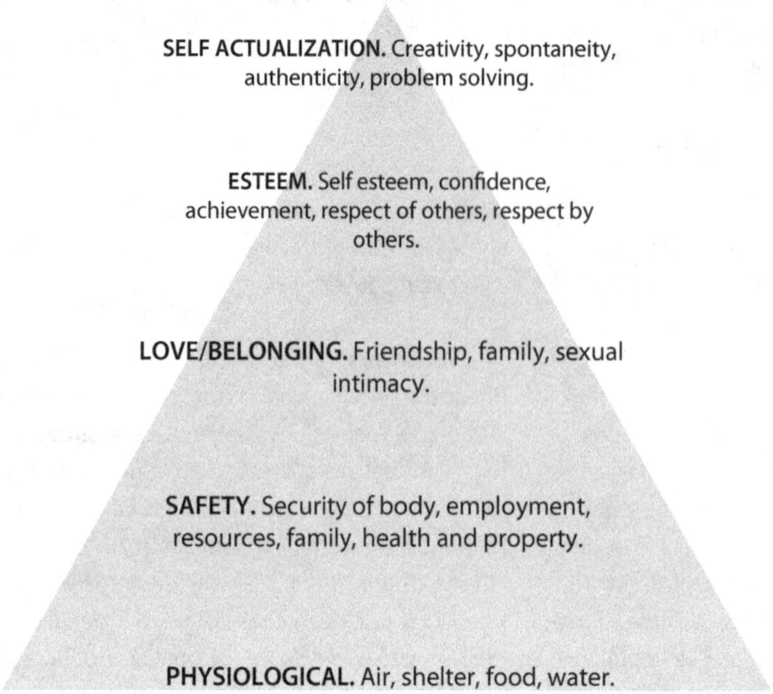

SELF ACTUALIZATION. Creativity, spontaneity, authenticity, problem solving.

ESTEEM. Self esteem, confidence, achievement, respect of others, respect by others.

LOVE/BELONGING. Friendship, family, sexual intimacy.

SAFETY. Security of body, employment, resources, family, health and property.

PHYSIOLOGICAL. Air, shelter, food, water.

FIGURE 5-2. Maslow's Hierarchy of Needs

Understanding the retail environment in which multicultural consumers shop is important, because these consumers may encounter unique experiences in the marketplace. Instances of marketplace discrimination continue to be reported, including employees following and monitoring customers in a store or providing diverse customers inferior service.[4] Small business owners catering to a diverse customer base should ensure that the retail environment is welcoming. This includes elements in the physical environment as well as employees' verbal and nonverbal cues. The physical environment and social setting can affect a multicultural customer's buying decision process and motivate customers to buy, or not buy, a product. A study conducted with Hispanic and lesbian, gay, bisexual, and transgender (LGBT) consumers showed that customers assess the congruency between their self-identity and an establishment (e.g., restaurant, retail store), referred to as place identity.[5] The researchers found that customers were more likely to patronize a place that is more congruent with their self-identity and avoid a place that is incongruent. Customers perceived an establishment to be more congruent with their self-identity when there were employees and other customers with whom they shared ethnic background. In addition, some Hispanic and LGBT customers reported uncomfortable stares or lack of recognition from employees, both of which contributed to their discomfort. However, bilingual signage and products/services with wide appeal created a more welcoming environment. The study found that customers' perceiving higher levels of congruency with the retail store or service provider are more likely to engage in positive word of mouth, return to the establishment, and refrain from complaining. For multicultural customers who rely heavily on the opinions of friends and family, positive word of mouth can greatly affect their purchase intentions. In addition, a positive experience helps alleviate purchase regret, which is a risk during a customer's postpurchase stage in the customer decision-making process.

Small businesses trying to appeal to a diverse market should train their employees to create an inviting environment for customers and should avoid verbal abuse. Employees can intervene when customers are verbally abusing other customers. The previously mentioned study showed that businesses can reap the financial benefits by creating a welcoming environment for diverse customers. Hiring diverse employees is perceived positively by multicultural customers. A related study found that when a customer shares similar ethnic background with a service provider, she may benefit from an enhanced service experience.[6] Interestingly, this study found that customers are more likely to experience comfort and friendship than receive free products or discounts based on their shared ethnic background. Therefore, when appealing to multicultural customers, businesses should strive to create a welcoming environment and when possible, hire and train diverse employees to provide excellent and friendly service, which is perceived as an important factor in assessing place identity.

USING THE MARKETING MIX

Once a small business has carefully identified a target market and developed a positioning strategy to compete within the market segment, the next step is to develop an action plan that makes full use of the marketing mix. *Marketing mix* is a term coined by Neil Borden in 1965 to cover the elements of marketing tactics. The marketing mix is also referred to as the four P's of marketing: product, price, place, and promotion (Figure 5-3).

Depending on the personality of the entrepreneur, the tendency may be to focus on too many or too few elements of the marketing mix. Developing too many tactics with not enough resources dooms the plan to failure. For overachieving entrepreneurs, it is important to focus efforts on those that are most easily accomplished and will give the best return. Achieving one or two initial successes will likely lead to more in the future.

For other entrepreneurs, previous experience may fall within a very narrow band of tactics. These entrepreneurs continue to work with what is most familiar and neglect other areas that may yield greater opportunities. It is important to consider all elements of the marketing mix and to think outside the box when developing the tactics discussed in detail later in this chapter.

Product

Once the customer value proposition is articulated, product or service features are created to address customers' needs. To be effective, the business must objectively analyze what is important to the customer. Why does the customer buy the product or service? What functionality does it serve? What need does it meet? It is important to keep in mind the core product that the customer is buying. In the case of an African American beauty salon, an African American woman can get her hair styled in a way consistent with her concept of beauty. This may not be possible at other salons. Along with this functionality, the woman may be looking for a chance to socialize, an important attribute of beauty salons in her culture. The appearance of the salon and the people who serve the clientele may be important. Time may also be a critical factor. It might be assumed that shortening the time cycle is what the customer wants, when in fact the customer might want to luxuriate in the salon, similar to how others might enjoy a coffee experience at Starbucks and others might enjoy in camping. Thus, the unique experience offered by the beauty salon may be the core product sought and may be an important differentiator for the small business. The quality of the service must be suited to the customer's expectations. Service must be consistent. Clients will not return if the client perceives the hairstyle or cut to be excellent one time and a disaster the next. If a product is sold, the packaging, warranty, and support may be a factor. These factors must be considered along with a cost-benefit analysis to properly assess product value.

The articulation of the customer value proposition for services is particularly difficult for emerging businesses. Minority business enterprises that have operated solely in co-ethnic markets may lose the value that close identification brings as they expand to new customers in different racial/ethnic markets. Shifts in population or increasing sophistication of co-ethnic markets may take away location as a customer value proposition. As such, the MBE

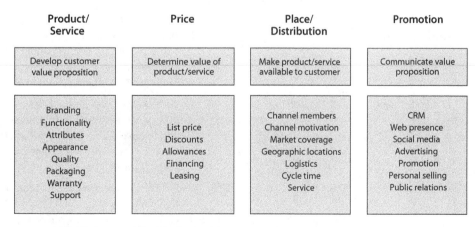

Product/Service	Price	Place/Distribution	Promotion
Develop customer value proposition	Determine value of product/service	Make product/service available to customer	Communicate value proposition
Branding Functionality Attributes Appearance Quality Packaging Warranty Support	List price Discounts Allowances Financing Leasing	Channel members Channel motivation Market coverage Geographic locations Logistics Cycle time Service	CRM Web presence Social media Advertising Promotion Personal selling Public relations

FIGURE 5-3. Elements of the Marketing Mix

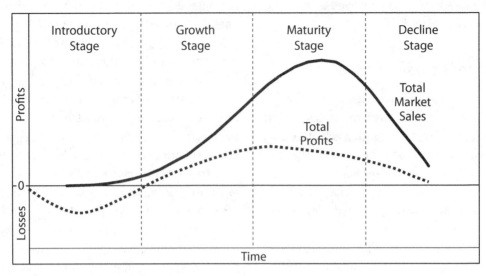

FIGURE 5-4. Product Life Cycle

must develop and communicate a different value. This could be customized services or personal attention. Successfully delivering these values may require a major redesign of the firm's service or other modes of its operation.

Similar to larger firms, small businesses must consider where the product or service lies in the product life cycle, shown in Figure 5-4. For example, if the product or service is in the introductory stage, emphasis should be on creating product awareness. For mature products, the emphasis should be on creating new uses or users or developing a line extension, such as a new flavor, size, or color. Table 5-2 outlines characteristics and marketing strate-gies for products and services at each stage of the product life cycle.

Branding. A brand is the image the customer has of the product or company. It conveys the nature of the user, a personality, core values, a culture, product benefits, and product attributes (Figure 5-5). Attributes may include price, safety, quality, and performance. Benefits are what the customer gets from the product, which may include functional or image benefits. A strong brand will have a strong emotional appeal that results in loyalty, repeat patronage, or other positive responses in the marketplace.

TABLE 5-2. Marketing Strategies for Each Stage of the Product Life Cycle (PLC)

Stage of PLC	Sales	Profits	Marketing Strategy
Introductory	Low	Negative (recovering research and development costs)	Product and service features are basic, distribution is limited, and the marketing goal is customer awareness and trial
Growth	Growing rapidly	Growing	Product and service features are increasing, distribution is increasing (e.g., expanding to online sales), and the marketing goal is consumer preference (your product offering chosen over competitor's)
Maturity	Flat to declining	Flat to declining	Consider adding new product or service features and promoting new uses, distribution is maximized, and the marketing goal is consumer preference. Increase sales with line extensions, new users, and new product or service uses.
Decline	Declining	Declining	Reduce product and service features, reduce distribution outlets, and the marketing goal is survival. May consider discontinuing the product or service or reformulating to launch a new product or service.

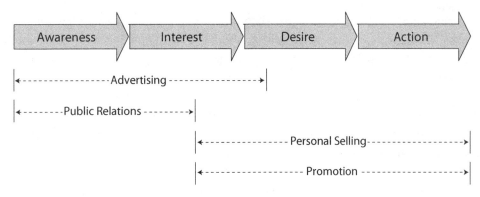

FIGURE 5-5. Branding

For small business entrepreneurs, who must compete with much larger enterprises that have considerably more resources, their marketing arsenal often includes emotional branding. The entrepreneur's story is woven into the business so that it has meaning for marketing the enterprise. This approach strives to persuade the customer to connect with the business or business owner. With minority entrepreneurs, this is relevant because many have overcome significant barriers to beat the odds and become successful. Their struggles become part of the fabric or essence of the business; or their commitments to supporting their communities can be compelling attributes of a product or service offering. Successful minority entrepreneurs are often pioneers for their communities, and many contribute to the welfare of others by creating jobs where none were available before. These individuals become role models for younger people to emulate. Their stories are inspiring.

Emotional branding can be helpful when competitors are offering products with a similar value proposition. Even if a business has competitive pricing and high quality, it needs something to set it apart. The bootstrapping owner of a fledgling business can use his/her personal story to get customers to take an interest in the business. This can be the differentiating factor in getting a foot in the door.

For B2B firms, corporate clients are looking to source products and services that will improve their competitive position. Many small firms tend to focus on competing on price when corporate clients value technological breakthroughs that can deliver sustainable competitive advantages. Often corporate clients look to small businesses for more timely responsiveness to orders and to firms that are able to cost effectively deliver unique, small batch orders.

Brand elements include the brand name, logo and symbols, slogans, packaging, colors, and so on. These elements can influence customers' perceptions of the brand. It is important that these elements are used consistently and work well together to convey a consistent brand positioning. In addition to the brand name, a brand logo is the most prevalent brand element. A logo is a graphical representation of the company that embodies its brand image from customers' perspectives. An ideal logo will say volumes about the company in a very economical way. Often, emerging businesses are so busy producing goods or delivering services that they do not take the time or spend the money to develop a logo that draws new customers and forms an attachment with existing customers. For the first-generation immigrant entrepreneurs who come from different business cultures where branding logos are not valued, creating these may not be viewed as important.

In the US context, every company should have a logo that is appropriate to the business and communicates clearly and unequivocally what the business wants its customer and community to think of the business. It is preferable to get professional help in designing the logo, but talented student teams have developed excellent logos. Once the company has decided on the logo, it should be tested on customers and vendors. If it communicates what the business wants, the logo must be trademarked. Then all company communication, marketing programs, and collateral elements (stationery, business cards, postcards, brochures, etc.) should make use of the logo in a consistent manner.

Pricing

The main influences on pricing generally include customer demand, competitor actions (including competitor prices), quality and related services, costs (including regulatory costs), technological conditions, and capacity or other resource constraints. A company's responses to such influences are shaped by its strategic and operational decisions. These include pricing objectives, strategies to accomplish those objectives, the structure of prices offered by the firm, and general pricing conditions in the markets in which the firm competes.

Important questions to ask about pricing include, What is the value of the firm's offering compared to competitors? How are the firm's products or services perceived by different market segments? Are there sustainable competitive advantages that can be identified for the firm that can lead to premium pricing? Answers to such questions will provide clues regarding how much discretion, if any, management will have in its pricing policies and decisions.

Often with emerging businesses, the rationale behind pricing is the entrepreneur's desire to make a certain profit margin regardless of what customers are willing to pay for the product or service. Prices may have been set in reaction to competitors or based on other factors. Some common pricing tactics are illustrated in Table 5-3.

In most businesses, one strategy will be used in combination with another. All pricing strategies should be evaluated against competitors. Financial analysis is mandatory for any pricing changes, and the effect of the changes should be monitored and adjustments made as necessary. An important factor in setting prices is to recognize that price is also a signal of quality. If a company is a subcontractor to a major manufacturer and they offer a product at a substantially lower cost than their competitors, the buyer may perceive the product as inferior.

An analysis of competitive pricing lets the business know how it is positioned against the competition. In the case of an African American coffee shop, the consultant team walked a ten-block radius of the shop and found seventeen competitors. They mapped the locations of each of these. Next, they collected pricing information for the most frequently purchased types of coffee. They found that the client business was in the tenth percentile of pricing. Pricing coffee lower than the competition may give away profits unnecessarily or convey infe-

TABLE 5-3. Pricing Tactics

Tactics	Description
Value pricing	Adjusting prices to offer the right combination of quality and service at a fair price. Requires competitive analysis to determine what constitutes the right price for the value that the business gives. Small businesses (despite often having cost advantages) should not attempt to compete on price alone.
Cost-based pricing	Cost-plus and markup pricing, return on investment, or other cost methods may be used to determine price. Requires careful accumulation of product costs to include both variable and fixed components. Costing based on variable cost can only pave the way to bad pricing. Small businesses sometimes do not track product line profitability. However, this can be easily gleaned from looking at financial statements and speaking to the owner. This can be educational for the business owner.
Competitive pricing	Matching prices with the firm's main competitors is a common method of pricing. Most small businesses do not have time to get a complete listing of competitor prices. This analysis can be invaluable in determining how the firm stands competitively. Includes finding the price ceiling or highest price and the pricing floor or the lowest price. In several student consulting analyses, this strategy has shown that the business charged prices that were too low.
Promotional pricing	A business may cut prices to gain customers in the short term. Done by the industry as a whole at certain times of year. For example, furniture is typically discounted in summer, when sales are low. For any promotions, it is important to assess the benefit achieved. If prices are lowered but no new customers or sales are gained, the promotion should not be repeated.
Discount pricing	Reducing prices to reward customer loyalty or purchase behavior and other incentives to reward for patronage. As in other cases, when prices are reduced, it is important to evaluate the benefit.
Tiered pricing	After a business determines that it is charging too little for its products or services, it is often difficult to raise prices without alienating customers. With tier pricing the business can identify products or services that are premium and charge more for those while keeping old prices as a baseline.
Dynamic pricing	Negotiation is a common form of dynamic pricing where two or more parties determine price based on negotiation power and skills. Yield management allows the business to price based on inventory and time of purchase. Used for perishable resources such as airline seats and hotel rooms. Auctions such as eBay can use competitive bidding to determine prices. With increasing online and mobile purchases of products, businesses are able to use a variety of dynamic pricing strategies to determine prices.

rior quality, when convenience is the key factor in the customer base.

When dealing with large volumes of customers, small businesses may have to offer volume discounts. Going into these negotiations armed with the correct numbers will let the business owner know the price range in which he or she can negotiate. Allowances, financing, and leasing may be other ways that small businesses can assist their customers in meeting the price.

Place/Distribution

From a cost standpoint, distribution processes can add to or reduce total costs to the small business, which can be passed along to either individual or business customers. For example, it is widely quoted that as much as 20% of what consumers pay goes toward the physical distribution of goods. Thus, a significant distribution management objective is to minimize the costs of performing order-filling tasks while delivering goods to customers. In a B2B context, locating a production facility near a major customer can reduce both delivery time and delivery costs. Overall, the goal should be to perform distribution activities in order to ensure the swift, safe, and low-cost delivery of goods and services to customers.

The first step in a good distribution program is a detailed market analysis to identify the locations of the target market by mapping customer locations. With emerging businesses, there is no room for any waste. Often a detailed neighborhood market analysis can identify significant savings for a small business. Careful business process analysis (discussed in chapter 7) can be very helpful in determining what improvements can be made in distribution. In the case of a parking lot cleaning service, the business was able to significantly reduce travel time by mapping upcoming jobs and taking the most efficient routes. This reduced costs of staff time and gas while also allowing the company to book additional business due to increased efficiency. For an MBE technology firm headquartered in New Jersey, opening a Seattle-area office to focus on its work with software companies in the Northwest ensured that the MBE was able to interact with product developers on a more regular basis to deliver more timely solutions.

Suggested questions to ask about place or spatial attributes include:

- How accessible is my place of business for customers compared to my main competitors?

- Is my location compatible with the other elements of the marketing mix that I offer?
- Am I making the best use of available marketing channels for delivering goods and services to customers?
- Can I afford to gain more control over the marketing channels that are currently being used?

As an emerging business, it is tempting to focus on a narrow part of the distribution channel. For example, an Indian American promotional products firm provides products that companies give away to enhance the customer relationship or promote a product. This could include eye-catching T-shirts or pens with the company logo. The promotional products company could focus on providing products only when the customer asks for them. If, for example, the customer has a trade show in two months and wants two thousand mugs as giveaways, the company must scramble to find a source for the mugs, print the logo, and get the shipment to the customer on time. This makes the business very reactive and subject to short lead-time requests. Instead of reacting, if the business, in close relationship with its customer, suggests an innovative high-tech giveaway that it has already sourced in anticipation, then logistical problems are reduced significantly. At the same time, the business better serves the customer. This is a win-win situation for the business and its customer. The business took a broad view of its customer's overall marketing strategy. Then it recommended effective products and promotional campaigns to help the customer achieve its goals. In the process, this promotional products firm created circumstances where it fulfilled orders most profitably.

As with other parts of the marketing mix, it is important to explore all feasible options in developing a distribution program. Look within the company for how warehousing, inventory management, shipping, and order processing are achieved. Analyze vendor and customer processes to determine where the value is in the chain and what efficiencies could be achieved.

Promotion

Integrated marketing communications refers to a consistent brand message across all promotional tools, which may include advertising, public relations, direct marketing, sales promotion, branded promotional products, social media platforms, and personal selling. The Awareness Interest Desire Action (AIDA) model, shown

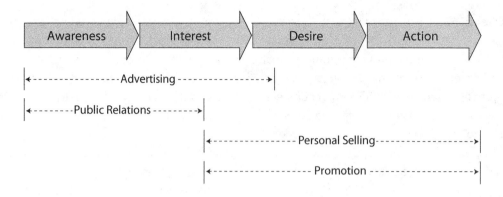

FIGURE 5-6. Awareness Interest Desire Action (AIDA) Model

in Figure 5-6, can help small business owners develop an effective communications mix based on the business's objectives. Advertising and public relations are most effective in generating product awareness and interest, but less effective in moving customers to actually buy the product or service. Personal selling and sales promotions are effective in stimulating desire and moving customers to buy, but less effective in building awareness. Ideally, a business will employ a mix of these tools, using a low-cost option such as public relations to generate awareness and using personal selling to close the deal.

Promotional tactics are more effective with emerging businesses in multicultural and hyperlocal markets. The use of broadcast media is less effective for small businesses because those methods are expensive and often ineffective in reaching a targeted hyperlocal market or a B2B market. For some first-generation immigrant consumer markets, promoting a product or service though native language media while being engaged in the targeted community is critical to success. At the same time, even though most immigrant Asian Americans and Hispanics read English, they sometimes prefer to read in their native language. The ethnic press can be a more effective means of attracting customers from ethnic markets than the mainstream press. For some small businesses, sponsoring a local event may increase brand name awareness and demonstrate an interest in the local community.

Suggested questions to ask about promotion programs and strategy include:

- Are our promotion messages clear, concise, consistent, and compatible with our position in the marketplace?
- Have we designed our promotion strategy in ways

that are cost effective in achieving our order-getting objectives?
- Are we evaluating our promotion efforts to ensure that we get "the best bang for our buck"?
- What changes should we consider making in our overall marketing communications strategy?
- Have we adopted state-of-the-art integrated communications methods and media?

Table 5-4 summarizes various promotional strategies. Three promotional strategies particularly relevant to small businesses are public relations, personal selling, and social customer relationship marketing, including online marketing and social media.

Public Relations. Marketing to ethnic markets may take the enterprise into religious and community institutions, where it is important to generate goodwill. For African Americans and Hispanics, the church may be a good place to reach key market segments. For other groups, family associations and community service organizations may be effective. Affinity groups are an excellent way to reach markets, and people are less apt to be skeptical when reached within their own community. However, sensitivity must be exercised in approaching these respected institutions. The communication must be authentic and appropriate, and it is most effective when delivered by someone from within the community.

Public relations, also referred to as earned media as opposed to the paid media associated with paid advertising, can be an effective way of implementing an emotional branding strategy. The business owner who has overcome the odds can be an excellent story for the local press. A company producing a line of hair care products for "curly and kinky hair" can choose to focus on getting

TABLE 5-4. Promotional Strategies

Media	Method	Cost	Small Business Advantages
Direct mail includes flyers, postcards, e-mail	Use of word-processing software allows person-alized mailings, use of desktop publishing allows business to design its own materials	Costs typically range from $1.50 to $5.00 per mailed piece, with additional cost for mailing-list acquisition when seeking new customers. E-mailing can cost consider-ably less.	Advantages include an effective way to communicate with current customers, with research showing that e-mail marketing is most effective when targeting existing cus-tomers rather than new ones. Provides an opportunity to communicate with different customers in their native language.
Print media	Create ads and place in local newspapers	Ethnic newspapers and maga-zines can offer reasonable cost due to lower circulation than mass media publications	For small businesses moving to adjacent markets, ethnic newspapers are an effec-tive way to reach another multicultural market, and ads can be placed in different languages. Increasing print media is mov-ing online.
Yellow Pages	Place ad or listing in Yellow Pages. Often includes a listing in online Yellow Pages.	Can range from a few hundred to over $1,000 a year depend-ing on size of the ad	In general, B2C companies that compete on price or service time availability find advantage with this strategy. Although many Yellow Pages are also moving online, print versions still exist in some markets.
Outdoor	Billboard, awnings, or other signage in high-traffic areas	Cost runs about $1,000 a year	Can be very effective for reaching local markets, especially if signage is placed in high-traffic areas. As messages online become increasingly oversaturated, sig-nage is making a comeback for getting attention. Local zoning laws need to be checked to see what is allowable.
Sales promotions, including online coupons, contests, samples, point-of-purchase displays	Sales promotions can be in-store or part of mailings or ads	Determine costs and exposure or reach prior to use or rollout	The small business often works with very little margin for error. Inexperienced busi-ness owners may want to pursue promo-tions because they think that will generate new business. A breakeven analysis should be conducted before application to ensure new business generation.
Social media	Promotion via Facebook, customer review sites, blogs, and Twitter	The most significant cost is staff time to update infor-mation and correct errors or respond to customer complaints	Encourages customer intimacy and requires little out-of-pocket expenditures beyond staff time

its product line reviewed in hairstyling blogs written by independent reviewers. In the case of an architectural firm, a photo spread of a design in a local magazine's home section is much more effective than running a generic ad in the same magazine. Having a comprehen-sive website with extensive information about the firm can be a good way of generating press interest. Reporters conduct Internet searches on community-related topics. If the website is professional and includes all the excellent credentials of the business owner, the reporter will often follow up for more information.

Simple and low-cost steps can be taken to create an effective public relations plan. All employees should be trained in explaining what the business does and its role in the community. Usually the business owner is the spokesperson for the business, but if he or she is uncom-fortable with the role, a designated spokesperson should be trained to answer any inquiries. The business should create a high-quality press kit outlining all its accomplish-ments as a business and its contributions to the commu-nity; the kit should be is adaptable to print, e-mail, and Web. The firm should regularly update its website with photos, videos, and other information that show these accomplishments. Cultivating a relationship with local reporters or bloggers in the industry might encourage them to write about the business or ask for a quote. A calendar of events that the company will participate in, such as community festivals (for B2C firms) or trade shows (for B2B firms), will keep the public informed. Producing and distributing press releases is not as effective as cultivating relationships with reporters who can then be reached by phone when the business owner has a story idea to pitch.

B2C businesses can issue regular newsletters electronically and can cultivate a community of supporters on Facebook, Instagram, Pinterest, Twitter, or other social networking sites to reach customers as well as develop relationships with online and print reporters and reviewers. B2C businesses can use Facebook, LinkedIn, and Twitter to enable followers to discuss new product or service offerings. Social media used to reach online or print reporters and reviewers can also be used as a vehicle for promoting participation in community events, trade shows, awards, or other developments in a business. Business anniversaries and other landmarks can be celebrated with the community. Developing partnerships with nonprofit organizations may provide name recognition in press releases issued by the nonprofit. Heartfelt participation in the community will create trust within the community for the business. In using online forums, the business should manage its community so that negative feedback does not foster more negativity. This requires an employee or service charged with monitoring and moderating all posts. Often the moderator is assisted by "power customers" who will respond in support or defense of the business. A response from another customer is often more credible than one from an employee of the business. Building this community of customers who will respond is an important tactic with social media. More information about using social media to deepen relationships with customers is at the end of this chapter.

Personal selling. An entrepreneur serves as the firm's main salesperson in its initial years; therefore, having strong sales skills is crucial to a new business's success. The founder of the company is the main salesperson in 82% of ventures. Sales skills are all the more essential because almost 90% of a fledgling enterprise's early sales are from direct sales.[7]

The key to any successful sales strategy is discerning the needs of the customer and finding the product or service to meet that need when information is not totally accessible. It is in this role that the business owner should be creative and responsive in shaping and meeting the undefined requirements of a new and upcoming market niche. Being the frontline salesperson for the firm allows the entrepreneur to have direct access to customer wants and needs. It gives him or her the opportunity to customize offerings as needed to get the sale. Having this close contact with the customer provides a significant advantage over large firms, where sales departments do not connect so intimately with product development or manufacturing teams. Personal selling is especially important for complex or expensive products or services and allows for relationship building, which can lead to long-term sales growth.

In executing a sales strategy, the business owner must have the tenacity to get a foot in the door. For this reason, having worked in the industry before provides a strong advantage if the business owner had a customer-facing role prior to starting the new business. Because of past relationships with the owner in another capacity, potential customers may be more willing to begin a relationship with the new small business.

Networks. A major constraint with small businesses is lack of financial, human, and other resources. Bootstrapping with a small staff and hiring whoever is available in the employment pool, the business owner does not have a reserve of sales support to fall back on. To overcome this, business owners need to develop networks. Such networks or clusters have been found to work very effectively in emerging economies, to such an extent that these networks of smaller firms can compete globally with much larger enterprises. For example, small businesses in Brazil developed clusters to compete in the shoe industry.[8] During boom times, the business is able to outsource to other businesses in its cluster to meet demand. Businesses pass sales leads that they cannot fulfill to other companies in the cluster. They group together to purchase equipment.

In a start-up, it is essential that the business owner use her or his selling skills to develop a network. As noted before, immigrant businesses tend to cluster in areas where they can find co-ethnic workers and a community more conducive to the lifestyle of the business owner. Clustering among Korean American entrepreneurs has assisted in creating a pool of capital to start businesses.

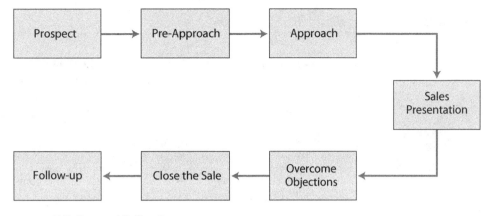

FIGURE 5-7. Personal Selling Process

The same clustering has occurred in various US industries, including Internet, biotechnology, and medical instruments firms. The creation of entrepreneur support systems that include large corporate partners, government, and supply chain partners is important to the success of gazelles, MBEs, and immigrant businesses.

Business-to-business selling process. Salespeople in B2B environments typically follow a seven-step personal selling process as outlined in Figure 5-7. Through networks, small business owners can identify prospects and determine their potential for being good customers. The pre-approach stage refers to researching and understanding the prospect's key decision makers, current suppliers, and business practices. The small business owner will contact the prospect during the approach stage to gain access and schedule an appointment for the sales presentation. It is very important that the business owner develop a sales pitch that effectively sells the company to any potential customers or referral sources.

Some business owners who come from Asian and other cultures where it is inappropriate to "boast" about oneself may initially find this difficult. The owner also has to learn to ask for the order, overcome objections, provide information on how the product matches the needs of the customer, and close the sale. These may be behaviors that are contrary to the owner's culture. The owner must be taught to be diligent in getting as much information as he can from the customer so that the sales pitch can be tailored to the needs of the specific customer. Basic to a good sales pitch is a strong belief in, indeed a passion for, the product and company. Additionally, the owner must back this up with impeccable customer service. Every employee who has contact with customers must show the same diligence and impeccable service. Finally, the business owner follows up with the customer to make sure that the order was received as expected. This helps reduce the potential for buyer's remorse and helps build a long-term, profitable relationship.

CUSTOMER RELATIONSHIP MANAGEMENT

Customer relationship management (CRM) is a process that uses technology to capture and analyze customer data to precisely identify customer needs as a means of developing deeper customer relationships. These customer needs are translated into business processes such as campaigns, generating leads, developing contacts, making the offer, and creating the contract. However, it is a mistake to think of CRM as mainly applying computer software. It is more about adopting technology and strategy to expand marketing opportunities. Businesses that adopt CRM as a strategy are likely to be more successful. The software allows the business to customize by using an automated set of rules. CRM has made the servicing of micromarkets economically viable. In effect, at its best, CRM eliminates the advantages of economies of scale enjoyed by larger enterprises and levels the playing field for emerging businesses (Table 5-5, Figure 5-8).

Customer Value Proposition

Providing customers something of value should be a cornerstone of a firm's marketing effort. The basic idea is straightforward. A business should articulate to the customer what value it provides that is better than its competitors. Keep in mind that value does not always involve the lowest price. Customers may value better service or a product that is more environmentally friendly because

TABLE 5-5. Customer Relationship Management (CRM)

CRM Concept	Description	Emerging Business Issues
Create a customer value proposition	Knowing the customer well and creating a value proposition for the customer that is uniquely identified with the business	There is often a disconnect between what the business assumes and what the customer truly finds of value. It is important for businesses to determine customer needs and tailor products/services to be of value to a market segment that is seeking these benefits.
Target customer share versus market share	It is less costly to retain existing customers than to acquire new ones. Use customer lifetime value to evaluate which customers to target.	Emerging businesses often focus on gaining new customers rather than selling more products and services to existing customers
Cultivate the customer	Use customer relationship management to increase customer share and acquire new customers	Without major resources for marketing programs, the best way for a business to grow is by growing the share of its existing and adjacent customer bases. Can be done through testimonials and referrals, especially via use of social media.
Manage information about your customer	Maintain a customer database and use every opportunity to add to the database	With low-cost options for software as a service, smaller enterprises can compete effectively. Emerging businesses must develop the discipline to collect, maintain, and mine customer information.

it reduces risk and fits with their image. In fact, more successful businesses are able to communicate the value provided to customers in ways that resonate with the customers. Typically, the customer value proposition in B2C companies centers on selection, quality, service, and price (Table 5-6).[9] In B2C firms, on-time delivery and being able to deliver products with zero defects increases the value proposition. The business may include technical, economic, service, or social benefits. If the business offers the best customer service in the local market, that could form the basis of the customer value proposition.

Although most small businesses have a customer value proposition, they fail to articulate it. This omission can result in a lack of focus in the firm's marketing efforts and indecision when it comes to what direction to take. In other cases, the business owner may wrongly define its customer value proposition. For example, one African American coffee shop owner thought his customer value proposition was high-quality coffee. When a focus group was conducted with his customers, they stated that the quality of the coffee was inconsistent; rather, they purchased coffee there because it was convenient. A packaging wholesale supply company thought timely delivery of products to its business customers was the value proposition. However, the firm was able to grow its profits by successfully integrating its supplier network into a customer's distribution system, thereby delivering more products than it could from one location. Coupling extensive customer analysis with

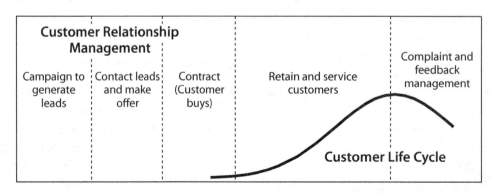

FIGURE 5-8. Customer Relationship Management and Customer Life Cycle

TABLE 5-6. Customer Value Proposition

Selection, Quality, Service, Price	
Customer benefits	Customer costs
Product	Price
Service	Cost of acquisition
Image	Maintenance
	Disposal

a careful review of the benefits and value the business can deliver is key to developing a good customer value proposition. The business must communicate clearly how it is similar to its competitors and how it is different. Then the business must deliver a value proposition that resonates with each customer.

Customer Share

A fledgling business typically targets an underserved niche market. Customer requirements for the product or service may be fuzzy, so the business makes its way by selecting paths that require relatively low amounts of invested capital but show the promise of high returns, even if the probabilities of success are low. New businesses often rely heavily on the sales skills of the entrepreneur to persuade customers to take a chance on a new business. Customers are acquired one by one; thus, each plays a large role in the success of the business.[10]

Given this scenario, much evidence suggests that the concept of customer share can be beneficial to emerging businesses. The first tenet of gaining customer share is to know the customer. In an initial direct sales contact, the business owner should collect as much information as possible on the customer and put this information into a database. In the experience of the student consulting program, even fledgling businesses with a small customer base sometimes do not know the customer. For example, a catering company owner may know that she sells five hun-

dred meals a week. But she might not be clear as to which customer is buying the most meals. The owner may also not be able to answer a range of other customer-related questions, including:

- How many customers are also buying from a competitor?
- Which competitor(s) are customers buying from?
- What other kinds of food do these customers like?

If the customer spends $4,000 on catering a month, the business owner might only be getting 10% of that customer's business. Focusing on growing customer share rather than market share will lead the business owner to focus on selling more products or services to high-potential existing customers. If a business owner can get 50% to 80% of a customer's business when each customer spends $4,000 per month, it will take only five hundred existing customers to generate $1 million in revenue, rather than thousands of new customers.

A careful analysis of customer sales can also yield more profits. A business that has 80% of its customers generating 20% of sales is in a different position than one where 50% of the customers are generating 30% of sales. Because new customers cost more to acquire than it costs to sell more to existing customers, it is advantageous to focus on increasing sales with existing customers. A rule of thumb estimates that it costs five times more to acquire a new customer than it does to maintain an existing customer. To get new customers into a store, there might be the cost of placing an ad in the newspaper, the cost of discounting a product to draw them in, the cost of printing and mailing postcards, or the cost of using a Web-based coupon service. For B2C companies the sales cycle can be shortened when selling more products and services to existing customers rather than seeking to acquire new customers. Getting more sales from existing customers will cost considerably less. If the business is able to capture the most ardent customers of the product and is able to get those customers to buy most of their product from the business, the highest profitability will result.

Ironically, the mission of CRM is to return the large enterprise to its small business roots. Yet small businesses tend to forget how important it is to manage the customer life cycle by cultivating the customer. To conceptualize CRM, consider the example of the neighborhood family Mexican restaurant. When entering the res-

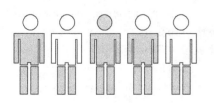

Get the most sales out of each customer

Capture percent of market

FIGURE 5-9. Customer Share versus Market Share

taurant, the customer is greeted by name and shown to her favorite table. Instead of being handed the standard menu, the owner recommends a dish based on current availability of the freshest ingredients, careful to avoid the customer's dislikes and with a good sense of what the customer might prefer on that day, given the time of year and the weather. The owner automatically brings a glass of the customer's favorite wine and ensures that the water has a fresh slice of lemon, just as the customer likes. The owner knows that the customer has a family celebration coming up and suggests that she can host the dinner party at the restaurant or have the event catered at her home if she so desires. The owner spends time talking to the patron and knows all the other restaurants she patronizes. He knows how often she dines out. He knows all the major events in her life that might require a dinner party. On her birthday, he will prepare a special cake as a present.

Using social media can be a part of a CRM strategy. Using the same neighborhood Mexican restaurant example, customer birthdays and anniversaries can be tracked online and proactive messages can be sent without waiting until a customer comes to the restaurant. Even in B2C relationships, use of social media can be a key part of a CRM strategy, but rather than tracking birthdays on Facebook, a salesperson may track career milestones on LinkedIn.

This kind of personalized service can do much to engage the customer, and it is quite conceivable that the business owner can gain a large share of this customer's restaurant spending. A recent study that included Asian and Hispanic customers showed that friendly and personalized service, especially from service providers with whom they shared ethnicity, resulted in increased satisfaction and loyalty and positive word of mouth.[11] Satisfied customers more likely recommend the restaurant to their friends. The owner can adjust his service experience to meet customers' expectations, especially for Hispanic or Asian customers in the previous example, and thus draw more customers.

A similar story is told by other entrepreneurs. Great benefits can come when entrepreneurs focus on the customer. For example, one business owner described how he started his business subcontracting for a large Fortune 100 company. He got to know his customers well and found out that they were outsourcing other kinds of production and services. The business owner followed up by providing whatever the customer wanted, often

pursuing products or services that were completely different from his core business. By providing for customer needs, the business was able to grow quickly and discover new markets.

Customer Lifetime Value

The concept of customer lifetime value is an important one to develop within a business. When a customer walks into a business and buys a product or service, most businesses value the customer for that single transaction. The next customer who buys a product or service is valued for that single transaction. In fact, when a customer walks into a business, he or she represents many more purchases than that single transaction.

To properly determine what a customer is worth, innovative and successful businesses will calculate a customer lifetime value. For large and sophisticated enterprises, this is often done with statistical modeling. The model will incorporate the customer's past performance plus other factors such as demographics, preferences, or psychographic factors that might determine how much the customer will buy and for how long. The model is updated using information about similar customers. This is possible in large enterprises because they have databases that capture all customer transactions, which they can combine with other databases they acquire. It is even simpler for a small business. The key is to capture the information through customer databases.

A B2C illustration of this concept is given here, but the same principles can be applied in a B2B context. Consider customers of a popular independent coffee shop. The average tab for each customer is $6, and a typical customer visits on average four times a week. Customers continue to patronize the coffee shop for around for six years, and about 90% of customers are retained from year to year. The coffee shop has done a careful analysis and has calculated that the incremental profit per customer is 20%. The coffee shop updates its customer analytics and costs annually.

A simple nondiscounted calculation of customer lifetime value would be the gross revenues for each new customer. In the coffee shop scenario, this would be achieved by multiplying the following: $6 average revenue per customer multiplied by 4 visits per customer per week multiplied by 52 weeks per year equals $1,248 in revenues per year per customer. For lifetime revenues per customer: $1,248 in revenues per year per customer multiplied by the 6 years the customer stays with the

TABLE 5-7. Customer Lifetime Value Analysis

	Year 0	Year 1	Year 2	Year 3	Year 4	Year 5	Year 6
Revenue per customer per year ($)		1,248	1,248	1,248	1,248	1,248	1,248
(Average tab × frequency for year)							
Profit per customer ($)		250	250	250	250	250	250
(Revenue per customer × 20% gross profit)							
Cumulative retention rate		100%	90%	81%	73%	66%	59%
Cumulative discount rate (8%)		93%	86%	79%	74%	68%	63%
Expected present value in year ($)		231	193	160	134	111	93
(Profit × retention rate × discount rate)							
Cumulative net present value ($)		231	424	584	718	829	922

shop equals $7,488. To get the simple nondiscounted profit, multiply the revenues by the 20% gross profit percentage, for $1,498 ($250 profit per year).

More complicated calculations of customer lifetime value include discounting and retention rates. Using such an analysis, the lifetime value of a customer at the coffee shop would be $922 (Table 5-7). Therefore, the coffee shop would evaluate the cost of marketing programs against this lifetime value. If there are opportunities to cross-sell or if the customer refers other customers, additional profit streams might be possible. A focus on customer lifetime value as opposed to profit in a single year allows more accurate cost-benefit analysis of marketing programs.

As with any model, it is important to continue to test it. If a typical customer does not stay for six years, does not purchase $1,248 per year, or does not generate a 20% gross margin, or if the customer retention rate does not stay at 90%, this will affect the calculation.

Also critical to the usefulness of this model is making sure that the costs are correct. When a marketing program is designed and implemented, it is important to track all costs associated with it. This requires careful analysis. For example, in the case of an online store, although most such businesses track the costs of designing and maintaining a store website, they fail to determine what additional costs they incur when fulfilling the orders. Order sizes may decrease, and more handling and shipping costs might be incurred. However, if it is assumed that handling and shipping are the same, these costs will not be included in the accounting of customer profitability. Additionally, the business must be careful to track all customers acquired through the marketing program. How many leads are generated from a marketing program?

How many conversions to sales are made from these leads? If conversion rates fall, the program cost per customer will rise.

Tracking costs and customers meticulously allows the business to determine the difference between the cost to acquire customers and the cost to retain customers. It will become evident in fairly short order that retaining a customer is much more cost effective than acquiring a new customer. Even the most targeted marketing programs reach a small portion of the market.

Each marketing program will differ in the number of customers it generates. There is less information on new customers than on existing customers. Will they buy again? Will they recommend to other customers? These are open questions when new customers are acquired and depend on good customer relationship management. For existing customers, a history of buying behavior helps the business determine what is possible.

Once accurate accounting of the "cost to acquire" and the "cost to retain" a customer is obtained, the business can perform calculations to determine where to allocate resources. Often the business finds that it is much more cost effective to design and deploy programs to retain customers versus those needed to acquire customers.

Defining profitability. Businesses that have an accurate accounting of profitability by customer or customer type have a tremendous advantage over those that do not. It is possible for these businesses to differentiate customers. The 80/20 rule, while not actually a rule like supply and demand, often holds when customer sales are analyzed. Some customers buy many times and recommend to their friends. As such, this 20% of customers may account for 80% of revenues. These are the customers that the business wants to cultivate with customized marketing programs or offers. Other customers buy infrequently, and when they do, they complain, they require much support, and they return the product more frequently than others. These customers cost the business time, expense, and morale. With emerging businesses, often these high-maintenance customers will occupy a large part of the business owner's time. They are unlikely to be profitable and in fact take up resources that could be used to generate profitability elsewhere. Some business thinkers feel these customers should be "fired."

It is important to divide all customers into groupings that define their profitability. The business should identify good customers and give them the attention they are due. Some businesses will assign staff to high-value customers. They take the opportunity to develop a deeper relationship with these customers. They will call them to get feedback on their experience. They will thank them for being good customers. They will collaborate with them to customize the product or service so that it better fits their needs. They can be targeted to be viral marketers of the business by recommending the business to their friends through social media.

Groupings can also be used to organize the business's customers so that the business is responsive to specific needs. Most minority businesses serve a combination of ethnic and mainstream markets. These markets cannot be treated in the same way. It is important that the business define groupings and focus staff, customer service, and marketing programs appropriately. In the same way, the business must market to and service different age and gender groups or other types of market segments.

Touchpoints. For fledgling and growing businesses alike, every interaction between the business owner and customers is important in building the relationship with the customer. There are many opportunities to interact with the customer, and each customer "touchpoint" should be exploited to build trust with the customer by getting to know the customer. The key touchpoints that are useful in consulting projects are illustrated in Figure 5-10.

Direct sales are the main route for getting information about a customer. The business owner should make sure that each meeting allows enough time to get to know the customer. What are the goals of the customer? What problems is the customer trying to solve? Whom does

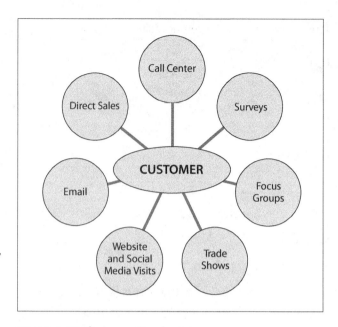

FIGURE 5-10. Customer Touchpoints

the customer partner with? Whom does the customer buy from? All this information should be kept in a database for future reference. The fledgling business wants to be an integral part of the customer's value chain.

Phone or e-mail ranks next in terms of getting information, and the business owner should make sure that the employees responsible for responding to e-mail make note of any relevant data. Quick response to e-mail queries can build trust with the customer, while phone meetings are opportunities to get more nuanced information. Even with the advent of numerous platforms for social media, phone and e-mail remain the most cost-effective means of generating customer leads and retaining customers.

Customer service (which may include e-mail, telephone, and face to face) is another major touchpoint for customers. Customer service staff must be courteous and integrate any information they obtain from the customer in the database.

Website and social media site visits are also important, and many B2C businesses give incentives to their customers for signing in when they visit the site or connect by social media. Such incentives could be access to information about new products in advance of other customers, access to order status, or access to other information. Having customers identify themselves helps the business track information about what kinds of questions customers have about products, or their browsing may

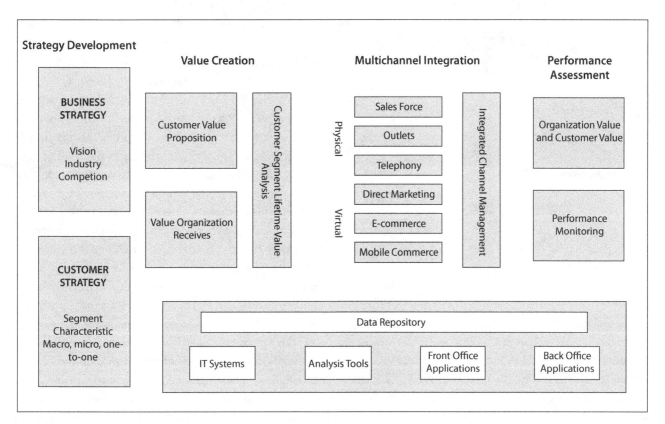

FIGURE 5-11. CRM Strategy

give indications of other types of products in which they may be interested.

For much of B2B marketing, trade shows play a crucial role in distributing information about products and services. Trade shows also provide direct contact with buyers. There are approximately eleven thousand trade shows every year. Businesses must be aware of when their industry's main trade shows are scheduled. In some industries, such as clothing design and manufacturing, buying is predominantly done at trade shows at certain times of the year to coincide with the selling season. As buyers can encounter fatigue with this venue, it is important to develop ways of appearing fresh and new.

Finally, surveys and focus groups can be used to elicit customer information. Response rates for customer e-mail surveys can be 10% to 20%. For the emerging business with no resources, the student team survey can provide invaluable information to help the business move forward. More information on these specific tools is presented in chapter 6, on market research.

Some practitioners believe that a CRM strategy should be at the core of a business's strategy and should encompass a broad spectrum, including strategy devel-opment, value creation, multichannel integration, and performance measurements.[12] Figure 5-11 depicts how such a strategy may be mapped out.

SOCIAL CUSTOMER RELATIONSHIP MANAGEMENT, ONLINE MARKETING, AND SOCIAL MEDIA

In a 2014 survey, the Pew Research Center found that 87% of American adults now use the Internet. Usage among those living in households earning $75,000 or more was 99%. Among young adults ages eighteen to twenty-nine, it was 97%, the same as among those with college degrees. Further, 68% of adults connect to the Internet with mobile devices like smartphones or tablet computers, and 58% of adults use smartphones.[13] As noted previously, some multicultural populations such as young Hispanics and Asians have higher rates of online and mobile use than the general population.

As Web usage evolved, it became evident that Web interactions were an extension of customer relationship management, where customer leads are generated through the Internet rather than in a physical location.

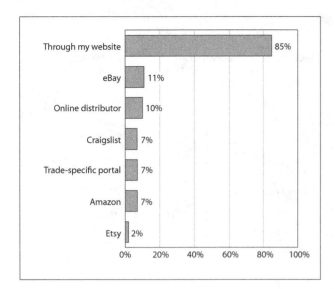

FIGURE 5-12. How SMEs Sell Online, 2013. Source: National Small Business Association

Business campaigns shifted to the Web, and online ad spending (desktop Internet and mobile) grew to 20% of all ad spending in 2013, surpassing newspapers at 17% and magazines at 8%, with mobile ad allocation expected to double by 2016.[14] The use of paid online searches (or placement on search engines through words searched) will continue to be the largest component of online advertising. E-mail, classified, and display ads are contracting as channels. With the growth of social platforms like Twitter and Facebook, display ads have regained prominence as effective means of targeting according to customer profiles.

As advertising moves increasingly away from print to the Internet, small businesses are given the opportunity to compete effectively with large companies, as it is possible to target very small segments of the market. This requires that small businesses better segment their potential customer base and conduct analyses to determine strategies to best reach their target customers.

The National Small Business Association (NSBA) conducted a technology survey of small businesses in 2013 (Figure 5-12). It found that 82% of businesses have a traditional website, while 18% have a mobile website and 5% have an app. The majority of businesses (66%) maintain their website internally, while 30% (down from 41% in 2010) outsource this.

The NSBA survey found that more small businesses are selling their products online: 28% in 2013 compared to 26% in 2010. Of the businesses that sold online, 85% did so through their own website. Credit and debit cards

were accepted by 69% in 2013, a drop from 91% in 2010 as many businesses moved to third-party vendors such as PayPal (up to 47% from 22%) due to a desire to provide higher levels of cybersecurity.

Regarding the use of social media as a sales platform, the survey found that the most frequently used site was LinkedIn, followed by Facebook (Figure 5-13). It is notable that 85% of small businesses used social media to do business networking rather than as a customer-facing tool.

For small businesses that do use social media as a customer-facing tool, most use it as a form of broadcast advertising. The "like" app on Facebook allows customers to signal to friends that they like the business or support the brand. Customers use social media to receive promotions, to get updates on future projects, to learn more about the company, and to be informed about upcoming sales; all forms serve to advertise and promote the business. This is also a means for small businesses to incorporate permission marketing, a way for customers to opt in to marketing communication. Listening in on social media can assist the enterprise in adding wanted product and service features, developing new products, projecting future trends, and anticipating possible negative trends or crises. Some low-cost means of listening include Google Alerts, Technorati blog searches, Twitter searches, Facebook searches, and YouTube searches on keywords that may be of interest to the business.

Large corporations have already integrated social media as part of the CRM strategy, using social media as a marketing communication channel to provide brand and product information. Social media is also used to discover, expand, and evaluate knowledge about customers by analyzing data from profiles, postings, and links. Service is provided and products are sold on social media platforms. The collaborative power of social media has

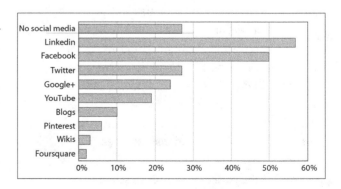

FIGURE 5-13. Small Business Use of Social Media, 2013. Source: National Small Business Association

CRM Processes		Social Media Data	Social Functionalities	Social CRM Process
1. Campaign management	Social Media Use	1. Posting body	1. Search	1. Monitoring
2. Lead management	1. Provision of content	2. Posting envelope	2. Social media monitoring	2. Management
3. Contact management	2. Analysis of content	3. Profile body	3. Business intelligence	3. Interaction
4. Offer management	3. Channel for transaction	4. Links	4. CRM system	
5. Contract management	4. Platform for cooperation		5. Social media management	
6. Retention management			6. Community	
7. Service management			7. Social network analysis	
8. Complaint/feedback management				

FIGURE 5-14. Social CRM

been used to develop products and define marketing campaigns. A company like Dell uses social media throughout it CRM processes—campaign launches, lead management, contact management, offer management, contract management, retention management, service management, and feedback management.[15] Figure 5-14 shows the areas where social CRM has an impact.

Creating a Web Presence

A business website or social media site can be an effective marketing tool, although some B2C firms have begun to adopt the use of only social media platforms. When developing a website, a business must have very clear goals about what it hopes to achieve. Websites provide the opportunity to improve relationships with existing customers. A company can provide in-depth detail about its products and services at very low cost. A website or social media site provides the small business with the ability to reach new markets both nationally and internationally. It can cut costs and increase efficiencies by allowing customers to access information at any time and from anywhere. In a B2B context, websites are no longer an optional vehicle for providing current and prospective customers with information.

When properly designed and used, company websites and social media sites are very effective in reaching current and new customers. As with every aspect of marketing, the design of a website or social media site starts by asking the customer what he or she wants and ensuring ease in finding this information in a manner that can lead to a sale.

For the most part, it is recommended that the business contract a Web design company to create a website. Student teams that are working with a small business can assist in developing the content as well as the architecture of a site by asking the following questions:

1. What is the objective of the site? (Examples: online shopping, electronic brochure, develop relationships, gather market research, manage events, build awareness, gather sales leads, or provide service.)
2. What type of visitors will the site attract?
3. Is the website effective in meeting its established objectives?
4. What are the aesthetics and overall visual appeal? Is the website memorable, well differentiated, or fairly standard? Are the branding, aesthetics, and information on the website consistent with all other touchpoints?
5. What are the key differences (positive or negative) between this website and competitors' sites? (Differences could be in terms of aesthetics, ease of use, extent of information and options, or any other aspect of website evaluation.)

A competitive website analysis is the best way of determining the best features to include. A business should identify its competitors, ask customers who they consider competitors, and conduct a search on keywords to see which competitors emerge. Figure 5-15 maps out the key characteristics in effective websites, and Table 5-8 outlines typical ways to assess competitors' websites and their capabilities.

Information quality can be measured by asking questions about the website's depth, scope, and completeness. Updating information is crucial to keeping the website current. The information has to be clear and easily understandable. Service quality is particularly important on an e-commerce website. Empathy is the care and attention the business gives the customer. Reliability ensures that the service can be performed dependably and accurately. Responsiveness is prompt service. Customers are more likely to be satisfied with systems quality if the website is easy to navigate, pages load quickly, the site is personalized to the customer, and there is a sense of reality (telepresence) in the virtual environment. For business-specific quality, the brand of the business should be evident. A reputable business

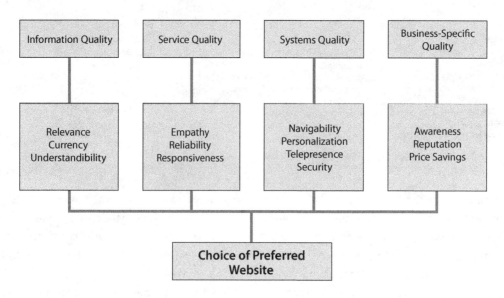

FIGURE 5-15. Evaluating the Effectiveness of a Website

TABLE 5-8. Evaluating a Website

Feature	Reason	Tools
Ranking and traffic	Ranking shows how high up the website will appear in a search. Traffic gives an indication of how many visitors come to the website. Comparative page ranks help the business understand where its website stands against competition.	Alexa provides overall ranking and general demographics Searchmetrics provides ranking on search as well as links PageRank Checker is another site that provides ranking
Keywords	Keywords give the business an indication of what words customers use to search a product or service. The business can add keywords to capture more searches.	Google AdWords provides metrics on keywords used Google Trends provides current hot topics. Wordtracker has a free basic keyword search
Search engine speed		Google page speed insights can indicate how quickly the page loads
Social media	Use of social media by the competitor can show which platforms are most effective	Check the website to see links to social media Check the platform to determine likes and followers Open Site Explorer provides an accounting of links HubSpot's marketing grader can provide an overall evaluation
Branding	Quality and consistent branding can lead to more customer trust and purchases	Check aesthetics to see if high-quality images are used. Check for errors in copy. Is the communication consistent with the customer value proposition?
Call to action	Websites are strongest when they encourage the potential customer to contact the company	Is there consistent call to action throughout the site? Does the website encourage customers to contact the business or to buy?
Other features	Websites can provide a wealth of competitive information	For B2B websites, a catalog may be included along with order form. It is often possible to determine turnaround times on requests for bids Customer lists and testimonials provide information on the type of industries the business serves

Bunky Boutique
A Case Study on Social Customer Relationship Management

When Rachel Malloy moved to downtown Phoenix, she felt that there were too few local businesses. To remedy this, in 2007 she launched Bunky Boutique. She brought in an architect to design a space that gives the perception of a larger shop, with its unique walls creating small cutout areas in which customers can shop privately for clothing and other accessories. Malloy can also open (or close) up her shop with the movable "walls," since the adjacent locally owned coffee shop operates separately. Her store layout is just one unique aspect of Bunky Boutique.

In 2013, Malloy brought in student consultants to assess her marketing and branding strategies. They began by evaluating her brand elements, including the brand name ("Bunky" was Malloy's grandmother), logo, and consistency of her marketing collateral. Like many small business owners, Malloy has a strong personal connection to the Bunky Boutique brand, and her product offerings reflect her passion for supporting unique designers and the local community.

The student consultants gathered customers' perceptions of Bunky Boutique using an online survey, and they conducted several customer interviews. Malloy was anxious to "learn more about her customers, confirm hunches, and act on the data." The students found that customers strongly associated Malloy and her brand with a unique local Phoenix vibe. They recommended a brand mantra (core essence of the brand), Unique Phoenix Fashion, which she implemented as part of her new branding strategy. The survey also revealed that her customers were more interested in unique clothing and accessories than discounts. She now offers fewer promotions (about once a year) and sales are up. She learned where many of her customers live, such as Phoenix historic districts, which helped her target the right customer.

Her online marketing strategy offered more opportunity, especially her website and use of social media. The website was not an accurate reflection of her unique

retail store. The students suggested featuring Malloy and her unique product offerings more prominently. She also wanted to use social media as a hub for communicating what was new with the brand. She uses Facebook to share images of new clothing and accessories and promote new inventory. Customers are encouraged to act fast, as there is high product turnover due to limited supply of the locally designed merchandise. The students created #Howdoyoubunky as a way for customers to share photos of themselves wearing the boutique's clothing and accessories. Malloy also maintains a blog that is consistent with the "Bunky voice." She also sends out an e-newsletter, but her resources have shifted to other social media tools that are more immediate and enable her to share customer or product images.

One of the student consultants stayed on after the project was completed and helped Malloy launch her newly designed website in 2014. Malloy found her new website to be a manageable and worthwhile expense. She now has total control over the content compared to previously, when she outsourced the site's development and maintenance. Although she thinks about opening up a second shop, she feels that she still has an opportunity to maximize her current location. She wants the business to "work for her," and she is able to delegate some of the operations to well-trained employees.

Bunky Boutique has won numerous awards and kudos, such as the *Phoenix New Times* best new boutique (2007) and inclusion in *USA Today*'s ten best places to shop in downtown Phoenix.

builds trust with the customer. The customer should also perceive value with price savings. The business website that ranks high on information, service, and systems and business-specific quality will be the preferred website.[16] A survey of both external and internal users will give a good indication of how effective a website is.

Search Engine Optimization

Search engine optimization (SEO) is a means of bringing traffic to the business owner's website. Potential customers overwhelmingly use search engines as a means of finding the products and services they need. These search engines provide and funnel the traffic based on a number of factors that the business owner should seek to maximize.

The key is to get the business website link on as many other sites as possible and have those inbound links direct traffic to the site. This includes creating free listings on sites such as Yelp, Google, and the Yellow Pages as well as on industry-specific websites. Search rankings are based on link popularity. The more clicks on the link, the higher the resultant ranking. Business owners should also limit the number of outbound links that take people off the business website. The business could track website traffic by using free services such as Google Analytics and improve SEO tactics as necessary.

Social Media

Social media have become major forms of marketing. Examples include forums, blogs, comments, review sites, and Twitter. For example, most business owners start by using Google Alerts to track any keyword or brand mentions. This communication tool informs business owners of the specific keywords that customers search for when looking for their products or services. This information can be used to adjust the keywords attached to business websites.

Twitter is the real-time media that keeps users current on happenings and various types of chatter. This might be the first place a rant (negative comment) or rave (positive comment) will be mentioned. From Twitter, posts can quickly go viral, making it difficult to implement the right damage control (for example, a customer may post a complaint about the business). Business owners should monitor Twitter and other social media sites to determine both positive and negative feedback on the business.

Creating a blog for the business is another way to drive traffic to its website. The more content and density on the business website, the higher its search engine rankings will climb. Businesses should encourage their loyal customers to post reviews on sites such as Yelp.

Online coupon services such as Groupon and Living Social have been used to drive new customers to businesses. It is important to do a careful break-even analysis to determine at what level couponing is effective. Review services such as Yelp can also bring customers into the business. It is important that the business encourage loyal customers to post reviews. At the same time, the business should monitor reviews so that any negative reviews can be dealt with quickly. All marketers need to be aware that social media platforms will continue to evolve, and selecting the appropriate sites for a company will take careful analysis.

Maintaining the Website

For most small businesses, it makes sense to use an Internet service provider (ISP) to host the website rather than rely on the business's own servers. It is difficult for a small company to ensure that servers are up twenty-four hours a day, seven days a week, and that it has adequate security to ward off malicious hackers or other online criminals. In fact, large companies spend a significant amount of money to ensure security. For relatively low cost, a small business can get enough space at an ISP to satisfy all its Web requirements. Cloud computing services allow even more cost controls and reliable operations, as clients pay for only the amount of server space used (which can be expanded as demand increases or lowered when demand is down). If a small business buys broadband service such as a DSL line, the provider may include a website in the package.

Neglecting a website may lead customers to distrust the company. Customers may perceive the company to be disorganized and to not care about its products, or worse, not care about its customers. The business must maintain the website regularly. Monthly reviews to check information accuracy and links are very important. Make sure someone within the business has been trained to do this and that the person is accountable for what he or she does.

MARKETING PLAN

The marketing plan brings together all the concepts covered in this chapter. Like the business plan described in chapter 1, it includes a description of the business's current market situation and provides a road map for marketing activities over a specified period of time, typically one to five years. A marketing plan contains about 60% to 70% of the content included in a business plan and provides direction not just for marketing but for the entire organization. For some small businesses, a marketing plan is often used in place of a business plan. The following provides the elements of a marketing plan. Keep in mind that many of these elements are covered throughout this book.

FIGURE 5-16. Components of a Marketing Plan

Executive summary. This section briefly describes the plan's highlights and objectives. As cautioned in this book's epilogue, executive summaries take time to write and should be revised several times.

Current market situation. Situational analysis identifies internal and external environmental factors that may affect the small business. SWOT, PESTLE, Five Forces, and other tools covered in chapter 1 may be used. The current market situation, including top competitors, is characterized.

- What are the current or projected sales of or demand for the business's product/service in this market?

- What are the major industry trends?
- Who are the major competitors, and what are their market positions in terms of sales? What are their positioning strategies?
- Who are the customers in the market and what products/services are they buying?
- What customer needs are satisfied by the business's product/service? How profitably is this done?

Target market, positioning strategy, and customer analysis. This section describes the target market. Include market segmentation factors such as geographic (e.g., city, region, zip code), demographic (e.g., age, gender, family size, family life cycle, income, occupation, education, race, and religion), psychographic (e.g., lifestyle), or behavioral (e.g., consumption by occasion, benefits sought, user status, usage rate, or loyalty status)

The positioning strategy is defined. Competitive advantage and core competencies are identified. A positioning strategy is created based on meaningful differentiation. A customer profile is developed. The customer decision-making process is described for the product/service, including key influencing factors.

Objectives. Objectives should be specific, measurable, attainable, relevant, and time-bound (SMART), given environmental opportunities and threats outlined in the SWOT analysis. They should also be consistent with the business's mission, goals, and priorities, in addition to supporting the strategic direction of the marketing plan. Objectives should be aligned with the business's resources, strengths, and capabilities.

Marketing strategy. The marketing mix provides the basis for marketing strategy. Key questions to ask about the four elements of the marketing mix are outlined below.

PRODUCT
- What products or services are being offered?
- How does each product support the business strategy and objectives?
- How do each product's features and benefits, quality, packaging, services, and branding provide value for customers?
- What product or service enhancements, or changes to the product lines, would add value to customers and help the business reach its goals?

PRICE

- How can pricing be used to support the business objectives and brand positioning?
- What are each product's costs, and how do they affect the profits? How does this compare to competing products?
- How do channel and promotion decisions affect pricing?
- How do customers perceive the product's value? Are customers price sensitive?
- What price promotion tools can be used (e.g., quantity discounts, etc.)?

PLACE/DISTRIBUTION

- How do product, data, and money flow through the value chain, and how can participants add more value for customers?
- How and where do customers expect or prefer to buy products, and how does that affect channel decisions?
- Who will manage inventory, orders, billing, shipping, and payment, and how will this be tracked?
- Who will transport and store supplies, parts, and finished products? How will this be done, where will products be stored, and when will this happen?

PROMOTION

- How is the value proposition communicated to customers?
- How do customers respond to certain types of media and messages?
- Is the message consistent across all marketing communication tools, such as ads, social media, personal selling, and direct marketing?
- How are social media being used?

Market research. This section asks what type of research (secondary or primary data) the business will use to achieve its goals. An example in new product development might be to use concept testing, surveys, and focus groups to identify product/service features and benefits that customers value. Regarding marketing communications, the business could measure promotion effectiveness by tracking coupons used or sales that result from promotions or discounts. Customer satisfaction feedback could be solicited through surveys.

Marketing programs. A marketing program spells out specific activities to achieve goals and responsibilities. It provides the "who, what, when, and how" of the marketing plan. A timeline is also included.

Financial and operational plans. Financial projections and budgets are a crucial part of the marketing plan. They outline expected revenues and profits. Schedules and responsibilities are also articulated in this section.

Metrics and implementation control. As discussed in chapter 1, plans are only as good as what the business can measure. The business must create metrics, such as new customers acquired by month, quarter, or year. It might measure customer lifetime value. Results are assessed after the plan is implemented. Any problems or performance variations are identified, and corrective action or contingency plans are developed when necessary.

DISCUSSION

1. Using US Census data on the zip codes surrounding the client business, compile a profile of the most attractive target markets. Select one of the targeted groups and identify how it could be reached effectively through a local advertising medium.
2. Emerging businesses often need to have very low-cost marketing programs that reach a local market. Brainstorm some ways that a business could use low-cost methods to promote the business.
3. Review the section on Web marketing. Create a checklist and evaluate the current effectiveness of the client business's website. Suggest ways in which the client can use social media to increase customer engagement.
4. Analyze and discuss how the client incorporates the customer life cycle to increase revenues and profits. Discuss specific programs at each phase of the customer life cycle.
5. Based on what you know about your client's community engagement activities and relationships, what public relations program could be effective at relatively low costs?

NOTES

1   Jerome D. Williams, Wei-Na Lee, and Curtis P. Haugtvedt, *Diversity in Advertising* (Mahwah, NJ: Lawrence Erlbaum Associates, 2004).

2   Antonieta Reyes Echezuria, "Brand Engagement: An Analysis of Motivation," in proceedings of the annual conference of the Association of Marketing Theory and Practice, March 2012.

3   A. H. Maslow, "A Theory of Human Motivation," *Psychological Review* 50 (1943): 370-96.

4   David Crockett, Sonya A. Grier, and Jerome A. Williams, "Coping with Marketplace Discrimination: an Exploration of the Experiences of Black Men," *American Marketing Science Review* 4 (2003): 1-21.

5   Mark S. Rosenbaum and Detra Y. Montoya, "Am I Welcome Here? Exploring How Ethnic Consumers Assess Their Place Identity," *Journal of Business Research* 60 (2007): 206-14.

6   Detra Y. Montoya and Elten Briggs, "Shared Ethnicity Effects on Service Encounters: A Study across Three U.S. Subcultures," *Journal of Business Research* 66 (2013): 314-20.

7   Amar Bhidé, *The Evolution of Businesses* (New York: Oxford University Press, 2000).

8   Michael Porter, *Competitive Strategy* (New York: Free Press, 1980).

9   James C. Anderson, James A. Narus, and Wouter van Rossum, "Customer Value Propositions in Business Markets," *Harvard Business Review*, March 2006.

10 Don Peppers and Martha Rogers, *The One to One Future* (New York: Currency/Doubleday, 1996).

11 Montoya and Briggs, "Shared Ethnicity Effects on Service Encounters: A Study across Three U.S. Subcultures."

12 Adrian Payne and Pennie Frow, "A Strategic Framework for Customer Relationship Management," *Journal of Marketing* 69 (October 2005): 167-76.

13 Susannah Fox and Lee Rainie, "The Web at 25 in the U.S.," Pew Research Center, February 27, 2014, www.pewinternet.org/files/2014/02/PIP_25th-anniversary-of-the-Web_0227141.pdf.

14 Zenith Optimedia, *Executive Summary: Advertising Expenditure Forecasts*, December 2013, www.zenithoptimedia.com/wp-content/uploads/2013/12/Adspend-forecasts-December-2013-executive-summary.pdf.

15 Olaf Reinhold and Rainer Alt, "Social Customer Relationship Management: State of the Art and Learnings from Current Projects," *BLED 2012 Proceedings*, Paper 26, http://aisel.aisnet.org/bled2012/26.

16 Younghwa Lee and Kenneth A. Kozar, "Investigating the Effect of Website Quality on E-Business Success: An Analytical Hierarchy Process (AHP) Approach," *Decision Support Systems* 42 (2006): 1383-1401.

6. Research and Data Gathering

This chapter illustrates the methods and techniques used in conducting business and marketing research. Most consulting projects require some form of research to obtain information and data needed to effectively solve problems and make sound business decisions. Small businesses rarely have the luxury of using paid, professional consultants to conduct their research. Consulting by teams of business students, supervised by faculty and business professionals, offer client firms and organizations valuable access to research that otherwise would not be available to them (see chapter 2). The completed research studies can often have a sizable impact on current operations and future strategic directions. The information is typically most useful to businesses when it is presented in terms of analytical results and relationships that the business owner can understand and apply.

In the first part of this chapter, task and functional research questions are used as a way to illustrate how the process works. The questions illustrate how and why certain methods and techniques are used in carrying out the main tasks of research. The second section focuses on secondary research. Compiling information from published sources or using data collected by someone else can be a cost-effective means of getting valuable information. The third section covers primary research, whereby the consulting team will itself collect the data. Qualitative research, which emphasizes the context and content of what is being reported rather than what is counted, measured, or quantified, is covered in the fourth section. Observational methods are included in this type of research.

Business and marketing research is a systematic process of collecting, analyzing, interpreting, and presenting information or data on a defined question, issue, or topic pertaining to market exchange transactions and relationships. The findings and results produced from the research process are used mainly to support decisions and solve problems.

After Studying This Chapter

When the student consulting team has reviewed this chapter, it will be able to frame key questions that business owners ask in order to move forward. Such questions need to be answered based on research rather than on guesses, hunches, and intuition.

After studying this chapter, students will be able to:

- Define, select, and compile published (secondary) information useful in making a business decision.
- Design, use, and analyze the results from a survey or questionnaire (called primary research).
- Describe, use, and interpret the results of focus group interviewing, ethnographic studies, and other qualitative research methods.
- Apply standard research methods to help solve multi-cultural business and marketing problems.
- Help a small business answer important research questions.

RESEARCH PROCESS

Questions in Figure 6-1 provide a way to explore the research process. The sequence of questions begins with how the research can help to accomplish project objectives and moves through to the evaluation of the costs and benefits of the time, talent, and other resources required to complete the research. For emerging businesses with few resources, even the time involved in

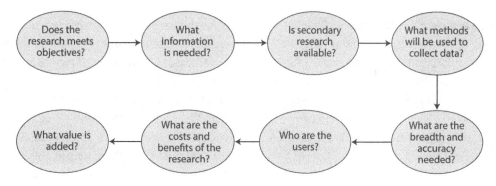

FIGURE 6-1. Key Questions about the Research Process

completing such a survey can represent tremendous cost to the business. The results must justify the costs, or the research should not be done.

Does the Research Meet the Objective?

In completing the consulting project on time and within budget, the consultant cannot afford to engage in any activities that are not directly relevant to the project mission. The initial question asked is, What are the basic objectives of the project that require information to be collected and analyzed? Answers should focus on the definition of the problems that the consultant is being asked to investigate. Often there will be issues related to finding new opportunities in the marketplace (e.g., different markets to serve or ways to increase sales and revenue among present customers). If the needs of the business have been described in terms of finding new

customers, increasing the frequency of store visits of existing customers, or satisfaction with service timeliness, the research will need to provide reliable information for taking appropriate action. From the beginning to the end of the project, the aim should be to provide information and knowledge that will help the client make better decisions. It is important to keep the objective of the research at the forefront throughout the research process.

What Information Is Needed?

In answering this question, it is important that the consultant team cover the full range of factors that affect the business. A sampling of these factors is shown in Table 6-1.

These factors illustrate that marketing itself is very broad in scope. The more clearly information needs are identified, the more effectively the consultant will be able

TABLE 6-1. Categories of Marketing Information

Customers	The Firm	The Market
Demographic Age, race, national origin, ethnicity, education, household size, gender, income	Financial Growth rates, financial characteristics, business model, cash flow	Economic Conditions Local employment, economic growth, housing starts
Geographic Region, state, county, city, community, census tracts,	Competitors Branding, positioning, merchandising, locations, advertising, product offerings, pricing, size, and resources of competitors	Industry Trends Sector growth, industry dynamics
Socioeconomic/psychographic Lower, middle, or upper class, lifestyle, occupation	Experience Human capital, owner's capabilities, successes	Regulations Federal, state, and local regulations
Cultural Religious traditions, ethnic customs, music preferences, artistic sensibilities	Managerial Benchmarking or other performance measures, elements of strategy	Sociocultural Issues Religion, racial, ethnic, sexual orientation, and other factors
Business Customer life cycle	Businesses Place in the supply chain, cash flow needs	Businesses Industry trends, sustainability issues, resource costs, outsourcing trends

to define and follow steps in the business and marketing research process. With minority business enterprises (MBEs), it may be important to supplement the information obtained through analysis with information on racism and the effect of discriminatory practices on buying from particular companies. This type of information can be crucial to understanding the barriers the business faces in the current marketplace.

In determining the needed information, time constraints (or in the case of professional consulting, client money constraints) must be considered. While there is a lot that consultants or business owners may want to know, secondary research takes time, and the more primary research data that is needed not only increases data collection time but can decrease the responsiveness of those being surveyed, as they may not want to take a lot of time in answering questions.

Are Secondary Data Available?

Data are generally classified as primary or secondary. Primary data are collected directly from the group, sample, or population of interest. Primary data include all forms collected by a researcher, such as surveys, focus groups, and observational or other qualitative data. Data collected or compiled by someone else are called secondary data. US Census data are a commonly used form of secondary data. Census data can provide secondary data on the trade areas covered by any business. Racial/ethnic composition of the market area, including household size or other demographics, is also available through census data sources. The US Census Bureau, the US Department of Commerce, and a range of private sector sources publish information on businesses and industries that can be used in secondary research.

What Methods Will Be Used to Collect Data?

Secondary data such as client financial statements can be useful in defining benchmark standards for the firm. Other examples include store invoices, sales records, product return or rejection rates, and other company documents. There may be additional internal sources of information such as marketing materials or reports. Other data will be collected from external sources such as government websites, newspapers, periodicals, and library databases. Local government economic development agencies are an excellent source of secondary information. Keep in mind that the detailed niche information required for ethnic small businesses may not be available

in mainstream sources. In these cases, it may be helpful to identify industry benchmarks. Secondary sources should include community/ethnic newspapers and the Yellow Pages.

Methods used to collect primary data include observation, focus groups, ethnographic studies, and surveys (by telephone, mail, online, and personal interviews). Primary data regarding customer preferences and shopping experiences could be collected by customer "store intercept" interviews. Survey questions can also be asked of preselected customers (or convenience samples) and others who shop near where the data are collected.

What Are the Breadth and Accuracy Required?

This question gets to the heart of asking what kind of research will be conducted. There are basically three categories of research: exploratory, descriptive, and causal. Exploratory research is broadest in scope because its purpose is to define and clarify problems, gain insight into situations and relationships, and form hypotheses that can be examined in more rigorous and narrowly defined research.

Descriptive research focuses definitively on answering specific questions about who, what, when, where, and how in relation to a topic or problem. It is generally considered to be more rigorous than exploratory research and should provide answers regarding product choices and decisions, provide estimates of what will occur in the future, and generate an empirical basis for understanding the problems and issues being studied.

Causal research is the most rigorous of the three types because the results are expected to yield explanations of the cause-and-effect relationships between and among variables. Under ideal conditions, causal research is conducted through laboratory and field studies using experimental designs.

Consider these issues in choosing research methods:

1. If the research is exploratory, the scope will need to be broader and more tentative than when it intends to describe, evaluate, or confirm a previously established condition or relationship.
2. If the research is descriptive, it will be more rigorous and definitive than if it is exploratory, but it is generally less rigorous and more inclusive than explanatory research.
3. If the research is causal, it will focus on meeting the requirements of experimental design and manipula-

tion of variables to ensure the valid determination of cause-and-effect relationships among the variables being studied.

Of the three types, descriptive research is the most inclusive as to methods and uses. It ranges from basic statistical analysis of means and frequencies to more elaborate multivariate methods of statistical analysis. Often statistical software packages such as SPSS will be used to execute the analysis. Explanatory research is less likely to be used in project studies and research because of time, resources, and its generally more theoretical and analytical orientation and purposes.

Two types of research—qualitative and quantitative—are related to the types of data and methods of analysis used in data collection. Qualitative research focuses on answering research questions based on the content and context of understanding people, behavior, or other aspects of business and marketing. This is done through the use of observational studies, open-ended interviews, focus groups, and ethnographic studies. These methods provide important emotional and contextual understanding of behavior and relationships.

Some observations should be made about sampling methods. In quantitative research using surveys, it is expected that those selected for inclusion in the research will be representative of the population being studied (e.g., sample). The size of the sample is a strong determinant of validity. Validity is important because it means that the results actually and accurately describe what they purport or claim to describe.

The trade-off between cost and accuracy may be the main determining factor in selecting sampling methods. If general background information is needed that will be broadly representative of the larger population in the community, a convenience sample might be adequate. But if precise statistical estimates are to be developed, with specified levels of confidence in the estimates that are to be presented, more rigorous statistical or probability sampling must be developed.

In such a case, the expected results would be accompanied by a precise statistical calculation about the expected error or confidence associated with the numerical results. The terms applied to such a relationship or concerns are the *validity* and *reliability* of the results of the study. Clearly, if decisions involve considerable risks, substantial investments, or commitments of resources, higher levels of reliability would be imposed. This means that the sampling could be duplicated and that comparable results would be expected.

Who Are the Users of the Research?

The primary users of the research are typically the business owners or clients. However, the business owner may make use of the research to achieve other objectives, such as justifying financial projections to bankers and investors. The results may also provide evidence for the size of a market niche.

The design and execution of the project must meet generally accepted analytical standards. This could include a certain number of years of financial data to establish a trend, designated size of a sample survey to provide a given level of confidence in the statistical results, or other measurable categories of relationships and outcomes of the research. Such standards are likely to be indicated and applied by the mentors and advisors as well as the professors who are supervising a given project. In conducting the research and analyzing the results, all these audiences should be considered.

What Are the Costs and Benefits of the Research?

Many forms of research can be quite expensive and particularly prohibitive to small businesses. Care should be taken that the methods used are appropriate and cost effective. Businesses want to make the best use of all their resources. The costs should not be any higher than what is needed to provide the necessary information. It should also be recognized that benefits from research can be quite subjective and even intangible. The value to the client should be determined, not assumed. The expectation should be that the benefits will be greater than the costs.

Costs to the client would be the owners' time and any financial support provided to cover out-of-pocket costs, such as travel for personal interviews or incentives for participation. Consultants, whether they are paid or not, should quantify their time spent in completing a research project.

Benefits from marketing research are commonly associated with gains that the business can realize from using the results of the research. In a retail gift shop project, for example, the owner needed to be able to make better selection decisions in buying merchandise. This could lead to improved inventory control, reduced inventory carrying costs, increased efficiency of allocation of financial resources, and ultimately increased sales.

Broadly speaking, the benefits associated with such research are increasing sales and market/customer share, uncovering needs and preferences, finding alternative ways of attracting and serving customers, and reducing business risk.

What Is the Value Added?

The final work product of the business and marketing research is a written report to the client. This will be evaluated with respect to its technical, managerial, and other dimensions that lead to increased profitability. By technical evaluation, it must be ensured that the coverage includes the most up-to-date information deemed adequate to solve the problems being studied and support sound marketing decisions. In managerial terms, the business improvement ideas generated from the project should be sound and help guide buying decisions and sales projections or meet other managerial needs. The owner must be able to implement the recommendations that were supported in the research. The reported results should be actionable and effective.

SECONDARY RESEARCH

Whatever the questions, problems, or issues that require research, the process should begin with secondary research due to its low cost and high availability of data. Most likely the first search will be on the Internet to identify relevant information sources. This can sometimes prove overwhelming. More productive searches begin with library resources that limit the search to more fruitful areas.

The research objective needs to be as clear as possible. If the topic has not been fully clarified, ask advisors, team members, and faculty how to gain greater clarity. This is especially pertinent with small businesses that are inexperienced with the consulting process. It is important to spend time figuring out exactly what needs to be researched. Time taken at the outset to ensure clear problem definition and project focus will save time for completing other tasks later in the process.

It may be beneficial to re-ask the question about how the research results will be used. If the research is completed, what difference will it make? What actions can be taken on the basis of it? Inexperienced consultants are often enamored with "nice to know" data. If the results of the research are not actionable or do not directly answer project questions, then the research should not

be done. What value will be added to the business when the information is obtained? Take the time to come up with the mission or objective in writing and share it with the business owner and team advisors. Time is a scarce commodity on any consulting project, and the team needs to be right on target. Being slightly off target at the beginning can pull the team far away from the goal by the end.

Budgeting Time

The deadline for the finished project may be a few months away, but research takes time. There can be wide variation between teams in the amount of time used to complete projects. The amount of time can vary by a factor of five or six. Needless to say, the more time spent on the project, the higher the probability that it will be done correctly. In fact, it is possible to miss the mark completely if not enough time is spent. Beginning researchers are likely to make missteps or run into dead ends before finding the right direction. They should allocate even more time than experienced researchers for task and project completion. The more experienced the researcher becomes, the less time needs to be allowed for misdirected effort.

Start early and budget blocks of time (two to three hours) adequate to do serious searching. It can take forty to sixty hours to thoroughly research a relatively small topic. Finding the information itself is not difficult once the important sources are known. Filtering, sorting, organizing, and coming up with relevant conclusions can take considerably more time. If the consultant is new to a research area, she or he needs learning-curve time to process and better understand the information being generated. It is necessary to build a framework for processing the information in a meaningful way. Often the framework does not become clear until the consultant has "lived" with the data for a while. Starting early also allows time for more feedback from the business owner and advisors.

Using the Library Effectively

The library is the best place to begin research, as it contains databases that are not available on the open Web. Additionally, there may be a reference librarian who can assist with starting the research. The resources of libraries may vary; however, most public libraries contain useful business databases, and college or university libraries will have access to considerably more. To begin your search it is helpful to come up with relevant keywords.

It is also helpful to find the relevant industry code by looking it up in the North American Industry Classification System (NAICS). Download a substantial number of articles to assist in getting knowledgeable about the general environment for the client business. Start with articles about industry size and dynamics. Find articles on a particular product or service. Reading SWOT (strengths, weakness, opportunities, and threats) analyses of larger companies in the same industry might give insights about how to approach the client business.

Trade journals or magazines are also a good resource for examining a particular industry. Three examples in retailing include *Stores*, *Chain Store Age*, and *Progressive Grocer*. For multicultural entrepreneurship, the list of trade publications would include *Black Enterprise* and *Hispanic Business*. Many mainstream publications also carry articles about multicultural entrepreneurship and marketing. Just about every industry has a trade publication from a trade association, and many are available at the local library or on the Web. Often there is an annual issue that gives industry statistics for the year. Student teams have the added advantage of industry mentors who often have access to expensive market research done by private firms. These are available only through subscription or membership. They include directories of firms in an industry, restaurant association summaries of cost structures, and projections of industry growth.

Some of databases such as EBSCO Host provide citations in American Psychological Association (APA) format (used for business research), which can be useful for the team's final report. Keep in mind that it takes substantial time and effort to become knowledgeable about any business area. A good rule of thumb is to continue to accumulate articles until duplication is found. Here are some of the most frequently used business databases:

- ABI/INFORM Complete. ProQuest, indexes, abstracts, and full text from thousands of business periodicals. Many periodicals have annual issues that give statistics for the year.
- Business Insights: Essentials. Industry rankings, profiles, market share data, company histories, company fundamentals, and investment reports.
- Business Source Premier. EBSCO Host, coverage of all business, including marketing, management,

management information systems (MIS), accounting, finance, and economics. Also includes market research reports, industry reports, country reports, company profiles, and SWOT analyses.
- Datamonitor360 MarketLine Advantage. Company analyses, SWOT analyses for major companies, company financials, and executive biographies. Three thousand industry profiles using Porter's Five Forces. Political, economic, social, technological, legal, and environmental (PESTLE) analyses. Country, company and product database with market shares
- Factiva. Combination of the *Wall Street Journal*, the *Financial Times*, Dow Jones and Reuters newswires, and the Associated Press, as well as Reuters Fundamentals, and Dun and Bradstreet company profiles.
- IBIS World US and Global Industry Reports. Reports on US industries written at the five-digit level of the NAICS. Each report of about 25–30 pages uses Porter's Five Forces framework.
- MarketingResearch.com Academic. Access to more than five hundred market research reports that cover a variety of sectors such as beverages, food, office supplies, personal care, and telecommunications. The reports are detailed and international in scope and application.

Evaluating Research

The key to business research is to find recent, relevant information. For most business topics, information older than twelve months may not be very useful. It is also important to evaluate sources for credibility. A major business publication will be fairly reliable (although some have been known to be wrong) but may be biased. An article from an individual's blog may be based on the individual's opinion and therefore is not a credible source. At the same time, the individual may have unique expertise or insights or have particularly influential views that will be important to consider in your research. For company publications or industry association publications, assess the potential accuracy of the information. The mission of an industry group is to promote the industry; thus its information might paint a much brighter picture than is actually the case.

CARS (credibility, accuracy, reasonableness, and support) is a simple acronym that helps in evaluating research. A summary checklist is provided in Table 6-2.

TABLE 6-2. Checklist for Evaluating Research

High	Low
Credibility	
Author's education or experience relevant to the issue	Anonymous author
Contact information given	No contact information
Organization that author or website belongs to is reputable and unbiased on the issue	Periodical not well known, known or suspected bias in content or authorship
Author has reputable position	Reviews are mostly negative
Author has good reputation	Author is not convincing
Periodical is of good quality in content and presentation	Writing contains bad grammar and numerous misspelled words
Accuracy	
Up-to-date information, dates are current	No date or old date
Any historical data includes the latest year	Use of vague or sweeping generalizations
Comprehensive, many sources of data, cites all relevant sources of information	Limited information or sources, limited coverage of topic
Considers the audience for the information	Hidden messages of persuasion, inappropriate for audience
Reasonableness	
Fair, presents all sides	Angry or spiteful tones, not balanced
Objectivity, controls biases, discloses any conflict of interest	Conflict of interest
Moderateness, most truths are ordinary (some truths are not, but check to see if they are real)	Sweeping statements
Consistency, writer avoids contradictions	Writer exaggerates or overclaims
Worldview, writer identifies his or her religious, political, etc. points of view	Writer obscures his or her biases and viewpoints
Support	
Source of information is cited	No identified source for numbers
Corroboration, may want to triangulate, find three sources of information that agree	Absence of documentation when it is needed
Agrees with outside sources of information	Cannot find other sources that agree with information

Consumer Data

Having basic demographic data on potential customers and using it to inform marketing strategies are essential to any business's success. Yet small businesses are often in the dark as to the profile of their customers. This is especially ironic because much of this information is readily available to the public.

Many examples of national data sources and references are described in the following list. While all of them may not be as readily available as census sources, they are still quite accessible and generally considered to be economical sources of information.

- American FactFinder. A query function to a variety of government databases, including the Survey of Busi-

ness Owners, American Community Survey, American Housing Survey, Annual Economic Surveys, Annual Surveys of Governments, Census of Governments, the Decennial Census, the Economic Census, Equal Employment Opportunity (EEO) data, and the Population Estimates Program. Detailed data can be extracted into Excel files for analysis and visual display.

- US Census Bureau. This US Department of Commerce website provides a huge amount of demographic information and is likely to be the most valuable source of data. Using the site, it is possible to create custom reports for specific communities and their population, housing, economic, and other data. Information can be retrieved for state, county, and city levels as well as by census tract and zip code. Detailed information is available, such as the number of African Americans living in a specific census tract, but the search may take time to figure out.

- Current Population Survey (CPS). A monthly survey of about fifty thousand households conducted by the Census Bureau for the Bureau of Labor Statistics. The CPS is the primary source of employment status of people sixteen years and older. Data include employment, unemployment, earnings, hours of work, and other indicators. They are tracked against demographic characteristics, including age, sex, race, marital status, and educational attainment. They are also available by occupation, industry, and class of worker. Additional characteristics to produce estimates on a variety of topics include school enrollment, income, previous work experience, health, employee benefits, and work schedules.
- FedStats. This website offers links to current demographic statistics on a wide variety of American population factors from a dozen US government agencies.
- Consumer Expenditure Surveys. This Bureau of Labor Statistics website provides data about consumer spending in the United States. Demographic information, such as the average number in consumer unit, percent male and female, education level, age, and income, is detailed along with average annual expenditures consisting of fourteen main categories: food, alcoholic beverages, housing, apparel and services, transportation, health care, entertainment, personal care products and services, reading, education, tobacco products and smoking supplies, miscellaneous, cash contributions, and personal insurance and pensions.
- Survey of Consumer Finances (SCF). This triennial survey of the balance sheet, pension, income, and other demographic characteristics of US families also gathers information on the use of financial institutions.
- American Housing Survey (AHS). This survey collects data on the nation's housing, including apartments, single-family homes, mobile homes, vacant housing units, household characteristics, income, housing and neighborhood quality, housing costs, equipment and fuels, size of housing unit, and recent movers, National data are collected in odd-numbered years, and data for each of forty-seven selected metropolitan areas are collected about every four years, with an average of twelve metropolitan areas included each year.
- US National and State Data. This Population Reference

Bureau website provides annotated links to sources of national and state data on the Web, including Census Bureau population data, the Urban Institute, and many other organizations.

- IRS Tax Stats. This Internal Revenue Service website offers information about the financial composition of personal, business, nonprofit, and other taxpayers.
- Simply Map. A Web-based mapping application that enables users to develop interactive thematic maps and reports using thousands of demographic, business, and marketing data variables. It may be available through local or institution libraries.
- Pew Research Center. The Pew Foundation has funded extensive research aimed at informing the public, improving public policy, and stimulating public life. Areas of research include arts and culture, children and youth, computers and the Internet, corrections and public safety, economic policy, education, environment, family financial security, health, Hispanics in America, media and journalism, religion, science, and civic initiatives.

Competitive Information

Company descriptions or profiles, financial performance, and other information can be useful as "competitive intelligence." Knowing what competitors are doing can be important in making decisions about how to seek and sustain a competitive advantage. Examples in this category include the following sources, some of which are available at libraries that subscribe to them:

- Hoovers Online. Hoovers provides brief information on several dozen industry sectors and four dozen industry snapshots, available by clicking on "Companies & Industries." The site also includes extensive information on approximately fourteen thousand companies worldwide, both public and private.
- ReferenceUSA. This provides directory information for approximately twelve million companies in the United States. Companies can be searched by name, business activity, size, and location. With this database, it is possible to identify businesses by geographic area and type of business, as well as by number of employees and gross annual sales.
- Dun and Bradstreet. D&B is another directory of information on companies. It covers approximately one million US companies with sales greater than $1 million or total number of employees greater than twenty.

- Telephone Directories. While most phone listings have been moved to digital format, some neighborhood chambers or ethnic business associations continue to publish hard copy listings. These sources can be searched to determine who local competitors are and where they are located.
- Bizstats. This website provides information compiled from IRS data about business profit and loss and balance sheets. It provides enough detail for businesses to benchmark their financial performance against businesses of similar size.
- Online Mapping. Search engines such as Bing and Google and rating sites such as Yelp have a mapping function that allows researchers to search on a business category and find competitors within a determined radius.
- *Inc. Magazine*. This magazine focuses on small business issues. The Inc. 500/5000 list can be used to find companies that may qualify as high-impact companies and to provide competitive information. This source may be particularly helpful when working with B2B clients.

Small Business

The focus up to this point has been on sources that are national in scope. Yet most projects are likely to be highly localized. Thus familiarity with local resources is quite important. Key sources and references are as follows:

- Kauffman Foundation. The foundation funds extensive research on innovation and entrepreneurship. It also maintains an entrepreneurial index and continuing studies on a number of business issues.
- US Small Business Administration. This website provides tools such as business plans and other resources for small businesses. The Office of Advocacy has studies on a number of business issues.
- 2007 Survey of Business Owners. This US Census Bureau survey provides extensive data from the 2007 Economic Census on ownership of business enterprises by minorities and women. The Economic Census is conducted every five, years and searches can often be narrowed to the city or county level.
- Minority Business Development Agency. Part of the US Department of Commerce, this agency provides information on various trends pertaining to demographics, industry characteristics, exports, and other important dimensions of minority small businesses.

- National Black Chamber of Commerce. This nonprofit, nonpartisan, nonsectarian organization is dedicated to the economic empowerment of African American communities. The NBCC reaches 100,000 black-owned businesses.
- US Hispanic Chamber of Commerce. This organization works to advocate, promote, and facilitate the success of Hispanic business. The national body has a network of nearly two hundred Hispanic chambers of commerce and Hispanic business organizations.
- US Pan Asian American Chamber of Commerce. This national nonprofit association represents Asian businesses and Asian professionals in business, sciences, the arts, sports, education, entertainment, community, and public service.

Industry or Trade Associations

Just as there is a trade journal for just about every industry, there is also a trade or industry association for just about every industry. Some of these associations publish yearbooks that give industry statistics or monthly reports on industry trends. Some will answer inquiries by e-mail. Many have websites. Just remember that industry associations try to paint the industry in the best light, so it is important to evaluate the information carefully. To contact trade associations, use the *Encyclopedia of Associations* or try the Internet Public Library list of associations.

Trade associations could also include country trade associations, whose purpose is to develop trade for their country. In order to do this, they might maintain extensive statistics. To get a listing of international trade associations, access the Federation of International Trade Associations.

Social Media

Social media can also be mined for consumer research. Monitoring Twitter posts can reveal shifting trends or moods. It is possible to search the thousands of groups on LinkedIn to find out how communities are formed around products or services. The number of Facebook likes and Twitter followers can quantify consumer interest and brand awareness. Reading customer reviews on Yelp can give an idea of a business's strengths and weaknesses and those of its competitors. Monitoring books and topics on Amazon.com can give an indication of trends. In certain high-tech industries, influential blogs are the best source of information. Research should also be conducted on discussion forums.

PRIMARY RESEARCH

Once secondary research has been completed or is well under way, consideration can be given to primary research. One of the most basic and widely used methods of primary research is a survey of an identified group of respondents (i.e., a sample). Surveys can be very labor intensive and costly. They should be defined, designed, and completed with these factors in mind. Recognize that professional marketing research firms typically price telephone surveys at $50 per completed call, while a mall intercept survey may cost anywhere from $20,000 to $50,000, depending on the sample size, length and complexity of the questionnaire, and standards applied regarding validity and reliability of the results. The team should ensure that the right direction is taken before starting the survey process.

Preliminary Research

Most small B2C businesses serve a local market, so it will be necessary to understand local factors. Make sure to carefully explore available market data. This refers again to secondary research. Before refining a primary survey instrument, talk informally with a few customers. Ask open-ended questions or questions that provide more insight or details. For beginning researchers, it is important to gain enough knowledge to ask the right questions in the finished survey. Ask customers why they buy the product or use the service. Talk to potential customers as well. Ask them why they do not buy and what they buy instead. Talk to suppliers; they are great sources of information about the industry and competitors. Allow enough time to pretest the survey with a small group of likely respondents before deciding on the final set of questions to be used.

B2B customer research can pose unique challenges in obtaining responses. Corporations tend to keep their vendor lists confidential, and finding the decision maker(s) involved in a purchase decision can be difficult. While the buying function may be done by someone in a purchasing or supply chain management group, the actual people who evaluate a product or service offering may be in the department that will use the product or service.

Refine the Purpose

A balance must be struck in creating surveys. If too few questions are asked, the purpose will not be achieved. If too many questions are asked, the respondents may experience fatigue and fail to complete the survey. The optimal path is to ask just the right number of questions. This should be based on determining the most essential information needed and then testing the survey instrument before it is actually placed in the field to determine the amount of time it takes to complete the survey. Creating an effective survey is similar to hitting a small bull's eye. It is important to focus on the "need to know" versus the "nice to know" questions.

There are additional complications in conducting research when working with a business that is new to customer/client data collection. The client business is likely venturing into new and unfamiliar territory. The business owner may not be quite sure what she or he wants to know or do. The consultant has to make sure that the business owner also goes through the educational process. As the business owner learns more, she/he will want to be more involved. The scope of the project can change. However, projects can be refined to perfection and not accomplish anything. It is important to stay focused on what must be accomplished. At the same time, allow the increasingly educated client to inform the process. This should help to build his or her confidence in the project. In some ways this could be considered part of the effort to get the client's buy-in to the final results and recommendations of the project.

Who Is to Be Surveyed?

First, avoid the common mistake of surveying people (respondents) because it is convenient to do so. This may seem a low-cost approach to getting information, but it is likely an incorrect one that will produce misleading or even useless results. This could mean asking the right questions of the wrong people and getting obviously irrelevant answers. Such a survey would likely miss the people who should be targeted and questioned.

Consider the consequences of surveying the wrong group: Time and effort are misused. Correct segments of the market that should be questioned are omitted or overlooked. And as stated above, the information obtained is likely to be incorrect or irrelevant.

Two examples highlight the issues involved. One relates to a mall intercept survey and the other to a telephone survey. A consumer is intercepted in the mall and is asked a few questions. Marketers may use the results from this survey and extrapolate to all consumers. However, there are major drawbacks to doing this. If respondents are limited to mall intercepts, people who do not shop at malls are excluded, as are those who work during the times malls are open. Similar exclusions can occur with telephone surveys. People who are not home when calls are made or who only have mobile phones are excluded, as are people who screen calls. Omissions may be even more basic. It could be that by using these convenience sampling methods, the wrong people are sampled. These survey design errors can result in getting the wrong information. It is important to think carefully about who is to be surveyed and how best to reach the targeted population.

For example, a consulting team was working with a farm implement manufacturer who was interested in entering the home gardening market. The company asked a student team to gather information about gardener interest in high-quality, premium-priced cutting tools. The challenge was be to identify this target group and determine how to reach them. Getting to know the buying behavior of garden club members would be one possibility. Looking at participants attracted to garden shows might be another. Investigating patrons of certain nurseries could be still another. Clearly the emphasis needed to be on reaching the serious gardener who would want quality tools. Casual gardeners who find gardening a chore would not be interested in paying a premium for tools. For most small businesses, the challenge will be similar. The researcher must devise a method of surveying a small segment of the market.

After doing secondary research, the team determined that serious gardeners join associations so that they can enjoy their pastime together. The team identified the Master Gardener program as the best population from which to choose their sample. Master Gardeners are volunteers who instruct people on gardening. There are fifty Master Gardener associations, approximately one in every state. The team located the Master Gardener coordinator and was able to get a list of serious gardeners to survey.

What Do You Need to Know?

Trying to define exactly what the client needs to know is not as easy as one might think. In the example of the team working with the garden tool business, the business needed information about the consumer gardener. But demographics may not be among the need-to-know questions. If demographic data would be useful, then secondary research is the best way to get it and is considerably more efficient than administering a survey. How about the growth rate of the market? This is likely to be obtained from secondary research. It is expedient to get as much data as possible from secondary sources and then compile a list of what is missing.

The team consulting with the gardening business did this, but many questions remained. What kind of cutting tools are important to gardeners? How do they judge quality? Would gardeners pay a premium for the tool and if so, how much of a premium? How do serious gardeners use the Internet to purchase items? There may be too many questions for the survey to be effective. Questions must be filtered, and the researcher must get agreement from the business on what is actionable.

Often, "guerrilla" marketing research is necessary given the short time period of the student consulting engagement. There are seven key principles to keep in mind when designing market research:[1]

- Behavior-based. Make the survey behavior-based instead of attitude-based. It is more important to know what the customer is going to do as opposed to what the customer prefers. Attitudes often do not match behavior. Ask behavior questions: What have they bought? What will they buy?
- Actionable. If the business cannot do anything about the issue, do not ask. Make sure that all questions will lead to actions that will improve circumstances for the business.
- Extendable. The instrument should allow the researcher to redirect the focus on the business. Ask questions that test this: Which tools are most highly valued? Is brand loyalty an important factor in buying?
- Focus. The survey should focus on what information is needed to achieve the goals of the project. There should not be any extraneous questions. Most respondents will only give a small window of time, and the researcher must use this to the best benefit of the business.
- Validation. Beyond the specific questions, use the survey instrument to validate one issue in the marketing strategy. Determine what this is and then incorporate questions that will address it. Do not miss the opportunity to validate the strategy.
- Directional. The survey is directional rather than empirical. It is a convenience sample, fast and furious. As such, be careful how the results are used.
- Repeatable. Make an instrument that can be reused

by the business. The business environment changes often, and surveys have to be redone. Create an instrument that the business owner can use again, and give instructions on how often it should be used.

Type of Survey

Professional researchers will choose between regular mail, e-mail and online, telephone, or face-to-face surveys. When making these decisions, they weigh the cost of the survey against the likely or expected response rate. They also must take into account the complexity of the questions and kind of information being requested and how the results will be used.[2] Finally, they need to determine the likelihood that the target market will respond to a certain type of survey. For example, when surveying B2B customers, online surveys and e-mail may be more effective than phone surveys, as the former allows respondents to answer at a time convenient for them. Young B2C customers may prefer surveys they can complete using mobile devices or social media platforms, while senior citizen B2C customers may prefer phone surveys. For good examples of survey questions, check out surveys used by the Pew Research Center.

Recognize that response rates vary widely, even for a specific type of survey. The prospective respondent's level of involvement determines the extent of participation. With high-involvement respondents (people who care about the issue), response rates will rise. Response rates can be high for any survey method if the right tactics are used. Repeated reminders are helpful. Using different methods (telephone with mail or telephone with e-mail) can increase response rates.[3] The format should include an initial explanation, an invitation to prospective respondents, and possibly an accompanying incentive offer to respondents. Much higher rates are sometimes reported for topics that generate unusual interest. However, even when invitations or requests for participation are made by telephone, often only 10% to 20% who agree to participate will actually return the e-mail questionnaire. Internet surveys must be shorter than mail surveys and must be personalized rather than sent as part of a newsletter, flyer, or other form of communication. Costs are also relatively low per completed response. Under special circumstances, costs can be much higher. For example, in a Hispanic tax-preparation service, the business owner entered all survey respondents into a drawing for a DVD player.

When considering methods that involve direct contact by telephone, there are distinct advantages over impersonal, pencil and paper, or even Internet interactive contact. Telephone surveys have the advantages of flexibility and ability to deal with topics that could not be addressed in regular mail or Internet surveys. Response rates also tend to be much higher, in the range of 20% or more depending on the topic. But they must usually be brief (fifteen to twenty minutes or less). They are relatively expensive, at $30 to $50 per completed interview.

Face-to-face interviews can cover the most complex and sensitive topics. Response rates can be very high. An expected range is from 20% to 40%, lower for consumer surveys and higher for B2B surveys. This method is obviously labor intensive, as allowance must be made for travel time and other incidental expenses of the interviewers, along with the actual cost of interview time.

In large national surveys (such as national opinion polls completed by telephone), it is customary to interview about one thousand randomly selected American adults. These results are generalized for the entire population of the United States using mathematical relationships involved in calculating standard errors of means and proportions in randomly selected samples. As a practical matter, random sampling is not feasible in most small business consulting projects. It is far more likely that convenience or judgment samples will be used. The consulting team will target a local segment that pertains to the trade or market area served by the client.

But even with convenience and judgment samples, careful consideration should be given to the selection of survey respondents. Who should be surveyed? Often one of the most difficult tasks is finding a viable list of customers to survey. Customer lists should be tested to ensure that they are not "dead" lists or do not have a high rate of wrong contact information. Sometimes student teams will contact community groups to survey their members. Nonprofit associations are often sympathetic to student projects. Industry advisors and mentors may call upon their networks to come up with a list of possible respondents.

The short timeline involved in academic consulting assignments makes it likely that either an e-mail, online, or telephone survey will be selected. All kinds of tactics can be used to improve the response rate. Mailing a postcard before and after, using first-class mail, addressing a letter personally to the respondent, having a person of authority sign the letter that accompanies the survey, making a charitable donation if the respondent answers, making follow-up phone calls, or running a sweepstakes can increase the response rate. Affiliation with a community organization or university can also increase the response rate.

For exploratory surveys, adhering to strict random-sample design is not expected. It is likely that teams will survey far fewer than five hundred respondents in a convenience sample. Although the findings cannot be inferred to the entire population, such sampling is often more than adequate for the bootstrapping small business. In many student consulting projects, a sample size of one hundred is adequate to provide acceptable results. Surveying fewer respondents would definitely be considered a small sample. But even this might be sufficient for some forms of qualitative research.

Keep in mind that the more concise the survey, the higher the response rate. If the survey is online, it should be completed in five to seven minutes. For a telephone survey, two to three minutes may be all the time that respondents will give. Face-to-face interviews can be longer. It is important to set expectations beforehand; if the survey instructions state that there are ten questions and it will take three to five minutes to complete, respondents are more likely to comply.

Formulating the Questions

Once the content of the survey is decided, the researcher can proceed with creating the questions. Survey questions must be worded very carefully. It is easy to introduce bias or to direct respondents to an answer if care is not taken. Poorly worded questions can give bad information, which is costly, since it is likely to be misleading.

Take, for example, the simplest kind of question: one that respondents answer either yes or no. Do you approve (disapprove) of the way the president is handling the economy? The way the question is worded, the respondent is more likely to say yes. In order to overcome this bias, marketing research firms like the Gallup Poll rotate the order of approve and disapprove when they ask questions. Be aware that respondents may have other ways of reacting to questions that give the wrong information. For example, if a list of TV brands is presented, some respondents will say they own the most prestigious brands even when they do not. It might be more accurate to ask them to list or rate the brand(s) that they own. But recognize that this option might increase the costs of coding and completing the data analysis. Such trade-offs are commonplace in research.

Include at least one question on demographics or characteristics of the customer so you can understand behaviors of different market segments. Have more important questions in the middle or at the end, when people are already invested in the interview process and are unlikely to stop or walk away. Although not everyone will comply, ask for a contact e-mail in case the research team has a lingering, burning question.

Open-ended questions provide valuable insight into directions that the research might not have pursued otherwise. But the questions should not be completely open ended, or the customer will not be able to answer them. Provide guidance as to the direction or choices, such as "What three words come to mind when you think of Brand X?"

If a fair number of surveys are being administered, it is more efficient to have answers fall into categories of a rating scale. This makes tabulation of results easier. Some of the common types of questions that involve the use of rating scales are illustrated in Figure 6-2.

Five-point Likert scales are the most common types used in marketing and business research. There are technical and analytical reasons for using seven- and even nine-point scales. Basically, the choice depends on how much sensitivity or scope is allowed for measurement and what effect the extended scales have on reliability. When using a rating scale, be aware that the midpoint, or the "neither satisfied nor dissatisfied," rating can be misinterpreted. Some respondents interpret that rating to mean the middle. Some believe it represents a neutral position. Some respondents who do not care or do not want to answer will use that rating as well. Researchers sometimes eliminate the midpoint rating so that they can do a majority count of either positive or negative. Others include a "don't know" rating so that respondents who cannot answer the questions can be properly categorized. A "not applicable" designation can also accurately capture situations in which respondents are not in a position to answer a question appropriately.

Rank-order questions can determine what is more important to respondents. They can be used to determine product, feature, and attribute preferences. But they are limited in terms of statistical analysis and may not give information on how much the respondent likes one option over the other. For example, a college student was asked to rank order his favorite beers; the options included Coors, Bud, and Miller. It could be that the respondent liked Coors much more than the other two or that he liked Coors just slightly more. It would be

Unbalanced scale with named categories for each point on the scale			
Would you buy this product or service?			
Definitely will not buy	Probably will not buy	Probably will buy	Definitely will buy
1	2	3	4

Balanced scale, without naming the intervals or points on the scale				
How important to you is the availability of a sales associate in shopping for hardware?				
Not at all important				Very important
1	2	3	4	5

Balanced scales, with naming of intervals or points on the scale				
To what extent are you satisfied with this store?				
Very dissatisfied	Somewhat dissatisfied	Neither satisfied nor dissatisfied	Somewhat satisfied	Very satisfied
1	2	3	4	5
What is your position on this issue or statement?				
Strongly disagree	Somewhat disagree	Neither agree nor disagree	Somewhat agree	Strongly agree
1	2	3	4	5

FIGURE 6-2. Sample Rating Scales

impossible to determine this from his answer. One way to get around this is to ask respondents to allocate a specific number of points (for example, 100) to their choices. In that case, the respondent may give 75 points to Coors, 15 points to Bud, and 10 points to Miller. This gives a better idea of how much more important one beer is than the other.

Another popular tool is the semantic differential scale, which uses opposites to gauge psychological impressions. This can be used to determine the subtleties of brand imaging or consumer attitudes. For example, a company may test the impression given by its website using the semantic differential scale shown in Figure 6-3. Be aware that bias can be created in a semantic differential question by putting all the positive words on one side. The respondent becomes accustomed to checking certain ratings and continues without really reading the words.

Once questions are formulated, assess whether the wording and meaning are clear ("How many bottles of beer do you drink in a week?" might not generate the information wanted if the bottles of beer are different volumes), that the language is accessible to the respondent ("How many containers of alcoholic liquids do you imbibe in a week?"), and that questions are not biased ("Are you pleased with the great taste of Coors?").

To determine if respondents are being truthful, researchers often incorporate several questions asking for the same information. If a respondents answers the questions differently, this may indicate that the individual is less than forthcoming. This respondent may be eliminated from the sample.

Most surveys will be of an exploratory nature and will have a relatively small number of respondents (i.e., fewer than five hundred). For quantitative information, ask respondents to give number answers rather than predetermining categories. For example, instead of creating categories like "fewer than one," "two to five," "six to ten," and "over ten," ask the respondent to give the exact

	1	2	3	4	5	
Modern						Traditional
Unreliable						Trustworthy
Friendly						Unfriendly
High quality						Low quality
Bargain						Expensive

FIGURE 6-3. Semantic Differential Scale

number. This gives more raw data that can be categorized by the researcher. Include some open-ended questions to capture information that otherwise would not be considered.

The exception to this is demographic data. Be aware that respondents may be especially sensitive to demographic questions such as nationality. For example, who likes to answer the question, How old are you? To overcome this, use age categories and keep them as broad as possible. The same can be done with income level. Some researchers just use two categories, over and under $50,000 in household income, to differentiate households with discretionary income. By asking for zip code, it may be possible to then use census data to deduce income levels.

Psychographic information requires the clustering of information to create profiles of customers. Interpreting or giving meaning to the answers from a psychographic perspective could be based on some categorical description among the market segments responding to a survey, such as whether a respondent is considered to be an achiever, successful, and work oriented and favors established products that showcase his or her success, versus a striver, a person who has the same aspirations but is unable to achieve them. Such categories are used in comparison with demographics and socioeconomic categories to understand groups of people from a lifestyle or psychographic perspective. Achievers and strivers are two groups in what are called VALS-2 types of psychographic segmentation. Be aware that most established psychographic profiles do not routinely consider multicultural populations. Often such groups do not show up in psychographic profiling because they do not meet income levels considered attractive by marketers. As such, student teams have the opportunity to create new profiles of use to marketers who see the opportunity in these markets.

Typical questions in student projects focus on the following:

- How does the customer get information about the client?
- What attracts the customer to the client?
- What are the customer's reasons for using the product or service?
- What product or service features are desired?
- What does the customer like about the client?

- What competitive products are used and how much?
- How does the business compare to competitors?
- Why does the customer prefer the competitor over the client?
- What factors are important in making the buy decision?
- What price is the customer willing to pay for various attributes?
- What mode of communication or marketing does the customer prefer?
- What is the optimal timing and frequency of marketing promotions?
- What is the level of customer satisfaction with key attributes of the product or service?
- What improvements would the customer like to see?
- What are customer characteristics, such as age, gender, income, or frequency of purchase?
- What incentives will motivate sales staff?
- How can relationships, processes, or pricing with suppliers be improved?

Ordering the Questions

Most projects do not allow the luxury of a list from which good respondents can be selected. Often the first questions on a survey are used to screen respondents. For most consumer research, interviewers will look for women between the ages of eighteen and fifty-four. They are most likely to be the decision makers in a household when it comes to buying goods and services. There may be other types of screening questions, depending on the objective of the research. For example, in a gardening survey administered by students, the screening question asked was, How many hours do you garden in a month? Those who responded with more hours were more likely to be serious gardeners.

Once the researcher has screened the right respondents, it is important to begin with a question that the respondent wants to answer. With the gardening survey, the team started out with the gardener's area of specialty. Gardeners want to talk about what they are interested in, and asking this question opens up the respondents and makes them more willing to respond. Then the survey moves on to more general questions that warm the respondent up. These questions might get the respondent to start thinking about the product or service. The middle of the survey is the place for the questions that require more thought or consideration. Timing is very important. Consider whether the respondent will be tired

TABLE 6-3. Survey Question Order

Screening	Used to qualify respondents for survey
Warm-up	Easy questions to get respondent in the mind space of answering questions
General	Related to survey but not difficult to answer
Difficult	These questions take more thinking and effort to answer
Classification and demographics	Some respondents find demographic questions to be sensitive

or bored and incorporate strategies to keep interest up. Tough and sensitive questions (like demographics) are placed last. Respondents are less likely to walk away when they have invested all that time and effort in answering the questions. And even if they do, some valuable information will already have been gathered. Table 6-3 summarizes the order of survey questions.

If the survey is to be administered over the telephone, have a script for the survey administrator to use. It is important that each survey be administered in a consistent manner.

Pretest the Survey

The best way to ensure that the survey works is to pretest it on a few typical respondents. Incorporate this pretest in the timeline for the project. The purpose of the pretest is simply to ensure that the questions are understandable and that the answers give the information required. All kinds of problems can be uncovered when the survey is tested. Respondents might interpret questions completely differently from the intended meaning. They might misread words. They might be confused. Surveys may need to be translated into another language. Questions may need to be corrected. Test respondents under the same conditions that actual respondents will experience. Gather information on what happened. Meet with the team and spend sufficient time revising the questionnaire. In revising, ask hard questions about the objective of each question and whether the objective was achieved.

Evaluate the Research Process

Review the results with a strong critical eye. Does it make sense to act on the findings? Does more research need to be done? Be aware that the biggest flaw of surveys is that people do not always do what they say they will do.

Service Firm Surveys

A number of surveys are widely used to evaluate service firms. These surveys have the advantage of being validated by researchers. Three of these are presented in this section. SERVQUAL is a survey instrument that measures service quality as the gap between the expected level of service and customer perception of the level of service, using five dimensions. Tangibles are the physical manifestation of the firm through its facilities, equipment, and employees. Reliability is the ability of the firm to perform its services correctly, consistently, and in a timely manner. Responsiveness is the willingness to help customers and provide prompt service. Assurance is the ability of employees to nurture trust and confidence through their knowledge and courtesy. Empathy is the caring and personalized attention.[4]

In Figure 6-4, SERVQUAL has been adapted to a Latina-owned community fitness center, a business that provides fitness equipment, classes, and personal training for its customers. The survey uses a seven-point Likert scale (1 as strongly disagree and 7 as strongly agree) to determine how the customers perceive service quality compared to what is expected. Customers are asked about the tangibles, which include the facility, equipment, and employees. Reliability is interpreted as providing the right service at the right time. Note that under responsiveness, the survey reverses the statements so that they measure the opposite of responsiveness. This breaks the respondent out of replying according to pattern, requires the respondent to read the question more carefully, and might encourage a more accurate response. The same reversal is used in the empathy category.

The following set of statements relate to your feelings about Fuente Fitness. For each statement, please show the extent to which you believe Fuente Fitness has the feature described by the statement.

There are no right or wrong answers. All we are interested in is a number that best shows your perceptions about Fuente Fitness.

Checking a 7 means that you strongly agree that Fuente Fitness has that feature, and checking a 1 means that you strongly disagree. You may check any of the numbers in the middle that show how strong your feelings are.

Tangibles   1   2   3   4   5   6   7

a.   Fuente Fitness has up-to-date equipment.

b.   Fuente Fitness's physical facilities are visually appealing.

c.   Fuente Fitness's employees are well dressed and appear neat.

d.
     The appearance of the physical facilities of Fuente Fitness is in keeping with the type of services provided.

Reliability

e.   When Fuente Fitness promises to do something by a certain time, it does so.

f.
     When you have problems, Fuente Fitness is sympathetic and reassuring.

g.   Fuente Fitness is dependable.

h.   Fuente Fitness provides its services at the time it promises to do so.

i.   Fuente Fitness keeps its records accurately.

Responsiveness

j.
     Fuente Fitness does not tell customers exactly when services will be performed. (-)

k.   You do not receive prompt service from Fuente Fitness's employees. (-)

l.   Employees of Fuente Fitness are not always willing to help customers. (-)

m.
     Employees of Fuente Fitness are too busy to respond to customer requests promptly. (-)

Assurance

n.   You can trust employees of Fuente Fitness.

o.   You feel safe in your transactions with Fuente Fitness's employees.

p.   Employees of Fuente Fitness are polite.

q.   Employees get adequate support from Fuente Fitness to do their jobs well.

Empathy

r.   Fuente Fitness does not give you individual attention. (-)

s.   Employees of Fuente Fitness do not give you personal attention. (-)

t.   Employees of Fuente Fitness do not know what your needs are. (-)

u.   Fuente Fitness does not have your best interests at heart. (-)

v.   Fuente Fitness does not have operating hours convenient to all their customers. (-)

Note: (-) designates reverse statements to encourage more accurate response. This would not be shown on the actual survey.

FIGURE 6-4. SERVQUAL Survey for Latina-Owned Fitness Business

Keep in mind that the sample surveys presented here are much longer than a student consulting team will use in their projects. Customers and clients are not willing to spend more than a few minutes completing a survey. It is likely that the team will take key elements from a sample survey and eliminate questions that do not serve the goals of the research.

SERVQUAL can also be categorized by the three primary dimensions of interaction: quality, physical environment quality, and outcome quality. Under these primary dimensions, there are subdimensions of attitude, behavior, expertise, ambient conditions, design, social factors, waiting time, tangibles, and valence. Figure 6-5 shows how this would be used to survey customers for a fine art gallery. Each of these subdimensions uses the SERVQUAL factors of reliability (r), responsiveness, (sp) and empathy (em) described previously.[5] For the art gallery, the establishment of trust is very important, as customers often purchase pieces that cost up to $1,000. Employees must be knowledgeable and be able to relate to the customers. The experience at the gallery, which includes customer interaction with tangibles, must be enjoyable. Because building a strong customer relationship is crucial to getting the customer to purchase more and up, the gallery should survey customers to determine if there is a gap between expected and perceived service. The inclusion of all these dimensions and subdimensions makes this survey particularly onerous. The student team must prune all elements that do not address the outcomes of the consulting project.

In some cases, the business may have determined that key drivers determine the value of the marketing. The business may translate this to customer equity. The final survey model shown in Figure 6-6 uses survey items to measure drivers for customer equity. In this case, a community bank has isolated value, brand, and relationship as key to driving customer equity. These are all factors that contribute to return on marketing.[6] The survey attempts to get at customer share by asking about competitors.

Checklist for Conducting a Survey

1. Conduct secondary research first. Typical research instruments may be available, or trade associations may have done research already.
2. Conduct preliminary research. If the survey involves customers, find a few customers and ask them explor-

atory questions. If the primary research involves businesses, ask the client to recommend some current business clients or ones that are representative of the industry the client company is seeking to target. The goal is to understand as completely as possible the issues that are to be studied. Recognize that it is more helpful to ask open-ended questions in preliminary research.
3. Ensure that respondents are available. Pretest any customer lists to see if they are viable.
4. Create a research instrument and review it with advisors and faculty. Specify the objective of each question. Revise the instrument based on feedback and approval from the client.
5. Pretest the instrument on a few typical respondents. Revise the instrument based on observations and feedback.
6. Submit the instrument to advisors or faculty for final approval. Include a description of what the sample will consist of and how the respondents will be selected.
7. Administer the instrument.
8. Analyze the results using a statistical analysis software.
9. Deliver a report on the survey findings to the client.

QUALITATIVE RESEARCH

The term *qualitative* refers to methods that focus more on the context and meaning or subjective aspects of information than on the numerical or *quantitative* aspects of what is being studied. Data collection and research design procedures are shaped by the purposes and uses of qualitative methods. With regard to MBEs and promising businesses in new markets, these methods can provide valuable insights into the direction of the market. They are also cost effective and can be accomplished in a relatively short period of time; therefore, they are relevant to the guerrilla marketing environment of most MBEs. Types of qualitative research are summarized in Table 6-4.

Focus Groups

A focus group is typically six to twelve people who are led by a skilled moderator in an in-depth discussion on a topic. The discussions are exploratory in nature.[7] They may be used to learn and understand how people feel about an issue, product, or service. Interaction among the people in the group is important. One person's response can be the stimulus for another person to speak. This

The following set of statements relate to your feelings about James Fine Art Gallery.

Circling a 7 means that you strongly agree and circling a 1 means that you strongly disagree. You may circle any of the numbers in the middle that show how strong your feelings are.

There are no right or wrong answers. All we are interested in is a number that best shows your perceptions.

	1	2	3	4	5	6	7

Interaction Quality

Overall, I'd say the quality of my interaction with this firm's employees is excellent.

I would say that the quality of my interaction with James Fine Art Gallery's employees is high.

Attitude

You can count on the employees at James Fine Art Gallery being friendly (r).

The attitude of James Fine Art Gallery's employees demonstrates their willingness to help me (sp).

The attitude of James Fine Art Gallery's employees shows me that they understand my needs (em).

Behavior

I can count on James Fine Art Gallery's employees taking actions to address my needs (r).

James Fine Art Gallery's employees respond quickly to my needs (sp).

The behavior of James Fine Art Gallery's employees indicates to me that they understand my needs (em).

Expertise

You can count on James Fine Art Gallery's employees knowing their jobs (r).

James Fine Art Gallery employees are able to answer my questions quickly (sp).

The employees understand that I rely on their knowledge to meet my needs (em).

Service Environment Quality

I would say that James Fine Art Gallery's physical environment is one of the best in its industry.

I would rate James Fine Art Gallery's physical environment highly.

Ambient Conditions

At James Fine Art Gallery, you can rely on there being a good atmosphere (r).

James Fine Art Gallery's ambiance is what I'm looking for in a gallery (sp).

James Fine Art Gallery understands that its atmosphere is important to me (em).

FIGURE 6-5. Survey with Subdimensions for Fine Art Business

Market Share and Transition Probabilities
List the banks that you use.

The next time you go to a bank, what is the probability that you will go to any of the following (list provided in actual survey)? Provide percentage for each.

Size and Frequency
What types of banking services do you use?
_____ Checking account
_____ Savings account
_____ Loans
_____ Credit Cards
_____ Investment services
On average, how often do you use banking services in a week?
_____ Once
_____ Twice
_____ Three times
_____ Four times
_____ More than four times

Value-Related Drivers
How would you rate the overall quality of the following banks? (5 = "very high quality," 1 = "very low quality")
How would you rate the competitiveness of the interest rates of each of these banks? (5 = "very competitive," 1 = "not at all competitive")
These banks provide the service I want when I want. (5 = "strongly agree," 1 = "strongly disagree")

Brand-Related Drivers (5 = "Strongly Agree," 1 = "Strongly Disagree")
I often notice and pay attention to the bank's media advertising.
I often notice and pay attention to information the restaurant sends to me.
The bank is well known as a good corporate citizen.
The bank is an active sponsor of community events.
The bank has high ethical standards with respect to its customers and employees.
The image of this bank fits my personality well.

Relationship-Related Drivers (5 = "Strongly Agree," 1 = "Strongly Disagree")
I have a big investment in the bank's loyalty program.
The preferential treatment I get from this bank's loyalty program is important to me.
I know this bank's procedures well.
The bank knows a lot of information about me.
This bank recognizes me as being special.
I feel a sense of community with other customers of this bank.
I have a high level of trust in this bank.

Note: These questions would be used to determine customer equity. Competitor banks will be listed. This survey is longer than would be used in actual research. Select the most relevant items.

FIGURE 6-6. Survey for Customer Equity Drivers of Community Bank

TABLE 6-4. Types of Qualitative Research

Method	Benefits	Limitations
Focus groups: Usually a group of 6–12 people led by a moderator in a discussion of a specific topic	Provides information (opinions, experiences, etc.) to understand what people want, like, and how they respond to new ideas and products	Subjective and judgmental, difficult to quantify results, relatively expensive to administer, record, and complete
In-depth interviews: Long, probing individual interviews without use of a formal questionnaire	Designed to uncover motivations or reasons behind behavior, attitudes, and perceptions	Data based on thoughts of a single individual, heavily reliant on the meaning given by the interviewer
Ethnographic studies: Participant-observer exchanges that reveal insights into psychosocial and cultural aspects of behavior	Uncovers the lived expressions and meanings that explain behavior in defined cultural contexts, groups, and institutional arrangements. Can be important in understanding the cultural context of a multicultural market.	May require considerable academic and technological resources (understanding of ethnography, videography) to use effectively
Observational studies: Obtaining information by observing and recording behavior	Captures behavior as it occurs in the moment	Insights limited to what can be observed, description that requires attribution and explanation
Mystery shopping: Interviewer simulates buying or other transactions in a store	Provides detailed evaluations of actual performance and shopping satisfaction	Heavily reliant on interviewer recall from the interview experience

major strength of focus groups can also be their major drawback. Individuals can dominate the discussion or lead others to think like them. Nonetheless, the researcher can experience the reaction of participants in ways not possible with surveys. He or she can catch nuances and emotions that are impossible to capture in a survey. An example may include determining how assertive a person is relative to being an innovator and adopter or a follower and laggard in responding to ideas, products, and brands.

Typically, a researcher will form a group of about eight and run the focus group for one and a half hours. More than eight participants will have to be recruited, as some people will confirm their attendance yet not show up. Financial incentives to participate increase attendance rates, thus most people are paid to participate. For a small business, free meals or low-cost giveaways can serve as incentives for customers to participate. Focus groups can be done quickly and are sometimes less expensive than surveys. The moderator is crucial to a successful focus group. She or he needs to demonstrate unconditional acceptance and positive regard. Any negativity will stifle discussion and elicitation of responses. The moderator needs good observational skills to manage the discussion and accomplish objectives. In some instances, focus groups are videotaped so that the moderator can focus solely on leading the discussion. Moderators cannot exhibit a bias toward any point of view

and must be neutral in discussion. They cannot impose or suggest direction to any questions asked, and they must be able to make quick decisions about how to direct the discussion to get the most out of it. Often moderators have the ability to become trusted quickly.

In preparation for a focus group, the researcher will create a discussion guide. The first step is to explain the purpose of the group and what the researcher wants the participants to do. It is important to disclose all recording devices or whether people are watching from behind two-way mirrors. Initial stages of the focus group may concentrate on introductions and getting people to participate. The middle part of the focus group is the most intense. Participants will discuss the major issues. The final stage might be to summarize the discussion and get clarification. A focus group can be a combination of writing and discussion. Sometimes moderators will ask participants to put their feelings in writing first, followed by a more thoughtful discussion. This ensures that important comments are not lost.

The transcript of the focus group is analyzed by coding the respondent comments and summarizing patterns that emerged in the discussion.

One-on-One In-Depth Interviews

Spending thirty minutes or more for an interview with one respondent may seem like an unacceptably costly or time-consuming method of obtaining information from

Explorer West Middle School
Creating an Identity in the Education Marketplace

Education is about creating an experience that will change a student's life. Explorer West Middle School redefines the experience of middle school by offering a distinct award-winning program that focuses on sustainability and outdoor education. Explorer West attracts a diverse student body of about ninety students per year, with nearly 25% students of color.

Every seven years, Explorer West participates in the Pacific Northwest Association of Independent Schools accreditation process. The process begins with a self-study, which is an opportunity for the school to self-reflect and examine its mission and philosophy. The result of the self-study process is a comprehensive document that highlights the school's self-identified strengths and weaknesses, in addition to a self-assessment on how the school is fulfilling its mission. This self-study is shared with a peer review team of educators who then provide a report of their findings to the association's accreditation committee and board of governors.

In order for a school to begin the self-study, it must provide an assessment of how the school is meeting its major standards, such as its mission and core values. Typically schools outsource this task to professional consultants. However, in 2009 Explorer West called upon a team of student consultants to conduct this crucial assessment in preparation for the school's self-study. Evan Hundley, the head of the school, confirmed that the student team conducted an assessment on the most important major standard, the school's mission statement and core values.

The student consultants conducted an extensive series of surveys with Explorer West students, faculty, administration, and stakeholders such as parents, alumni, and board members to inform the forthcoming self-study. The results from a SWOT (strengths, weaknesses, opportunities, and threats) analysis and surveys provided

insight into Explorer West's strengths and areas that needed improvement. For example, a survey of seventh and eighth graders, alumni, and parents revealed that the outdoor education program contributed to higher levels of self-esteem. The majority of eighth graders, alumni, and parents also reported that Explorer West helped prepare the students for high school.

The student team conducted a thorough evaluation of the school's mission statement. Specifically, team members tested the validity of core phrases in the mission statement among the various stakeholders. The team observed that although the school was highly committed to cultural diversity, the mission statement did not reflect this important focus. The team recommended that Explorer West look for more opportunities to inform the community about its commitment to diversity. As a result of the student team's recommendations, Explorer West revamped its mission statement. The improved and more representative statement also affected the school's curriculum: the school faculty evaluated the course curriculum in light of the new mission statement and made necessary adjustments.

The student team presented its findings to Hundley and the school's board of directors. Hundley notes that the research conducted by the team of student consultants was comparable to that of professional consultants and proved to be invaluable to the school's reaccreditation process.

a small group of individuals. Yet for some studies this could be an acceptable trade-off between the relatively brief period of per-respondent time in focus group research. The argument for the in-depth interview is that it offers more quality and quantity of information per respondent. By definition, it allows a topic to be explored in greater depth than other techniques. By providing more detailed information, the results can also be representative of the feelings and perceptions of the respondents. Thus, it can be argued that there is more value in the information that is obtained. Those who use this method argue that it offers more information for less money without some of the limitations imposed by focus groups.

The method is especially strong when key informants and gatekeepers are the targets of the investigation. This format can also be beneficial in a B2B environment where there are only a limited number of people who make buying decisions and thus a large sample size may not be possible. As an example, one student team interviewed hotel and wedding event planners to determine how they selected caterers. Each interview took one hour, but only a few respondents were necessary to get valuable information. For a project in which a considerable amount of risk is involved or in which relationships should be examined with especially detailed critiques, this method should be considered. As with focus groups, it is important that interviewers have adequate knowledge of the subject being investigated as well as familiarity with interviewing techniques.

Ethnographic Studies

Both surveys and focus groups have their drawbacks as research methods. Typically, low response rates for mail-only surveys decrease their effectiveness. Focus groups may be dominated by a few individuals, or participants may feel pressure to say the "right" thing. Market researchers are increasingly turning to ethnographic studies to gather information. Ethnographic study is a well-established form of research used by anthropologists.

An ethnographer begins with extensive reading on the topic. Once knowledgeable about the topic, she or he proceeds to do research in the natural environment. He or she may administer questionnaires in the field or take photographs of the participants and their surroundings. The process involves videotaping the subjects while they use products or go about their normal tasks. The

researcher interviews and records observations while participating and observing the subject's environment.

Ethnography is the subjective alternative to the quantitative approach of behavioral research. The ethnographic method acknowledges that the researcher is immersed in the process. Researchers like it because it may bring about more original ideas. Long, open-ended interviews allow people to tell their stories. In this case, the researcher does not follow a script. Respondents are allowed to say anything they want. Ethnographers believe that these very open-ended interviews capture spur-of-the-moment thoughts as well as deep truths that the respondent feels. The respondents speak in their own words and are free to roam to any subject.

The researcher may watch the respondents act naturally in their environments. In one case, the researcher was interested in consumers' relationships with their motorcycles and with other riders. He actually joined a Harley-Davidson owner's group (HOG) and became immersed in the environment alongside the consumers. In another case, BMW dashboard designers rode in cars with customers to see what was important to drivers. They observed drivers talking nonstop on cell phones, writing notes, eating lunch, and shaving while driving—all activities they would not have known about otherwise.

This type of participation helps researchers get very close to the subject and allows them to notice potentially important areas for new ideas on positioning. When they participate in what the subject does, they see firsthand the objects, movements, gestures, and processes that help them understand what the customer thinks and feels. The researchers may even re-create the environment in which the subject uses the product. They might collect articles used in conjunction with the product. The Hartman Group, a market research firm based near Seattle that focuses on food company research, observes what families have in their refrigerators and cabinets, rather than their reported consumption, to determine their actual buying behaviors.

Some researchers will focus on the product and follow it throughout its life. This tells the story of what happens to the product from the time it is designed to when it is discarded by the consumer. A more complete understanding of what the product means to the customer is created. Most businesses focus on the relationship only at the time of purchase or when it is used. Understanding the whole process might produce breakthroughs in marketing.

Ethnographic studies are based on the understanding of behavior within the context of cultures and cultural influences. Broadly, this could be the norms and customs associated with music, art, and language. In a marketing context, more concern is placed on material culture. The functions, symbols, and status associated with products and brands are artifacts of material and consumer culture. Thus ethnographic studies are particularly pertinent to ethnic markets. It is important to be familiar and comfortable with, if not immersed in, a group-specific cultural environment to understand how to best communicate and market to these communities. For students, hip-hop and punk-rock cultures might be familiar examples of where ethnography would be an effective way of understanding how being a part of these cultures influences aspects of lifestyle and consumption behavior.

Observational Studies

In situations where customers or users can be watched in the buying or consumption process, observational studies could be especially valuable. Mystery shopping is a form of observational study. It is commonly used by most large retail chains to assess the quality of customer service. People are contracted by the store to behave as regular shoppers. As they proceed with trying to buy an item, the mystery shoppers make notes about how service is delivered. The exact measures for assessment differ depending on the type of store. Some businesses have specific requirements of their sales staff, and they measure against these requirements.

While mystery shopping is a popular form of observational study, there are other uses of this type of qualitative research. Consulting teams can conduct competitor observational research, gathering information on competitor store hours, displays, pricing, in-store promotions, number of customers, nearby environment, and other factors. One set of competitor evaluation questions is illustrated in Figure 6-7. Another student team observed, recorded, and later questioned customers at a local fast-food restaurant about wait time, ease of ordering, and shopping experience. Based on the results, the team was able to design a more customer-friendly and effective

---

Student consultants will visit competitors, observe, and gather the following information:

1. Date and time.

2. Availability of parking and access to public transit.

3. Surrounding environment (number of stores, residential units, 15-minute car count on street, etc.).

4. Hours of operation.

5. Signage – include description of awnings and window display.

6. Square footage and store layout.

7. Amount and display of merchandise.

8. Number, quality and special features of services or products offered.

9. Pricing.

10. Customers (type and number).

11. Customer service (wait time, quality of customer service, etc.)

12. Social media (Facebook, Twitter, Linkedin, blogs, Yelp, Urban Spoon, Google, Zagat, etc.)

FIGURE 6-7. Competitor Observation

layout of the reader board. Customers and the client firm benefited from faster order processing, better service, and reduced transaction time. The team was able to combine its marketing research results with business process analysis (discussed in chapter 7) to help the business improve operations and increase sales. The relevance of this brief summary is to suggest that if customer responses in an actual store setting can serve as a guide to improving the business, consider how an observational study might be used. For example, consider observing different days of the week and/or times of the day. It is important to be consistent with measures across observations.

DISCUSSION

1. Go to the Pew Research Center website. Choose a study and describe its survey methodology. Evaluate the purpose of the survey. Indicate the extent to which each question in the survey relates to the purpose. Look at the questions and summarize the following aspects of the research: use of open-ended questions, clarity of the answers obtained, whether the survey missed any important questions.
2. Create a survey to satisfy a purpose. Administer the survey to five people. Analyze whether the survey was effective. Suggest improvements.
3. How would qualitative research be used to find out crucial information about the client that could not be obtained by quantitative research?
4. With three other students, conduct a competitor observation of four different retail stores in a shopping mall. Compare and contrast your results. Which store had the best customer service?
5. Create metrics to evaluate the client business against its competitors.

NOTES

1   Brooks Gekler, class materials developed at the University of Washington–Bothell, 2010.
2   D. A. Dillman, J. D. Smyth, and L. M. Christian, Internet, Mail and Mixed-Mode Surveys: The Tailored Design Method (Hoboken, NJ: Wiley, 2009).
3   D. A. Dillman, G. Phelps, R. Tortora, K. Swift, J. B. Kohrell, J. Derck, and B. L. Messer, "Response Rate and Measurement Difference in Mixed-Mode Survey, Using Mail, Telephone, Interactive Voice Response (IVR) and the Internet," Social Science Research 38 (2009): 1–18.
4   A. Parasuraman, Balarie A. Zeithamal, and L. Leonard, "Servqual: A Multiple-Item Scale for Measuring Consumer Perceptions of Service Quality," Journal of Retailing 64, no. 1 (Spring 1988): 12–40.
5   Michael K. Brady and J. Joseph Cronin Jr., "Some New Thoughts on Conceptualizing Perceived Service Quality: A Hierarchical Approach," Journal of Marketing 65, no. 3 (July 2001): 34–49.
6   Roland T. Rust, Katherine N. Lemon, and Valarie A. Zeithami, "Return on Marketing: Using Customer Equity to Focus Marketing Strategy," Journal of Marketing 68 (January 2004): 109–27.
7   P. Hague, A Practical Guide to Market Research (B2B International, 2006), www.b2binternational.com/b2b-blog/ebook/practical-guide-to-market-research.pdf.

7. Business Processes

In previous chapters we have focused on the firm from a departmental or functional point of view, such as marketing and sales. Here we shift to a process and performance point of view. This means analyzing the related tasks and activities involved in delivering something of value, which could be selling a product or delivering an invoice to a customer. In this context, the "customer" could also be inside the firm, as when human resources selects and hires a skilled sales person or bookkeeper to perform the business's tasks effectively. Beyond describing and analyzing business processes and performance, in this chapter we illustrate how businesses manage processes by mapping them and communicating their value to the firm. We emphasize how businesses turn strategy into business action. Special attention is given to how firms look for ways to continuously improve processes and overall business performance. The balanced scorecard (BSC) methodology is used to show how businesses evaluate four dimensions of firm performance: financial, customer, internal, and organizational learning and growth. Other process management tools and techniques discussed briefly include total quality management (TQM), key performance indicators (KPIs), and lean manufacturing.

RELATIONSHIPS BETWEEN THE BALANCED SCORECARD AND BUSINESS PROCESS ANALYSIS

The balanced scorecard (BSC) is one of the most widely used tools for moving from strategy to implementation.[1] It also provides a comprehensive method for aligning vision and strategy. It provides a means of communicating the strategy so that individuals up and down the organization structure can understand and follow the indi-

cated results. Goals are not focused solely on financial metrics. While the BSC tool has been taught in business schools and used in some large corporations for years, it is a relatively new concept among small business owners, and thus an explanation of its benefits and drawbacks may be necessary before the BSC is adopted by a small business client.

Business process analysis is a component of the balanced scorecard and has expanded with its own set of advocates. The experience of student consulting teams is that business process analysis has been effective in helping emerging businesses make the leap from marginal to promising firms. Having inefficient or inconvenient operations and customer transaction procedures often constrains an emerging business from growing quickly and may prevent it from growing at all. Completing a good business process analysis does much to document what the business does. The business can articulate where value is added. Efficiency improvements can be highlighted. A template for replication is created that allows the business to move from slow to higher growth. As many of the businesses that students consult with are service businesses, we have included the service blueprint in this chapter, with its stronger focus on customer-facing activities.

Other concepts in this chapter include total quality management, key performance indicators, and lean manufacturing. Common in all these methods is the propensity to map and measure the activities of the business to determine if the business has met its goals. These metrics have been extended to national and international organizations, such as the International Organization of Standardization (ISO), which issues more than 19,500 standards in areas such as manufacturing quality management, the environment, food safety, information management, and social responsibility. Numerous ISO studies show the impact of these metrics on economic development and sustainability. In a business-to-business (B2B) environment, large corporations often require suppliers to follow ISO900 and other business process certifications, especially in manufacturing industries.

After Studying This Chapter

After reading this chapter, students will be able to:

- Articulate a strategic vision in clear and concise language and translate the vision and strategy into goals and measured results.
- Describe the key drivers in small business adoption of technology.
- Map a business process across functions and determine where value is created.
- Create documentation to scale-up the business.
- Select key performance indicators for a business dashboard, with leading and lagging indicators to give appropriately frequent feedback.

- Create a service blueprint to deliver memorable customer experiences.

THE BALANCED SCORECARD

The balanced scorecard (BSC) was one of the first frameworks that encouraged using measurements beyond purely financial ones as a way of evaluating how enterprises performed. As shown in Figure 7-1, the BSC added questions about the customer, internal business processes, and learning as a means of achieving the firm's strategic vision. Bear in mind that objectives, measurements, targets, and initiatives to achieve the vision of each category must be articulated.

Moving performance evaluation away from a single (financial) perspective allows businesses to integrate new measures that are relevant to the knowledge economy, such as innovation and human capital. Financial metrics focus on the past and may not allow the business to be proactive in capitalizing on opportunities or preventing problems. Lagging indicators, such as financial

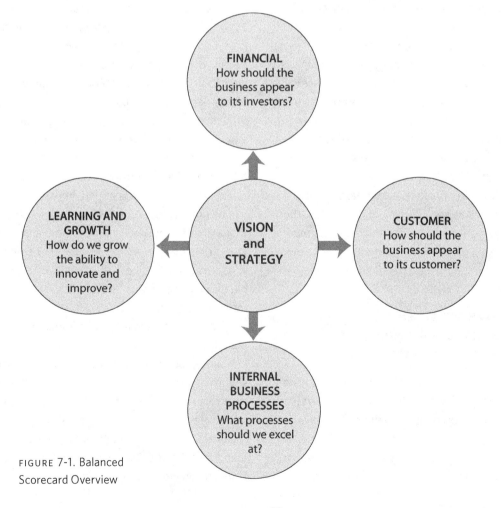

FINANCIAL
How should the business appear to its investors?

LEARNING AND GROWTH
How do we grow the ability to innovate and improve?

VISION and STRATEGY

CUSTOMER
How should the business appear to its customer?

INTERNAL BUSINESS PROCESSES
What processes should we excel at?

FIGURE 7-1. Balanced Scorecard Overview

statement results, also represent the outcome of strategic planning. In contrast, the BSC emphasizes evaluation of leading metrics, which allow business owners to be proactive rather than reactive in executing strategy. The BSC also gives managers tools that enable them to see how their activities may lead to the company's future financial success.

Implementation of strategic plans often hit roadblocks because stakeholders are not clear on the plan or are not held accountable for achieving the goals. The BSC serves as a method of simply and clearly communicating the strategy to the rest of the organization. It also allows the organization to customize the strategic planning process to its own culture. The BSC has been used in business, health care, and education throughout the world.

Student consultants can assist business owners by taking the following steps outlined by Robert Kaplan and David Norton:[2]

- Translating the vision. The role of the student team is to refine the strategic vision for the business owner. A business owner will often have generic or vague visions, such as an art gallery owner who wanted to revitalize the art imagination in the local marketplace. The goal of this business owner was to have sustainable and growing revenues with a quality brand image. The refinement of this strategic vision involved identifying the target customer and determining what constituted a quality brand image. Students often fall prey to nonspecific language in strategic visions as well. The vision must be deconstructed into specific, measurable objectives. In addition to clarifying the vision, the student team must also ensure that there is consensus. This means communicating with all the key stakeholders and ensuring that each is clear about the vision.
- Communicating and linking. Managers must communicate strategy up and down the organization so that it is linked to departmental and individual objectives. The best results will be achieved when the job performance of each individual in the firm supports the strategy. Each individual unit of the business and each employee must have personal scorecards that link them to the overall strategic vision of the company.. Often, strategies are mapped across functions to ensure that these linkages are present.
- Business planning. Although most businesses that student teams work with are not large organizations

where functions may operate as silos, there is still the danger that functions within a business will operate independently. Managers must stay focused on the strategic plan and decide the most influential drivers of success. Then resources must be allocated and priorities set so that goals can be met. A strategy map can help identify common themes as well as guide resource allocation decisions.
- Feedback and learning. Strategic learning is essential to the ongoing sustainability of a business. One of the first factors that student consultants look for is whether the business or business owner has repeatedly made the same mistake. If yes, the business's chances of survival are slim. Getting feedback through effective metrics is one way for businesses to learn.

SMALL BUSINESS ADOPTION OF TECHNOLOGY

Business process analysis evaluates the firm's mission-critical processes to determine how the business can enhance value. This often involves assessing whether technology should be incorporated to increase capacity or effect efficiencies. The use of technology no longer provides a competitive advantage for the small business but has become ubiquitous in businesses large or small. However, small businesses continue to have varying levels of technology adoption, with low adoption resulting from a focus on short-term costs as opposed to long-term benefits. Researchers have identified the technology adoption model as a robust framework for explaining why technology is adopted.[3] Usefulness and perceived ease of use are the two most important drivers in this model. It has proved effective in explaining when and why small businesses adopt technology. Usually the perceived usefulness is market driven. Either customers, competitors, or the desire for growth can drive small businesses to adopt technology. Perceived ease of use could include factors such as the small business's level of technology sophistication. However, the most salient driver is the business owner's commitment to technology.[4]

As noted in previous chapters, more than 80% of firms have a website. Most businesses have also adopted essential function software for accounting, payroll, and e-mail. It is increasingly required of small businesses who work on government contracts or as part of the supply chain of larger corporations to integrate their processes with those of much more sophisticated customers or suppliers. Figure 7-2 shows the levels of information tech-

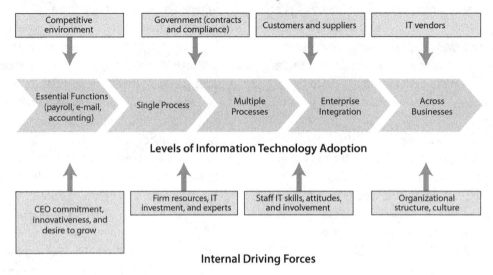

Levels of Information Technology Adoption

Internal Driving Forces

FIGURE 7-2. Small Business Adoption of Technology

nology adoption in a small firm, along with the external and internal drivers.[5]

Use of cloud computing in small businesses has grown exponentially, from 5% in 2010 to 43% in 2013, according to the *2013 Technology Survey*, conducted by the National Association of Small Businesses.[6] Small businesses are also concerned about cybersecurity, with nearly half of businesses falling victim to cyberattacks that interrupted service. According to the European Network of Information and Security Agency, 68% of businesses use cloud computing to avoid capital expenditure and 64% want flexibility and scalability; about a third want more computing capacity and business performance.[7]

As shown in Figure 7-3, business preference for cloud services is spread across services such as individual software packages, for example, accounting, human resources, and procurement (software as a service, or SaaS); complete operating system and software (platform as a service, or PaaS); and infrastructure, for example, storage or network capacity. Figure 7-4 shows that businesses are more likely to use customer relationship management (CRM), project management, and payroll services in the cloud. Business concerns with cloud computing are privacy, integrity, and confidentiality, along with availability. However, for many businesses investment in technology and its proper adoption are worthwhile.

BUSINESS PROCESS MANAGEMENT

Business process management is analysis and coordination of a set of activities or tasks needed to deliver value to customers or fulfill a strategic goal. It involves a cross-functional and, increasingly frequently, a cross-business perspective, as when a firm works with its vendors and customers in supply chain management. Although common in large corporations and the manufacturing industry, business process management can also assist restaurants in shortening customer service time, office cleaning companies in optimizing the deployment of staff, and agricultural packaging houses in moving fresh product to market. Business process analysis can come in the guise of business process reengineering, Six Sigma, total quality management, process management, kaizen,

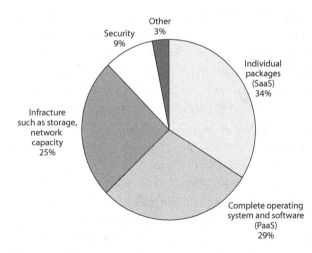

FIGURE 7-3. Business Preference for Cloud Services

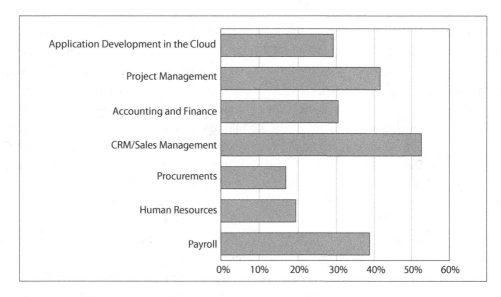

FIGURE 7-4. Services Most Likely to be Outsourced to Cloud

and lean management as well as process maps of enterprise resource planning (ERP) systems. Business process management both maps and remodels business processes, deploys processes as part of software, and allows for the improvement of those processes. Despite this, some researchers report that as many as 60% to 80% of business process management initiatives have been unsuccessful.[8]

Small businesses often fail to reach critical mass because they are unaware of the shortcomings or inefficiencies in their operations and thus they deploy resources (financial and human) inefficiently, which drives up costs and reduces profits that could have been reinvested in company growth. Also, firms may not understand their core competencies and core business processes. Typically, businesses have not documented their processes so that they can be replicated for regional or national expansion. They may not have considered the use of the Internet and the ability to link anyone, anywhere, anytime in terms of increasing their part of the value chain with their

suppliers and customers. Generally they have made little use of business process analysis.

The basic concept of what constitutes a business process is very simple: input, conversion, and output. According to the diagram in Figure 7-5, complexity is added based on the specific characteristics of individual businesses. In *The Balanced Scorecard*, Kaplan and Norton created an internal business process diagram to describe the processes within an enterprise. The key to their model is that the processes important to the business are mapped out, at which point it is possible to work on ensuring that each process meets stated goals and that the cycle time for each can be improved. This process mapping can identify bottlenecks that cause the entire process to slow down and result in wasted resources.

In the area of systems analysis and implementation in large enterprises, business process analysis has been taken to increased levels of sophistication with certified training by organizations such as the Institute of Configuration Management. The following brief summary of

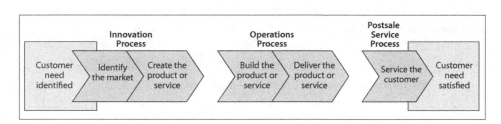

FIGURE 7-5. Internal Business Process. Source: Robert S. Kaplan and David P. Norton, *The Balanced Scorecard* (Boston: Harvard Business School Press, 1996)

steps in *Configuration Management II* is similar to the process described later in this chapter.[9]

1. Determine the basic requirements for the system, including regulatory, business, mission, and objectives.
2. Establish all inputs and outputs for the system or process. Define stakeholders and what must be included and excluded. Determine what information and resources go into the system. Determine what information and resources are the product of the system.
3. Map out the process by establishing the link between inputs and outputs. Define how all information and resources are processed to satisfy the output requirements. Evaluate the process for weaknesses and revise it to mitigate them. Document the process and assign a process/document owner.
4. Plan the implementation process. Determine the impact of implementation. Establish roles and responsibilities for managing implementation.
5. Deploy the new process. Manage the deployment using good project management practices. Track and monitor the progress of the implementation. Revise, document, and implement changes as needed.
6. Evaluate the process. Establish metrics for system performance. Monitor the system performance according to these metrics. Evaluate where improvements or changes need to be made based on how well the system performs.
7. Revise the system as needed. Define the scope of the change. Determine how to accomplish the change. Document the change and establish an effective date for its implementation. Track and monitor implementation of the change.

Who Are the Customers and What Do They Value?

In business process analysis, start with the top-level issues. Find out what the business is all about. This is not as simple as it seems. What the business is today may not be what the owner wants it to be in the future. Perhaps the owner has not thought about what it should be in the future at all. What is the mission or overall goal of the business? Business missions are about customers, so start by asking questions about the customer. Who is the customer? How has that customer changed in the past? How will the customer evolve in the future? What are the customer segments? What does the customer value? What does the product or service do for customers? Look at the product life cycle in relation to the customer. Why do customers leave? Who are the firm's potential customers? What do they want? What would make the customer's life easier? Are there new technologies entering the market or likely to enter the market that will change what customers are looking for? Determine where the product or service is in its life cycle. Look at the customer life cycle.

Once answers to these questions are determined, a clear picture of business goals will emerge. The business goals then have to be broken down into specific business outcomes, such as market share and profitability. These become key performance indicators or metrics for the business. It is important to note that metrics must be detailed at the start.

Target the Critical Processes

Once the business goals are determined and it is decided how these will be measured as outcomes, consider the business and determine its core processes. These processes are usually documented in block diagrams or flow charts. In more sophisticated operations, analysts can use Business Process Modeling Notation (BPMN) or Unified Modeling Language (UML) to map the process. To make this analysis process accessible to students and employees, a simple set of notations is used here.

Typically, an analysis will start with a clear focus on the main steps in the process. These are mapped by asking questions, watching how people operate, and following the paperwork trail. Time-motion studies can identify how much time each part of a task takes. Tracking work-in-progress inventory can help identify parts of the process that move slower or faster than others. Next, the steps are broken down into subprocesses. In complex organizations, the subprocesses are broken down into several other levels. A student consulting project with a photography studio provides an example of business process analysis (Figure 7-6). This service business is similar in nature to other small businesses such as legal, financial, or health services.

Map the top view. The core process of a photography studio is booking the client to come in for a photo shoot. Afterward, the client selects the proofs that she likes and the frames she likes, if a frame is desired. The photographs are processed and then delivered to the client.

Photography Studio Business Process

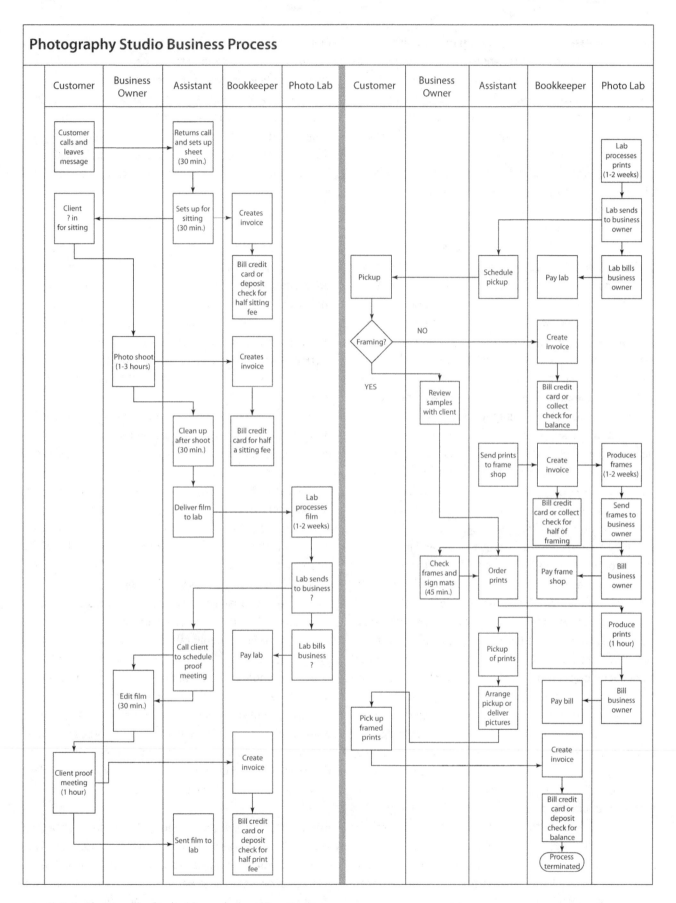

FIGURE 7-6. Photography Studio Mapped across Functions

Map subprocesses. The clear focus on the overall process may appear straightforward, but even such a simple process is more complex than this overview suggests. These steps must be broken down into subprocesses. The consulting team spent time with the business owner and mapped out a process flow chart (see Figure 7-6). They documented each step, how each step linked to or drove other steps in the process, and the amount of time taken. Like many bootstrapping small business owners, this business owner had higher staff turnover than a larger enterprise would have. She could not afford to provide the extensive benefits that larger enterprises could, nor could she afford high salaries. She often used interns to assist in her business. As a result, the business owner was often performing many of the tasks listed to keep the business going, without analysis of what was important for her specifically to do. Although the business was extremely promising and new clients called daily, this resulted in a major constraint in her ability to grow. Time tied up in these tasks was time taken from doing the core value-added task of photography shoots.

Mapping the subprocesses was the first step in analyzing where efficiencies could be obtained. The mapping showed that this business owner, although never trained in business, was very astute about payment. Clients were asked for payment upon booking the first appointment rather than upon delivery of service. This ensured that the client turned up for the appointment, and it brought cash into the business immediately. The client paid the balance for the shoot immediately after the shoot, again reducing the chances of bad debt and ensuring that the client would show up for the next stage of the process. By mapping such mundane tasks as invoicing and collecting payment, the team could work to reduce the cash disbursement cycle (discussed in detail in chapter 8, on analyzing accounting processes), increase the throughput of service processing, and shorten the service processing cycle.

An African American–owned moving and storage company sought help from the student team to increase sales. Discussions with the owner pointed to possibly losing business due to poor customer service and poor follow-up to bid inquiries. The process chart in Figure 7-7 shows the process both prior to and after reengineering. As shown in the figure, in the original process there was no follow-up, either with customers who did not respond to the firm's bid or with customers who did contract the firm's services. The consulting team proposed some simple changes to the process. The team suggested that all inquiries for bids be logged into a database, that a quality assurance check be added for completed jobs, and that customers be contacted for follow-up business.

By adding a database, the company was better able to track clients, ensure high customer satisfaction, and seek repeat business. Additionally, the database allowed the company to become a learning organization and to improve its pricing, service offerings, and customer service over time.

Map across functions. A cross-functional analysis breaks down steps by the function or person who performs them. In larger enterprises, the transfer between functions often results in inefficiencies that can be captured in process analysis. In the case of the photography business, and typical with small businesses wanting to grow, the tasks were not broken down by function. Most of the work was performed by the principals in the firm. This lack of differentiation made it difficult to delegate the work to others.

Figure 7-6 shows the student team's careful analysis of the firm's processes. This revealed that processes could be broken down into crucial value-added tasks that only the business owner could do and those that could be delegated. It was obvious that the business owner was the only one who could do the photographic shoot. In addition, as is typical with promising businesses, the business owner was the firm's best salesperson. Therefore, it was important that she was the key touchpoint with the customer when buy decisions were made.

Further, the analysis showed that an assistant could take care of the mundane scheduling and logistical tasks, while a bookkeeper could take care of the billing and payment tasks. The functional analysis also revealed the need for a photo lab and framing shop; these outside firms played an important role in fulfilling the service. Although most small business owners would not think of these vendors as part of their business processes, any improvement in a vendor's production time can decrease the main firm's cycle time, which allows the firm to take on more customers and convert to cash more quickly.

Break out the value added. A detailed analysis of each step in a firm's processes yields additional ideas for improving them. Including the photo lab and framing shop in the analysis allows the photography studio to explore improvement in its part of the value chain. Questions can be asked about reducing production time at both the photo

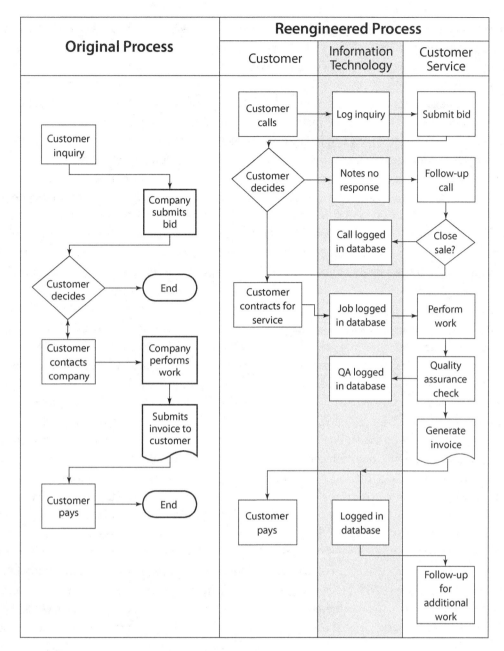

FIGURE 7-7. Reengineering a Moving Company

lab and framing shop. Could the photo lab pick up and deliver, thereby reducing travel time for the assistant? Consultants could explore whether credit card processing could be faster or cheaper. Perhaps the customer could be asked to decide on the frame when the proofs are approved, versus scheduling another appointment. This would enhance the customer experience by reducing one trip to the studio while decreasing the order fulfillment time. Another option would be using a cloud service for customers to view and choose photographs over the Web, thereby saving both the photographer and the customer time.

Most important, the documentation of the business's processes allows the business owner to easily delegate tasks to others. If staff turns over, this documentation will reduce training time. Additionally, having a picture of the entire flow allows staff to see how each task is interdependent with the others. Staff will be better able to suggest other ways of improving operations.

Create metrics. Most enterprises rely on traditional financial measures to evaluate their processes. They look at return on capital, return on investment, or net present value. These measures favor investing that offers faster returns and involves less risk. But they are biased toward short-term gains and emphasize results for specified time periods. Recognize that quality (or other value that allows a firm to charge more than its peers), customer loyalty, and brand value may better reflect a firm's long-term performance. In order to survive for the long run, the business may need to do something risky and innovative. Thus, an investment in product development could lessen immediate returns while offering quite substantial returns in the future. It is important that the student consulting team develop metrics that are understandable and manageable for the business owner. The student team should also help the business owner learn to interpret and use metrics that give a comprehensive picture of business performance.

Metrics need to be accurate and objective, and they need to measure more than one dimension. They need to make effective trade-offs. They need to be crystal clear to everyone at all levels in the business. They must take into consideration the future, not the past. The balanced scorecard is an alternative to depending exclusively on financial measures. As described above, the BSC uses a combination of financial outcomes, customer metrics, internal processes, and enterprise innovation and learning. These measures have to tie in to the specific strategic objectives of the business. Table 7-1 shows the application of BSC to a law firm.

Gather metrics. The business sees improvements from process reengineering with the development of metrics and measures that show progress. With process mapping, it is important that information be gathered to provide a baseline to measure changes. Often the information is there but it has not been used. Less easily available information can be obtained by sampling a segment of the population or data.

Once measurements are gathered, they need to be assessed for how they contribute to the goals of the enterprise. It is helpful to divide the measurements into lead indicators (measurements that assist in predicting) and lag indicators (which measure whether goals have been reached). Lead indicators are similar to economic indicators such as production capacity or housing starts, which give economists an indication of what might be in store for the economy. A key lead indicator for a photography company, for example, would be client inquiries. For a payment processing company, it may be the quantity of payments from customers of existing clients. For a video game design company, it may be increased sales of tablets, televisions, and mobile phones. Keeping track of all potential clients who called and how they learned about the firm is important but rarely done in small businesses. It lets the business owner know the effectiveness of individual advertising programs. For the emerging business, the effectiveness of a few thousand dollars in expenses can have a tremendous impact on the profitability and even the survival of a firm.

The percentage of inquiries converted to appointments is the next important metric. In the photography company example, if few inquiries are converted into actual clients, the business owner will revisit the sales pitch. For a machine tool shop, if the conversion rate following shipment of samples to automobile or yacht building businesses is low, then examining the consistency with which they deliver parts within tight tolerances may be examined. Leading indicators give the busi-

TABLE 7-1. Balanced Scorecard Measures

Financial		Customer	
Goals	*Measures*	*Goals*	*Measures*
Survive	Cash flow	Brand image of excellence	Client surveys
Succeed	Sales/profit growth		Cross-marketed revenues
Thrive	Increase market share		Number of clients by revenue categories
	Increase return on equity		Share of top-20 client spending
Internal Business		*Innovation and Learning*	
Goals	*Measures*	*Goals*	*Measures*
Service excellence	Industry benchmarking surveys	People development	Growth in billing rates
	Staffing ratios		Ranking in *Best Lawyers of America*
	Blend rates realized		Lawyer turnover

TABLE 7-2. Sample Key Performance Indicators

Manufacturing	Retail	Construction
Percent on-time delivery	Same-store sales	Cash flow
Customer returns and complaints	Sales per square foot	Labor productivity
Lead time	Loss prevention	Schedule variance
Time to resolve complaints	Gross margin percent	Margin variance
Inventory turns	Inventory turns	Unapproved change orders
	Average sales per customer	Backlog
	Labor costs as percent of sales	
	Staff turnover	
E-business	Restaurant	Hair Salon
Conversion rate of marketing campaigns	Spend per head	Percent repeat customers
Number of visitors	Costs per cover	Spend per head
Number of unique visitors	Table turnover	Value per chair
Cost per thousand views	Percent of prebooked tables	Inventory turns
Average order	Labor cost as percent of sales	Rent as percent of sales
	Customer satisfaction	Cash flow

ness owner an idea of whether goals will be met. For emerging businesses, focusing on a breakeven number of clients is important to the survival of the business. For example, in the photography business, 50% of calls are converted to sales. If not enough inquiries are made in a given month, sales will not be achieved in the next month. Consequently there is a good chance that breakeven will not be reached in three months' time. This leading indicator signals the business owner to put more effort into generating initial inquiries rather than into converting inquiries into sales.

In the photography studio case, once the photo shoot is completed the business owner will track the effectiveness of cross-merchandising. Did the client buy additional prints beyond what was in the original contract? Did the client purchase framing services? If not, the business owner will explore the factors that prevented these add-on sales.

Lagging indicators measure success or failure in reaching goals. They include revenue, profits, customer lifetime value, market share, and return on investment.

The business should work with internal and external stakeholders to determine key performance indicators. Some consultants suggest having twenty-five to thirty performance indicators. The indicators need to be accessible, relevant, and easily understood. All employees and relevant suppliers should understand what the metrics are and how they work. There should be a balance between leading and lagging indicators. The indicators should measure performance against long-term and short-term goals. The metrics should not be contradictory. One measure cannot be improved at the expense of another. Table 7-2 shows typical key performance indicators for industries that are commonly part of student consulting projects.

Map the customer's point of view. The picture is not complete until the firm's business processes are mapped from the customer's point of view. This could be done by in-depth interviews with one or two customers, talking to them about their experience. Anyone who has gone through a service process can give a detailed description of its foibles. The best businesses will always look at their processes from the customer's point of view. What can be done to make life easier for the customer? When business processes are looked at in this way, it becomes obvious that there are many opportunities for improvement.

Who Owns the Process?

At the same time that core processes are being mapped, an assessment must be made of the business's readiness to change. Larger enterprises conduct a survey of employees' attitude to new ideas or elements of the change, such as technology. Some test instruments rank the enterprise on a scale of one to five regarding readiness for change. With small businesses, it is most important to assess the owner's attitude to change. The owner is the primary decision maker and key to the change process. Some owners are ready and even eager to change; others are reluctant. Keep in mind that just because the

Soul Carrier

Where Value Is Created in Business Processes

"Here's to asking where you want to go, and here's to having the courage to pursue your journey to authenticity."

Jennifer Boonlorn was an undergraduate marketing major attending Arizona State University (ASU) when tragedy struck. Her parents lost their lives in a fatal car accident, and that accident changed Boonlorn's life forever. Boonlorn learned to embrace the idea that she had a mission to fulfill in her life. Upon graduating from ASU, she began working with a public relations firm in Phoenix in addition to taking fashion courses at a local community college. As part of her coursework, Boonlorn went on a weeklong tour to New York City to learn more about the fashion industry. She was so inspired that she decided to move to New York City. She applied and was admitted to Parsons: The New School for Design.

She gained valuable experience there and interned at major fashion industry leaders, such as Oscar de la Renta and *Women's Wear Daily*. She remained in New York when she graduated from Parsons and began working at a major clothing manufacturer. But Boonlorn longed to return to the desert, and in 2009 she moved back to Arizona and pursued opportunities in the local fashion industry. She participated in an art project called "The Mannequin Is Our Muse," where designers created art with a mannequin to be displayed at the Scottsdale Fashion Square. Boonlorn's mannequin design was made with recycled materials, and this became the inspiration for Soul Carrier. From there, she began making clutches, which eventually evolved into handbags.

As her business began to grow, Boonlorn looked carefully at her business processes to determine where value was created. She found that it no longer made sense to manufacture her handbags locally. As a small business owner, it was difficult for her to buy small quantities of material on her own, and she did not have the capacity to expand in response to demand. She explored suppliers in India and manufacturers in New York and Phoenix. In

2013, she created a partnership with a Mexican family based in Léon, Mexico, one of the world's leather capitals. The Mexican family runs a small leather shop and produces high-quality handmade leather products. Boonlorn met and hired a local translator, since she is not fluent in Spanish. The translator not only helps with communication but helps oversee the manufacturing process, as Boonlorn's business is located in Arizona. Boonlorn was pleased with the quality of the initial batch of handbags, and she now works exclusively with this small family-run leather manufacturer in Mexico.

In 2014, with her manufacturing processes handled in Mexico, Boonlorn was able to concentrate on her core competency of design. She launched her "Authentic Change" collection of leather handbags inspired by Boonlorn's friends, a line that includes the Kelly Beth, Sarah Elizabeth, Jaime Leigh, and Olivia handbags. In addition, the clutch named Blake Emery, after Boonlorn's niece, represents playfulness and having no fear. It is with these original designs, inspired by real people, and through marketing via social media that value is created for her business.

Boonlorn aspires to expand to retail outlets in Arizona and California and would like to evolve Soul Carrier into a "lifestyle brand" to include home products and yoga-related accessories.

owner is not ready, this does not mean the change will not happen. Small business owners are smart and agile. Education can go a long way in making the business owner and the business ready for change.

The appropriate level of change is the next assessment made. With the abundance of technological solutions available, it is tempting to recommend the latest and greatest. But often the business is not ready to adopt this type of technology. Simpler solutions that employees can understand and maintain prove superior in many cases. For example, an Excel spreadsheet may be more appropriate than sophisticated accounting software.

In order to effectively implement change, the process owner needs to be intimately involved. The process owner is not always the business owner. Other key people in the business may be responsible for critical processes. Just because the business owner has bought in does not mean that everyone else is on board. The process owner is accountable for the process. She has the authority to make decisions. The process owner coaches and mentors others in learning the process. He or she is the advocate for procuring resources for the process.

Excellent processes have excellent process owners who are accountable for the outcomes of the process. They are responsible for a program of continuous improvement. They have a team orientation and value disagreement and opposing views. They make the best use of the business's knowledge assets.

So the consultant should make an assessment of process owners in the business. Evaluate their ability to lead excellent processes. Determine what kind of development is needed. If this will enhance support for process improvement, communicate what you have learned to the client or owner.

Metrics should be customized to the business or organization in which they are applied. Unless they are meaningful to the stakeholders, metrics become just another administrative burden. Organizations often make use of dashboards, or a compilation of key performance indicators, to clearly and simply convey the status of metrics. Figure 7-8 is the dashboard that was devised for a displaced persons center in Indonesia.[10] Instead of financial, customer, internal processes, and learning, the center's perspectives have been customized to health facilities, community, service provision, and staff. The metrics used as key performance indicators fit the center's mission. Notice how the color coding assists in identifying problem areas.

Consultants and software have long since entered the realm of key performance indicators and dashboards. All

Measures	Clinic 1	Clinic 2	Clinic 3	Clinic 4	Clinic 5	Clinic 6	Clinic 7
Staff							
Job satisfaction	4	3	4	4	4	3	3
Weeks since last pay	3	3	3	3	3	18	18
Months since training	1	1	1	1	1	1	1
Months since supervision	1	1	1	1	1	0	0
DHO supervisory visit	no	no	no	no	no	no	no
Disposal of used needles	fair	poor	poor	poor	fair	fair	poor
Needle reuse	excellent	excellent	excellent	excellent	excellent	excellent	excellent
Thermometer skills	excellent	excellent	excellent	excellent	excellent	fair	fair
Sterilization skills	fair	fair	fair	fair	fair	fair	fair
Health facilities							
Running water	yes	no	yes	no	yes	yes	no
Overall facility	fair	fair	excellent	fair	excellent	fair	poor
Waste disposal	poor	poor	excellent	poor	poor	poor	poor
Equipment (%)	65	61	61	61	61	61	48
Supplies (%)	83	94	94	94	88	75	94
Drugs (%)	73	48	58	91	58	54	64
Community							
Satisfaction (%)	100	100	100	100	100	25	67
Knowledge (%)	83	75	57	100	60	0	33
Outreach (%)	58	100	57	83	60	63	100
Active kaders (n)	9		7	10	5	5	3
Service Provision							
Hours of operation	no	yes	yes	no	no	no	yes
Child health (1–9)	7		4	7	6	6	
Antenatal care (1–9)	4		4	4	4	4	
Postpartum care (1–9)	0			7		6	
PPH clinic (1–9)	6		7	6	5	4	
PPH barracks (1–9)	6		7	6	5	4	

Met Target	Partially Met Target	Below Target

FIGURE 7-8. Balanced Scorecard for Indonesian Health Clinic System

enterprise resource planning systems have the capability to produce reports and dashboards from operational and financial data. However, for most small businesses, it will be the student consultants who develop the capacity to use these tools to help the business survive, grow, and thrive.

OTHER METHODS OF BUSINESS PROCESS ANALYSIS

Before we turn to the challenges of managing service delivery processes, three other frameworks for business process management and evaluation of firm performance deserve brief descriptions.

Total quality management. Because it focuses on what it takes to gain and retain customers, total quality management (TQM) should appeal to consulting teams and business owners alike. Two related principles are continuous improvement of products and services and the idea of building quality into each stage of the process of production and delivery. Such practices can be closely linked to strategy because they foster a leadership approach that empowers employees and managers through participation in and support of the strategies that drive company decisions and actions. TQM methods can also be used to strengthen supplier performance and relationships. When this happens productivity, quality, and improved performance can be realized throughout the firm's supply chain. Within the firm, statistical quality control can be adopted as a means of measuring and ensuring that decision making, monitoring of process stages, and adherence to quality outcomes are all contributing to implementation of strategies as well as improved firm performance.

Key performance indicators. Arguably the most flexible of all the approaches to aligning strategy and measuring firm performance, key performance indicators (KPIs) are ideal for their variety and adaptability in tracking business outcomes. KPIs can be quite simple and straightforward, as the average time to complete a task or the number of orders shipped by value. Sorting out business from new and repeat customers by value, among different product types for varying time periods, could be a bit more challenging. Regardless of complexity, the underlying premise in using KPIs is that tracking and measuring are essential requirements in the process of performance improvement. One notable caution in using this approach is to make sure that the indicators measure what is most important to the customer and to achieving the firm's strategic goals. A reminder of this focus, perhaps, would be to begin by defining what is "key" to achieving the firm's strategic goals and objectives.

Lean manufacturing. Lean manufacturing focuses on efficiency and reducing waste or unproductive time and effort. A common example relates to inventory: keeping it to a minimum and only holding what is essential for sustaining production and satisfying customer demand. Stated positively, the higher the volume of sales per unit of inventory, the more efficient the firm's performance. But this simple statement, or ratio, does not tell the whole story about inventory levels. Recognize that inventory, work in process, working capital, and sales must all be in synch across these functions to achieve the right mix of decisions for each of these process areas. Nevertheless, gaining owner support for the adoption of lean production processes can go a long way toward controlling costs, reducing waste, and increasing efficiency in the firm.

SERVICE BLUEPRINT

Services account for an increasing proportion of economic activity. Typically, student consultant teams work with businesses or organizations that provide professional, retail, financial, education, and health care services. Because business process analysis has its roots in manufacturing, little work has been done to create a business process model that considers the exigencies of services. Some experts believe this lack of attention stems from the human and interpersonal nature of services. Services are also fluid, ever changing, and intangible. This intangibility contrasts with products that can be perceived through touch, smell, sight, or taste. In such cases, measurements of quality are easier to discern. But as products become more commoditized, services that create meaningful customer experiences have become important. These experiences are essential to creating strong customer bonds and loyalty.

Innovation in service is just as important as innovation in products, and service blueprinting has emerged as a useful approach to address the challenges of service design and innovation.[11] Businesses use a service blueprint to visualize the service process from the customer's touchpoints. The blueprint maps points of contact, all service processes, and the physical evidence associated with the service experience. The blueprint also connects to the firm's underlying support systems. As with business process modeling, the blueprint can be used for very large or very small activities.

Orchestrating memorable customer experiences requires management of all customer experiences with the business and ensuring cross-functional coordination. The business has to have a clear vision of how design and development will improve customer satisfaction and achieve the business's goals. As with all goals and measures, this has to be communicated to all members of the business or organization so that everyone participates in supporting the vision. Part of the problem with service design is that it is often informal and there is a lack of concrete terminology to communicate what is to be achieved. Additionally, activities of a specific function are often seen in isolation, and relationships and interdependencies are not spelled out. Successful organizations move through clear steps that are very similar to the product development process:

1. Create clear objectives.
2. Generate ideas.
3. Develop concept.
4. Design service.
5. Prototype service.
6. Launch service.
7. Obtain customer feedback.

Service blueprinting began as a process control technique that could solve problems preemptively and identify failure points. It evolved to a focus on customers and mapping customer process against organizational structure. Later, onstage and backstage activities were differentiated. Physical evidence was added to bring the total to the five components shown in Table 7-3.

After mapping out these five components, consultants should identify each time the customer crosses the line of interaction as a moment of truth. In some cases, analyzing moments of truth may bring about the opportunity to make backstage actions visible. For example, a sushi restaurant may have the sushi master interact directly with customers. This may reinforce brand image and justify higher prices by showing not only the skills to assemble the meal but also the freshness of the ingredients.

External pain points are real or perceived problems that the customer encounters. Where is the customer

TABLE 7-3. Service Blueprinting

Physical Evidence	Physical evidence is what the customer sees. This could include the website; the physical location, including interiors, building, parking lot, and landscaping; the staff's appearance, including dress and demeanor; and forms and paperwork.
Customer Actions	Customer actions are are all the steps that customers undergo as part of the service process. Actions are mapped in chronological order and are central to the blueprint. Typically, this is the first component mapped. Customer actions are the foundation of all elements in the blueprint. It is important to identify which service is to be blueprinted and why. As the business may have many variations of the customer process, it is best to map the most typical process. Include any Web interactions. Often, observational studies can be used to supplement employee descriptions of what the customer does.
Line of interaction: crossed when customer connects with employee	
Onstage/Visible Contact Employee Actions	Onstage employee actions capture the interaction of the business with the customer. This could involve an employee who greets, responds to queries, processes an application, or assists with sale of the product. Self-service technology should also be included in this.
Line of visibility: everything above this line is seen by the customer	
Backstage/Invisible Contact Employee Actions	Backstage actions are not seen by the customer. These include telephone calls, making arrangements, or even physical actions that are not seen by the customer, such as moving baggage to the airplane in the airline check-in process.
Line of internal interaction	
Support Processes	Support processes usually cover the firm's underlying support services, including facilities maintenance and management and information technology

process unsatisfactory, blocked, or broken? Is there a delay, confusion, or lack of accessibility when the customer undergoes his or her actions? Often these pain points can be determined through customer surveys or observing customers as they go through the process. Web analytics can show when customer patronage drops off.

Internal pain points are where there is inefficiency, waste, or delay with backstage or support processes. For example, if a supplier frequently ships late or orders are incorrect, this is not visible to the customer but may cause problems in on-time delivery of the product to the customer. The service blueprint can have additional annotations that show minimum and maximum delivery times.

Opportunity to improve may not be part of the customer actions but may enhance the customer experience. This includes improvements to the facilities or the look and feel of the website. Figure 7-9 shows the service blueprint for a Latina-owned tax service firm. Analyzing each moment of truth or touchpoint with the customer can give ideas for how to innovate the process to better create customer loyalty.

This business targets the Latino population in its area by providing services in Spanish. Even with a relatively simple process such as a tax service, there were eleven

moments of truth where the customer came in contact with the firm. The business had not focused on its website because it mainly perceived itself as a personal service business. However, the student team found that the Latino population did search online to evaluate products and services. Competitors used the website to establish trust and evaluate the reputation of the firm. Completing the website competitive analysis (described in chapter 5), the student team was able to make recommendations about how to improve the firm's Web presence.

The firm was located on the second floor above a popular bakery. Only street parking was available and signage was very poor. This was a lost opportunity, as the student team determined that the street was a high-traffic arterial. In addition, local businesses did not know that a tax firm was there. Details such as the appearance of the reception area and the conference room where clients meet with the accountant were also instrumental in creating a welcoming environment for the customer.

As shown in the service blueprint, the receptionist plays a crucial customer service role, working with the customer in five frontline interactions and one backstage interaction. The firm had hired a receptionist who spoke Spanish, but it relied heavily on the owner to provide the tax services, because she was unable to find a Spanish-speaking bookkeeper, and hiring an accountant was pro-

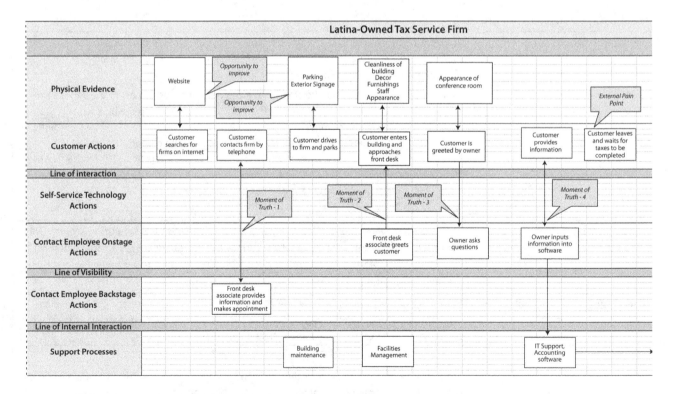

FIGURE 7-9. Service Blueprint Latina-Owned Tax Service Firm

hibitive. However, relying so heavily on the owner to provide services resulted in delays in the actual preparation of the tax return. The information had to be input into the accounting software, and then there was a day's delay in getting and analyzing the output. This required that the customer make another appointment to review the tax return, creating an internal and external pain point.

The firm determined that it could train the receptionist to gather information from the customer, and it could hire or train a bookkeeper to input information into the accounting software prior to the appointment. The customer could be asked to provide any missing information prior to the appointment with the owner. As the bookkeeper only provided backstage actions, it was not necessary to hire a Spanish-speaking bookkeeper.

Completing a service blueprint enabled the business to consider details such as the appearance of the tax return and invoice. These were opportunities to establish trust or market to the customer. The firm began to attach flyers to its tax returns, advertising a list of other services such as payroll and accounting, providing the opportunity to cross-sell other services.

DISCUSSION

1. Map out the process for student registration at your educational institution, including the selection of courses, securing financial aid, registering for courses, and procuring textbooks. Where is the value added? What improvements can be made?
2. Identify one high- and one low-performing retailer with regard to customer service and timely delivery of products. Analyze the business processes for the low-performing retailer and discern the causes of poor service. Identify lessons the business can learn from the processes used by the high-performing firm.
3. Map out the service blueprint for a casual dining restaurant. Show what the customer sees as physical evidence, the actions the customer takes, visible contact employee actions, invisible contact employee actions, and support processes. Determine the moments of truth, opportunities to improve, external pain points, and internal pain points.
4. Identify key performance indicators for a tax preparation service.

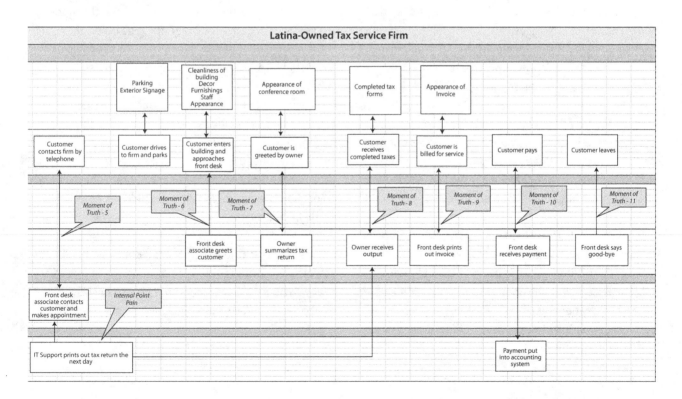

Flowers on 15th

Business Process Improvement

"We are not in the flower business. We are in the emotion business."

Flowers on 15th is a neighborhood flower shop in Seattle, Washington, owned by Alex Soto. As a young boy, he enjoyed playing with flowers; his dream was to pursue a career that would enable him to play with and enjoy flowers in abundance. He began his journey as an international flower broker. He recalls a life-changing experience that occurred while he was traveling in Hawaii to buy tropical flowers. Soto received a phone call from his father asking him to reroute his trip to San Juan, Mexico, as part of a religious pilgrimage. Soto carried out his father's wishes and traveled to Mexico. When he arrived in San Juan, he observed an array of carnations that were part of an offering to the Virgin of San Juan de los Lagos; he realized that he needed to follow his dream of "playing among the flowers." He returned to Seattle and opened Flowers on 15th.

None of the floral arrangements in the shop are premade. Although Soto sources flowers both internationally and domestically, the majority (about 80%) are locally grown.

In 2008, a student consulting team provided Soto with recommendations to improve his business operations. The students identified several areas for improvement, including the website, the physical organization of the store, cross-merchandising, and the shop's accounting processes.

First, the students created content for Soto's website and ensured that the site was fully operational. A good website is important because it is often a customer's first impression of the business. Next, the students conducted observational research in the flower shop. They determined that the physical layout of the store was too

crowded and that it did not showcase the unique floral arrangement process. The team recommended that Soto bring the flower design station to the front of the shop so customers could observe the staff creating the floral arrangements. The custom floral arrangements are an important differentiating factor for Flowers on 15th, especially given that there is a large grocery store across the street that predominantly sells bundled flowers.

Following the update to the shop layout, the students suggested that Soto cross-merchandise other gift items in the store. Soto heeded their advice and now displays a variety of items sold on consignment. He is able to support other local businesses by promoting their products. The students also recommended that Soto reduce storage units (reducing his costs) and use both doors to enhance customer flow in the store (increase sales). Finally, the students helped Soto understand his accounting systems and encouraged him to look at his business objectively. He has been able to sustain his flower shop partly because he followed several of the students' recommendations.

Soto is dedicated to serving the community with his flowers. He attributes his success to his strong faith and happy customers. Each day, Soto is able to live his dream of creating something uniquely beautiful for his customers.

NOTES

1 Robert S. Kaplan and David P. Norton, *The Balanced Scorecard* (Boston: Harvard Business School Press, 1996).

2 Robert S. Kaplan and David P. Norton, "Using the Balanced Scorecard as a Strategic Management System," *Harvard Business Review*, July–August 2007.

3 Yu Chung William Wang, Chwe-Wei Chang, and Michael S. H. Heng, "The Levels of Information Technology Adoption, Business Network, and a Strategic Position Model for Evaluating Supply Chain Management," *Journal of Electronic Commerce Research* 5, no. 2 (2004): 86–100.

4 Chia-An Chao and Aruna Chandra, "Impact of Owner's Knowledge of Information Technology (IT) on Strategic Alignment and IT Adoption in US Small Firms," *Journal of Small Business and Enterprise Development* 19, no. 1 (2012): 114–31.

5 Morteza Ghubakhloo, Mohammad Sadegh Sabouri, Tang Sai Hong, and Norzima Zulkifli, "Information Technology Adoption in Small and Medium-Sized Enterprises: An Appraisal of Two Decades Literature," *Interdisciplinary Journal Research in Business*, 1, no. 7 (July 2011): 53–80.

6 National Association of Small Businesses, *2013 Technology Survey*, www.nsba.biz/wp-content/uploads/2013/09/Technology-Survey-2013.pdf (retrieved September 29, 2014).

7 European Network and Information Security Agency, *A SME Perspective in Cloud Computing*, November 2009, www.enisa.europa.eu/activities/risk-management/files/deliverables/cloud-computing-sme-survey (retrieved March 6, 2015).

8 N. Abdolvand, A. Albadvi, and Z. Ferdowsi, "Assessing Readiness for Business Process Reengineering," *Business Process Management Journal* 14, no. 4 (2008): 497–511.

9 Vincent Guess, *CMII for Business Process Infrastructure* (Scottsdale, AZ: Holly Publishing, 2002).

10 Grace J. Chan, Kristen B. Parco, Melva E. Sihombing, Susan P. Tredwell, and Edward J. O'Rourke, "Improving Health Services to Displaced Persons in Aceh, Indonesia: A Balanced Scorecard," *Bulletin of the World Health Organization* 88, no. 9 (September 2010): 709–12, doi:10.2471/BLT.09.064618.

11 Mary Jo Bitner, Amy L. Ostrom, and Felicia N. Morgan, "Service Blueprinting: A Practical Technique for Service Innovation," *California Management Review* 50, no. 3 (Spring 2008): 66–94.

8. Accounting and Financial Analysis

ABOUT THIS CHAPTER

Proper accounting is vital to the success of any business. For small businesses, the importance of accounting, and particularly the management of cash flow, is magnified by the impact it can have on the survival of the business. Resources are scarce. Business owners often operate with little margin for error. If the business owner has the wrong information regarding any number of accounting issues, it can be fatal for the business.

The financial sophistication of the business owner sometimes determines the amount of financial reporting the company does. Some business owners do their own bookkeeping. They ensure that transactions are recorded, prepare the financial statements, and generally have an intimate knowledge of the business's financial condition. These business owners create budgets to control the business. They perform cash flow projections to anticipate funding needs. A business cannot be properly managed unless its owner uses budgets and financial statements. The more financially sophisticated the business owner is, the more credible he or she is to potential investors and lenders.

Other business owners hire an accountant or bookkeeper to do the accounting for the business. Hiring a certified public accountant (CPA) gives some comfort that financial statements are compiled correctly, but it is not a guarantee that transactions will be properly accounted for. Because of the cost, most business owners will hire bookkeepers to do day-to-day transactions and accountants to prepare the quarterly and annual financial statements and the tax returns. Having an accountant does not exempt the business owner from understanding and being responsible for the financial statements. Not having good accounting and financial analysis can disadvantage businesses in evaluating growth opportunities, measuring where the firm is successful, and securing capital. The student consulting team can perform a great service to the business if it integrates these into the core processes of the business.

Many entrepreneurs have a passion for solving problems and meeting customer needs. This may pull a business owner's attention away from the time and detailed effort it takes to create financial statements. Thus, it is not unexpected that small businesses, including many high-impact firms, may have less than optimal financial management systems for making decisions. The job of a good consultant is, in part, to help the business owner and managers understand the important financial drivers for a small business and help them manage their business using these drivers.

After Studying This Chapter

After reading this chapter, students will be able to:

- Articulate the steps in setting up an accounting system.
- Describe how the order processing and fulfillment cycle relates to financial statements.
- Describe how the purchasing cycle relates to financial statements.
- Complete income statement and balance sheet analysis.
- Describe ways of improving cash flow from the receipt, disbursements, and conversion cycles.
- Select the proper tool and perform financial analysis for a new business opportunity using payback period, net present value, return on investment, internal rate of return, and sensitivity analysis.
- Analyze a recommendation using breakeven, benchmarking, and cost/benefit analysis or outsourcing analysis.

ACCOUNTING ANALYSIS

Accounting is used to measure the performance of a business. It reports how large a business is, how much it is growing, and whether its parts are contributing their share. Accurate numbers can point the business in the right direction, while inaccurate numbers can steer a business totally off course. It is common knowledge that bookkeeping is a frequent source of problems faced by small businesses.

Even the smallest businesses use an accounting system. For fledgling businesses, the system is often Quick-Books or Sage. A basic system can be purchased for about $250, with premium systems available for up to $1,000 per user. Cloud computing solutions are also available for various pricing schemes. These systems are tailored for small businesses, and their features are relatively simple. Some industry associations have also developed accounting and other software systems for small businesses within their industry. The advantage of these systems is that they are easily deployed, with step-by-step menus to take the business owner through the process. These systems do not require a deep understanding of accounting or computers in order to install or use them. Their disadvantage is their limited number of features; they cannot be used as the business grows because they do not allow for much complexity. More sophisticated systems cost $5,000 and up. As discussed in the previous chapter, cloud computing applications, or software as a service (SaaS), are also available to business owners as another relatively low-cost option.

Accounting processes are fairly standard across businesses, as are the requirements for tax or government reporting. Resource-strapped business owners are often more focused on generating sales or providing services than they are concerned about the more mundane tasks of keeping their accounting or tax situation under control. Often, when the business is small, the entrepreneur takes a seat-of-the-pants approach rather than systematically determining what makes sense in the long term. Since accounting issues are tied to cash management, and cash management is the number one cause of small business demise, taking this tack is dangerous and myopic. Poor accounting can trigger time-consuming audits by government agencies that can tie up the entrepreneur for several weeks. Poor accounting can also cause the entrepreneur to make the wrong decision about a growth strategy. With careful deployment of an accounting sys-

tem, however, a business can improve its own processes so that minimum accounting requirements are met and growth can happen.

Setting Up Accounting Systems

Small business accounting systems have templates for typical sole proprietorships or single-owner LLCs such as construction contracting, retailers, or health care practitioners. It is important at the outset for accounting systems to be set up properly. Often this involves the creation of a set of files that provide the basis for transactions (Figure 8-1). These need to be logical for the business, consistent, and kept up to date.

Chart of accounts. A chart of accounts is the listing of accounts to which transactions are posted. They include the typical items that are part of financial statements, such as revenues, expenses, cash, and accounts receivable. Charts of accounts are specific to the business and, although the accounting system will suggest typical accounts, it is up to the business to ensure that there is enough detail to generate information to make relevant decisions. Typically, this is done by breaking accounts into subaccounts. For example, a business will separate sales, cost of goods, and other expenses by product line.

If the business owner sets up the chart of accounts without the assistance of an accountant, there may be problems with its logic and consistency. Even when bookkeepers or accountants are used, the chart of accounts may be set up for tax reporting but might not allow for management reporting. It is helpful to review the chart of accounts to determine if changes are required to better fit the firm's needs. Business owners need profit and loss broken out by location, products, and customer to really understand how to grow.

Payroll. Processing payroll requires business owners to calculate compensation based on hourly or other rates. Social Security (FICA) and Medicare costs are included according to annual tables provided by the government for employees and the employer. A third category includes federal withholding taxes, state unemployment costs, and deductions for company benefits such as 401(k) savings or medical plans, including complying with the requirements of the Affordable Care Act, which require that companies with fifty or more full-time equivalent

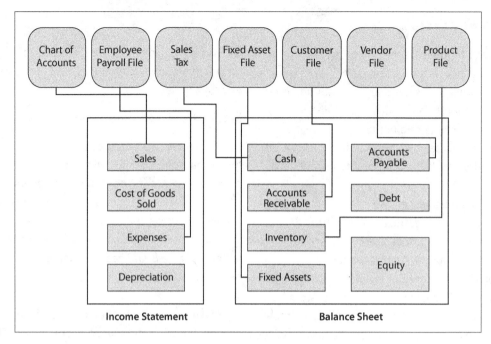

FIGURE 8-1. Setting up Accounting Systems for Small Businesses

employees provide health care benefits or pay a penalty. Businesses should also be aware that tax credits are available for companies with fewer than fifty full-time equivalent employees.

Payroll checks have to be generated. Reports and payments to government are done on a regular schedule, and penalties and interest are assessed for inaccurate reporting and late filings. Another important reason for timely processing and deposits is employee morale. Not filing the proper forms gives the impression of disorganization or instability and can create problems that result in disgruntled employees.

Providing incorrect W-2 information will also lead to problems with the Internal Revenue Service. So it is in the best interests of both the business and the employees to make sure that payroll records are up to date and accurate.

Sales taxes. Sales taxes can be extremely burdensome for retailers and restaurants to account for because they often involve hundreds of transactions. Some items are taxable, while others are not. Often sales taxes must be collected for more than one tax agency. Some states have sales taxes and others do not. Accounting systems will keep track of the sales tax collected and create the necessary forms to report and pay various tax agencies. Again, the key is for the business owner to ensure that these forms and payments are done correctly and on time. The best way to do this is to employ an accounting system

and diligently enter all sales into the system on a regular basis. Sales tax audits are extremely time consuming and can tie up a business owner for weeks.

Because tax payments are due on a monthly, quarterly, or annual basis, some cash-strapped business owners may use the cash that is sitting in their tax payment accounts for short-term financing needs. The co-authors of this textbook have seen firms that do this go out of business when they have been unable to replenish these tax payment accounts in time to meet payment deadlines. These funds do not belong to the business (they are being collected for the government by the business), and this use of "diversion financing" should be avoided, as sole proprietors may not survive their first five years mainly because of cash flow problems. Relying on such inappropriate sources of financing may cause the business to improperly manage its other sources of cash generation.

Customer data. For companies that extend credit to individual or business customers, a simple customer database will include billing address, ship-to address, contact information, billing terms, current orders, and delivered orders for the past few years. These data should be accurate and up to date. Each customer will be tracked by a unique customer number. Customer files will also include customer payment information. Prior to taking on any business customers, it is important that the business conduct a credit check on the customer to determine whether terms should be extended.

One of the key strategies for a business at any stage of development is to deepen an understanding of its customers. As we discussed in an earlier chapter, customer relationship management (CRM) systems enable the vigilant business owner to add other pieces of information about the customer that will help with follow-up sales. If this information is carefully analyzed and systematically collected at the early stages of the business, it can both foster and accommodate growth. Well-connected CRM and accounting systems will facilitate ease in tracking customer needs and avoid multiple entries of the same data.

Vendor data. The vendor database should include contact information, payment terms, the business's credit limit with the vendor, and various levels of discounts for quantity ordered. If the vendor is a subcontractor, this will be noted in the file along with the requirement to generate a Form 1099 for IRS reporting purposes. Vendors may be categorized as cost of goods sold or expenses.

As small businesses increase their vendor lists, they may neglect to ensure their accuracy. Yet outdated or inaccurate vendor information may cause the business to pay redundant invoices or invoices incorrectly. If quantity discounts or extended payment terms are not used, the business has incurred unnecessary expenses. Other information should be added as the vendor relationship grows. The business should track delivery times, defects, and other measures of vendor performance. Vendors should be evaluated to see if better service and cheaper prices can be obtained. Many business owners do not feel they have the time to seek competitive bids, thereby losing an opportunity to save money.

Product data. Product files serve both the order processing system and the inventory system. Each product should have a unique product number. Linking the product to a vendor allows the business to differentiate between the same product provided by two different vendors.

Inventory systems will track products and provide information on when the product has to be reordered. Keeping product supplies to just-in-time levels can be a real benefit to the business.

Fixed asset data. A business needs to keep track of property, equipment, and other assets that it uses to generate revenues. As the business acquires these assets, they should be posted to a fixed asset listing that is accurate and up to date. Small business owners often start businesses with their own funds or equipment and do not initially distinguish between their personal and business assets. They may neglect to record every purchase of equipment. This can cause incorrect tax to be paid and other problems.

Order Processing and Fulfillment

Fulfilling an order is a process common to most business-to-business (B2B) firms. As shown in Figure 8-2, a new customer is acquired through the hard work of the business owner or employees. A credit check is conducted, and terms are negotiated with the new customer. There may be additional negotiation about the specifications of the product to be delivered. A customer order is created. Since most businesses use an accounting system, the system will automatically assign a unique number to each order. This is important for tracking order progress. The business procures the materials it needs, employs workers, and produces what the customer wants. It ships the product. The customer is billed (again with a uniquely numbered invoice), and payment is collected.

In the best case, the business has targeted creditworthy customers who will repeat-buy. The product meets customer requirements and is manufactured efficiently and with high quality. If business processes run smoothly, and accounting is straightforward and automatic. Problems occur when the processes do not work as they should. For example, if the product specifications are not clear or if the business fails to deliver as promised, the customer will reject all or partial delivery of the product. If price and terms are not clearly communicated within the business, the customer will reject the invoice. If the order fails to arrive on time, this may cause the customer to demand a discount. If the customer is not creditworthy, payment may not be collected. These problems will obviously have business consequences, including unwarranted shipping, redo, and administrative costs. Each of these must be dealt with on a case-by-case basis. Dealing with exceptions is time consuming and prone to error and, much as we talked about in the previous chapter, inefficient processes in billing and accounting systems drive up costs within a business.

When businesses do not have an accounting system or if they use some combination of manual and automated systems, it is important that both orders and

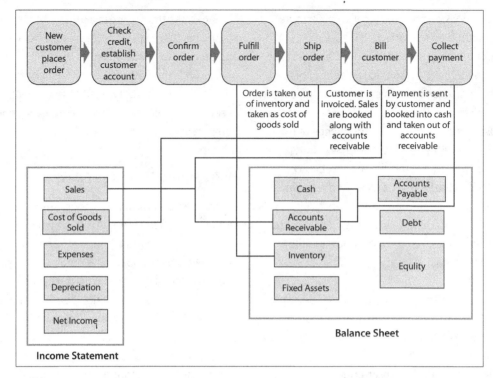

FIGURE 8-2. Order Processing and Fulfillment Receipt Cycle

invoices be uniquely numbered and dated. (Often this is accomplished by using prenumbered forms.) This allows for information to be collected about how long it took to fill the order and for the order to be tracked.

Purchasing Disbursement Cycle

Most fledgling businesses begin with very little cash, so they need to be very resourceful in how they spend their money. Success of the business is highly dependent on how well the entrepreneur can bootstrap or do a lot with very little. In the purchasing disbursement cycle outlined in Figure 8-3, the business needs to find the vendor with the most value for the best prices. For most start-up businesses, being "lean and mean" is the only way of surviving. Some entrepreneurs are able to start their businesses for very little by buying high-end computer equipment from bankrupt Web-based firms much as start-up restaurants will buy used kitchen equipment from bankrupt restaurants. Other businesses scour the used furniture market for fixtures at a fraction of the cost of new. Businesses that do not spend the time soliciting competitive bids or doing comparison shopping often end up paying more than they need to for items that do not drive profitability. Some business thinkers believe that bootstrapping for survival may be essential to business growth.[1] Businesses that spend too much in the start-up phase are not resourceful enough to flourish and grow. At the same time, business owners and managers need to understand the concept of "opportunity cost," in which looking for bargain deals may consume time that can be better used to drive sales. Likewise, buying inferior or used scientific equipment may reduce costs but may result in poor quality in companies that do technology research and development.

When purchasing involves products or services the business sells to the customer, the vendor must be dependable. The business's reputation may be staked on the quality and timeliness of work produced by the vendor.

Often, a small business with no credit rating will have to prepay for its orders or pay cash on delivery. It is important to establish a good credit record quickly so that terms will be extended. The business owner will often have to work directly with vendors to convince them that the firm has long-term viability and that favorable terms are warranted.

As with the receipt cycle, the better the business processes, the easier it is to manage the accounting. If terms are negotiated, the vendor data file is accurate, and the goods are received in quality condition, the accounting system will pay the invoice on the due date and book the transactions. If terms are uncertain or not entered correctly into the system, intervention is necessary. If the goods do

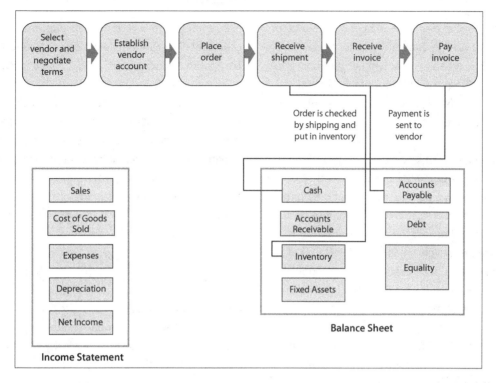

FIGURE 8-3. Purchasing Disbursement Cycle

not arrive according to specifications, both business and accounting problems ensue.

FINANCIAL ANALYSIS

Corporations report financial statements following generally accepted accounting principles. These rules on how financial statements should be compiled are set by the Financial Accounting Standards Board. For the most part, small businesses do not have to adhere to all the same requirements as public companies. They are not subject to Securities and Exchange Commission regulations, for example, because they do not sell their stock to the public.

Most small companies hire accountants to review their financials, but few pay for a full audit by an accounting firm unless their customers, bankers, or investors require it. Three financial statements are typically prepared by accountants: the income statement, the balance sheet, and the cash flow statement.

- Income statement. The income statement (also called the profit and loss statement) gives an account of what the company sold and spent in an accounting period. Sales (also called revenues), or what the company sold in products and services, less any expenses

(expenses are divided into a number of categories), and less taxes equals the company's net income.
- Balance sheet. The balance sheet is a financial snapshot of what the company owns (assets), what it owes (liabilities), and what it is worth free and clear of debt (equity). A balance sheet gives an indication of the company's financial health.
- Cash flow statement. For most small businesses, it is often more productive to start with the cash flow statement. Unlike the income statement, which may involve noncash entries, the cash flow statement deals only with what came in and what went out in cash. Looking at the actual cash flow gives an indication of how well the company can meet its current-period obligations and whether it requires additional capital.

Not all financial reporting is covered here; for example, tax returns must be prepared. Also, for its own internal purposes, the business will compile management reports that focus on locations, product lines, customers, and other activities or projects. This allows the company to get a good picture of how profitable these activities are and how fast they are growing. If reports are not generated, business owners may not know if the activity is profitable at all.

All financial statements rely on the company exercising a certain amount of discipline in how it accounts for everything that occurs. A company needs to have careful procedures for bookkeeping, resolving exceptions, and reconciling everything to cash accounts. Bad numbers foster bad decisions. Not instituting good accounting procedures when a business is in its early stages also creates a barrier to growth.

An in-depth analysis of a company's financial situation requires looking at the business's financial statements and the audit trail of documents that create them. For smaller B2B businesses, it is possible to look at account registers and review the actual transactions (because they are relatively small in number) to find transaction details. For businesses with more sophisticated accounting systems or for business-to-consumer (B2C) companies with many transactions, the general ledger (for details on administrative costs and cash balances), fixed asset listing (for details on property and equipment), accounts payable ledger (for details on vendors, timing of payments, and payment amounts), accounts receivable ledger (for details on customers, timing of receipts, and receipt amounts), and inventory listing (for inventory by item, cost, and time in inventory) would have to be reviewed.

Before analyzing the financial statements, most consultants will assess how much they can rely on the numbers given. One quick check is to compare bank statements against cash accounts. Most auditors will take a random sample of transactions and assess whether they can trace them to the bank statements. If they cannot, it is likely that the financials are not accurate. In general, business owners should make it a practice to reconcile bank statement to financials on a monthly basis. Small and large errors can be caught and corrected quickly. Incorrect transactions that are allowed to remain on the books often develop into much larger problems.

Another quick method of assessing the relative accuracy of small business financial statements is to compare the firm's ratios (i.e., cost of goods sold, or COGS, as a percentage of sales; selling, general, and administrative, or SG&A, as a percentage of sales; and liquidity ratios) against industry norms. If ratios are relatively close to those of hundreds of similar companies, then you can make a reasonable assumption that the business's financial statements are relatively accurate.

With small businesses, accounting procedures should also be reviewed to ensure completeness or to confirm that all transactions are tracked. A review of the general

account registers will show individual sales, expenses, and other detail. A random selection of transactions can be compared to documents. The account registers should also be reviewed for exceptions and how they are resolved.

A business owner's personal and business lives may be hard to separate in sole proprietor companies, but it is important to do so to enable better business decision making. Having personal transactions in business accounts is an administrative nightmare to untangle and can lead to inaccurate financial statements. It may also prevent objective decision making. The business owner needs distinct bank and credit card accounts for all business transactions.

Income Statement Analysis

Historical income statements should be analyzed for trends (Figure 8-4). Comparing monthly and annual statements for trends provides data for planning purposes. Trend analysis is essential for materials forecasting, inventory control, capital budgeting, human resource scheduling, marketing, advertising, promotional campaigns, and profit maximization.

Revenues. For small businesses, reaching a critical mass in revenues is essential to business survival. For food service establishments, only 64% of sole proprietorships were profitable in 2008. Of these businesses, those with higher revenues were more likely to be profitable. Similar trends are seen in other industries.

Whether or not a business will reach financial sustainability and hit critical mass depends on its sales and marketing programs and its ability to control costs. Keep in mind that profitability and cash flow generated may be more important than revenue growth for some companies.

The business needs to identify its profitable customers. Analyzing sales by customer will let the business know which customers buy the most. It will also identify the potential for additional sales. Matching this list with cost of sales and expenses associated with that customer will let the business know customer profitability.

By the same token, the business needs to categorize sales by product line. Businesses will often adopt products on an opportunistic basis without conducting an analysis of whether the product will be profitable. Unless sales and cost of sales are broken out by product line, the business owner will be unable to conduct an analysis. Profitability by product line lets the business owner

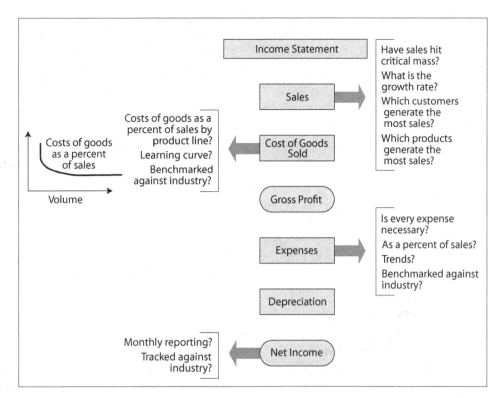

FIGURE 8-4. Income Statement Analysis

know where to focus his or her efforts, identifies areas of best potential growth, and determines which products to drop.

Analyzing a small business's historical income statements helps to determine its future prospects. If a company's revenue grew at 15% last year, a 15% growth might be expected in the next year. But analyzing growth rates is not as simple as straight-line extrapolation. It is difficult to have continued double-digit revenue growth or to sustain a growing rate of revenue growth. Growth projections need to be based on assessments of potential new sales, not simply on historical trends.

If sales growth slows or stagnates, serious analysis has to be done about the direction of the company. Companies with stagnant revenues may need to pare expenses and figure out more efficient ways to make the product and get it to customers. Even if sales are not growing, a business can still grow profits.

Cost of goods sold. The cost of making or buying the product a business sells is aptly named the cost of goods sold. In order to respond quickly to customers, businesses will have an inventory of products to draw from when they receive an order. Although these products may have been manufactured weeks before, they are not counted on the income statement or expensed until the product is shipped

to the customer. This adheres to the accounting principle that expenses must be matched to revenues.

The calculation of cost of goods sold (COGS) as a percentage of revenues (also called gross margin) is a key indicator of business performance. Over short periods of time, COGS is typically a consistent percentage of sales. Over longer periods of time, if companies are growing, COGS may decrease if the company is able to negotiate better terms for raw material inputs. Likewise, as commodity prices fluctuate on the world market, COGS as a percentage of sales may fluctuate. For retail businesses, COGS can reflect buying the right merchandise that can be sold at good prices. Careful attention to COGS and its relationship to sales can lead to overall improved profitability.

Operating expenses. Operating expenses (sometimes referred to as selling, general, and administrative, or SG&A) is a catchall category for every other kind of expense. It includes payroll, marketing costs, utilities, office supplies, insurance, legal costs, and the like. Many small businesses necessarily spend very little on these types of expenses. But there might be a tendency to spend unwisely because the business lacks the time or expertise to do proper research.

A process known as benchmarking is used to compare the business to its peers. The business will evaluate its spending as a percentage of sales against others in the same industry with the same level of revenues. Benchmarks will be discussed in detail later in this chapter.

If a firm's expenses as a percentage of sales are above or below the benchmark, it does not necessarily mean that the business is performing better or worse than its counterparts. It could be that the business is underspending in the category, or that it sells a different mix of products or services that drive the excess expenses. Essentially, benchmarking gives a business owner and consultant a chance to explore areas of potential concern more closely to determine ways to potentially increase profitability.

Profitability. Most small business owners are clear about the size and trends of their overall profit but may not track sales by customer or product line. In both B2B and B2C businesses, setting up an accounting system to track profits by product line and by customer (or in some cases customer type) can assist in making management decisions. Most accounting systems allow for both product line profitability and customer profitability, the latter as long as customer information is entered along with expenses.

Timeliness. Income statements are required on a quarterly or annual basis for tax purposes, but owners of a business should have monthly budget and actual numbers at their fingertips. These numbers need to be timely and accurate. Often, variances between actual numbers and the budget can point to small problems that will throw the business out of kilter if they are allowed to continue.

Not knowing how the business is doing financially is a major reason for small business failures. Managing the business by activating the accounting system, completing some basic financial analysis, and staying constantly in touch with the business's financial status are all critical for adequate profit.

Balance Sheet Analysis

A company needs a variety of assets in order to operate, including inventory to sell, cash to pay staff and suppliers, and buildings to house its operations. The balance sheet summarizes what a company uses to operate (assets) and what it did to finance those assets (equity and liabilities). The balance sheet by its very nature measures financial health at a point in time.

There are several key ratios that are calculated and compared to industry averages. Knowing how a business compares financially helps the business owner who is seeking loans or expansion opportunities. Knowing that a business's financial ratios compare favorably to the industry gives the owner a psychological and planning advantage. It adds to the owner's general awareness of the industry and provides an early warning system for industry fluctuations and trends. A full balance sheet is complicated, but most small business analyses focus on a few elements (Figure 8-5).

Cash. Most businesses generate cash when customers pay for goods. Having a healthy cash balance is a good sign because it means that the business is generating profit, but having too much cash can mean that the company is not deploying its assets to maximize profitability. Assessing a business's cash position and its ability to meet current liabilities guides a business owner in making decisions about how best to use the available cash.

Accounts receivable. In many types of business, customers have thirty days to pay a bill or invoice, though there is often an option to receive a 1–2% discount if invoices are paid within ten days. While the company is waiting for the customer to pay, the outstanding balance appears on the balance sheet as an account receivable. As a measure of financial health, analysts often look at accounts receivable as a percentage of revenues. For some businesses, having small accounts receivable as a percentage of sales shows that the enterprise is quickly collecting on its sales. Yet this can also mean that the company is forgoing sales due to its tight credit terms compared to competitors.

When dealing with accounts receivable, a business also needs to develop an aging schedule to monitor the timeliness of payments by customer. Because of the cost to the business in financing accounts receivables, slow-paying customers may actually be unprofitable. If this is the case, the business should explore the potential of raising prices, altering credit terms, or discontinuing business with a particular customer.

Inventory. Most businesses want to fill orders quickly. To satisfy this customer service requirement, the business needs to have product on hand to ship to its customers as quickly as possible when orders comes in. Products or parts waiting to be assembled are kept in inventory in anticipation of these orders. On the other hand, compa-

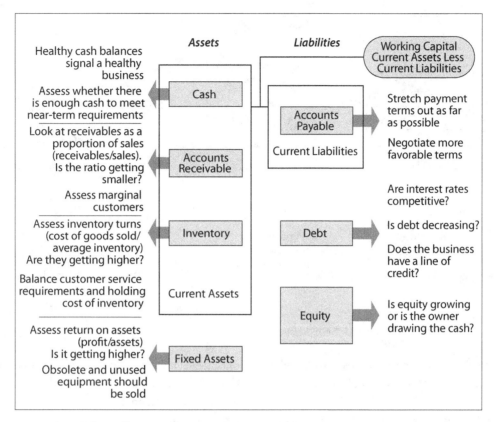

Healthy cash balances signal a healthy business

Assess whether there is enough cash to meet near-term requirements

Look at receivables as a proportion of sales (receivables/sales). Is the ratio getting smaller?

Assess marginal customers

Assess inventory turns (cost of goods sold/ average inventory) Are they getting higher?

Balance customer service requirements and holding cost of inventory

Assess return on assets (profit/assets) Is it getting higher?

Obsolete and unused equipment should be sold

Assets

Cash

Accounts Receivable

Inventory

Current Assets

Fixed Assets

Liabilities

Accounts Payable

Current Liabilities

Debt

Equity

Working Capital Current Assets Less Current Liabilities

Stretch payment terms out as far as possible

Negotiate more favorable terms

Are interest rates competitive?

Is debt decreasing?

Does the business have a line of credit?

Is equity growing or is the owner drawing the cash?

FIGURE 8-5. Balance Sheet Analysis

nies may try to keep very little inventory because there are financing, maintenance, insurance, and administrative costs to keeping inventory. Striking an effective balance between maintaining high service levels and holding down costs is important in any business.

Inventory is sometimes measured by the days of sales it will support. The fewer the days, the more efficient the company is; yet having too few days runs the risk of not being able to deliver products to a customer. Inventory turns is another measure used to determine inventory efficiency. Cost of goods sold divided by average inventory (inventory levels may be seasonal) gives inventory turns. A higher rate of inventory turns means that the company is operating at higher levels of efficiency. For most businesses there is an optimal amount of inventory to carry to ensure prompt service to customers without tying up financial resources in inventory. Comparing an individual business to industry norms, particularly in inventory days or turns, is a typical way of determining if sufficient or insufficient inventory is being carried.

Working capital. Working capital refers to current assets (such as receivables and inventory) less current liabilities. While this is not a balance sheet ratio, it is often com-

puted to determine the business's cash requirements. As a business grows, it typically needs more working capital. This may be figured into financial projections.

Fixed assets. These are buildings and equipment that the company owns and uses to make money. Fixed assets need to be productive. Assets that do not generate money tie up capital that could be used elsewhere and usually have financing and holding costs. While all companies need some level of fixed assets, a consultant can help a business owner determine necessary versus unnecessary fixed assets by analyzing the potential impact of an asset's sale on the company's profitability.

Accounts payable. Just as some customers get thirty days to pay their bills, so do some businesses when they buy from vendors. Vendor payable accounts act as short-term financing for a business. Companies may want to stretch this out as much as possible as an inexpensive means of borrowing. Cost-benefit analysis should be done to evaluate how effective discounts are. For example, if a 2% discount is offered on accounts payable within ten days, it is often less expensive to use a bank line of credit to so the firm can capture these

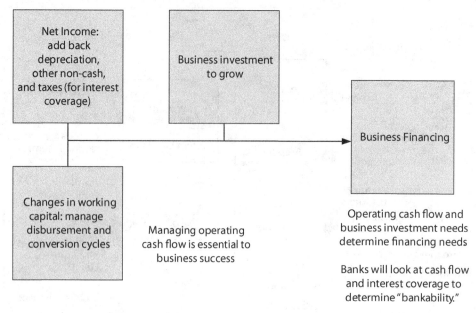

FIGURE 8-6. Cash Flow Analysis

discounts. A consultant can help a business owner determine the most profitable accounts payable strategy.

Debt. For each industry and each company there is an optimal level of debt as a percentage of equity. A consultant can help a business determine its debt-equity ratio, compare it to industry standards, and determine if the company is properly leveraged. A debt-equity ratio that is too high for a particular business can result in inability to pay creditors, while a ratio that is too low means the business is using expensive equity financing rather than relatively low-cost debt financing. The debt-to-asset ratio (debt as a percentage of total assets) can be used in the same way.

Equity. Equity, net worth, or book value is what the company is worth according to its books or balance sheet. Equity is what the business owner or other investors put into the company and any earnings the company keeps or retains to grow the business. Sole proprietors may draw from retained earnings rather than take a salary.

Bankers and investors look for book value to grow, signaling that the business owners are interested in reinvesting earnings to grow the business rather than drawing the cash for themselves. If the business is going to be sold, book value will be one of the determining factors in what price it gets.

Cash Flow Analysis

In larger enterprises, the cash flow statement is used to differentiate where cash is generated (through opera-

tions, by selling assets, or financing from a bank) from what it is being used for. Cash flow is also used to determine whether the enterprise can meet its debt obligations. It is sometimes used to verify the income statement, because accounting is complicated with many noncash items.

Small businesses are less complex in scope. Investing activities, capital structure, and often their income statements are very close to their cash flow. However, it is still important to complete a cash flow analysis to determine if the business will be able to meet its obligations in the future (Figure 8-6).

Operating cash flow. The cash flow statement starts with the company's net income and then adds back any expenses that are not cash, such as depreciation. If the business needs more cash for working capital, that is added in. Making these adjustments gives the operating cash flow. Operating cash flow tells how much cash the business generates.

Bankers look at operating cash flow to determine if the business can support interest payments on the loan it has taken or will take. An interest coverage ratio (earnings before depreciation, interest, and taxes divided by interest payments) can be calculated to give an idea of how well the company can support its debt.

Providing credit to customers can often increase sales volume and is standard practice in some industries. The business needs to take the time to do credit checks before

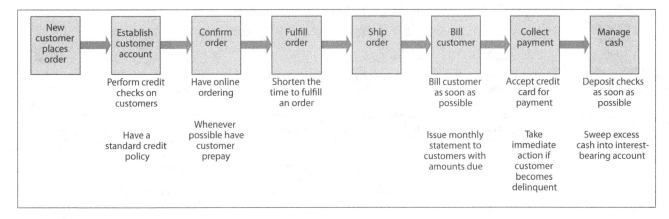

FIGURE 8-7. Managing Cash Flow: Receipt Cycle

extending credit to a customer. Not extending credit does not mean a sale is lost. Most businesses require new customers with no credit rating to prepay for orders until credit is established. If credit is extended, the business should have a written credit policy and should enforce it. Otherwise the business stands to lose more money on bad debts than it can bring in in sales. Written credit policies can speed debt collection when discounts are given for early payments. Small businesses have shown a marked improvement in cash flow after credit policies were implemented.

Having an online ordering system can speed up the receipt cycle. In an enterprise, processing a purchase order can exceed $100 and extend over weeks. The longer it takes to process a purchase order, the slower the cash receipt from that order. Online ordering can be done twenty-four hours a day, seven days a week, and saves considerable administrative costs. Careful design of the online ordering system can eliminate errors and expedite ordering. Additionally, the business can provide extensive information on the product and save costly telephone inquiries.

Whenever possible, the business should have a customer prepay for an order or pay immediately upon receipt. Prepayment is standard for any industry where the product is customized for the customer. Because many fledgling businesses create unique products for their customers, it is possible to require prepayment or payment upon receipt.

If prepayment or payment upon receipt is not used, the business should bill the customer as soon as possible. Some firms process and mail the invoice prior to shipping, so that the invoice and the shipment are received at the

same time. It helps to maintain and monitor an accounts receivable aging report that shows money owed by the customer. The company should know which customers are most timely with payment. Late fees may be charged if payment is not received on time.

The company should have a debt collection procedure to ensure that all debts are collected. Smaller businesses may be taken advantage of by customers who think small businesses do not have the resources to collect. The company should develop a system to collect debts. This includes sending monthly statements and late-payment letters and calling the customer. These are extremely effective in getting customers to pay.

Credit card payment systems provide timely cash turnaround and put the financing burden directly on the customer. Small businesses sometimes see the costs of setting up credit card payment systems as a barrier. Setup costs are up to $500 and the per transaction cost is 10 cents, plus a monthly fee of about $10. Credit card companies charge from 1% to 2% of the purchase value. However, the ability to collect immediate payment without having the expense associated with staff time to collect debts can outweigh these costs.

A basic principle of cash management is to get it in the bank as soon as possible. The faster cash moves from the customer to the bank and into appropriate short-term investments, the better. Some small businesses consider a run to the bank every day a burdensome task and will collect checks over a few days. This has two drawbacks. First, money not in the bank does not generate interest. Second, this practice increases the possibility of loss or other bookkeeping problems. Once in the bank, large cash amounts can be swept into

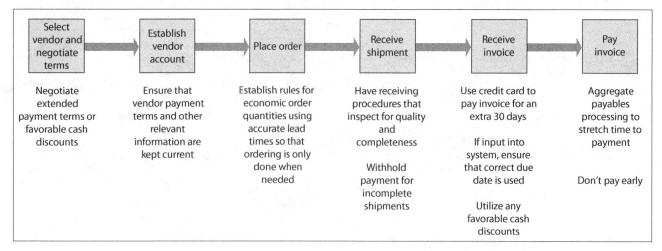

FIGURE 8-8. Managing Cash Flow: Disbursement Cycles

interest-bearing accounts. The business should work with a banker to ensure that money does not accumulate without generating interest.

A small business should work very quickly to establish a good payment record so that it has a good credit history. This will allow the business to negotiate more favorable payment terms with creditors. Whenever possible the business should revisit these terms with the vendor. Often, as a business grows and becomes more stable, better payment terms can be negotiated.

The business needs good receiving procedures so that payment is not made for a product that was not delivered. Once the invoice is received, accounts payable procedures should ensure that the business pays the invoice only when it is due. Some clerical staff will aggregate invoices and pay them weekly, often pulling in invoices that are due in a few days. Aggregating procedures should

try to stretch time to payment out as long as possible without incurring penalties.

Managing the production process can do much to improve the cash flow within a business. Large enterprises like Dell have shown that changing the customer ordering process and working closely with vendors can cut production time. In most business models, the business makes a forecast of orders and manufactures for inventory according to the forecast. If the forecast is wrong, costs are incurred. If the forecast is too high, surplus inventory must be sold at deeply discounted prices. If the forecast is too low, expediting orders can cause production costs to go sky high.

Developing a business model in which goods are not manufactured until ordered can save considerable expense and makes business sense if customers are willing to wait for their order. This strategy often involves

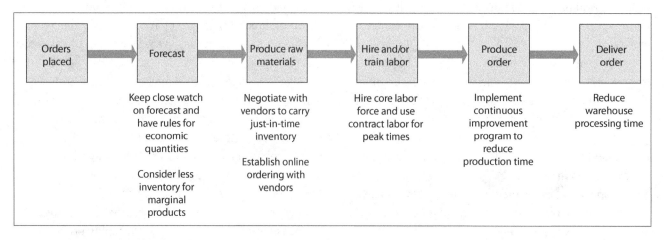

FIGURE 8-9. Managing Cash Flow: Conversion Process

working closely with vendors to reduce the lead time for getting raw materials and component parts. Establishing online ordering with vendors and having the ability to check their inventory via the Web can assist in saving time in the production cycle.

Additionally, carefully controlling inventory so that only frequently turning items are stocked reduces the amount of money tied up in financing and maintaining inventory. In terms of the labor force, a core labor force with additional contract or seasonal labor for peak times can save on labor costs, though it can reduce quality in some industries that require high-level skills. The practice of hiring seasonal labor at the year-end holiday shopping period in retail, or additional skilled or unskilled laborers during peak building periods in construction, is common.

Lack of tax planning and not filing tax returns in a timely manner is a sign of poor organization. Among business owners filing for bankruptcy, 20% gave the cause as problems with the IRS. Procrastination can be the downfall of small business owners. Taking the time to file taxes gives the business a chance to review its performance for the year. Additionally, most bankers look to timely filing of taxes as the first sign of financial responsibility.

Accounting and Financial Metrics

In addition to the financial analysis above, the student team may want to calculate the following ratios to determine trends in the company's financial performance. All ratios compare the business to competitors in the same industry.

Horizontal analysis. Analysis of the firm's growth rates (percent change from previous year) for revenues and net income gives an indication about trends in the company's revenues and profits. For the company in Table 8-1, sales appear to be slowing in 2016, but the firm is still able to increase net income by controlling expenses.

TABLE 8-1. Horizontal Analysis

	2016	2015	2014
Net Revenues	408,214	404,374	377,023
Growth Rate in Revenues	0.9%	7.3%	
Net Income	14,335	13,400	12,731
Growth in Net Income	7.0%	5.3%	

TABLE 8-2. Profitability

	2016	2015	2014
Net Revenues	408,214	404,374	377,023
Cost of Sales	304,657	304,056	284,137
Gross Margin (Net Revenues minus Cost of Sales divided by Net Revenues)	25.4%	24.8%	24.6%
Net Income	14,335	13,400	12,731
Net Margin (Net Income divided by Net Revenues)	3.5%	3.3%	3.4%

Profitability. There are several measures of profitability. Merchandising firms typically examine gross margin, or gross profit ratio (net revenues minus cost of sales divided by net revenues). This profit ratio indicates if a merchandising company is purchasing product effectively and getting a good price from the customer. The company in Table 8-2 has been able to increase its gross margin, showing that it purchased at better prices. The net margin also increased because other expenses were reduced.

Current, quick, and working capital. Current ratio (current assets divided by current liabilities) and quick ratio (current assets minus inventory divided by current liabilities) are liquidity measures and thus show the company's ability to meet its obligations. The higher these ratios, the more liquid the company or more able it is to pay its short-term obligations. In Table 8-3, the supermarket company's quick ratio has improved slightly from 2015 to 2016. Its current ratio has worsened. It has negative working capital, but that is not necessarily a problem, as supermarkets use accounts payable to finance their operations.

Inventory turnover. Inventory turnover (COGS divided by average inventory) measures how often a company sells its inventory. The company in Table 8-4 is increasing its inventory turnover, which means it is getting more efficient.

Receivables. Receivables turnover (net receivable sales divided by average net receivables) is a measure of the times, on average, that receivables are collected. The company in Table 8-5 has very high receivables turnover, suggesting that the firm collects its customer payments in cash.

TABLE 8-3. Current Ratio, Quick Ratio and Working Capital

	2016	2015	2016	2015
Current Assets			Quick Ratio: Quick Assets divided by Current Liabilities	
Cash and cash equivalents (Quick)	7,907	7,275	0.217	0.202
Receivables, net (Quick)	4,144	3,905		
Inventories	33,160	34,511		
Prepaid expenses and other	2,980	3,063		
Other current assets	140	195	Current Ratio: Current Assets divided by Current Liabilities	
Total current assets	48,331	48,949	0.870	0.884
			Working Capital: Current Assets minus Current Liabilities	
Current Liabilities	55,561	55,390	-7,230	-6,441

TABLE 8-4. Inventory

	2016	2015	2014
Cost of Sales	304,657	304,056	
Inventories	33,160	34,511	35,180
Average Inventory (Calculated by taking the average of the beginning and ending inventories)	33,835.5	34,845.5	
Turnover (Cost of Sales divided by Average Inventory)	9.00	8.73	

TABLE 8-5. Receivables

	2016	2015	2014
Net Sales	405,046	401,087	373,821
Net Receivables	4,144	3,905	3,654
Average Receivables (Calculated by taking the average of beginning and ending receivables)	4024.5	3779.5	
Receivables Turnover (Net Sales divided by Average Receivables)	100.65	106.12	

TABLE 8-6. Payables

	2016	2015	2014
Cost of Sales	304,657	304,056	
Accounts Payable	30,451	28,849	25,180
Average Payables (Calculated by taking the average of beginning and ending payables)	29,650	27,014.5	
Turnover (Cost of Sales divided by Average Payables)	10.3	11.3	

TABLE 8-7. Debt-to-Asset Ratio

	2016	2015
Total Debt	36,401	34,549
Total Assets	170,706	163,429
Debt divided by Total Assets	21.3%	21.1%

Payables. Payables turnover is calculated by taking average payables and dividing by COGS. Payables days are calculated by dividing 360 days by payables turnover. Typically a company will negotiate or take full advantage of any credit terms it receives (Table 8-6).

Debt-to-asset ratio. The debt-asset ratio (total debt divided by total assets) measures the amount of the company's assets that are a result of debt. The debt-to-asset ratio is compared to the industry as a measure of company solvency (Table 8-7).

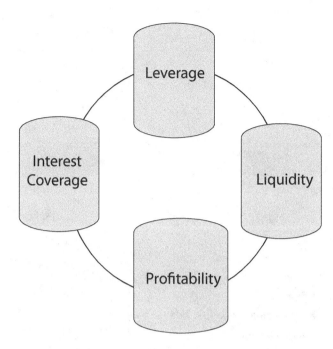

FIGURE 8-10. What Banks Look At

Regarding the predictors of bankruptcy, banks look at a combination of factors, including leverage (debt to equity), liquidity (cash to total assets or, as a substitute in student projects, quick or current ratios), profitability (retained earnings over total assets), and coverage (earnings before interest, tax, depreciation, and amortization to interest expenses).[2] In order to be "bankable," or eligible for bank loans, a business must ensure that its ratios are strong relative to its industry (Figure 8-10).

FINANCIAL PROJECTIONS

The consulting team may develop recommendations that involve both increased revenues and increased expenses. In small business consulting, financial projections that support the proposed expenditures or expected revenues should be in the final report.

Inherent in any projection is the risk that assumptions about revenues or expenses may not be accurate or perfectly predictable. The risk of inaccurate assumptions is higher for smaller businesses, which have limited borrowing capabilities or cash on hand than larger firms, so special care should be taken in producing a financial pro forma for a small business. Typically sensitivity analysis is completed so that business owners have an ability to manage finances should assumptions and projections be higher or lower than anticipated.

Opportunity. The first order of business is to assess the size of the opportunity. This is best done by conducting the market and business research described earlier in this book. Potential revenues figure prominently in financial projections. It is important to get evidence to support these projections. It is also important to be realistic about the business's chances. Even if the market potential is large and the opportunity looks attractive, if there are competitors it is unlikely that the business will be able to get a large share of the market.

Time frame. Projections for investments should be made to the end of the useful life of the investment. Many IT systems become outdated in three years, so financial analyses of computers and software should extend to three years. Other investments—for example, buildings and equipment—can extend farther. The key for a consultant is to determine the length of the investment's value, which can be done by working with a business accountant. The longer the time period used in projections, the harder it is to accurately project sales and expenses with any amount of certainty, and thus determining the value of an investment becomes more difficult.

Gathering the numbers. Fledgling business owners with few resources are often more concerned with downside risk than with upside potential. They rarely invest large amounts of money in new opportunities. Instead they iterate their way to success with small investments. That said, there is financial risk in undershooting demand projections. If demand significantly outstrips a company's ability to finance the additional production, or requires it to carry significant trade debt for a growing period of time required to meet that demand, a business may go under.

The key to maximizing opportunities is to accurately project revenues and ensure that all costs and risks are captured. Take the case of a small business considering e-commerce. When the consultant focuses on costs, they are first divided between up-front investment and ongoing costs. In the simple example illustrated in Table 8-8, $10,000 is budgeted to develop the e-commerce site and catalog, and an additional $5,000 is budgeted in one-time marketing costs.

Next, cost of goods sold is examined. Although the business may have a storefront, cost of goods sold may be different on the e-commerce site, because there may be additional costs in packaging, handling, and shipping as well as reduced costs in warehousing the inventory.

CASE STUDY 8
Green Cleaning Seattle

The Triple Bottom Line

In 2006, Gea Bassett was completing a master's program in education. With just $25 and a prepaid cell phone, she started cleaning homes to earn extra money. It did not take long before she hired her first employee because of rapidly growing demand. By graduation, Bassett realized that this was a promising career opportunity. She focused her efforts exclusively on her new company, Green Cleaning Seattle—Eco-Maid Services, which offers a variety of ecofriendly cleaning services

Why green? Bassett worked at the Natural Foods grocery store when she was a teen; the experience sparked an interest in environmentally friendly products. She is intent on reducing pollution and chemicals in the environment while supporting the local economy. For example, clients are grouped by location to reduce drive time. Bassett also recognized the high demand for green cleaning in the environmentally conscious Pacific Northwest, as well as a growing demand among parents and pet owners for chemical-free home cleaning products.

Bassett realizes the importance of delegating tasks. She primarily focuses her efforts on marketing and business operations. As with many new start-ups, her marketing budget was small; she initially used Craigslist and Google AdWords to promote her business. In 2009, Green Cleaning was the second business in Seattle to be featured by Groupon. With very little competition in green cleaning at the time, she sold about 285 deals. The increased awareness due to this promotion was a turning point for the company. Today Bassett works exclusively with local advertisers.

Bassett focuses on developing and retaining employees. She offers flexible working hours to her employees, with set days on, weekends off, and workdays that end at 5:00 p.m. She uses a standard pay scale, paying more for

longer-term employees. She has a handbook and policies to guide employees and two lead cleaners to provide supervision. All cleaning products are provided; employees are not allowed to use clients' products. She also takes the time to review client evaluations each week.

Bassett has grown her company through internal sources of capital and has strategically hired employees. Most of her company's revenues come through cash payments and from having only cleaning products as inventory and vacuum cleaners as assets; accounting is straightforward.

In 2011, a team of student consultants worked with Bassett to enhance her financial acumen. Although Bassett had recently hired an accountant, the students recommended that she strengthen her own accounting skills. They provided her with templates, including a step-by-step process for how to input data and calculate common financial ratios. The students reviewed her pricing strategy, created a model to forecast future growth, and calculated key financial metrics to be monitored. She implemented several of their recommendations, including changes to her website, building team spirit, and enhancing her employee incentive package.

Bassett attributes her success to perseverance, creativity, and an interest in the local economy. She emphasizes the ethics behind the business. Green Cleaning's projected revenues for 2011 were nearly $390,000, with approximately seventeen employees—impressive growth for a $25 initial investment.

TABLE 8-8. Sample Up-Front and Variable Costs

	Year 0	Year 1	Year 2	Year 3
Up-Front Costs				
Marketing	5,000			
Site development	10,000			
Revenues		50,000	75,000	100,000
Cost of goods (50%)		25,000	37,500	50,000
Gross margin		25,000	37,500	50,000
Expenses			**Costs by Year**	
Hosting		3,000	3,300	3,630
Advertising		2,500	5,000	7,500
Ongoing maintenance		1,000	1,100	1,210
Personnel		10,000	11,000	20,000
Profit	-15,000	8,500	17,100	17,660

Selling on the Internet involves a new way of marketing to the customer. There are affiliate programs, new promotional programs, and advertisements that have to be developed. Additionally, there are site maintenance and hosting costs.

Once the costs have been determined for the first year, projections have to be made into the future. For some costs, such as hosting costs, the business might add an estimated cost increase based on a multiyear hosting contract or an analysis of past years' trends in hosting cost increases. Other costs, such as personnel, behave in a not strictly variable, or step function, way—they take a jump (additional person needed) when they hit a certain level of sales. Assumptions for all numbers gathered must be stated, and if circumstances change, assumptions may have to be rethought.

Different kinds of costs can affect the financial calculations. Figure 8-11 defines the costs typically used and how they behave.

Fixed costs are costs that stay the same no matter what volume is produced. Rent is an example of a fixed cost. Fixed costs may change over a very long period of time but not for the period being evaluated.

Step-function costs are similar to fixed costs except they stay the same for a shorter period of time. An example of a step-function cost is a teacher. If any students enroll, a teacher must be hired. Once thirty students are enrolled, another teacher must be hired, but a new teacher will not be hired for each additional student from two to twenty-nine.

Variable costs increase as volume increases. For example, the food costs in a restaurant increase with each new customer. If there are no customers, there is no food cost.

Semivariable costs have a minimum fixed component and then they rise based on volume. Utility costs sometimes behave this way. There is a base cost for having the service and then costs increase linearly based on volume.

Once the behavior of the cost is determined, it can be classified as direct and indirect. Direct costs are directly attributable to the product, service, or cost center being analyzed. If utilities are directly metered to the cost center, they would count as a direct cost. If utilities are metered to the entire building, they would be allocated based on business procedures and would be an indirect cost. Table 8-9 describes what costs to use for various types of analysis.[3]

Payback Period

This is the simplest measure of return on investment and calculates the time to breakeven. Using the investment of $15,000 in the Table 8-8 example above, take the profit for each year and determine in what year the investment will be recouped. In this case, the payback period occurs in the second year. The year 1 profit of $8,500 plus the year 2 profit of $17,100 equals $25,600, which covers the original $15,000 invested.

When using the payback period of analysis, the faster the payback period, the better the investment is determined to be. Payback is often used to determine which

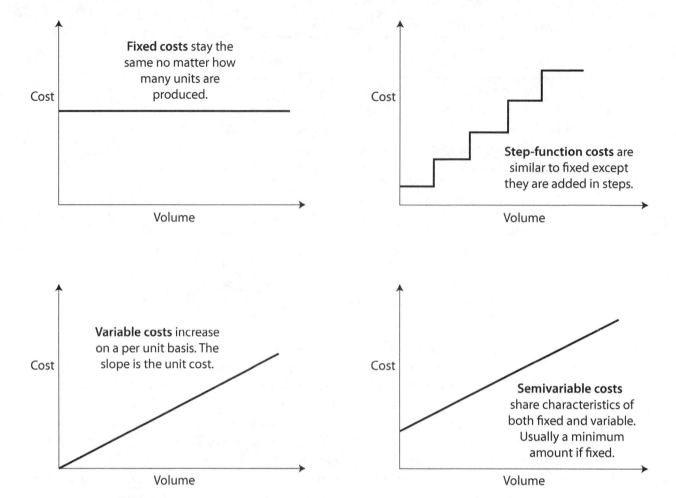

FIGURE 8-11. Cost Behavior

investments to make when companies have constraints on their access to capital—which is true for almost all small businesses. Some enterprises require eighteen-month payback periods for certain levels of investment. While large enterprises, which focus on net present value calculations to make investment decisions, do not put much credence on payback, small businesses with scarce money resources and tight cash flow find that the payback period, simple as it is, is the main criterion for a go or no-go decision on an investment.

TABLE 8-9. Costs and Type of Analysis

	Full-cost accounting	*Differential cost accounting*	*Responsibility accounting*
Costs	Direct versus indirect	Fixed versus variable	Controllable versus uncontrollable
Method	Assign costs to cost center based on direct and indirect	Analysis of cost behavior Cost volume profit analysis Contribution analysis	Programming Budgeting Variance analysis Reporting
Analysis	Pricing Product profitability	Eliminate product Outsource Pricing Dispose of assets	Cost control Performance assessment

TABLE 8-10. Sample Net Present Value Analysis

	Year 0	Year 1	Year 2	Year 3
Investment	15,000			
Profit		8,500	17,100	17,660
Calculation of present value		$\dfrac{8,500}{(1+0.08)^1}$	$\dfrac{17,100}{(1+0.08)}$	$\dfrac{17,660}{(1+0.08)}$
Present value	(15,000)	$7,870.37	$13,574.53	$15,140.60
Net present value (-15,000 + 7,870.37 + 13,574.53 + 15,140.60) = 21,586				

Net Present Value

Net present value (NPV) gives the size of the return from the investment. It incorporates the time value of money, which is not included in the payback period calculation, and the cost of capital to a firm. NPV is a tool to use in determining the long-term profitability of an investment. To construct an NPV analysis, a consultant first determines the profit from each year in which a new product is available as a result of the investment. Following this, the profit from years beyond the first one are discounted back, using this cost of capital. When the calculation is performed in the example in Table 8-10, the net present value is $21,586.

For small businesses, the cost of capital, or discount rate, is typically the interest rate they are charged for a bank loan. Cost of capital can vary depending on the size of the company.[4] For large enterprises, the cost of capital is typically a weighted average of their borrowing costs and the cost of equity.

Net present value allows the business to evaluate if the initial investment in setting up an e-commerce site is worth the return it will generate over three years.

Return on Investment

Return on investment (ROI) evaluates the results of an investment without factoring in the time value of money. It is useful in helping a small business decide between two different investments of the same size. To calculate an ROI, simply sum the total profits over a given period and divide by the dollar amount of the investment.

The drawback of ROI is that large projects are not differentiated from small projects. Also, it does not give any measure of how long it takes to achieve that return (Table 8-11).

Internal Rate of Return

The internal rate of return (an iteration process) finds a yield that fits future earnings to the investment today. This is relevant when comparing investments against each other.

Internal rate of return does not give the magnitude of the investment or what the investment will bring in dollars to the business. Another drawback is that if there is zero cash flow in any year, the calculation does not work (Table 8-12).

Sensitivity Analysis

To anticipate the uncertainty of future revenues and expenses, most financial projections will include a view of different scenarios. The focus of this analysis should be to anticipate what downside risk the investment brings as well as the impact on the business should sales exceed expectations. When sensitivity analysis is done, the busi-

TABLE 8-11. Sample Return on Investment Analysis

	Year 0	Year 1	Year 2	Year 3
Investment	15,000			
Profit		8,500	17,100	17,660
Return on investment (8,500 + 17,100 + 17,660) / 15,000			288%	

TABLE 8-12. Sample Internal Rate of Return Analysis

	Year 0	Year 1	Year 2	Year 3
Investment	15,000			
Profit	-15,000	8,500	17,100	17,660
Rate of return (calculation iterates a return that fits the cash flow)			67%	

TABLE 8-13. Sample Sensitivity Analysis

Most Likely Case	Year 0	Year 1	Year 2	Year 3
Marketing	5,000			
Site development	10,000			
Revenues		50,000	75,000	100,000
Cost of goods (50%)		25,000	37,500	50,000
Gross margin		2,5000	37,500	50,000
Expenses				
Hosting		3,000	3,300	3,630
Advertising		2,500	5,000	7,500
Ongoing maintenance		1,000	1,100	1,210
Personnel		10,000	11,000	20,000
Profit	-15,000	8,500	17,100	17,660
Present value	-15,000	7,870	13,574	15,140
Net present value	21,585			

Worst-Case Scenario	Year 0	Year 1	Year 2	Year 3
Marketing	5,000			
Site development	10,000			
Revenues		30,000	45,000	50,000
Cost of goods (50%)		15,000	22,500	25,000
Gross margin		15,000	22,500	25,000
Expenses				
Hosting		3,000	3,300	3,630
Advertising		5,000	7,500	7,500
Ongoing maintenance		1,000	1,100	1,210
Personnel		10,000	11,000	20,000
Profit	-15,000	-4,000	-400	-7,340
Present value	-15,000	-3,703	-317	6,292
Net present value	-25,314			

Best-Case Scenario	Year 0	Year 1	Year 2	Year 3
Marketing	5,000			
Site development	10,000			
Revenues		75,000	125,000	200,000
Cost of goods (50%)		37,500	62,500	100,000
Gross margin		37,500	62,500	100,000
Expenses				
Hosting		3,000	3,300	3,630
Advertising		2,500	5,000	7,500
Ongoing maintenance		1,000	1,100	1,210
Personnel		10,000	11,000	20,000
Profit	-15,000	21,000	42,100	67,660
Present value	-15,000	19,444	33,420	58,007
Net present value	95,872.32			

ness owner and consultant are asking "what if" questions. What if sales do not take off? What if marketing expenses are higher? What if it costs more to buy the product? What if ongoing maintenance is higher? What if sales are higher than expected and I need to hire new staff?

Table 8-13 shows some sensitivity analysis on the level of sales and the amount of advertising expenditures. This analysis shows that the business stands to lose $25,000 in the worst-case scenario.

Taking into consideration all the likely scenarios, the business owner can plot a distribution of the expected returns with assigned probabilities. Analyzing this distribution, the business owner can decide whether the investment is worth the risk.

Financial Plan for a New Business Opportunity

All entrepreneurs benefit from starting a business with a plan. Most investors and lenders know that the key people in the business are the main determinants of its success. They will look for people who are experienced in the industry and who have a track record of success. Usually these people are very cognizant of the business model, industry benchmarks, how to manage risk, and how to increase profitability.

Take the example of a new restaurant business. Although student consulting teams rarely work with a start-up business, their work often involves evaluating a new business or product line. Compiling the financial plan would be similar to a financial plan for a new business. The financial plan starts with a detailed listing of start-up costs. An entrepreneur knowledgeable about the restaurant industry knows what costs to include and how to make the optimal choices between low-cost and high-quality items that will produce quality products. New entrepreneurs might spend more up front and take longer to generate sales. This is illustrated as an S-curve; experienced entrepreneurs have a shallower S, with less up-front costs, while inexperienced entrepreneurs would likely have more up-front costs. As consultants, it is important to advise the business on how to minimize up-front costs without compromising quality and to ramp up sales as quickly as possible to reach breakeven. Any new venture is risky. Adopting such a strategy will mitigate the risk to some extent. Table 8-14 shows detailed start-up costs for the new restaurant.

Next, a detailed month-by-month projection of the income statement is prepared . It is helpful to follow the conventional format shown in Table 8-15 when compiling

TABLE 8-14. Sample Start-Up Costs for a Restaurant

Security	$10,000.00
Construction rent	10,000.00
Construction utilities	2,000.00
Licenses	5,000.00
Deposits	2,500.00
Marketing	5,000.00
Printing	5,000.00
Architects	10,000.00
Legal	3,000.00
Inventory	10,000.00
Furniture, fixtures	75,000.00
Leasehold improvements	60,000.00
Other	35,000.00
Total	232,500.00

projections. The data collected start with daily projections of the number of covers, or meals served, and the average price of a meal. This comprises the unit sales and price data needed to calculate revenues. This is further multiplied by the number of days in a month to arrive at the monthly unit sales. The business owner should be a good source for this information.

Seasonality has been incorporated in these projections, and this can affect cash requirements. In this case, the restaurant is assumed to have more revenue during the summer months than during the first quarter of the year. Payroll is projected from the number of workers needed, the hours they will work, and the appropriate pay rate. Other expenses are projected based on market rates or by accessing comparable financials from services like BizStats.com. The amount of detail necessary to make valid projections is critical. Student teams that are new to financial analysis can call on their mentors, advisors, and faculty to guide them through how to gather costs for financial projections.

After projections are compiled and verified, the expenses as a percentage of sales are compared to the industry benchmarks. In this case, a return on sales of about 5.7% is very close to the benchmark for restaurants with $1 million in revenues.

Adding back the depreciation and amortization, it appears that the business will have about $77,000 to pay interest and debt. The financial projection should factor in a ramp-up period when customers are just getting to

TABLE 8-15. First-Year Projections for a New Restaurant

Month	1	2	3	4	5	6
Seasonality	6%	6%	8%	10%	10%	8%
Covers	4,020	4,020	5,360	6,700	6,700	5,360
Revenues	60,300	60,300	80,400	100,500	100,500	80,400
Cost of Goods	24,120	24,120	32,160	40,200	40,200	32,160
Gross Profit	36,180	36,180	48,240	60,300	60,300	48,240
Management (Fixed)	3,350	3,350	3,350	3,350	3,350	3,350
Salaries and Benefits	13,266	13,266	17,688	22,110	22,110	17,688
Rents (Fixed)	5,443	5,443	5,443	5,443	5,443	5,443
Advertising	1,675	1,675	1,675	1,675	1,675	1,675
Other Expenses	11,474	11,474	11,474	11,474	11,474	11,474
Depreciation and Amortization	1,675	1,675	1,675	1,675	1,675	1,675
Taxes	3,433	3,433	3,433	3,433	3,433	3,433
Total Operating Expenses	40,316	40,316	44,738	49,160	49,160	44,738
Net Profit	-4,136	-4,136	3,502	11,140	11,140	3,502

know the restaurant; sales in the first few months will thus be less than they are when the restaurant is established. To cover the ramp-up period and the seasonality of sales, the business needs a cash reserve. If the business is able to achieve the projections used in this example, the payback period will be about five years.

Breakeven Analysis

In evaluating the investment, the concept of breakeven is important. Breakeven analysis is defined as the time when total invested costs (both start-up and operating) equal the amount of revenue received. The breakeven is noted as the time when investment plus operating expenses equal total revenue (Figure 8-12).

For the small business, it is equally important to determine a breakeven for year-to-year or even month-to-month fixed costs. By focusing on sales goals, the business can aim for the revenues (usually translated from the number of customers served or manufactured items sold) it takes to get to breakeven and to keep the business viable.

In the case of the new restaurant, it is helpful to calculate breakeven meals that need to be sold on a monthly basis. A monthly goal for meals helps the entrepreneur focus on profitability and take action as needed to increase the number of customers. To do this, break

out monthly fixed costs. This includes rent, utilities, a core staff, marketing costs, and other costs that will be there as long as the business is open. In this case, assume that fixed costs are about $40,000 before depreciation and amortization. A gross profit of about $40,000 would be required to break even. Working backward from a 60% gross profit, or $9 per cover, 4,500 covers or meals will be the breakeven number (Figure 8-13).

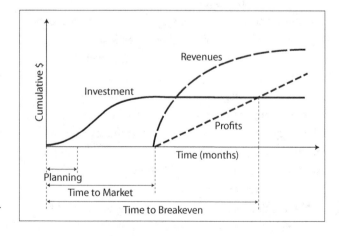

FIGURE 8-12. Breakeven Analysis

7	8	9	10	11	12	Annual Total	
6%	8%	8%	10%	10%	10%		
							Average
4,020	5,360	5,360	6,700	6,700	6,700	67,000	Meal $15
60,300	80,400	80,400	100,500	100,500	100,500	1,005,000	
24,120	32,160	32,160	40,200	40,200	40,200	402,000	40%
36,180	48,240	48,240	60,300	60,300	60,300	603,000	60%
3,350	3,350	3,350	3,350	3,350	3,350	40,200	4%
13,266	17,688	17,688	22,110	22,110	22,110	221,100	22%
5,443	5,443	5,443	5,443	5,443	5,443	65,316	6%
1,675	1,675	1,675	1,675	1,675	1,675	20,100	2%
11,474	11,474	11,474	11,474	11,474	11,474	137,688	14%
1,675	1,675	1,675	1,675	1,675	1,675	20,100	2%
3,433	3,433	3,433	3,433	3,433	3,433	41,196	4%
40,316	44,738	44,738	49,160	49,160	49,160	545,700	54%
-4,136	3,502	3,502	11,140	11,140	11,140	57,300	6%

Cost-Benefit Analysis

A cost-benefit analysis is often a key part of the business case. Financial analysis to determine if a strategy, solution, or program generates more cash than it will cost is basic to most consulting projects. Yet it is surprising how often this analysis is left until the end of data gathering. Keep in mind that a cost-benefit analysis must be completed for every recommendation. If the student consultants cannot provide evidence of a net benefit, the recommendation is not viable.

Basically, cost-benefit analysis takes the acquisition (fixed) costs of an investment and the projected benefits or cash flow generated and determines whether any

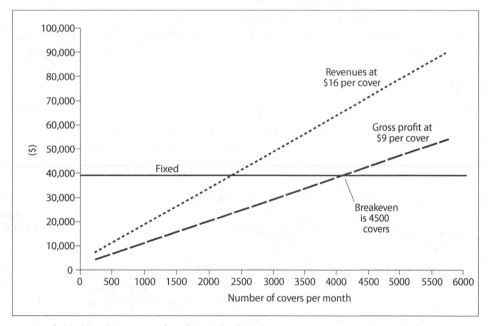

FIGURE 8-13. New Restaurant Breakeven Analysis

financial benefit will result. Students often expect that costs will be given to them, and they find it difficult to quickly estimate costs or benefits. For example, one student team recommended that a company use a postcard campaign. The student consultants were able to get printing and mailing costs but could not estimate what benefit would accrue from the campaign. It may be possible to look at company records to capture the response rates of past campaigns. Or, the students could do research to determine what response rates are typical for postcard campaigns. If this proves unfruitful, then the student consultants can make a reasonable estimate with sensitivity analysis, for example, 5%, 10%, and 15% response rates. Alternatively, the students could determine how many new customer visits would need to be generated in order to break even and then they could assess the likelihood of reaching that level. A more extensive cost-benefit analysis will incorporate intangible benefits such as improved customer service, better competitive position, or better information. Note the quantitative and qualitative analysis given to the cost-benefit analysis of a new truck (Table 8-16).

A frequent student consulting recommendation is to hire an intern to provide labor. This can be a net benefit, but often it is a net loss. Interns require training and supervision. Because they are usually inexperienced, they require a clear description of their duties and, possibly, step-by-step procedures. Most small businesses do not have these readily available. Often the small business does not have a human resource professional to conduct a proper search nor the manpower to supervise. Interns can result in substantial cost and loss of time for the business.

Benchmarking

Comparing a business with other businesses in the same industry, or benchmarking, is an important analysis for any business to perform. It can be done by gathering key financial ratios such as gross margin, profit margin, inventory turnover, receivables turnover, return on capital, return on equity, and revenues per employee. Benchmarking is not limited to financial data. Other key indicators to measure are new products developed, marketing programs, and distribution systems. Large enterprises might benchmark efficiency measures such as the number of transactions per employee in functions such as accounting and customer service.

When benchmarking, the business must be compared to similar businesses in terms of industry and size. Financial ratios for common businesses are available at websites such as BizStats.com. Some industry associations keep these statistics for their member businesses. A restaurant owned and run by a sole proprietor with $300,000 in annual sales would be benchmarked against similar-sized restaurants. It would not be compared to Starbucks or other large enterprises that have hundreds of millions in revenues, nor would it be compared to a restaurant with annual sales of $75,000.

Students recommending business growth strategies can assess the financial ratios that a company should aim for when it reaches its growth goals as a way of projecting future expenses. Such a comparison may yield areas of cost savings. For example, Figure 8-14 benchmarked an Indian restaurant against industry statistics for similar-sized restaurants. The restaurant was found to be high in terms of both food cost and payroll. This led the consult-

TABLE 8-16. Cost-Benefit Analysis

	Cost	Benefits	Financial Analysis
One-time	Purchase or financing of a new cleaning truck costs $125,000	Trade-in price received from an old truck (if any) or increased efficiency of the new vehicle (i.e., lower fuel costs, increase speed of project completion that reduces staff expenses)	Cash sufficient to cover purchase, or cash flow sufficient to cover financing
Continuing	Cost of maintaining, financing, and using the new truck in excess of the cost of the old truck; depreciation of truck	Increased revenue	Net present value, return on investment, and internal rate of return may be used
Time	Useful life of the new truck	Longer life of the new truck	Payback period
Other factors	No increase in customers prompts competitive response (pricing), recession, quality issues, start-up problems	High-quality service, customer satisfaction, customer retention, efficiencies with other product lines	May not be included in financial analysis

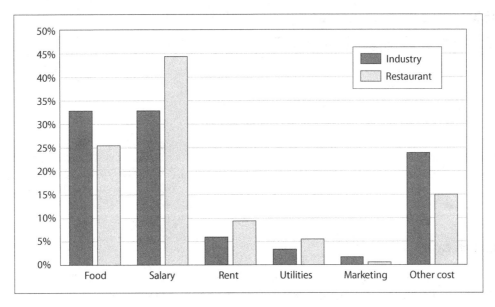

FIGURE 8-14. Benchmarking

ing team to recommend that the restaurant schedule wait staff only when needed. The team also pointed to areas where spending was below industry averages for marketing. This suggested that more funding should be put to marketing.

Benchmarking can help the business set goals to help it become more competitive. For example, a business might have profit margins of 7%, but benchmarking lets it know that the best businesses in its industry have profit margins of 10%. The business can then set higher goals. Benchmarking can also point to strengths and weaknesses that should be exploited or corrected, respectively.

DISCUSSION

1. Compute and interpret several balance sheet, income statement, and cash flow financial ratios for the client business. What conclusions would you draw from your analysis?
2. Complete a breakeven analysis on the client business using an online coupon such as Groupon or Living Social. Specify what level of new business (number of customers) is necessary to break even.
3. Complete a financial analysis of a new business opportunity. Give an analysis of qualitative as well and financial factors. Conduct a sensitivity analysis.
4. Conduct a cost-benefit analysis of a recommendation for your business. Be sure to include all factors that contribute to value.
5. Find industry statistics and benchmark your business. What strengths does the business show? What weaknesses?

NOTES

1   Amar Bhidé, *The Origin and Evolution of Business* (New York: Oxford University Press, 2000).
2   Edward I. Altman and Gabriele Sabato, "Modeling Credit Risk for SMEs: Evidence from the US Market," *Abacus* 43, no. 3 (2007): 332–57.
3   David O. Renz, ed., *Non-Profit Leadership and Management* (San Francisco: Jossey-Bass, 2010), 602.
4   Craig R. Everett, *Capital Markets Report 2014* (Los Angeles: Pepperdine University, 2014).

Epilogue: The Final Client Oral Presentation and Written Report

ABOUT THIS EPILOGUE

Most student consulting projects culminate with a final presentation where the hard work of the student team is showcased and celebrated. Often mentors, advisors, and other business professionals will be part of the audience along with the business owners. In some cases, this is the students' first experience presenting to a professional audience of business practitioners. Standards of performance are higher than for the typical student presentation. Preceding and following the final presentation, the student team will prepare the findings and recommendations for the final report. Students are expected to write a report that will pass the scrutiny of their mentors, advisors, or faculty and provide documentation for the business owner to implement the recommendations and improve the performance of the business. The effectiveness of the student project will likely be measured in a follow-up review some months after the engagement. All this puts pressure on the team to produce a report that will stand the test of time.

An effective final presentation and written report are predicated on excellent data gathering, analysis, and creative thinking in coming up with recommendations. As noted before, the nature of the student consulting project is such that the team does not arrive at a point where all prerequisites are satisfied until the final quarter of the time allotted. As such, most teams are under pressure to get the job done quickly when it is most imperative to reflect and be inclusive.

Although most consultants no longer provide hundred-page reports to their clients, writing an extensive final report provides an important pedagogical function. Students learn how to complete evidence-based analysis in a complex situation. There are no right answers in the student consulting project. The writing itself develops strong communication and critical thinking skills. At this phase of students' learning, detailed step-by-step compilation and analysis is required for students to fully understand how industry practitioners come up with their much more succinct versions. As yet, students do not have the foundation to produce presentations that communicate to and persuade business audiences.

After Studying This Epilogue

The goal of this epilogue is to provide a brief description of how to prepare for the final presentation and write the final report. After reading this epilogue, students will be able to:

- Understand the process for developing effective findings and recommendations.
- Articulate the steps in preparing a professional presentation.
- Describe factors in communicating the visual display of data.
- Define key elements that should be contained in the final report.

PREPARING FOR THE FINAL PRESENTATION AND REPORT
Developing Effective Findings and Recommendations

Providing detailed evidence for analysis and recommendations allows the student to understand how data builds analysis and leads to recommendations that may move the business forward. Typically the process for completing the final report starts with a list of recommendations. Then the student team will compile the appropriate data to support the recommendation. This usually takes the form of compiling the appropriate data and completing analysis that points to the recommendation. Some recommendations will be adopted by the business owner very quickly (often before the consulting project is completed), because the data and findings are within the business owner's realm of understanding. Recommendations that take the business owner out of his or her typical comfort zone will require more data and analysis. Additionally, the team provides comprehensive data and analysis to establish credibility.

With novice consultants, analysis and recommendations are often superficial because of inexperience. For example, a student team may recommend technology adoption without understanding that proper training and a certain level of technology sophistication are required before the recommendation can be implemented. Some student teams have recommended training employees when the business owner does not have the resources nor skills to do so. Others have recommended that labor or skill shortages be relieved by hiring interns, without understanding that interns often require more in training than the benefits they provide to a business.

The following reprises the checklists in chapter 2 as guidance for what teams should keep in the mind while developing the final presentation and report:

1. Recognize pitfalls and biases in data gathering. Assess and articulate all assumptions in the analysis. Keep in mind that a team may miss solutions because individual team members do not share information or assume that others in the team know everything that they know.

2. Be wary of using shortcuts and habit to guide analysis. With tight time frames and exponential workload at the end of a project, it is easy to fall prey to shortcuts. Expect that more time than anticipated will be required, and ensure that individual calendars are cleared to allow for thorough analysis.

3. Identify key benchmarks or ratios to evaluate recommendations for frequently made decisions. However, benchmarks or ratios should be evaluated critically and used selectively when novel situations are being evaluated.

4. Make sure that the recommendation is directly linked to the work areas in the consulting contract. This does not mean that the consulting team should exclude findings and recommendations that create opportu-

nity or solve problems, that arise serendipitously, and that are backed by good data and analysis. Also, ensure that the recommendation addresses the right problem. A recommendation for the wrong problem is an obvious mismatch that should be avoided.

5. Process and integrate the best available data into the recommendation. Even at this late stage in the project, if data are incomplete or inadequate, the correct data can be often acquired quickly because the team is experienced in where to look.

6. Base recommendations on an informed, rational choice-making process and not on beliefs or assumptions. Use a "bounded rationality" approach as a guide because it emphasizes analytical judgment based on facts, rational inferences, and consideration of other influences.

7. Recognize the value of intuition and creativity in making recommendations. There are limits to analytical inferences and judgments. Insights and sound choice making can be formulated on hunches, imaginative insights, and other nonquantitative grounds. Be inclusive rather than exclusive.

8. Assess the value and impact of alternative recommendations. All recommendations should have a cost-benefit analysis. Cross-check and triangulate the analysis and results to ensure accuracy and consistency.

9. Evaluate expected outcomes and develop contingencies for the process. It is important to develop sensitivity analysis because recommendations project future performance, which is subject to uncertainty.

10. Provide time, money, and other resources needed for implementation and follow-up on a recommendation, to make sure that it produced the expected results. Provide a means for the business to measure the results from the recommendation and a timeline for when results are expected.

Prioritizing Recommendations

The final report, including appendices, is often upward of one hundred pages and the business owner may find it difficult to review all the material. The consulting team's research findings and analysis must be prioritized in order to make them understandable, acceptable, actionable, and usable for the client. The team will choose how groupings will occur based on what the team is trying to communicate. For example, the team may group recommendations by functions such as marketing, operations, or finance.

Grouping recommendations by priority is another way of approaching the task. For example, recommendations may be grouped together for a strategy to acquire new customers by increasing services and streamlining operations. Getting suggestions from faculty and mentors is helpful. Of course the team's own ideas are key. In view of the team's work and interactions with the client, what are the most persuasive or effective findings to propose to the business owner? Thinking along these lines should make a challenging task easier in gaining client buy-in and implementation of the team's recommendations.

The Action Plan

The ultimate test of a project's value is determined by how well decisions and action steps are implemented by the client. Hence, it is very important that a detailed plan for decision implementation be articulated. Be clear about what the proposed action will require of the client, how the action taken is to be directed and measured, and what markers will measure results. The business owner must know what is expected and how to determine what is, and is not, working over the course of decision implementation. In addition, the client (or someone she designates) should be accountable for implementation. Therefore timelines, budgets, cash flow projections, or other measurement and control tools must be identified as part of the implementation process. If this is not done properly, accountability and follow-up is impossible. The following reprises another checklist from chapter 2:

1. What should the new arrangements/actions achieve? What level of performance? What quality of output?
2. How will the new situation differ from the old? Will there be different products, services, or activities? Different processes, equipment, and/or locations?
3. Are the effects likely to last? Are the business and the target market changing so quickly that there may be no need for the new product or service? Is it possible that people will revert to present practices?
4. What difficulties will arise in implementation? Will there be employee resistance or shortage of materials or other resources?
5. Who and what parts of the firm will be affected? Are employees receptive? What should be done to prepare employees? Do matching changes need to be made elsewhere?
6. When is the best time to change? Should it be at the end of a season, during down time, at the close of a financial period, or at the beginning of the calendar year?

Measuring Results

Recommendation follow-up should be guided by the performance expectations promised in the written client report. There must be sufficient detail and documentation so that anyone not part of the detailed work of the project can understand what is to be accomplished and how it will be measured.

The directions that the client will take following the completion of the project will depend heavily on the quality and persuasiveness of the recommendations made and the amount of buy-in to the changes that the team has generated during the consulting engagement. The final checklist of recommendations should do the following:

- Address project goals.
- Be supported by the data and analysis.
- Add value to the client and the operations of the firm.
- Consider resource availability or provide means of getting resources.
- Provide enough detail to implement.
- Provide the metrics and time frame for measuring success.

The ultimate test of the worth or value of student consulting projects must be measured in terms of how well they accomplish their stated goals and objectives.

COMMUNICATING RESULTS

The final step in the student consulting project is communicating recommendations in a client-based presentation and final report. While the student team may have contributed many hours of work on the project, the ultimate evaluation of the research and consulting is determined by the team's effectiveness in communicating its recommendations. The following section provides guidance for communicating the results orally, through a final client presentation, and in writing through a professional final report.

The Presentation

The final presentation takes the place of the typical meeting with the client where consultants present a clear and simple picture of the situation and the recommendations. Generally the presentation is structured to show the analysis of the problem and opportunity such that it naturally leads the client to the recommendations. The presentation must iterate the benefits of the solutions so that implementation is a foregone conclusion for the client.

The purpose of the presentation is to focus awareness on a manageable number of dimensions. It is not possible to cover all the work completed for the project, and doing so could overload the client. The presentation does not have all the answers. These will be provided in the final report. The final presentation is a key means to communicate the results to the client and provide a showcase for the team's work to mentors and advisors.

Plan as a group. Maintain constant and open communication with team members as the team prepares for its final presentation. This includes a commitment to strive to collaborate and actively listen. It is important that room be made for every team member's ideas to be shared; although there may not be consensus, there should be buy-in for the team's recommendations. Keeping communication open at this late stage in the process will be difficult. Team members will be tired. There will be the urge to get it over and done. Rehearsals may run late into the night. Resist the urge to "satisfice," and instead choose excellence to the finish. Plan for the unexpected. Computers crash, files can be lost, and printers run out of ink.

Analyze the situation. The occasion, setting, and purpose of the presentation, along with the many reasons for making the presentation, are all part of the situation analysis that should precede any oral presentation. For most project-related presentations, these elements are relatively straightforward. Early in the project experience, gaining agreements on project scope and priorities and defining problems more clearly are likely to be dominant issues and concerns. However, by the time of the formal presentation, considerations of credibility, persuasive evidence, and reinforcing the client's buy-in are likely to become important.

Regarding the physical surroundings of the presentation, give attention to seating, lighting, and other factors that may influence the comfort and attention of those in the audience. Another factor to consider is making sure that the content and focus of the presentation are appropriate for the client's needs.

Know the audience. In approaching this part of the planning process, consider several aspects of what makes

for effective interpersonal communications. Start with knowledge, education, and cultural background. Individuals must have some common ground in all these areas, at least with respect to language use and expectations. It is the speaker's responsibility to learn what the client knows about the subject and what he or she expects in the presentation. For example, the student team should be careful not to include too much business jargon if the client is unfamiliar with that terminology. Final recommendations can still be supported by research but may need to be communicated in a way that is easily understood. Additionally, to the extent that differences in age or other demographics affect the response to or understanding of the subject, adjustments will need to be made accordingly.

It is important to ask who will be in attendance. The business owner may bring employees or business partners to the presentation. For example, the team may need to accommodate individuals who may or may not be familiar with the consulting process or results that will be shared.

Also recognize that the team is being evaluated in the presentation process. Its ability to establish rapport or relationships, along with cultivating confidence and credibility, should be given consideration.

At this point in the consulting process, the business owner should not be surprised to see the results from the research conducted or be unfamiliar with the final recommendations. The student team should have been updating the business owner along the way to gain buy-in for the team's proposals. For example, if the student team is proposing a new website, the business owner should be aware of this recommendation so that he or she can provide feedback along the way. The final unveiling of the website may be saved until the final presentation, but the idea of a new website should not be new.

Identify the team's goal. Determine the purpose of the presentation by focusing on what the audience needs to know when they leave. Formulate a succinct statement that summarizes the basic point the audience must accept. The best presentations make the message stand out, easy to follow, and personally important to the audience.

Organize the body of the presentation. Once the key purpose is determined, select the main points to support the purpose, and determine the evidence that will be used to support the recommendations. The team will have an abundance of data, and it is important to select the findings and analyses that are the most persuasive in achieving the purpose of the presentation. Team members will often want to include the analyses that they invested the most work in or that result in the most interesting visual display. These can all be included in full detail in the final report. The findings, analyses, and recommendations in the presentation must serve the presentation purpose only. The presentation must be organized such that the audience will be persuaded to accept the team's recommendations. The focus of the presentation should be on presenting the final recommendations with an implementation timeline.

Develop the introduction. The introduction must gain the audience's attention. It should preview how the team will proceed and tell the audience when questions will be taken. The most important element of the introduction is to establish credibility with the audience. If the audience does not perceive the team as honest and trustworthy, they are unlikely to take the presentation seriously. When planning, ask how the team will be perceived and what can be done to enhance credibility. Determine similarities and differences between the team and the audience.

The introduction will include the full names of all the team members and the agenda for the presentation. It may acknowledge mentors and advisors. Keep the introduction brief yet complete.

Plan the conclusion. Recognize the importance of having a strong conclusion. It should accomplish several tasks. The conclusion reviews and highlights the main points of the presentation. The audience should be reminded of the importance and benefits. There might be some follow-up actions that should be conveyed as part of the conclusion. The conclusion should answer the question, "So what?" Be clear about what is in it for the client.

It is also customary to acknowledge the team's gratitude to the client, mentors, and advisors. Teams often end with a memorable statement that brings the presentation to a close.

Sharing research results. As student consultants, it is important to remain objective when sharing results from the research conducted throughout the consulting process. Some students are hesitant to share negative customer feedback, but in reality this could be a very important finding that contributes to a major recommendation. One way to share research findings that may be perceived

negatively is to remain objective and share them in the context of the project goals and as an opportunity for improvement. For example, if a customer says that service is slow, this could create an opportunity to blueprint the service process to identify possible solutions, such as a smaller menu, more staff, or a more efficient food preparation process. The student team should also keep in mind that the business owner may be sensitive to negative feedback, and the team should be prepared to offer solutions for improvement.

Practice the presentation. The adage "practice makes perfect" is apt. Rehearse the presentation in front of others who are unfamiliar with the material. Each team member should develop and repeat the presentation outline until he or she is fluent. This often involves hours of rehearsal for a twenty-minute presentation. Rehearsal should be done under presentation conditions. All speakers should be checked for eye contact, gestures, and voice inflection. The rehearsals should be timed.

Reading the presentation from a PowerPoint slide or sheet of paper is the least desirable choice because it tends to take away eye contact with the audience and reduces the likelihood that the presenter will be sensitive to audience feedback. Typically there is such a preoccupation with getting the words out that expressiveness and enthusiasm may be lacking. This method of presentation may also reveal a speaker's discomfort with a more conversational style. The delivery is likely to be stilted. It is best to avoid this manner of delivery. It tends to bring out the bad parts of public speaking and oral presentations.

The impromptu mode of delivery is one in which the team member speaks in a conversational tone with no notes. Eye contact is enhanced, along with a likelihood of keeping in touch with the audience and following their reactions. There is likely to be a readiness to answer questions that may arise. But there are serious limitations, particularly for novice presenters. They may be prone to forget the order of the presentation or leave out key points.

The term *extemporaneous* defines a mode of delivery in which the presenter speaks from prepared notes in a conversational manner. The speaker can adopt different methods that suit a particular presentation's need or situation. Audience contact can be encouraged. All forms of visual or other presentation aids can be incorporated into the presentation as well.

In most cases, the entire team will participate in

the presentation. Determine the order of the speakers. Team members will often present the part in which they were most involved. Ensure that there is a smooth transition between speakers. Teams should also identify each member's strengths and assign each presenter the most appropriate material to cover. In such a short presentation, it is usually not necessary to reintroduce the team members or say that the next team member will be presenting on a certain topic. This type of information can be easily communicated through the visual aids used (e.g., slides).

Use a keyword outline. Preparing a keyword outline of the presentation is a good way of bringing closure to the planning phase. Keywords can serve as cues for parts of the delivery phase. They can also reduce the reliance on memory at transition points or in other parts of the presentation. The outline can also serve as a checklist for or reminder of the flow of the entire presentation.

Establish or reinforce your credibility. How much of the audience's attention is attained rests on the team members indicating that they are prepared enough and confident during of the presentation. The team may emphasize the depth and care of the research and analysis for the project. Team members can establish common ground. Showing a passion for the project goes a long way toward establishing credibility.

Use your body effectively. Body language is very important in public speaking. Standing rigidly behind the podium or slouching on it can be signs of needing it as a defense between the speaker and audience or can indicate some discomfort in being in front of an audience. Do not use the podium as a crutch or point of separation.

The presenter should stand up straight, arms at sides, and face the audience. Establish and maintain eye contact with the audience as a way to welcome audience members into the presentation and give them a sense of their importance. Use gestures to complement voice changes or points of emphasis. Gestures should help give energy to the presentation. Other tips for effective use of the body include moving around, standing erect but relaxed, and using a variety of facial expressions.

Use voice effectively. Avoid speaking in a monotone. The voice should enhance the message. Be sure that the presenter can be heard by everyone in the room. Speaking too softly will convey a lack of confidence. Speaking too loudly could give the impression of being too brash and pushy. Change the pace or rate of speaking. Pause to get attention and to make a serious and complex point of information. Speed up the pace when there are details that do not need to be emphasized or remembered. Be clear and enunciate words clearly. If there is an accent in the presenter's speech, it may be necessary to slow the speech. Recognize differences between the articulation and the sounds that the audience will hear.

Preparing and using visual aids. Communication is usually best when it can be both verbal and visual. Visual aids should be an integral part of most formal presentations. It is rare for a business presentation not to have visual aids. Unfortunately this practice has some undesirable side effects, such as "information dumping." Presenters are so eager to get material before the audience that slides are overfilled with content. In preparing visual aids, be judicious in including only those that enhance the message.

It is prudent to visit the room prior to the presentation to check for any problems that might arise. Technical glitches can occur, and backup options such as additional laptops or external drives are convenient to have on hand. In addition, it is a foregone conclusion that the presentations with the most complex animation are the most likely to go wrong. Do not rely on visual effects to give the presentation its punch. All slides in the presentation should be proofread several times. There should be *no* typographical, grammatical, or spelling errors. Further, projectors can alter colors, and slides on a laptop may look different on a large screen. Using a white background with a dark-colored font is typically the safest color scheme.

Handling questions and answers. In terms of audience takeaways, handling questions and answers can be a very important complement to the presentation. It is best to try to anticipate audience questions and prepare answers before the presentation. Handling the question period well at the end of the presentation adds to the credibility of the team.

When answering the question, repeat it back to the audience. Be gracious, respectful, and positive, even if the question seems to cast doubt on credibility. Be truthful and sincere in answering the question. Defer longer questions until the team is finished with the presentation.

It is important that the audience feels that all concerns will be addressed. Some student teams prepare slides with additional information to aid in answering questions.

Professionalism. Student teams should plan to dress professionally, typically in business attire, for the final presentation. The delivery of the presentation should be professional and should avoid inappropriate uses of humor or language that is too informal. Engaging the business owner in a professional manner demonstrates a high level of respect for him or her and also contributes to the student team's credibility.

Nervousness and anxiety. Nervousness and anxiety are natural reactions to stressful situations. Even prominent entertainers and professional speakers report that they experience these emotions. The response and challenge for everyone is to find a way to cope with nervousness and anxiety. Extensive rehearsal is the best method for overcoming most of the problems with presentations. Before speaking, taking long breaths (four-count inhalations and four-count exhalations) while imagining relaxing words can also have a calming effect. When it is time to present, enjoy the moment, as the team has worked hard to be able to shine.

In preparing for the final presentation, take the time to watch several presentations at TED.com. Some of the best speakers present in that forum, which allows only twenty minutes per presentation.

Presentation outline. Student teams should keep in mind that the final presentation is intended to convey the major findings and recommendations of the consulting engagement. One suggested outline for a client presentation is as follows:

- Introduction. Student consultants introduce themselves and acknowledge the client and their mentors.
- Agenda. Team members give an overview of the presentation and the topics that will be covered.
- Project scope and consulting plan. Students review the project scope and the process to achieve project goals. For example, the project scope may have been to evaluate the viability of launching a new product. This may have required secondary and primary research and a competitive analysis.
- Research findings. The project will include more data, findings, and analysis than can be presented in the

short time allowed. Students should provide enough information to persuade the client that the recommendations should be pursued. This often means presenting highlights of the work produced. However, in order to establish credibility with the audience, the student team often provides details about research methodology, data collected, and analysis produced. It is best to present these visually and refer to the final report for more information.

- Key recommendations. The team should spend the bulk of the presentation time presenting and describing each recommendation. The recommendations should flow from the research presented and include enough cost-benefit analysis so that the audience finds the recommendations credible. For example, a student team should not recommend that the business owner hire a new employee without identifying the need for additional staff in the research section of the presentation.
- Implementation timeline. Students should conclude with an implementation timeline as shown in Figure E-1. The business owner may be very receptive to the student team's recommendations, but she may need help prioritizing her next steps.
- Conclusion. Student teams should conclude with a recap of the final recommendations, thank the business owner for her participation in the process, and ask for questions. The ability to answer questions will also speak to the credibility of the team.

The Final Report

Report writing can be among the most challenging and demanding aspects of the project experience. It must be a total team effort. Yet the report must be written and presented such that the client or reader sees it as the single voice of the team. To be really effective it must read as if one individual wrote it. Thus, at the outset, each team should develop a style sheet that details usage and spelling for the final report and have a primary editor.

The report writing process should extend throughout the term of the project. Various written assignments from the faculty are intended for later integration into some part of the written consulting report. A very early part of the process should involve developing a report writing plan. This means outlining and organizing before the team writes. It also means that each team member is assigned tasks that will ensure that all the research, analysis, and problem solving that will go into the report will be defined and completed in a timely way.

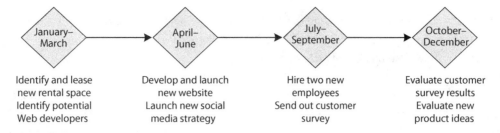

FIGURE E-1. Implementation Timeline

This should also mean that workloads are allocated fairly and with regard to the skills and strengths of each team member. Particular attention should be given to determining whose style will best complement the writing of the team. That individual should be considered for the role of primary editor. This also means that drafts need to be completed well in advance so that the primary editor has sufficient time to review them.

Most knowledgeable businesspeople agree that a project report should be about thirty to fifty pages. This means that the first draft may be significantly longer than the finished report. This length forces the team to sharpen its focus so that the resulting product will hold the reader's interest. This does not mean that the large amount of documentation that usually accompanies a project will be lost. Background materials can be contained in the appendices, and indeed some of the materials in such a section may be vital to proper execution of strategies and programs. Be concise yet ensure that you provide enough information to support your recommendations.

Display of Data

To communicate clearly to a business audience, it is important to make effective use of graphics, data, and text. When the data details must be shown, text is the most efficient means of communication. However, graphics are likely to be more influential in keeping the audience's attention. Visual display of information has the benefit of using many more elements—such as color, shape, pattern, texture, and dimension—to communicate. Graphs and text can be used to show relationships. Additionally, the creation of a visual display of information is in itself a means of critical analysis. Often, seeing data in the form of a map or other graphic can clarify the results of the analysis. Much of the guidelines presented in this section are from Edward Tufte, professor emeritus from Yale University.[1]

Pie charts. Pie charts are effective means of showing categorical data. An audience looking at a pie chart can quickly see the relative proportions of each category. Be careful to limit the number of categories used in a pie chart. Too many categories can overwhelm the display.

Bar charts. Bar charts are often used for frequency distributions of population in quantitative measures such as age or income. They also lend themselves well to showing year-to-year growth in measures such as sales and profit.

Line graphs. Line graphs are useful in communicating trends. A time series line graph is used to show what happens to a variable such as income over time. The horizontal axis is time or years, while the vertical axis shows variables such as income. Time series graphs are excellent for depicting patterns such as economic cycles.

Maps. By using a map and color coding, it is possible to show the geographic concentration of variables. Maps are also excellent for showing competitor locations and other geographic factors that might affect the profitability of a business.

Matrices. Matrices are tables that invite comparison. They are often effective as narrative tables. Matrices can be used to compare attributes of the business to those of its competitors. The key to an effective matrix is to select attributes that are important to the analysis.

Use combinations or multiples. Different types of graphs can be used in combination to show more variables.

Use color. Color is one of the most important elements of visual display. Unfortunately, using the default values of various software programs is sure to result in "chart junk." With computer screens it is tempting to use bright colors. But the temptation should be resisted. A good guide is to use colors found in nature. They tend to be muted. Bright colors used in moderation can be very effective in communicating. Also be careful of colors used in combination. They can have a subtractive effect or, worse yet, they can have an unsettling effect on the audience. As with text, projectors can alter colors and it is typically safer to use a white background.

Use text. There is no rule that limits the amount of text in a visual display, yet many novices use short, truncated titles that detract from good communication. Use the text to extend the explanation and make the analysis clear.

Keep display clear. Programs such as MS Excel make it easy to graph. Experts in the visual display of information say that this is very dangerous. It can lead to a proliferation of "chart junk"—that is, displaying images without much informational value. Chart junk is also about making the wrong choices and missing the mark in effective display. For example, using three-dimensional graphing does not increase the communication of information, nor does the use of strikingly bold colors or massive amounts of textures.

Be careful of the grid's impact on visual display. Grids, labels, and titles can often overwhelm the visual display with their intensity. Use them only when needed. Think carefully, too, about the scaling of data. Not all charts have to start at zero. Start at a point that allows the audience to understand the relationships and to make meaningful comparisons.

Most sophisticated forms of visual display need to be on paper. Data density on computer screens is one-tenth to one-thousandth of a printed page. If providing complex evidence, put it in print and allow the audience to look at it carefully and in detail.

Show the data. It might sound obvious, but good visual display actually shows the data. The Challenger explosion immediately after takeoff was blamed on O-ring failure. But the main culprit was poor visual display of information. Although data were given, no one could see the clear pattern of O-ring failure in low temperatures. In order to show the data, understand the data. In fact, the later Columbia explosion was blamed on simplified display of information through PowerPoint slides. Know the data inside out. This helps team members come up with the appropriate visual display. Experts in information believe that people with a passion for

what the data show come up with the best form of visual display.

Eliminate ambiguity. Good visual display of information is clear. Even when there is extensive data, the presentation must still be clear. Relationships and conclusions should be logical and meaningful. The message should be precise. There must not be any ambiguity or confusion. The presentation should be efficient and show what is necessary with a minimum of effort on the part of the viewer.

Do not distort data. Data, like truth, must have integrity; otherwise data are misleading. There are many temptations to distort data in the business world. Sometimes it might appear that bending the evidence will encourage adoption of a recommendation. Or a marketer might want to present products in the best light. A client could pressure the team to show one thing while omitting key facts that may lead to a different conclusion. In the long term, business relations are about trust, and distorting data erodes that trust. Strive to obtain and present only the most relevant and accurate data. If the truth has to be bent to demonstrate a point, the wrong path of communication is being pursued.

Excellent visual display requires excellent command of the data and an in-depth understanding of design. To communicate what the data show, the visual display must have a purpose. Once the mission is clear, use color, shape, layout, comparison, layering, dimensions, and other elements to tell the story.

Suggested Elements of the Final Report

Cover letter. The cover letter is addressed to the business owner and serves at least three purposes. First, it acknowledges that the report is being submitted to the client. Second, it provides a brief description of the project along with a few highlights of the findings, conclusions, and recommendations. Finally, it expresses gratitude to the client for his or her cooperation, support, and contributions to student learning that have been made along the way. Figure E-2 gives an example of a cover letter from a student team working with a Latina-owned financial services firm. The letter concisely summarizes the agreed upon scope of work, research done by the team, and recommendations in order of importance.

Executive summary. The executive summary provides much more than a summary of the entire project. In fact,

March 15, 2015

Ms. Aida Perez
Hispanic Professional Services
1000 Evergreen Way
Everett, WA 98203

Dear Ms. Perez:
Attached is the final report of the student consulting project. This report is a collaborative team effort authorized by our educational institution. At the beginning of this engagement, we agreed that the team would address marketing and customer service issues.

We conducted extensive competitive analysis, a potential customer survey of Hispanic businesses, and reviewed internal work processes. Our analyses show that there is growing demand in the state for payroll and tax preparation services for Hispanic businesses. Our research and analysis have identified the specific areas where there is a higher concentration of the target market and what key factors will attract this market to your business. The details of this are contained in the report including a listing of Hispanic businesses and contact information.

Our recommendations in order of priority are:

1. Grow business revenue through an effective tiered pricing system that will increase revenue while remaining competitive in the market.
2. Improve business management through the help of an additional employee skilled in QuickBooks software and accounting to increase service consistency and business productivity.
3. Implement a referral system to increase client acquisition through effective customer relationship management.
4. Implement the proposed design of the business website to reach the target market more effectively and expand the client base through a strong online presence.

Through strategic marketing utilizing the recommendations above, we estimate that the business can increase small business accounts by 50% and payroll accounts by 100%. Detailed analysis, recommendations, timelines, and metrics for evaluation of the effectiveness of these recommendations are contained in the final report.

We thank you for your cooperation and contribution to this project. We would like to express our gratitude and appreciation for your tremendous support, and for giving us the opportunity to consult with your business and the privilege of being a part of your team.

Yours truly,

Student Consulting Team

FIGURE E-2. Sample Cover Letter

it is the most widely read part of the plan, and its quality is often the deciding factor in whether the client will read the rest of the report. The executive summary succinctly focuses on what managers and decision makers need to know, yet it is complete enough to be persuasive. Executive summaries are difficult to write, and the team should take the time to think through all the findings and recommendations before tackling it. Typically executive summaries are drafted after the body of the report is complete. They must provide the highlights of the work and the call for action. Good executive summaries undergo many revisions.

Table of contents. The table of contents shows how the report is organized. Major headings (and sometimes subheadings) are indicated so that readers can find the portions of the report that are of interest. If headings are properly formatted while drafting the report, a table of contents will be generated automatically.

Background and introduction. This section includes an explanation of the project's purpose and scope and presents the methods of research and analysis. It provides background information on the company, financial performance, and management biographies. The business model may also be included. The business model definition calls for thinking of the company in terms of what value is being provided, what benefits are being offered in the marketplace, and how the business will profit from it. Differentiation adds further content and context by considering how the delivery of these values and benefits will be designed for competitive advantage of a given company in comparison with its competitors.

Situation analysis and the firm's environment. Assessments of the external and internal environments in terms of how the firm operates are an important part of any report. Such assessments must include the challenges, constraints, and influences that will determine the outcomes of the plans that are implemented. A detailed strengths, weaknesses, opportunities, and threats (SWOT) analysis may be included here as well as a competitive assessment. As noted before, caution should be exercised in presenting the SWOT analysis, as it can often be perceived as negative.

Findings and analysis. This main section of the report will include data analysis and presentation of findings on competitive analysis, business process analysis, market analysis, financial analysis, and other discussion. Because there can be many findings, it is important to group similar findings together and to prioritize the categories. When presenting primary research results such as a customer survey, these may be included:

- Identify the research objective and key research questions (e.g., what key factors contribute to customer satisfaction?).
- Describe the research methodology (e.g., an online survey was sent to current customers, with a 20% response rate).
- Discuss the results using the sample (e.g., 60% females with an average age of twenty-five years old), analysis used (e.g., regression analysis), and findings (e.g., 70% of customers indicate that they are very likely to return to the restaurant).
- Discuss the results (e.g., what are the key takeaways?).

Also be sure to discuss any limitations (e.g., limited time to collect data). In assessing the value of this section, readers will ask the following questions:

- Was the research sufficient, or was key information not sought?

- Was the methodology sound? Was the analysis done correctly?
- Were the conclusions drawn supported by the evidence?
- Were patterns or conclusions missed? Were incorrect conclusions drawn?

Recommendations. The recommendations that the consultant team makes to its client are critically important to the overall success of the project. They are the result of many hours of hard work. Recommendations should not be presented to the client before they are in final form. Past experience with novice consulting teams shows that they often have not completed all the necessary analysis or communicated the findings in such a way that the client will readily accept them. In these cases, it is important to review the findings and recommendations with faculty, advisors, or mentors before going to the client.

Recommendations should:

- Address project goals.
- Be supported by data and analysis.
- Add value to the client's firm.
- Consider resource availability or provide means of getting resources.
- Provide enough detail to implement.
- Provide the metrics for measuring success.
- Be fully documented in the report.

Recommendations should be grouped by category and prioritized. Teams often present will recommendations following the findings and analysis. Questions to be asked include:

- Were the recommendations supported by the evidence?
- What benefits will the recommendations provide to the business?
- Were costs and benefits quantified?
- Do the recommendations fit with the mission and vision of the business?
- Does the business have access to the resources necessary to implement the recommendations?
- Is there sufficient detail in the report for the business to know how to implement the recommendations?
- Were the recommendations time bound?

Recommendation

We recommend that the business owner proceed with development of his podcast portal and the creation of educational-based podcasts. However, this recommendation is contingent upon the owner's ability to sustain his livelihood from other sources of income during the early stages of development. If the business owner is not in the position to do so, then we recommend that the business does not move forward at this time.

Evidence

Demographic data, industry size and revenue, growth trends, interest levels, along with market strengths were utilized to support our findings that there is a viable and growing market for the development of an educational podcast portal and podcast production. Market demand is visualized when analyzing demographic and socio-economic trends, along with recent sales revenue of online content purchases ($2 Billion).

Currently there are more than 200,000 podcasts being produced. Today, the listener market that consumes these podcasts is estimated at over 6 million and projected to soar to 60 million by 2010. *The Yankee Group* estimates by the end of the year, 41.6 million consumers will own a digital audio player, and there will be more than 10,000 businesses and individuals publishing podcasts.

The content of podcasting is growing rapidly as demonstrated by the surging number of new podcasts listed at podcast directories. The number of podcasts listed at *iTunes* grew from 5,000 in June 2005 to over 20,000 in September 2005.

Podcasting is something that started and has continued to grow outside of the conventional media market. The audience growth is fueled by the rise in popularity of digital music player, and people's desire to take more control of their digital content, listening and watching what they want, when they want. The desire to —time and place shiftll content has been demonstrated by the success of digital video recorders such as *TiVo* that automatically record favorite television programs. Also the increasing use of the Internet and the availability and speed of broadband, means downloads are much faster and gives people the opportunity to get more from the Internet.

Cost Benefit

The cost of starting this business is quite low in comparison with many business start-up costs. We project the total costs for the first year of operation will be $29,790 and some revenues will be generated. The major investment will be the development of the Web site portal. Since the business is homed-based, tenant improvement and leasing costs are not involved. Setting up a quality podcast studio requires minimal investment to include recording and editing equipment, computer with Internet access, hosting and bandwidth service, and content inventory. Other miscellaneous expenses include logo design, business cards, and miscellaneous licensing fees. All financial analysis is detailed in the findings and analysis section of this report.

	Year 1	Year 2	Year 3	Year 4	Year 5
Total Expenses	-29,790	-26,395	-27,700	-28,999	-30,350
Net Cash Flow	-24,350	2,713	25,884	50,451	64,990
Cumulative Cash Flow	-24,350	-21,637	4,247	54,697	119,687
Net Present Value	74,365				

Action Steps

We believe it is important that the client move quickly as podcasting may have a 4-5 year time frame as reflected in the product life cycle. We think a reasonable time frame to have his business up and running would be within 9-12 months from today. In order to meet his production start deadline, we suggest that he use the following time line. All other following recommendations should also follow this time line.

FIGURE E-3. Sample Recommendation

- Have the risks been analyzed?
- How will the business measure whether it has been successful in implementing the recommendations?

Figure E-3 gives an example of a recommendation made by a student team tasked with determining the feasibility of a podcasting business. The team recommends that the business owner move forward with the business and gives a quick summary of the market size. The cost-benefit analysis is provided next. Keep in mind that detailed market and financial analysis are given in the findings and analysis section of the report. Specific costs and revenue are itemized in that analysis, with supporting evidence. The recommendation provides a concise review. An

Trade Show	Decision Go/No/Go	Locate Content	Web Design	Develop Business Model	Locate Sales Merchandise	Purchase Equipment	Podcast Production Starts	Start to Promote Business
Sept. 29	Oct. 1	Nov. 1	Nov. 15	Dec. 1	Jan. 1	Jan. 15	Feb. 1	Mar. 1–June 1

FIGURE E-4. Action Timeline

action plan with timeline is provided so the business owner can understand when and how the recommendation is to be implemented (Figure E-4).

Appendix materials. Copies of surveys, summaries of raw data, transcripts of focus groups, or significant interviews should be included in this section. Student teams often include data sets that provide valuable information to the business, such as potential customer lists. These should be included in their entirety in the appendices.

Style, Layout, and Presentation

The report should be written in a clear, concise, and direct style. Short sentences are usually better than longer sentences. Long sentences with clauses are harder to follow, since they are likely to contain more than one complete thought. Use bullet points any time there are three or more items in a sequence or list. This is more appealing than using a sentence containing a lot of commas.

Avoid complicated language that has to be explained or that is likely to require a great deal of effort to read and understand. When technical or complicated words must be used, provide an accompanying clarification or illus-

tration. Avoid sending the reader to a dictionary. Be sure to keep the client in mind as the primary reader. Recognize that if the client is going to have difficulty reading the report, its usefulness to him or her is likely to be limited. Moreover, it could reduce the likelihood of the client adopting or implementing ideas and solutions.

Keep in mind that the report informs, advises, persuades, and possibly even warns the client about some important issues that need his or her attention. In order to be clearly heard, make sure all findings and recommendations are expressed as positively as possible. For example, instead of describing the business as disorganized, specifically address what has to be improved, such as having a better database or documenting procedures.

The final report is often the part of the project that endures. Business owners may retain the project report and implement the recommendations over a long period of time. They may use elements of it to apply for financing. It is important documentation of the team's hard work. Often team members will show the report as evidence of the quality of work they can achieve. The team should take the time and effort to make it the best possible product.

DISCUSSION

1. Select two presentations from TED.com. Analyze the introduction and conclusion. How did the speaker establish credibility? What did the speaker do to grab interest at the beginning? How did the speaker make a persuasive and memorable point in the conclusion? Assess the speaker's style. Was eye contact maintained? Was the speaking style extemporaneous? What did you learn that you will consider using when you make your oral presentation?

NOTES

1   Edward Tufte, *The Visual Display of Quantitative Information* (Cheshire, CT: Graphics Press 2001).

Index